לַה' הָאָרֶץ וּמְלוֹאָהּ

מִסִפְרֵי

Ethics of Our Fathers

PIRKEI AVOS

Ethics of Our Fathers
*With a Blended Translation-Explanation,
Living Lessons, and Selected Insights and Stories*
Illustrations by Boris Shapiro

Published by Living Lessons
1375 Coney Island Ave. #207
Brooklyn, New York 11230
(347) 709-8660 • info@livinglessons.com

Distributed by Hachai Publishing
718-633-0100 • info@hachai.com

Copyright © 2018 by Living Lessons
Reprint: 2023

All rights reserved.

No part of this publication may be reproduced, stored in a retrieval system, or transmitted in any form or by any means, electronic, mechanical, photocopying, recording or otherwise, without prior written permission from the copyright holder.

ISBN: 978-1-935949-35-0
Printed in China

≫ THE WEISS EDITION ≪

Ethics of Our Fathers

With a Blended Translation–Explanation,
Living Lessons, and Selected Insights and Stories

Illustrations by Boris Shapiro

This Pirkei Avos is dedicated by

Rabbi Moishe & Ruty Weiss

Sherman Oaks, CA

In loving memory of

ר' ישכר דוב ומרים ווייס ע"ה
R' Yissochor Dov (Berel)
& Miriam Weiss ע"ה

ר' שלום וצפורה לפידות ע"ה
R' Sholom & Tziporah
Lapidus ע"ה

And in honor of their dear children

Sholom Eliezer, Menachem Mendel,
Yonah Mordechai, and Chana Pearl
Weiss שיחיו

Introduction

Our hearts are overflowing with gratitude to Hashem as we present this new milestone in our ongoing series of publications. This volume is dedicated in honor of the Bas Mitzvah of our dear daughter Chana Pearl, תחי׳, whose birthday is on the very special fifth light of Chanukah.

Pirkei Avos is the most widely studied masechta in Shas. The sayings of our sages, from Moshe Rabbeinu onward, have inspired our people since Sinai. Avos is studied by men, women, and children annually. Hundreds, perhaps thousands, of commentaries have been written on it, each with a unique approach.

Fifty-nine masechtos of the mishnah deal with the facts of the law. Pirkei Avos speaks to the person behind the actions—to one's character. While the Torah instructs us to protect the property and dignity of another, Avos pushes us to do so eagerly and joyfully, to go beyond the letter of the law, to be truly better people.

"He who wishes to become a chassid should fulfill the words of Avos" –Bava Kama 30a.

So, why is it called "Avos," a term that means "fathers," particularly our forefathers Avraham, Yitzchak, and Yaakov? Wouldn't it be more appropriate to name it "Middos" or "Derech Eretz?"

The commentaries offer many answers. We would like to share the answer that motivated us to partner with our dear friends at Living Lessons to publish this unique commentary:

We learn many things from our teachers, but it is from our parents and grandparents that we learn to be mentschen! To be properly behaved, refined, caring, and loving to those around us—this we receive from our Avos.

A loving father doesn't only teach his child the right path to take, but also how to walk it. So do the sages within this masechta hold our hands and walk us in the path of life.

We hope and pray that the present and all future generations of Klal Yisrael will continue to shine brightly, as we merit speedily, with Mashiach's imminent arrival, speedily in our days, Amen!

Rabbi Moishe & Ruty Weiss,
Sholom Eliezer, Menachem Mendel,
Yonah Mordechai, Chana Pearl שיחיו

Sherman Oaks, California

Foreword

Torah is both the blueprint and the guiding light of a Jewish person's life. But it can be very difficult—for our generation especially—to decode its relevance and envision the beautiful world that will emerge from following its instructions.

Living Lessons produces *sefarim* and curricula that employ thoroughly researched, highly relatable, and meticulously designed lessons to excite children with the practical significance of Torah to their daily development.

Unique among *Sifrei Kodesh*, **Pirkei Avos** is a flowing fountain of direct life-messages from Chazal, each one with layers of timeless meaning and practical relevance. Read it too quickly and valuable lessons may be missed; study deeply and become lost in a mishnah for hours.

With this exciting new Pirkei Avos, young readers will find a beautiful balance of readability and empowerment through an array of practical innovations and features:

Innovations & Features

Explanatory Translation: Facing the Hebrew text is a relatable translation (in bold type), enhanced with basic commentary (in regular type) to provide context. In this way, the translations convey a meaningful message that fits comfortably into the "pshat" of the words.

Living Lessons: Beneath each mishnah, the "Living Lessons" section contains real-life lessons for today. These will certainly help children improve their thought, speech and action, just as Chazal intended.

Tidbits: From thousands of classic and contemporary commentaries, we selected these extraordinary tidbits to fascinate, instruct and motivate children in their lives today. The tidbits are presented in six categories:

Biography
A brief biography of a quoted Tanna's life, based on sources in Chazal.

Did You Know?
Interesting general knowledge related to the mishnah.

Behind the Quote
A connection between the Tanna and his statement; why he taught this specific idea.

Sparks
Overall insights on the ideas discussed in the mishnah.

Word-Power
Insights or alternative meanings for words and phrases.

Connections
How one mishnah relates to the next, or how different statements within one mishnah relate.

Generations of Tannaim & Historical Timeline: On the inside back cover we present a beautiful chart showing the transmission of Torah from teacher to student during the period of the Tannaim. When you encounter a Tanna's teaching, you can refer to the chart to see who his teachers, students and colleagues were.

On that page there is also an historical time-line highlighting major events in Jewish history and when they occurred in relation to each other.

A note on the Pirkei Avos text: There are many variations of the Hebrew text of Pirkei Avos, including where to break mishnayos. Our version largely follows the Siddur Sha'ar Hashamayim from the של"ה הקדוש published in 1717, and the Siddur Harav from the בעל התניא published in 1803.

Acknowledgments

The Weiss Edition Pirkei Avos owes its creation to Rabbi Moshe & Ruty Weiss, Sherman Oaks, California, the visionary benefactors of numerous *sefarim* created to engage, educate and inspire children.

A project of this kind depends on the passionate commitment of many people. We gratefully thank those who gave of their time and talent to develop this sefer:

- Rabbis L. Gerlitzky, S. Gurevitch, O. Gutnick, S. Laine, L. Loebenstien, and L. Posner who conducted thorough research for the commentary, translation, stories, and biographies;

- Rabbi S. Laine for researching and compiling the Generations of Tannaim chart and Historical Timeline, and Z. Friedman and Z. Stock for crafting their clear and informative design;

- Renowned artist Mr. Boris Shapiro who brilliantly illustrated each page and Mrs. C. Witkes for coordinating the illustrations;

- Z. Stock, M. Muchnik, Z. Friedman, and the Spotlight team for their creative oversight, page styling and cover design;

- Mrs. C. Raskin for tirelessly and creatively laying out the text and incorporating the artwork into each page;

- Rabbi & Mrs. Y. Abrams, Mrs. R. Wechter, and Mrs. C. Chazzan for editing and Mrs. H. Cantor for proofreading;

- The directorship of Living Lessons, Rabbis Y. Benjaminson, S. Baumgarten, G. Eichorn, S. B. Ginsberg, S. Weinbaum, and Z. Glick for their leadership, passion, and guidance.

גְּדוֹלָה תוֹרָה שֶׁהִיא נוֹתֶנֶת חַיִּים לְעוֹשֶׂיהָ בָּעוֹלָם הַזֶּה וּבָעוֹלָם הַבָּא (אבות ו:ז)

Living Lessons

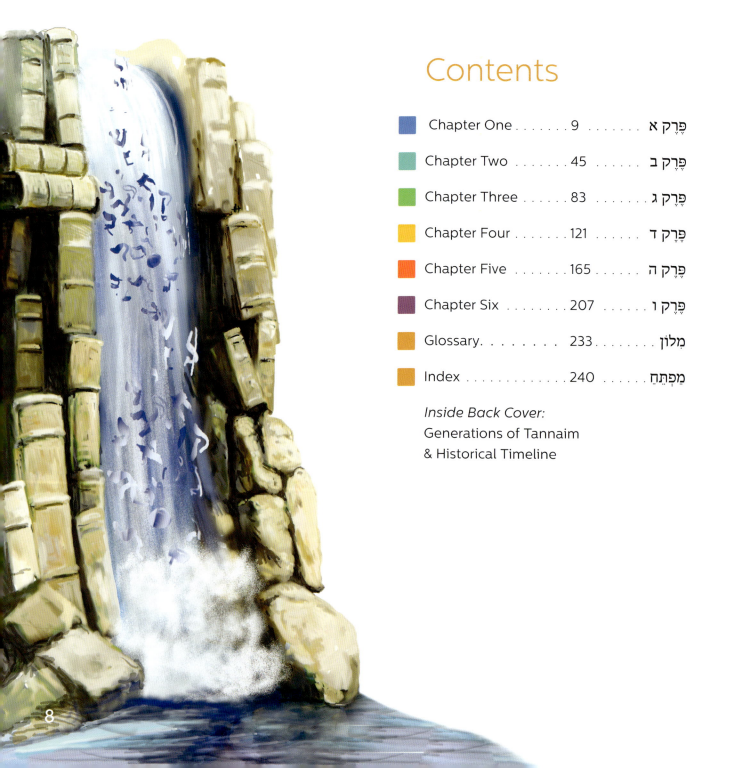

Contents

🟦	Chapter One 9	....	פֶּרֶק א
🟩	Chapter Two 45	....	פֶּרֶק ב
🟢	Chapter Three 83	....	פֶּרֶק ג
🟨	Chapter Four 121	....	פֶּרֶק ד
🟧	Chapter Five 165	....	פֶּרֶק ה
🟪	Chapter Six 207	....	פֶּרֶק ו
🟧	Glossary 233	....	מִלּוֹן
🟧	Index 240	....	מַפְתֵּחַ

Inside Back Cover:
Generations of Tannaim
& Historical Timeline

Chapter One

Kol Yisrael

Say this mishnah before beginning each new perek:

All B'nei **Yisrael have a portion in the World to Come.**

As it says in Yeshayah regarding B'nei Yisrael upon Moshiach's arrival: **Your people are all tzaddikim,** and **they will all inherit Eretz** Yisrael **forever**—they will never be exiled from it again.

All will recognize that they are **the branch of My planting and the work of My hands,** in which I, Hashem, **take pride.**

כָּל יִשְׂרָאֵל יֵשׁ לָהֶם חֵלֶק לְעוֹלָם הַבָּא,

שֶׁנֶּאֱמַר: וְעַמֵּךְ כֻּלָּם צַדִּיקִים, לְעוֹלָם יִירְשׁוּ אָרֶץ,

נֵצֶר מַטָּעַי מַעֲשֵׂה יָדַי לְהִתְפָּאֵר.

מֹשֶׁה קִבֵּל
תּוֹרָה מִסִּינַי
וּמְסָרָהּ לִיהוֹשֻׁעַ,
וִיהוֹשֻׁעַ לִזְקֵנִים,
וּזְקֵנִים לִנְבִיאִים,

וּנְבִיאִים מְסָרוּהָ
לְאַנְשֵׁי כְנֶסֶת הַגְּדוֹלָה.

הֵם אָמְרוּ שְׁלֹשָׁה דְבָרִים:
הֱווּ מְתוּנִים בַּדִּין,
וְהַעֲמִידוּ תַלְמִידִים
הַרְבֵּה, וַעֲשׂוּ סְיָג לַתּוֹרָה.

Moshe received the entire **Torah**—both the Torah Shebichsav and Torah Sheb'al Peh—**from** Hashem at Har Sinai. He then **passed it on** by teaching it **to Yehoshua,** who became the leader of B'nei Yisrael after Moshe passed away. **Yehoshua passed it on to the elder** leaders who led after he passed away. **The elders** passed it on to **the prophets,** beginning with Shmuel Hanavi.

The prophets passed it on to the Anshei Knesses Hagedolah, a group of Chachamim who led B'nei Yisrael after the times of the Nevi'im.

The Anshei Knesses Hagedolah **said** the following **three things: Be patient** in **judgment, establish many students, and make a protective fence for the Torah**—establish rules for yourself to keep you from doing aveiros.

Learn Like Them

Torah is not just another subject. It is Hashem's holy wisdom, and when we learn it we can connect with Him and know how to lead our lives. The five stages that the Torah goes through in this mishnah hint to five important steps in learning Torah:

1. **Humility**. Moshe Rabbeinu was the most humble person who ever lived. From him we learn that to be successful in Torah learning, we must be humble.

2. **Devotion**: Yehoshua was wholeheartedly devoted to his teacher, Moshe Rabbeinu. When Moshe Rabbeinu went up on Har Sinai to receive the Torah, Yehoshua waited for his return at the foot of the mountain for the entire forty days and nights!

From Yehoshua we learn that in order to succeed in Torah learning, we must devote ourselves to it completely, learning day and night.

3. **Diligence**: A זָקֵן (an elder) refers to someone who has gained much wisdom. We learn from the Zekeinim to work hard to understand Torah. Don't just say the words—try to really understand what you are learning.

4. **Hashem's Help**: The Nevi'im teach us that as smart as we may be, we need Hashem's help to understand Torah properly. Just as a navi receives his nevuah from Hashem, only with the help of Hashem can we be successful and accurate in our understanding of Torah.

5. **Application**: The Anshei Knesses Hagedolah established halachos from their Torah learning (referred to as תַּקָּנוֹת). We learn from them that our Torah study must also be applied to our practical lives.

Do Share

Sharing isn't only for toys and ice cream. The Anshei Knesses Hagedolah knew that if people wouldn't share their Torah knowledge, Torah would be lost. This is why the very beginning of Pirkei Avos teaches us about sharing Torah knowledge with others.

Biography

The Anshei Knesses Hagedolah was a group made up of 120 Nevi'im and Chachamim who formed the highest Jewish court until a few decades after the second Beis Hamikdash was built. Ezra Hasofer, who led the Jews back to Eretz Yisrael after the seventy years of Galus Bavel, headed this assembly. Some of its members were: Chagai, Zecharyah, Malachi, Daniel, Mordechai Hatzaddik, Nechemiah, Chananya, Mishael, and Azaryah.[1]

They established many of our daily practices, including the standard text of the main part of davening (the Shmoneh Esreh), brachos on food, Kiddush, and Havdalah.[2]

 ## Word Power

מִסִּינַי Why does the mishnah say that Moshe received the Torah "from Sinai" and not "from Hashem," or "at Sinai?"

Moshe received two important lessons from Har Sinai. Har Sinai was the smallest mountain, which taught the importance of humility. At the same time, Har Sinai was a mountain and not a valley, teaching the importance of Jewish pride. Being proud of your holy neshamah will give you the courage to fight for what's right.[6]

Behind the Quote

The Anshei Knesses Hagedolah were Torah leaders. The three things that they teach in this mishnah are critical for Torah leaders to know.[3]

 ## Sparks

Not Man-Made Why are the details of the mesorah mentioned at the beginning of Pirkei Avos?

Pirkei Avos is full of life lessons, morals, and guidance for life. Therefore, the mishnah begins right away by emphasizing that even these moral and ethical ideas of the Chachamim are not man-made ideas. They are also Hashem's wisdom that Moshe received directly from Him and passed down to us![4]

Torah Should Not Be Forgotten

Rav Chiya noticed that the Torah was being forgotten because there weren't enough teachers. So he made a plan to correct this, and got to work. He planted flax, made nets from the flax cords, and trapped deer. He shechted the deer, gave the meat to poor orphans, and used the deerskins to prepare scrolls of parchment. On the scrolls he wrote the five books of Chumash and the six sedarim of Mishnah. He traveled to many towns where there were no teachers, gave each scroll to a different child and taught it to him. Before leaving the town, he instructed each child to teach the scroll he had learned to the other children. In this way, he saved the Torah from being forgotten.[5]

Shimon Hatzaddik was one of the last members of the Anshei Knesses Hagedolah.

He would often say: The world stands on and was created in order to fulfill three things: Torah learning, avodah—serving Hashem with korbanos, or when there are no korbanos—through tefillah, and doing acts of kindness.

שִׁמְעוֹן הַצַּדִּיק הָיָה מִשְׁיָרֵי כְּנֶסֶת הַגְּדוֹלָה.

הוּא הָיָה אוֹמֵר, עַל שְׁלֹשָׁה דְבָרִים הָעוֹלָם עוֹמֵד: עַל הַתּוֹרָה, וְעַל הָעֲבוֹדָה, וְעַל גְּמִילוּת חֲסָדִים.

A World of Help

The entire world exists for the sake of Torah and mitzvos. Sometimes, there seem to be problems that stop us from doing mitzvos. Then we must remind ourselves, "Hashem created the world for Torah and mitzvos, and so it is impossible for that same world to prevent us from fulfilling them!" Obstacles to learning Torah and fulfilling mitzvos are really only challenges for us to overcome. As long as we don't give up, they can never overpower us.

The World – The Battleground

Learning Torah, serving Hashem, and helping others—that's a tall order! The mishnah teaches us that the world relies on all these three pillars, and that all three are critical.

Hashem wouldn't send a person on an impossible mission. Although you may be better at some things than others, you were given the ability to do everything you need to do.

 Did You Know?

 Word Power

Three Internal Pillars The three pillars that hold up the world correspond to the three types of expression: thought, speech, and action. Torah corresponds to speech, avodah to thought, and gemilus chassadim to action. The order that the mishnah lists them follows the order in the passuk that teaches us about fulfilling the Torah: כִּי־קָרוֹב אֵלֶיךָ הַדָּבָר מְאֹד בְּפִיךָ וּבִלְבָבְךָ לַעֲשֹׂתוֹ (For it (the Torah) is very near to you (and within your reach to fulfill) in your **mouth** and in your **heart** to **do** it.)"⁷

עַל שְׁלֹשָׁה דְבָרִים The three pillars of the world correspond to the three Avos: Gemilus chassadim corresponds to Avraham Avinu, who excelled in acts of kindness, and especially הַכְנָסַת אוֹרְחִים (welcoming guests). Avodah corresponds to Yitzchak Avinu, who is called עוֹלָה תְמִימָה (a perfect Korban Olah) since he was almost offered as a korban at Akeidas Yitzchak. Torah corresponds to Yaakov Avinu, who was יוֹשֵׁב אֹהָלִים (he sat in the tents [of Torah].) The mishnah, however, reverses the order, placing Torah first, because it is only through Torah that we know how to properly serve Hashem and help others.⁸

Biography

Shimon Hatzaddik was one of the last members of the Anshei Knesses Hagedolah. He served as Kohen Gadol in the second Beis Hamikdash for forty years. Many miracles happened there in his merit. For example, the western light of the menorah would burn longer than the others even though it had the same amount of oil. Also, on Yamim Tovim that occurred on Shabbos, when there were many kohanim serving, they would all feel satisfied after eating a mere kezayis (the size of an olive), or less of the Lechem Hapanim.⁹

Once, a Greek king in Shimon Hatzadik's time ordered that an idol be placed in the Beis Hamikdash, threatening that if it would not be done, he would cause great destruction. Frantically, B'nei Yisrael turned to Shimon Hatzaddik, who reassured them, saying, "Just as Hashem has always saved us, He will continue to save us." That Yom Kippur, while in the Kodesh Hakadashim, Shimon Hatzaddik heard a Heavenly voice announce, "The king has died and his decree has been annulled." A short time later they received a message that the king had died at the exact moment that he had heard the voice.¹⁰

Connections

The three pillars upon which the world stands correspond to the three teachings of the previous mishnah: **Torah**—Establishing many students. **Avodah**—Practical performance of mitzvos corresponds to the fences around Torah, which ensure that mitzvos are fulfilled properly. **Gemilus chassadim**—The previous mishnah taught the importance of patience before judging people, which is an act of kindness.¹¹

Behind the Quote

In this mishnah, Shimon Hatzaddik teaches that it is not correct to work on just one of the three paths at a particular time. Instead, a person needs to work on all three pillars consistently.

Shimon Hatzaddik valued consistency. He once remarked that he rarely ate from the Korban Asham brought by a nazir who became tamei. This was because often someone would vow to become a nazir at a moment of inspiration and would later change his mind. Since many nezirim's vows weren't sincere to begin with, they might not have been nezirim in the first place and thus their korbanos were invalid.

Shimon Hatzaddik was rewarded with "miracles of consistency" while he was the Kohen Gadol. One of them was that every Yom Kippur, when he drew the lots to determine which goat would go "to Hashem" (as a korban) and which goat would go to "Azazel" (to be cast from a cliff), the lot "to Hashem" came up in his right hand—a good sign for B'nei Yisrael. This happened for forty years in a row!¹²

Shimon Hatzaddik's Encounter

The Cusim, enemies of B'nei Yisrael, once asked Alexander the Great for permission to destroy the Beis Hamikdash, which he granted. Shimon Hatzaddik, Kohen Gadol at the time, heard that Alexander the Great was coming toward Yerushalayim, so he went out to greet him accompanied by some of the Chachamim, and wearing the majestic eight garments of the Kohen Gadol. Upon seeing him, Alexander asked, "Who are those people coming toward us?"

"Those are the Jews who rebelled against you," answered the Cusim.

As the two groups neared each other, Alexander suddenly dismounted his horse and bowed before Shimon Hatzaddik. The Cusim asked, "Why is a great king like yourself bowing before this Jew?"

"An image of this man appears to me before every battle and it is because of him that I win." Alexander explained. Turning to Shimon Hatzaddik, he asked, "What is the reason that you have come today?"

Shimon presented his plea, "Is it proper that the Beis Hamikdash, where the Jews pray for your empire every day, should be destroyed?" Alexander was so impressed that he not only revoked permission to destroy the Beis Hamikdash, but also granted permission to the Jews to kill the Cusim and destroy their temple of idolatry.¹³

Antignos from the city of Socho, received the teachings of the Torah from Shimon Hatzaddik.

He would often say: Do not serve Hashem as servants who work for their master in order to receive a reward. Rather, be as servants who work for their master out of love, and not in order to receive a reward. And let the awe of Heaven be upon you.

אַנְטִיגְנוֹס* אִישׁ סוֹכוֹ קִבֵּל מִשִּׁמְעוֹן הַצַּדִּיק.

הוּא הָיָה אוֹמֵר: אַל תִּהְיוּ כַּעֲבָדִים הַמְשַׁמְּשִׁין אֶת הָרַב עַל מְנָת לְקַבֵּל פְּרָס, אֶלָּא הֱווּ כַּעֲבָדִים הַמְשַׁמְּשִׁין אֶת הָרַב שֶׁלֹּא עַל מְנָת לְקַבֵּל פְּרָס, וִיהִי מוֹרָא שָׁמַיִם עֲלֵיכֶם.

The Real Motive

Rav said: לְעוֹלָם יַעֲסֹק אָדָם בְּתוֹרָה וּבְמִצְוֹת, וְאַף עַל פִּי שֶׁלֹּא לִשְׁמָהּ, שֶׁמִּתּוֹךְ שֶׁלֹּא לִשְׁמָהּ בָּא לִשְׁמָהּ—A person should always occupy himself with Torah and mitzvos, even with the wrong motives, for doing so for the wrong reasons will ultimately lead him to do so for the right reasons.

Rav used the words שֶׁמִּתּוֹךְ שֶׁלֹּא לִשְׁמָהּ (for doing so for the wrong reasons), which can be translated literally to mean "because from **within** the wrong reasons." Deep down, **within** every mitzvah that is done for some personal motive (לֹא לִשְׁמָה), there is really a desire to serve Hashem for the right reason, for His sake alone (לִשְׁמָה), as that is the true desire of the neshamah in every Jew.[14]

It's My Honor and Privilege

How would you feel if you were chosen to work in the king's palace? Would you feel the need to be paid? The honor of serving the king is enough without payment. This, the mishnah teaches, is the right attitude for serving Hashem. While there is great reward for every good deed that we do, the greatest reward for doing Hashem's will is strengthening our bond with Hashem.

The Gemara relates a story about Rabi Shmuel bar Susarti. Once, while visiting Rome, he found the empress's lost jewelry. The empress had declared a large reward for anyone who returned it within thirty days. Whoever was found with it after that date would receive the death penalty!

Yet Rabi Shmuel waited until after the thirty day deadline had passed and only then went to return the jewelry. The empress asked Rabi Shmuel if perhaps he had not heard the warnings.

"I have heard them," he replied.

"Then why didn't you return it within thirty days?" she demanded.

"I did not want it to be said that I returned it because I was afraid of you. I returned it only because of the commandment of my G-d, Who wants me to return it."[15]

Biography

Antignos was the leader of Socho, a city in the portion of shevet Yehudah. He was the head of the Sanhedrin after Shimon Hatzaddik, during the second Beis Hamikdash.

He had two students, Tzadok and Baysos, who misinterpreted this mishnah to mean that there is no reward for keeping the Torah and no punishment for transgressing it. They decided to stop keeping the Torah and tried to gain followers. When they realized that people wouldn't listen to their nonsense, they changed their approach. They began to spread the belief that only תּוֹרָה שֶׁבִּכְתָב (the written Torah—the twenty-four books of Tanach) are from Hashem, but not תּוֹרָה שֶׁבְּעַל פֶּה—the oral Torah passed down by the Chachamim. Sadly, the trick worked, and many people joined their group. Their followers were called Tzadokim.[16]

Behind the Quote

What enabled Tzadok and Baysos (see biography) to make such a terrible mistake was their lack of yiras Shamayim while learning. Therefore, Antignos, who saw firsthand the negative effects of learning Torah without yiras Shamayim, concludes his statement stressing the importance of having yiras Shamayim.[17]

Sparks

Fear Me, Not My Stick The mishnah says "let the fear of Heaven be upon you" rather than "...the fear of Hashem." This teaches us that one should serve Hashem with an awareness of His loftiness and greatness, rather than out of fear of His punishment.[18]

Word Power

לְקַבֵּל פְּרָס Usually, the word שָׂכָר is used when talking about a reward. The word פְּרָס is used here instead because it can also mean "a small piece." The mishnah is teaching that the reward for a mitzvah is only a small piece compared to the mitzvah itself. Don't do mitzvos because of that small reward—do it because it is the will of Hashem.[19]

וִיהִי מוֹרָא שָׁמַיִם עֲלֵיכֶם Another way to interpret this mishnah: If you will serve Hashem properly, without ulterior motives, then the fear of Hashem will be upon you—your enemies will fear you. As it says in the passuk וְרָאוּ כָּל עַמֵּי הָאָרֶץ כִּי שֵׁם ה' נִקְרָא עָלֶיךָ וְיָרְאוּ מִמֶּךָּ—and all the nations of the world will see that the name of Hashem is called upon you and they will fear you.[20]

Now I'm Free

The Ba'al Shem Tov once found himself in Istanbul before Pesach with no money and no matzah or wine for Pesach. He was distraught at the thought of not being able to perform the mitzvos of Pesach.

As the seder night approached, a Jew knocked on his door and introduced himself as a traveling businessman. He had all the provisions they would need to celebrate Pesach. The Ba'al Shem Tov was overjoyed! "Ask any request, and it shall be granted!" he told the man.

The man was wealthy, but did not have children, and so requested a blessing for children, which the Ba'al Shem Tov quickly gave him.

Immediately, there was a great commotion in Heaven. When a Tzaddik decrees something, Hashem will fulfill it. But this man and his wife were unable to have children. Hashem would have to perform a great miracle for them.

A proclamation was issued from Heaven: "This couple will have a child and the Ba'al Shem Tov will lose his Olam Haba as punishment for 'forcing' Hashem to perform a miracle!"

When the Ba'al Shem Tov heard this he exclaimed with great joy, "This is wonderful! Now I can be sure that my service of Hashem will be purely for the sake of serving Him, and not for any reward!"[21]

Yosei ben Yoezer of Tzreidah, and Yosei ben Yochanan of Yerushalayim received the teachings of the Torah **from them** (Antignos of the previous mishnah and his Beis Din).

Yosei ben Yoezer of Tzreidah says: Let your house be a meeting place for Chachamim. **Sit in the dust of their feet** and learn from them, **and drink their words** of Torah **with thirst**—listen closely to every word they say.

יוֹסֵי בֶּן יוֹעֶזֶר אִישׁ צְרֵדָה וְיוֹסֵי בֶּן יוֹחָנָן אִישׁ יְרוּשָׁלַיִם קִבְּלוּ מֵהֶם.

יוֹסֵי בֶּן יוֹעֶזֶר אִישׁ צְרֵדָה אוֹמֵר: יְהִי בֵיתְךָ בֵּית וַעַד לַחֲכָמִים, וֶהֱוֵי מִתְאַבֵּק בַּעֲפַר רַגְלֵיהֶם, וֶהֱוֵי שׁוֹתֶה בַצָּמָא אֶת דִּבְרֵיהֶם.

Living Lessons

Know Your Place

A person may feel very fortunate being able to turn his home into a meeting place where Talmidei Chachamim gather and study Torah. This mishnah tells us that a wise person will stay and learn from them and not consider himself an equal just because he is their host.

Always Wise

The mishnah says to drink their **words** with thirst. The mishnah is telling us to drink **all** their words, not just their teachings, including those that don't seem to be words of Torah. As Chazal tell us, שִׂיחַת חוּלִין שֶׁל תַּלְמִידֵי חֲכָמִים צְרִיכִים לִימוּד – Even the mundane talk of Talmidei Chachamim must be studied.

When a Talmid Chacham says anything, there is something to learn from it.[22] In addition to **what** he says, much can be learned from **how** he says it.[23]

Learning through Serving

הֱוֵי מִתְאַבֵּק בַּעֲפַר רַגְלֵיהֶם can also mean that one should serve Talmidei Chachamim and take care of their needs, such as cleaning the dust off their feet. In fact, Chazal say, גְּדוֹלָה שִׁמּוּשָׁהּ שֶׁל תּוֹרָה יוֹתֵר מִלִּמּוּדָהּ—serving Talmidei Chachamim is even greater than learning Torah from them.

The righteous Yehoshafat, king of Yehudah, went out to fight together with the king of Yisrael (and the king of Edom) against their common enemy, Moav. After seven days, they ran out of water. Yehoshafat asked the people, "Is there a navi here, so that we can ask Hashem what to do?" One of the men answered: "Elisha the son of Shafat is here, who poured water over the hands of Eliyahu [Hanavi]." Upon hearing that Elisha was the personal attendant of Eliyahu, Yehoshafat declared, "The word of Hashem is indeed with him."

By serving Talmidei Chachamim, one has the opportunity to observe the way that they act. From their actions one can learn a lot about proper conduct, even more than from listening to them teach Torah.[24]

Biography

Yosei ben Yoezer of Tzreidah After Antignos' passing, a new system of national leadership began, when B'nei Yisrael were led by more than one person. These Chachamim who led the nation together are referred to as זוגות—pairs, with one serving as the Nassi, responsible primarily for dealing with the nation's financial and political issues, and the other as Av Beis Din, in charge of the halachic matters. Five of these pairs are mentioned in this perek of Pirkei Avos. In this pair, Yosei ben Yoezer, who was a kohen, was the Nassi, while Yosei ben Yochanan was the Av Beis Din.

Yosei ben Yoezer lived in Tzreidah, which was in the portion of shevet Efraim. Due to his great piety, he was called the חָסִיד שֶׁבַּכְּהוּנָה—the most pious of the kohanim.[25]

Behind the Quote

Yosei ben Yoezer's generation was the first in which a halachic dispute wasn't resolved. This dispute was whether or not to perform semichah (leaning on an animal before it is offered as a korban) on Yom Tov.[26] This is why Yosei ben Yoezer emphasized the importance of people opening their homes as meeting points for Chachamim, so that when disagreements arose there would be many Talmidei Chachamim present to decide the halachah.[27]

Word Power

יְהִי בֵיתְךָ This mishnah can also be translated to mean that your "home"—the place where you are most comfortable and spend most of your time—should be in the Beis Medrash, where Chachamim sit together and learn.[28]

וֶהֱוֵי שׁוֹתֶה בַצָּמָא אֶת דִּבְרֵיהֶם The word "drinking" is used in reference to learning from Chachamim. Just as drinking carries nutrients throughout the body, learning Torah directly from Chachamim carries the teachings of Torah into every aspect of one's life.[29]

Sparks

My Agent The Torah commands us to connect ourselves to Hashem. But how can limited creatures like us connect to the infinite Creator? Chazal tell us that associating ourselves with Talmidei Chachamim is like being attached to Hashem Himself![30]

Light of the World Talmidei Chachamim are compared to the Beis Hamikdash. Just as the Shechinah rested in the Beis Hamikdash, spreading its light out to the rest of the world, Talmidei Chachamim draw down and spread the light of the Shechinah throughout the world.[31]

Did You Know?

House Full of Sefarim Even when one cannot actually host Chachamim in his house, he can make it a gathering place of Chachamim by having holy books. Then it is as if the Talmidei Chachamim whose teachings are written in the sefarim are actually in the house themselves.[32]

Hanging Around Pays Off

There were once two mute brothers who lived near Rebbi. Whenever Rebbi would enter the Beis Medrash to teach, they would follow him and sit at his shiurim. They would nod their heads and move their lips while concentrating on the shiur.

Rebbi davened for them, and they were miraculously healed of their muteness. Now that they could finally speak, it was discovered that their insistence of being at the shiurim had paid off—they were fluent in all mishnayos, midrashim, and the entire Shas![33]

Yosei ben Yochanan of Yerushalayim says:

Let your house be wide open for guests. Poor people should be treated like members of your own household.

Do not engage in too much idle chatter with the woman (your wife). This was said regarding one's own wife; how much more so does it apply to another man's wife.

Based on this, the Chachamim said: Whoever engages in too much idle chatter with the woman causes evil to himself, neglects the study of Torah, and in the end will inherit Gehinom.

יוֹסֵי בֶּן יוֹחָנָן אִישׁ יְרוּשָׁלַיִם אוֹמֵר: יְהִי בֵיתְךָ פָּתוּחַ לִרְוָחָה, וְיִהְיוּ עֲנִיִּים בְּנֵי בֵיתֶךָ,

וְאַל תַּרְבֶּה שִׂיחָה עִם הָאִשָּׁה, בְּאִשְׁתּוֹ אָמְרוּ, קַל וָחֹמֶר בְּאֵשֶׁת חֲבֵרוֹ.

מִכַּאן אָמְרוּ חֲכָמִים: כָּל הַמַּרְבֶּה שִׂיחָה עִם הָאִשָּׁה גּוֹרֵם רָעָה לְעַצְמוֹ, וּבוֹטֵל מִדִּבְרֵי תוֹרָה, וְסוֹפוֹ יוֹרֵשׁ גֵּיהִנֹּם.

Giving or Getting?

Giving tzedakah is compared to planting. A person who plants seeds of grain in the ground doesn't complain about his lost grain—on the contrary, he rejoices because he knows that from this one seed will sprout many more!

The same is true with tzedakah. When you give generously to the poor you will not lose, but in fact you will gain much more, since Hashem blesses those who give tzedakah.

Based on this idea, the mishnah can also be understood not only as an instruction, but as a promise: Your home will be wide open to the generous blessing of Hashem when you treat the poor as members of your household.[34]

Open to All

It's nice to be important, but it's more important to be nice! Opening our homes to the rich and respected makes us feel important, but Hashem wants our doors wide open for all people, rich and poor alike. The poor in particular should be made to feel comfortable in our homes.

Biography

Yosei ben Yochanan was the Av Beis Din of the Sanhedrin and leader of B'nei Yisrael together with Yosei ben Yoezer during the second Beis Hamikdash.

Together, they were referred to as אֶשְׁכֹּל—a cluster of grapes. The word אֶשְׁכֹּל is a combination of the words אִישׁ שֶׁהַכֹּל בּוֹ—a man who has everything in him. They were called this because they possessed all three essential traits: knowledge of the entire Torah, fear of Heaven, and acts of kindness.[35]

 ### Behind the Quote

Yosei ben Yochanan lived in Yerushalayim, a city always full of guests coming to the Beis Hamikdash. People might have been tempted to invite only the rich and important visitors, so Yosei ben Yochanan teaches to invite poor people, especially since they cannot usually afford to stay in a hotel.

 ### Connections

This mishnah adds to the previous mishnah that one's home should be open to all people, not just Talmidei Chachamim.[36]

 ### Word Power

וְיִהְיוּ עֲנִיִּים בְּנֵי בֵיתֶךָ These words can also mean "your children should be poor." This means that you should open your home to guests even if it will cause your own children to be like the poor, such as by giving up their comfortable beds or pillows for guests, or giving up their portion of food to feed a hungry visitor.[37]

וְיִהְיוּ עֲנִיִּים בְּנֵי בֵיתֶךָ Another way of explaining this teaching is that when you need to hire household help, you should hire poor Jewish people and provide them with a livelihood.[38]

Whose Honor Are You Seeking?

For many years the two holy brothers, R' Elimelech of Lizensk and R' Zushe of Anipoli, wandered from town to town disguised as simple beggars, inspiring people with words of wisdom and encouragement. Late one evening, the brothers arrived in the town of Ludmir. They knocked on the door of a large, regal home, asking to stay there overnight. "There's a poorhouse near the synagogue for wandering beggars. I'm sure you'll have no trouble finding accommodations there," the homeowner replied, and closed the door. Shortly thereafter, they came upon a simple-looking home, whose owner welcomed them in for the night.

Several years later, the two brothers once again visited Ludmir, this time as official guests of the community. A wealthy man approached them, "Rabbis!" he announced, "The town council has granted me the honor of hosting you during your stay." The brothers sent their coachman with the horses and luggage to the wealthy man's house, while they themselves continued on to the simple man's house.

When the wealthy man found out and protested, they replied, "The last time we were here and we did not have a fancy coach, you turned us away from your door. So it is not us that you want to host, it is our coachman, horses, and luggage—which are currently enjoying your hospitality!"[39]

Yehoshua ben Prachyah and Nittai of Arbel **received** the teachings of the Torah **from** Yosei ben Yoezer and Yosei ben Yochanan.

Yehoshua ben Prachyah says: Make for yourself a teacher from whom you can regularly learn, **acquire for yourself a** close and trusted **friend, and judge every person favorably,** even when he appears to have done something wrong.

יְהוֹשֻׁעַ בֶּן פְּרַחְיָה וְנִתַּאי הָאַרְבֵּלִי קִבְּלוּ מֵהֶם.

יְהוֹשֻׁעַ בֶּן פְּרַחְיָה אוֹמֵר: עֲשֵׂה לְךָ רַב, וּקְנֵה לְךָ חָבֵר, וֶהֱוֵי דָן אֶת כָּל הָאָדָם לְכַף זְכוּת.

Living Lessons

Unbiased Opinion

A person is always biased toward himself. So the mishnah tells even a great person to find a personal rav and a good friend, people who will help him objectively determine right from wrong.

Judge Everyone Favorably

When R' Yosef Yitzchak of Lubavitch was four years old, he asked his father why Hashem created man with one mouth and one nose, but two eyes. His father answered that at some things you need to look with your right eye, with love and warmth, and at others with the left eye, in a stricter, more discerning manner. Your siddur and fellow Jew should be looked at with your right eye—always seeing their beauty. A candy or toy, however, should be looked at with your left eye.⁴⁰

Healthy Self Esteem

The yetzer hara uses two types of thoughts to bring a person to do an aveirah. Sometimes he says, "You are so insignificant—your actions don't really matter." And so the mishnah responds—עֲשֵׂה לְךָ רַב, which can also be translated to mean "make yourself into a rav." Realize how important you are!

Other times, the yetzer hara might make you think, "I am so great, I don't need anyone to help me." The mishnah responds, "Acquire for yourself a friend" who will help you be honest in your service of Hashem.⁴¹

 Connections

The previous mishnah taught to make one's home into a gathering place for Chachamim. One who fulfills this might not feel the need for a personal rav, since Chachamim are always in his home! Yehoshua ben Prachyah responds that even if you are surrounded by Chachamim, you must choose one specific rav for yourself.

 Did You Know?

Tricks for Learning

The words עֲשֵׂה לְךָ רַב can also mean, "Make yourself like a teacher." Just as a teacher teaches aloud so that the students will hear, when you learn alone, be like a teacher—learn aloud. This will help you to better understand and to remember your learning.⁴²

 Sparks

On All Levels This mishnah teaches us a lesson on how to relate to three groups of people. From the first group—those who are spiritually greater than you—choose a master (rav). From those who are on a spiritually equal level, choose a friend (chaver). As for those who seem to be spiritually inferior, remember to judge them favorably.⁴³

Biography

Yehoshua ben Prachyah was the nassi after Yosei ben Yoezer during the time of the second Beis Hamikdash. When the wicked Chashmona'i king of the time wanted to kill all the Talmidei Chachamim, Yehoshua ben Prachyah fled to Alexandria, Egypt, and returned only years later, when his student, Shimon ben Shatach, reassured him that it was finally safe.[44]

Behind the Quote

Even though Yehoshua ben Prachyah held the highest position of leadership, he emphasized the importance of everyone having a rav.

Once, a student of Yehoshua ben Prachyah was acting inappropriately and was told to leave the yeshivah. He begged for forgiveness repeatedly, but each time Yehoshua ben Prachyah felt it wasn't right to let him back. One last time, the student approached for forgiveness, and this time Yehoshua ben Prachyah intended to let him finally return. However, since he was in the middle of davening, he motioned with his hand for the student to wait. The student misunderstood the wave of the hand as another dismissal, and he left, never to return. He eventually became an idol-worshiper and convinced other Jews to follow his ways.[45]

Yehoshua ben Prachyah regretted sending away his former student and not judging him favorably. He felt responsible for the student's becoming an idol-worshiper. This is why he says that one must judge every person favorably.[46]

Sparks

No Excuse Not to Excuse

We must always try to interpret another's actions in a positive way. When the actions are clearly wrong, we can still excuse it by assuming that it was the particular circumstances that pushed the person to sin.

In fact, Hashem only challenges a person with things that he can actually overcome. So even if you might see a Jew committing a terrible sin, remember that it reflects his great spiritual potential in that he received such a hard test![47]

Word Power

וּקְנֵה לְךָ חָבֵר These words can also be read וְקָנֶה לְךָ חָבֵר—let your pen be your friend. Writing things down helps greatly to clarify and remember your learning.[48]

Imagine If...

The Ksav Sofer was at a meal with a group of rabbanim when he decided to show them his most prized possession—a genuine half-shekel coin that was more than 2,000 years old! Everyone took a turn holding and admiring it. After a while, the Ksav Sofer requested that the coin be returned, but to everyone's shock, it had disappeared. Someone suggested searching everyone's pockets, but one rav, R' Yehudah Assad of Hungary, asked everyone to wait a few minutes. "After all," he said, "maybe the coin will turn up soon."

Twenty minutes passed, but the coin still hadn't turned up. R' Yehudah pleaded for some more time. After just a few more minutes, a waiter came running in with the coin, which had been found in the garbage that had been cleared off the table. Everyone was relieved that the coin was finally found, but were curious why R' Yehudah had been so insistent on searching more. With some embarrassment, he pulled out from his pocket an authentic half-shekel coin, identical to the one belonging to the Ksav Sofer!

"You see," he explained, "I, too, had one, but didn't want to say anything, as I wanted the Ksav Sofer to enjoy showing us his coin. After it disappeared, how was I going to be able to explain why I had one in my pocket? So I asked for some time and prayed that Hashem would spare me the embarrassment of being falsely accused."[49]

Imagine the scene if the Ksav Sofer's coin had not been found. Upon finding an identical coin in R' Yehudah's pocket, would anyone have believed his story?

Nittai of Arbel says: **Keep away from bad neighbors** who might influence you, **and do not be** too closely **connected to a wicked person,**

and do not despair when **punishment** is given for wrongdoings.

נִתַּאי הָאַרְבֵּלִי אוֹמֵר: הַרְחֵק מִשָּׁכֵן רָע, וְאַל תִּתְחַבֵּר לָרָשָׁע,

וְאַל תִּתְיָאֵשׁ מִן הַפּוּרְעָנוּת.

Good Friends

Some people aren't necessarily bad, but are likely to influence you in a negative way. Others might indeed be bad, but won't necessarily influence you in particular. The mishnah teaches you to be honest with yourself—keep away from bad neighbors that might negatively influence you. If a certain friend has a negative influence on you, don't wait for your parents or teacher to point it out—keep a distance.

Later, the mishnah says, "אַל תִּתְחַבֵּר לָרָשָׁע" – Don't **attach** yourself to him, but you may treat him with kindness and try to be a positive influence on him.[50]

Not Only Yourself

Often a person will not realize when he is being negatively influenced. If you see a friend who is being negatively influenced by another, point it out to him and try to help him distance himself from the bad influence. This is why the mishnah says הַרְחֵק, a word that is usually used in reference to distancing others.[51]

Constant Companion

Even once you have distanced yourself from negative influences, you are still not secure. The yetzer hara travels with you and will try to outsmart you, so be vigilant.[52]

 Word Power

וְאַל תִּתְיָאֵשׁ מִן הַפּוּרְעָנוּת These words mean not to give up hope when punished. When Hashem punishes, it is not out of vengeance or desire to hurt us. It's like a parent washing a baby to clean him from the dirt that covers him. The baby may cry, since he does not understand that the discomfort is really for its benefit. In the same way, we may be pained when we are punished, but we must remember that we are Hashem's precious children. When he punishes us it is only to cleanse our neshamah from the dirt that covers it.

Connections

In the previous mishnah we are told to judge everyone favorably. The mishnah continues now and clarifies that even though we must judge everyone with favor, we still should not put ourselves at risk in being too friendly with a bad person, or choose to live next to bad influences.[53]

Biography

Nittai of Arbel was the Av Beis Din when Yehoshua ben Prachya was the Nassi. He lived in Arbel, a city near Teveriah. He is only mentioned once more in the entire Mishnayos. He is buried on Har Arbel, near the burial places of Dinah the daughter of Yaakov Avinu and of Rabi Zeira.

Sparks

Don't Ignore Another's Suffering Although the mishnah tells us to distance ourselves from bad neighbors, it continues, וְאַל תִּתְיָאֵשׁ מִן הַפּוּרְעָנוּת. One way to explain these words is that when you see another person suffering, even a wicked person, don't ignore his pain, but try to help him. This may eventually even bring him to do teshuvah.[55]

Behind the Quote

Nittai of Arbel was the Av Beis Din. It was his responsibility to guide the people away from sin. Therefore, he instructs in this mishnah to keep away from negative influences so that hopefully there will be no need for punishment at all.

Did You Know?

Be Mindful, Not Worried The mishnah tells us not to worry excessively about punishment, which can prevent us from serving Hashem with joy. Still, we shouldn't feel invincible and think that we will never be punished.[54]

Story

Keep Good Company

There once was a Talmid Chacham who owned an inn. One day, some rough customers were arguing about how to divide profits from their latest business deal. The innkeeper decided to intervene and help them, because he was good at math and would likely earn a nice sum of money for his assistance.

He indeed settled the argument to their satisfaction and the ruffians were so impressed that they offered him to join their "company" and to become their bookkeeper. Before long, it became very clear to him that they were really thieves, but he nevertheless decided to continue working for them. "After all," he reasoned, "I'm only counting the money, I'm not actually stealing anything myself."

Slowly but surely, the scholarly bookkeeper joined in more and more of their activities, and eventually became a full-time thief. One night, on the way to a robbery, he met an old friend who was traveling to see their Rebbe, the holy Ruzhiner. He suddenly realized that what had started out as simply bad company had eventually caused him to fall so low! He now desperately wanted to do teshuvah. He joined his friend and traveled to the Ruzhiner, leaving his wicked ways behind him forever.[56]

ח

Yehudah ben Tabbai and Shimon ben Shatach **received** the teachings of the Torah **from** Yehoshua ben Prachyah and Nittai of Arbel.

Yehudah ben Tabbai says: When you sit as a judge on a case, **do not act as a lawyer** by advising those being judged. **When litigants are standing before you** in court, **consider both of them guilty** and don't favor either side. **And when they leave you** after the case, **having accepted the judgment, consider them both righteous.**

יְהוּדָה בֶּן טַבַּאי וְשִׁמְעוֹן בֶּן שָׁטַח קִבְּלוּ מֵהֶם.

יְהוּדָה בֶּן טַבַּאי אוֹמֵר: אַל תַּעַשׂ עַצְמְךָ כְּעוֹרְכֵי הַדַּיָּנִין, וּכְשֶׁיִּהְיוּ בַּעֲלֵי הַדִּין עוֹמְדִים לְפָנֶיךָ, יִהְיוּ בְעֵינֶיךָ כִּרְשָׁעִים, וּכְשֶׁנִּפְטָרִים מִלְּפָנֶיךָ, יִהְיוּ בְעֵינֶיךָ כְּזַכָּאִין, כְּשֶׁקִּבְּלוּ עֲלֵיהֶם אֶת הַדִּין.

ט

Shimon ben Shatach says: As a judge **you should investigate** and question **the witnesses thoroughly.** When questioning them, **be careful with the words you** use, because **perhaps they will learn from** your words what **lies** to say in order to win the case.

שִׁמְעוֹן בֶּן שָׁטַח אוֹמֵר: הֱוֵי מַרְבֶּה לַחֲקוֹר אֶת הָעֵדִים, וֶהֱוֵי זָהִיר בִּדְבָרֶיךָ, שֶׁמָּא מִתּוֹכָם יִלְמְדוּ לְשַׁקֵּר.

Living Lessons

When You are the Judge

When judging another person, the mishnah warns us to view them as guilty during trial.

This can be applied in a person's quest for good friends. When you need to make a judgment regarding whether a certain person would be a good friend for you, be very careful and selective. Ask yourself honestly: "Is this person going to be a positive influence on me?"

Don't Go Easy on Yourself

The mishnah speaks also to a person who is passing judgment on himself. אַל תַּעַשׂ עַצְמְךָ כְּעוֹרְכֵי הַדַּיָּנִין—Don't be your own defense lawyer, looking for excuses to justify your actions. Excuses may get you out of trouble, but they will not help you grow. Admitting that you must improve is the first step to becoming better.[57]

Biography

Yehudah ben Tabbai and Shimon ben Shatach were the third pair of the zugos. They lived during the time of the Second Beis Hamikdash, under the rule of the wicked king Yannai. There is a difference of opinion in the Gemara regarding which one was the Nassi and which was the Av Beis Din.[58]

Yehudah ben Tabbai Out of his great humility, Yehudah ben Tabbai did not want to be a leader. When the community wanted to appoint him to lead, he ran away to Alexandria, Egypt. The community begged him to accept the responsibility and eventually he agreed.[59]

Shimon ben Shatach The Chashmona'i king of his time held a personal grudge against Talmidei Chachamim and ordered them all to be killed. Shimon ben Shatach was saved by his sister, Shlomtziyon, who was married into the royal family and managed to hide him.[60]

When he came out of hiding, Shimon ben Shatach took back control of the Sanhedrin and legislated many decrees. One of them was a new rule that every father was obligated to send his child to school.[61]

 ## Behind the Quote

Shimon ben Shatach heard about a group of eighty witches living in Ashkelon. After he verified that they were indeed practicing witchcraft, all eighty were hanged in one day. In retaliation, relatives of the witches hired false witnesses to testify against Shimon ben Shatach's son, accusing him of commiting an aveirah punishable by skilah—stoning.[62] Shimon ben Shatach therefore warns that one must investigate and question witnesses extensively.[63]

 ## Word Power

הֱוֵי מַרְבֶּה לַחֲקוֹר אֶת הָעֵדִים

There are seven questions that the Beis Din must ask witnesses, such as what day of the month the incident occurred. However, the Beis Din may ask the witnesses the same question many times, because if a person is lying, the more he speaks, the more likely it is that he will trip up and the lie will be discovered.[64]

Alternatively, these words can mean that although only two witnesses are needed for the judges to be able to make a judgment, if more witnesses come forward, a judge should interrogate them as well, rather than passing judgment based on the testimony of just two witnesses.[65]

 ## Story

Way More Valuable

Shimon ben Shatach worked very hard to earn a living. He would pick chestnuts in the forest, carry them back to town, and make ink out of them. He would then sell the ink to support his family. Although he was very poor, Shimon ben Shatach did not complain. The only thing that bothered him was the time wasted carrying the nuts back to town, time that he could have used for Torah. Finally, one day he sold some of his possessions and bought a mule from a non-Jewish merchant to lighten his workload.

When he brought the mule home, his students went to see it and were delighted to discover a valuable precious stone hanging on the animal's neck. If they sold the stone, they realized, their teacher would no longer have to work to earn a livelihood, but could instead spend all of his time studying Torah! They joyfully informed their teacher about their incredible find. To their surprise, however, Shimon ben Shatach declared, "The praise that Hashem will receive when I return the lost gem is worth much more to me than any amount of riches!" He ran immediately to the market and returned the precious stone to the man who had sold him the mule. The astonished merchant proclaimed: "Blessed is G-d, the G-d of Shimon ben Shatach!"[66]

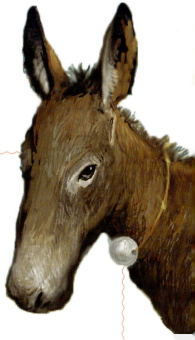

Shmayah and Avtalyon received the teachings of the Torah **from** Yehudah ben Tabbai and Shimon ben Shatach.

Shmayah says: You should **love work** and not consider yourself too important to work. **Hate positions of power** and do not choose them unless the responsibility is placed upon you. **Do not become too friendly with those in power.**

שְׁמַעְיָה וְאַבְטַלְיוֹן
קִבְּלוּ מֵהֶם.

שְׁמַעְיָה אוֹמֵר:
אֱהוֹב אֶת הַמְּלָאכָה,
וּשְׂנָא אֶת הָרַבָּנוּת,
וְאַל תִּתְוַדַּע לָרָשׁוּת.

Living Lessons

Laziness Doesn't Feel That Good

Some people think that the less they have to do, the happier they will be. However, the truth is that a person will naturally feel his best through working hard and succeeding at something. There is no greater feeling of accomplishment than seeing the fruits of your labor. Even when you don't succeed, when you put in work you can always be proud of your efforts! So next time you're feeling down, get up and get to work! You'll begin to feel much better.[68]

Doubly Sneaky

In the teaching וְאַל תִּתְוַדַּע לָרָשׁוּת—do not become too friendly with those in power—the word רָשׁוּת (those in power) can also refer to the yetzer hara. This is because the word רָשׁוּת also means "permission." The yetzer hara convinces a person that he is permitted to do things that are actually forbidden. Two things that lead a person into this trap of the yetzer hara are idleness—when a person has too much free time on his hands—and arrogance. So Shmayah says: love work and despise power. Remain humble, and that will ensure that you will not become too "friendly" with the yetzer hara![69]

 Sparks

 Behind the Quote

Remember Who is Really in Charge

Sometimes community leaders need to have connections with government officials. However, Shmayah warns, don't get too comfortable with them, and certainly don't rely on them. Remember, it is not the government officials who protect us and provide for our needs, but only Hashem Himself.[67]

Shmayah held the position of Nassi, which is very similar to the position of a king. Yet he exemplified humility and taught us not to seek power. For only a humble person who nullifies himself before Hashem can be a leader of the Jewish nation. In fact, the greatness of a leader is precisely his humility![70]

Biography

Shmayah and Avtalyon were the fourth of the zugos. Shmayah was the Nassi and Avtalyon was the Av Beis Din. Little is known about them, and there are very few stories told about them in the Gemara.

We do know that Shmayah and Avtalyon were descendants of Sancheiriv, the evil non-Jewish king who sent the ten shevatim into exile.[71] Some say they were converts, while others say they were born Jews but descended from converts. There are opinions that they were brothers.

Avtalyon was called by this name because he was the Av Beis Din—אַבְטַלְיוֹן can be taken to mean "father of the young" since טַלְיָא in Aramaic means a small child. Avtalyon acted in his position as a father to the young orphans.[72]

There is a tradition that both in life and death Shmayah and Avtalyon never separated. They are buried next to each other in Gush Chalav, a city on Har Meron in the Galil.

Connections

In the previous two mishnayos, Shmayah's teachers taught how to be a proper judge. Shmayah continues instructing the judge. He teaches that a person must not seek power, and when he is placed in a position of power, he must remain humble.[73]

Shmayah's teachers discussed how to judge court cases properly. Shmayah adds that if people would love work, they would earn enough, and not feel a need to borrow, steal, or cheat. This in turn would prevent most court cases dealing with monetary matters.[74]

Story

I Don't Want It

Rabi Yehudah bar Ilai was so poor that he once had to miss a special gathering because he didn't have a robe to wear. Rabban Shimon ben Gamliel sent him a robe as a gift but Rabi Yehudah refused it. Instead, he lifted the mat he was sitting on, revealing to Rabban Shimon's messenger a pile of gold coins that had miraculously appeared. "See, I could easily have lots of wealth, but I choose not to have it in this world," he explained. Rabi Yehudah bar Ilai was showing that if he desired money he could easily get it, but he preferred to earn his money through hard work.[75]

Avtalyon says: Chachamim, watch your words, for they can make you liable to be exiled. You may then be sent to a place of "bitter, unhealthy waters"—ideas that can damage the mind. The students who follow you to this place will drink from these "bitter waters," misinterpreting the Torah, and they will die spiritually, causing Hashem's Name to be desecrated.

אַבְטַלְיוֹן אוֹמֵר: חֲכָמִים, הִזָּהֲרוּ בְדִבְרֵיכֶם, שֶׁמָּא תָחוֹבוּ חוֹבַת גָּלוּת וְתִגְלוּ לִמְקוֹם מַיִם הָרָעִים, וְיִשְׁתּוּ הַתַּלְמִידִים הַבָּאִים אַחֲרֵיכֶם וְיָמוּתוּ, וְנִמְצָא שֵׁם שָׁמַיִם מִתְחַלֵּל.

Living Lessons

Total Avoidance

Why does the mishnah tell us to worry about such a far-off scenario—going to galus, which might be in a bad place and thus cause students to suffer? This teaches us that when it comes to chilul Hashem we must be concerned about even the most unlikely cause. Even if it seems extremely unlikely to cause something bad to happen, we must take into account any possible results. This includes even actions that are themselves positive; we must analyze them to make sure that all the results remain positive.

Be Clear

Sometimes you might say something and discover that it was understood very differently by the person you were talking to. Sometimes they are offended by your words even when you had no such intention. This often leads to hurt feelings or even fights, all based on a misunderstanding. It is therefore very important to carefully consider how people might understand what you say. Make your message very clear, leaving no room for misinterpretation.

 Did You Know?

Not Above the Law This mishnah can also be understood to mean, "Chachamim, be careful to fulfill your own words." Even someone who is very learned and pious must follow the decrees set up by the Chachamim to protect us from aveiros, even if he feels that he doesn't need that extra protection. The Gemara emphasizes this with a story: The Chachamim ruled that one may not read by candlelight on Shabbos because he may, per habit, tilt the candle in order to see better, which is forbidden on Shabbos. Rabi Yishmael was certain that he would not forget, so he read next to a candle on Shabbos. Sure enough, while engrossed in his learning, he almost tilted the flame. He exclaimed, "How great are the words of the Chachamim!"[76]

Word Power

מַיִם הָרָעִים Strong wine is diluted with water to make it drinkable. The Torah is compared to wine, while the explanations used to interpret it are compared to water. This is why the mishnah calls the misinterpretations of Torah "bad waters."[77]

Behind the Quote

Avtalyon was Av Beis Din and was greatly concerned with Torah learning and the wellbeing of Torah students. He therefore speaks about taking care of students and protecting them from any spiritual or physical harm.[78]

Sparks

With Love and Awe The mishnah tells us that those who misinterpret the words of the Chachamim will die—referring not to a physical death, but a spiritual death.[79] Spiritual death is just as bad as physical death, if not worse. We need to remember to tend to our spiritual health, just as our physical health. The best spiritual exercise is fulfilling mitzvos with feelings of love and awe of Hashem, which comes from learning about the greatness of Hashem.

Story

Huge Misunderstanding

A king once sent a letter to the king of a neighboring country with the following short request: "Send me a white horse with a black tail, and if not…"

The second king sent back a similar response: "I don't have such a horse and if I did…" and he did not elaborate.

When the first king received the response he became very angry and declared war on the other king. The battles went on for years, sacrificing many men, huge amounts of money, and destroying large areas of both countries. Eventually they made a truce. When they met, the second king asked the first, "What did you mean when you wrote 'and if not…?'"

"Obviously," answered the first king, "I meant to say that if you don't have a horse in those exact colors, then any horse will do."

"Oh! I thought you meant 'and if not I will attack your country,'" cried the second king.

Then the first king asked the second one, "And what did you mean when you wrote 'and if I did…?'"

The second king replied: "I meant that if I did have such a horse I would gladly send it to you!"

"Oh! I thought you meant 'and if I did, I would not give it to you,'" exclaimed the first king.

They realized how foolish they had been—they had fought a war only because they had not made themselves clear in their letters![80]

Hillel and Shammai received the teachings of the Torah from Shmayah and Avtalyon.

Hillel says: You should be students of Aharon HaKohen, and learn from his traits: be someone who loves peace and pursues peace by helping others to make peace, one who loves all fellow creatures and brings them close to the Torah.

הִלֵּל וְשַׁמַּאי קִבְּלוּ מֵהֶם.

הִלֵּל אוֹמֵר: הֱוֵי מִתַּלְמִידָיו שֶׁל אַהֲרֹן, אוֹהֵב שָׁלוֹם וְרוֹדֵף שָׁלוֹם, אוֹהֵב אֶת הַבְּרִיּוֹת, וּמְקָרְבָן לַתּוֹרָה.

A Friend to All

When Aharon Hakohen saw a person who needed to improve his character or behavior, he would greet him warmly, befriend him, and spend time speaking with him. The person would think to himself: "Aharon must think that I am a good person, and so he is spending time with me. If he only knew my true thoughts and deeds, he would not even look at me! Let me change my ways so I will be worthy of his admiration."

This teaches that the way to bring people closer to the path of Torah is through kindness and friendship. If you show them that you believe in their goodness, which everyone has within their neshamah—then you will certainly reach them.[82]

 Behind the Quote

Hillel was well known for his great humility and patience. Once, two men decided to challenge him and made a bet in which the one who would succeed in causing Hillel to lose his temper would win 400 zuz. On a very hectic Erev Shabbos, one of the men came to Hillel's house and repeatedly harassed him, but Hillel would not become angry!

Because Hillel was extraordinarily humble and patient with people, he emphasizes the importance of following in the ways of Aharon Hakohen, who went to great lengths in order to minimize arguments and increase tolerance.[81]

 Did You Know?

No Excuse Hillel was extremely poor. One wintry Friday, he didn't have enough money to pay the small admission fee for the study hall. But he refused to let that deter him. He climbed onto the roof and listened through the skylight to the holy words of Torah being taught. Eventually, the cold became too intense and he fainted. He was discovered the next morning buried under the snow and was quickly revived. When his determination to learn Torah at any cost was recognized, Hillel was allowed to enter the Beis Medrash without paying.

The Chachamim said in reference to learning Torah, "The poor are held accountable because of Hillel." Despite the little that he had, Hillel made sure to learn Torah. So can any person, no matter how poor, find a way to learn if he really wants.[83]

 Word Power

אוֹהֵב אֶת הַבְּרִיּוֹת At the end of the mishnah, Hillel says, "be… one who loves all fellow **creatures**," using a rather strange word to refer to people. Hillel is teaching that even someone who doesn't behave like a person, whose only apparent quality is that he is Hashem's creation, should be loved and brought close to Torah.[84]

Biography

Hillel was born in Bavel in the year 3648 (112 BCE) and, like Moshe Rabbeinu, lived for 120 years. He was renowned for his immense humility, patience, and love for his fellow Jews.[85]

At age forty, Hillel abandoned a life of wealth and went to Eretz Yisrael to learn Torah. There, he was very poor and would survive on a coin worth half a silver dinar a day. He would use half for his family and the other half to pay the admission fee to the Beis Medrash. Hillel had a wealthy brother named Shevna who offered him half his wealth in exchange for half of Hillel's portion in the World to Come, but Hillel refused, preferring to support himself.[86]

Hillel is famous for instituting a document called a pruzbul. In Hillel's times people wrongly avoided lending before shmittah because they could not collect the debt after shmittah. The pruzbul transfers the debt to a Beis Din, and is then allowed to be collected after shmittah. This encouraged people to lend money even when shmittah was approaching.[87]

Sparks

Torah Unchanged Hillel says "Bring people close to Torah." He doesn't say "bring Torah close to people." When trying to bring a Jew close to Torah, one must be very careful not to change the teachings of Torah, even to make it easier or more appealing to people.[88]

Warm Up The mishnah says first אוֹהֵב אֶת הַבְּרִיּוֹת—love people, and only then וּמְקָרְבָן לַתּוֹרָה—bring them close to the Torah. The best way to guide someone in the right way is to first shower them with love. Once they feel that you are rebuking them only out of genuine care, they will accept your words. Hashem did this with B'nei Yisrael, lovingly taking them out of Mitzrayim even when they were unworthy, and only afterward giving the teachings of Torah on Har Sinai.[89] Similarly, Moshe Rabbeinu only rebuked B'nei Yisrael after showing his care for them by leading them in conquering the lands of Sichon and Og.[90]

Even You Hillel teaches to learn from Aharon Hakohen to love peace, pursue peace, etc. This is to bring out the greatness of making peace: If the great Aharon Hakohen, the Kohen Gadol and the brother of Moshe Rabbeinu, wasn't too important to pursue peace between quarreling Jews or between a man and his wife, certainly we, who aren't on that great level, aren't too important to help make peace.[91]

Story

Anything for Peace

There was a woman who came to hear a lesson from Rabi Meir every week on Friday night. It happened one week that Rabi Meir taught longer than usual and by the time the woman came home, the Shabbos candles had already burnt out. Her husband, very angry, said, "I forbid you from entering this house until you spit in the face of Rabi Meir."

Eliyahu Hanavi came to Rabi Meir and explained to him what had happened. The woman arrived back in the Beis Medrash and Rabi Meir, pretending to have an eye ailment, announced, "Whoever knows how to cure my eye by saying special words and then spitting in the eye should please come and do so." The woman seized the opportunity and approached. Rabi Meir asked her if she knew what to say, and she became frightened. When she told him that she did not know, Rabi Meir told her "in that case, spit seven times into my eye." After she did so, he told her to go home and tell her husband, "You told me to spit only once, and I spat seven times."

His students asked him, "Why did you allow yourself to be disgraced in such a way?" Rabi Meir answered, "If Hashem forgoes His honor to bring peace between a husband and wife (by allowing His holy name to be erased in the waters of the sotah) certainly I can forgo my own honor to bring peace between a man and his wife."[92]

Hillel **would** often **say: Someone who tries to become famous** will end up **losing** any good **reputation** he already has.

Someone who does not work to continually **increase** his Torah knowledge will instead see it **decrease.**

Someone who is able to teach Torah and **does not teach deserves death,** because Torah is a source of life and he has withheld it from others.

Someone who uses the crown of Torah for personal benefit **will be destroyed**.

הוּא הָיָה אוֹמֵר:
נְגַד שְׁמָא אֲבַד שְׁמֵהּ,

וּדְלָא מוֹסִיף יָסֵף,

וּדְלָא יַלִּיף קְטָלָא חַיָּב,

וּדְאִשְׁתַּמֵּשׁ בְּתַגָּא חֲלָף.

Learn and Live

This mishnah emphasizes that Torah is our very life. Imagine if someone would say "I will take a short break from life and resume living tomorrow." Obviously that would not work at all! The same is with Torah—we must learn it continually to keep up our connection to it.

Another helpful tip brought out in this mishnah is that one of the best ways to retain your learning is by adding to your knowledge. When you learn new things you gain a deeper understanding of the things you already know, reinforcing what you learned previously so you remember it better.

 Connections

 Sparks

The first part of the mishnah warns against arrogance that stems from one's Torah knowledge. This might lead people to think that it's better not to learn at all than to learn with an ulterior motive. To this Hillel says, "He who does not increase his learning, his knowledge decreases." One must continue learning while simultaneously working to remove ulterior motives.[93]

Another mistake one might make is to decide not to teach others, since it could make one feel proud of his knowledge. To this Hillel answers, "One who does not teach deserves death." Even if it is likely to cause arrogance, one must teach anyway.[94]

Poor in Knowledge Tzedakah includes sharing Torah knowledge with those who know less.[95]

Biography

Hillel was famous for his patience, and is used in the Gemara as the symbol of a humble person. Once, a certain non-Jew came to Hillel's colleague, Shammai, and said to him, "I want you to convert me to Judaism, but only if you can teach me the whole Torah while I stand on one foot." Obviously that was an impossible request, and so Shammai sent him off. The man then went to Hillel, and made the same request. To his surprise, Hillel calmly said to him, "What is hateful to you, do not do to another. That is the whole Torah, while the rest is the commentary—now go and learn it!"[96]

Hillel had eighty students. The Gemara says that thirty of them were so great, they were worthy to have the Shechinah rest on them as it did on Moshe Rabbeinu. Another thirty were great enough to merit the sun stopping for them, just as it stopped for Yehoshua. Of all his students, the greatest was Yonasan ben Uziel, who is famous for writing Targum Yonasan.[97]

Hillel is buried in Meron close to Rabi Shimon bar Yochai.

Behind the Quote

Hillel was known for his humility.[98] The story is told of one isolated incident when Hillel showed a small hint of arrogance. When Hillel came to Eretz Yisrael from Bavel, the 14th of Nissan, Erev Pesach, occurred on Shabbos, and the Chachamim were unsure whether the shechting and offering of the Korban Pesach may override the laws of Shabbos. Only Hillel knew the halachah, and he explained that the Korban Pesach does override Shabbos. As a result, Hillel was immediately appointed as the Nassi, and he began teaching halachah to the other Chachamim. During the shiur, he rebuked the other Chachamim for not having properly honored the two great Tzaddikim Shmayah and Avtalyon.

As a result of the slight show of arrogance implied in the rebuke, Hillel forgot some of his learning.[99] It was because of this personal experience that he warns others to be very careful to avoid any arrogance.[100]

Word Power

נְגַד שְׁמָא אֲבַד שְׁמֵהּ These words can be read, "One who wishes to have a great name must first lose his name," by becoming exceedingly humble. When someone is truly humble, people will treat him with honor.[101]

חֲלָף Hillel uses the word חֲלָף to describe the result when one uses his Torah knowledge inappropriately. The same word also means to exchange. The greatest thing a Jew can achieve is to learn Torah and honor it, thereby connecting to Hashem. One who uses Torah for his own benefit has exchanged the real purpose of Torah.

Personal Gain

Rabi Tarfon owned many fields and orchards. Once, he was eating figs in his orchard and the watchman, not knowing who owned the orchard, mistook him for a thief. The watchman threw him into a sack and went to throw him into the river. Realizing that his life was in danger, Rabi Tarfon called out, "Woe is to Tarfon whom this man is about to murder!" Hearing this, the watchman realized his mistake and quickly ran off, leaving Rabi Tarfon unharmed.

For the rest of his life Rabi Tarfon was pained by the fact that he had used the crown of Torah for his personal benefit.[102]

Did You Know?

Tone Down the Rhetoric

The teachings of this mishnah are in Aramaic, the language that was spoken by the Jews in Bavel, where Hillel was from. Why did Hillel choose to say these teachings in Aramaic rather than Lashon Hakodesh?

Words spoken in Lashon Hakodesh are very powerful and tend to be fulfilled. Hillel did not want the harsh punishments mentioned in this mishnah to carry that power, so he said them in Aramaic instead.[103]

Hillel **would** often **say:**
If I do not try **to** help **myself, who** will do so **for** me?
But **if I am** selfish and try **to** help only **myself, what am I** worth? **And if I** do **not** do what I should **now, when** will I do it? I may not have the opportunity later.

הוּא הָיָה אוֹמֵר:
אִם אֵין אֲנִי לִי, מִי לִי,
וּכְשֶׁאֲנִי לְעַצְמִי, מָה אֲנִי,
וְאִם לֹא עַכְשָׁו, אֵימָתַי.

Motivate Yourself

The mishnah lists three thoughts that we can use to push ourselves to achieve more.

אִם אֵין אֲנִי לִי, מִי לִי? — To become a better person, you have to work on it yourself. Imagine a chicken that has become covered in dirt. If its owner wanted to clean it, he would have to spend hours wiping each feather, and still might not manage to remove every spot. Yet if the chicken would just give one good shake of its wings, all the dirt would fly off in an instant!

Parents, teachers, and friends can help you, but the only one who can really change you is you![105]

וּכְשֶׁאֲנִי לְעַצְמִי, מָה אֲנִי? — Working hard on yourself comes with the risk of becoming so absorbed with yourself that you forget to think about others. But what is all that work worth if you don't do anything for others?[106]

וְאִם לֹא עַכְשָׁו אֵימָתַי? — Something that is worth doing is worth doing now! This moment will never return and the opportunity might be lost forever![107]

 Connections

The first two statements in this mishnah together teach us something new. When it comes to yourself, don't wait for others to tell you what is right or wrong. At the same time, when around others, don't keep to yourself and expect them to figure out everything on their own. You should always be ready to help others.[104]

 Did You Know?

Missed the Purpose of its Creation Time, just like everything else, was created by Hashem and needs to be used to serve Him. Even if you do eventually do a good thing that you pushed off for later, the original moment not used in Hashem's service was not elevated as it could have been. And unlike most other things, once that moment has passed, it can never be recovered.[107]

Biography

Hillel tried very hard to help people in need, providing for them even things many others deemed unnecessary. There was once a rich man who lost all his money. Hillel hired a servant to run in front of the poor man's horse to clear the way for him, as he had been accustomed to when he was rich. One day, Hillel couldn't find anyone to do it, so he went and personally ran in front of the horse for a distance of three mil—almost two miles![108]

There was a time that the Chachamim were gathered in Yericho. They heard a Heavenly voice announce, "One of you is worthy of the ruach hakodesh of a navi, but your generation does not deserve this." All assembled turned immediately toward Hillel, understanding that the voice was referring to him.

When Hillel passed away they said of him, "He was a truly humble man and chassid, a leader of the caliber of Ezra Hasofer."[109]

Word Power

אִם אֵין אֲנִי לִי, מִי לִי These words can also be read "If I do not own myself, what do I really own?" What is the worth of everything else I possess if I cannot even control my own self?[110]

מִי לִי The word מִי can refer to Hashem, Whom we can never fully understand or describe and is therefore referred to as "Who." Accordingly, the mishnah can be read, "If I am not for myself"—if I am humble, then "מִי לִי—Hashem is with me."[111]

Sparks

It Only Gets Harder A young sapling growing the wrong way is relatively easy to straighten, compared to a grown tree. In the same way, the best time to work on yourself is in your youth. As the mishnah says, "if not now, when?" If you will not work to improve your character while you are young, when will you do it—when you are older, and it is even more difficult to change?[112]

Can't be Done for You Wealth and money can sometimes be earned without any effort, like when someone inherits a vast fortune. Spiritual growth, however, depends only on the effort that a person himself puts in. No one else can do it for him, nor stop him from doing it. It's entirely up to him.[105]

Start Again with Me

When the Maggid of Mezritch was a young child, his home was destroyed in a fire. He was surprised when he saw how greatly it affected his mother, and he asked her: "Is it right that the loss of physical possessions causes so much distress?"

"G-d forbid!" answered his mother. "I am not crying over the loss of the house. I am crying because of the loss of a very important document, which traced your lineage all the way back to the great Rabi Yochanan Hasandlar."

"If so," replied the boy, "you don't need to cry. A new prestigious ancestry will begin again from me!"[113]

Shammai says: Make your Torah learning a **permanent** thing that comes before everything else.

Say little and do a lot, and greet every person with a cheerful face.

שַׁמַּאי אוֹמֵר:
עֲשֵׂה תוֹרָתְךָ קֶבַע,
אֱמוֹר מְעַט וַעֲשֵׂה הַרְבֵּה,
וֶהֱוֵי מְקַבֵּל אֶת כָּל הָאָדָם
בְּסֵבֶר פָּנִים יָפוֹת.

Smile!

Think about the people you see every day from the moment you wake up until you go to sleep. They may include your parents, siblings, neighbors, classmates, teachers, bus driver, school guard, storekeeper, and others. Think what a difference it would make to their day if you would greet them the way this mishnah teaches, with a cheerful face. Sharing a friendly smile brings good cheer to them and to yourself!

 Did You Know?

Be a Do-a-lot Reshaim promise a lot, but fulfill very little. Tzaddikim promise little, but in actuality they do a lot. Efron originally offered Avraham his field to bury Sarah at no charge, but when it came down to it, charged him an outrageous price. Avraham, on the other hand, merely offered his guests some bread, and yet actually served them a full spread of butter, milk, bread, and meat.[114]

 Sparks

Under-Promise and Over-Deliver One of the situations where it is most important to take to heart the teaching "say little and do a lot," is when hosting guests. Sometimes guests are unsure as to whether their host really wants them there. It's when the host offers to his guests more than he'd promised that it shows that he truly desires their company.[115]

Biography

Hillel and Shammai were the fifth and last set of the zugos to lead the Jewish people. Hillel was the Nassi and Shammai served as the Av Beis Din. The students of Hillel and Shammai, referred to as בֵּית הִלֵּל and בֵּית שַׁמַּאי, are famous for their disagreements in regard to over 300 halachic rulings. Yet there are only three instances where Hillel and Shammai themselves are known to have argued.

Shammai was known for being very strict in his observance of mitzvos, and he encouraged others to do the same. One mitzvah he was especially particular about was keeping Shabbos in mind all throughout the week. If on a Sunday he would see a nice animal for sale, he would buy it to prepare for Shabbos. The next day, however, if he came across a nicer animal, he would buy that one for Shabbos, and eat the first one that night instead. The same thing could repeat itself multiple times in a week, and so it was said that Shammai ate all week in honor of Shabbos.[116]

Shammai is buried in Meron.

Behind the Quote

The Gemara relates three occasions when non-Jews came to Shammai asking to be converted, each one with his own foolish condition.[117] One wanted to learn only Torah Shebichsav. Another demanded to be appointed Kohen Gadol, and the third requested that Shammai teach him the entire Torah while he stood on one foot. Angered at their chutzpah, Shammai sent them off impatiently.

The men each went on with their request to Hillel, who gently found a way to correct their mistaken ideas. Shammai learned from Hillel how important it is to be kind, and therefore he teaches us to greet each person cheerfully.[118]

Sparks

Friendly to All A person who is very committed to Torah study might think to disassociate himself from others who don't talk about Torah, so as not to waste time that he could spend on studying. This is why, after stressing the importance of learning, Shammai concludes the mishnah, "greet every person with a cheerful face." Although Torah learning is extremely important, one must still treat every person in a kind and friendly manner.[119]

Did You Know?

Statistical Change In all the arguments between Beis Shammai and Beis Hillel, the halachah is like Beis Hillel, with only the following exceptions: in three cases the halachah is like Beis Shammai, and six where the halachah follows neither Hillel's nor Shammai's opinion.[120]

Some say that this rule will change when Mashiach comes, and the halachah will then be like Beis Shammai.[121]

Can't Be Disturbed

R' Efraim Margolis was a Talmid Chacham and a wealthy man. While he learned all day, his wife managed their business. She felt privileged to be able to support his Torah learning, and would only discuss business with her husband for a few minutes each day, while they ate.

One day, a businessman offered her a great deal that promised to earn them a huge profit. She didn't want to decide on her own whether to invest in the deal, so she went to the Beis Medrash and asked her husband to come out and to discuss the details. However, R' Efraim refused to interrupt his learning, even after his wife explained that the businessman could not wait and they would lose the opportunity. R' Efraim didn't budge. The businessman left and the deal was canceled.

Later, R' Efraim explained, "Chazal tell us that in order to acquire Torah you have to 'kill' yourself for it. This means that while you learn Torah, you must let nothing interrupt or distract you, just as if you were no longer alive. Tell me, if I weren't here in this world, would I be able to share my thoughts on this deal?"[122]

Rabban Gamliel would often say: Appoint for yourself a teacher in order to remove yourself from any uncertainty in Torah and mitzvos.

Do not give ma'aser by guessing how much you must give, even if it is more than the correct amount. Rather, make an exact calculation.

רַבָּן גַּמְלִיאֵל הָיָה אוֹמֵר: עֲשֵׂה לְךָ רַב, וְהִסְתַּלֵּק מִן הַסָּפֵק, וְאַל תַּרְבֶּה לְעַשֵּׂר אֲמָדוֹת.

Living Lessons

Verify First

The Gemara recounts many stories of great scholars who chose not to make decisions on their own, despite their great knowledge.[123] Every time a din Torah came to Rav Huna, he would bring ten students from the Beis Medrash of Rav to judge with him. Rav Ashi would consult with all the butchers in town when a sick animal was brought to him to rule if it was kosher.

Once, when Rav Mana had a question regarding a ladder that broke on Chol Hamoed, he asked his father Rav Yonah whether he was permitted to fix it. Rav Yonah told his son to find another rav to confirm his ruling, instead of relying on his own judgment.

This teaches us that even when you are confident in what you know, you should always still consult with a rav.[125]

 Did You Know?

Stricter is Not Always Better

Imagine some cheese fell into a pot of chicken soup on Erev Shabbos. You might think that it's best to be strict and to throw it all out, since it might not be kosher. This mishnah teaches us that it's wrong to do so without knowing the halachah. If the halachah is that the chicken does not have to be thrown out because the milk is nullified, then to be strict would be a waste of food. In fact, even if you are 99% sure of the halachah, that is a 100% valid question to ask the rav![124]

Word Power

וְהִסְתַּלֵּק מִן הַסָּפֵק The word סָפֵק—doubt has the same gematria as עֲמָלֵק, a total numerical value of 240. When the nations of the world saw the great miracles Hashem did for B'nei Yisrael, taking them out of Mitzrayim and splitting the Yam Suf for them, they trembled in fear. Only Amalek still had the chutzpah to attack, planting seeds of doubt in the minds of B'nei Yisrael. "Maybe Hashem won't always protect us?"

This is the tactic of Amalek: killing enthusiasm with thoughts of doubt. The mishnah's response to this is: "Remove yourself from doubt." Don't allow Amalek to cast a shadow of doubt on your belief, and trust in Hashem.[126]

Biography

Rabban Gamliel was the first leader after the period of the זוגות. He was also the first to be called by the title "Rabban," a new title generally used for a Nassi who was a descendant of Hillel.

Approximately forty years before the destruction of the second Beis Hamikdash, Rabban Gamliel decided to move the Sanhedrin out of its station in the Beis Hamikdash. This was because of the halachah that only when the Sanhedrin is in its place are all Batei Din authorized to judge capital cases. Since the Romans who ruled at the time were preventing the Batei Din from ruling according to halachah, Rabban Gamliel felt that it would be better not to judge such cases at all rather than be forced to rule improperly.[127]

Rabban Gamliel instituted many decrees for the people. For example, he instituted that all people use inexpensive tachrichim (burial shrouds) so the poor should not be embarrassed to bury their dead.[128] Rabban Gamliel was greatly respected even by the non-Jews of his time, and led the nation during the end of the era of the second Beis Hamikdash. He passed away a short time before its destruction.

Behind the Quote

From this mishnah on, it no longer mentions who received the teachings of Torah from whom. The previous generations understood clearly what their predecessors taught them, and had no questions on the meaning of their words. At this point, however, the teachings were no longer fully understood, resulting in disagreements as to their meaning. Rabban Gamliel, therefore, addressed his generation and said: "Make yourself a rav." Work tirelessly to delve into your teacher's teachings until you are like a rav for yourself—until you have come to a clear understanding without any doubts.[129]

Did You Know?

Golden Deal Someone came to Rabban Gamliel with a complaint against Hashem. "Hashem is a thief; He put Adam Harishon to sleep and then stole his rib!"

The man's daughter was present, and after asking Rabban Gamliel's permission to answer, she told her father, "I need a judge to pass a ruling: someone broke into our home, stole a silver vessel and replaced it with a golden one. We must receive compensation!"

The father laughed, "If only all thieves were so considerate to replace what they stole with items of greater value." The daughter answered, "You have just answered your own question. Hashem took one small rib from Adam and returned to him a wife to be his partner."[130]

Story
Bias Controls the Mind

When R' Shabsai Cohen, known as the Shach, was still a young man, he was hired to represent someone as a lawyer at a din Torah. The Shach skillfully explained his argument for the litigant he was representing. When he finished, the Rav said, "I cannot answer all your proofs but I still rule that you are wrong. I base my ruling on a new sefer recently published." The Rav pulled a sefer off the shelf and showed him the relevant point.

The Shach was stunned. "I am the author of that sefer! Yet I was so involved in the case that I saw it only from the perspective of my client, forgetting about that ruling."

The Shach was amazed at the wisdom of the words of Chachamim: a person does not see the faults in his reasoning on his own and must therefore always seek the advice of a rav.[131]

Sparks

A Teacher Removes Doubt "Appoint yourself a teacher (rav) and remove yourself from any doubt." A proper teacher answers any doubts regarding your path in life.[132]

Shimon, Rabban Gamliel's son, says: I grew up among Chachamim my entire life, and I have not found anything better for a person than silence.

Studying is not the most important thing, but action is.

Whoever talks too much brings on sin.

שִׁמְעוֹן בְּנוֹ אוֹמֵר: כָּל יָמַי גָּדַלְתִּי בֵּין הַחֲכָמִים, וְלֹא מָצָאתִי לַגּוּף טוֹב מִשְּׁתִיקָה,

וְלֹא הַמִּדְרָשׁ עִקָּר אֶלָּא הַמַּעֲשֶׂה,

וְכָל הַמַּרְבֶּה דְבָרִים מֵבִיא חֵטְא.

Wise Words

We often feel that we have so much to say and share with others. While that may be true, there is so much more to gain from listening to others, especially when around greater and smarter people.

Silence is the Best Cure

It is extremely painful to be humiliated in front of others. Chazal say that when one is insulted but doesn't answer back, he merits tremendous reward from Hashem. The pain he suffers from the harassment cleanses him from the effect of his aveiros.

The Chachamim taught: Those who are insulted but do not insult, hear themselves abused without answering, act with love and accept their suffering with joy (knowing that everything comes from Hashem and is ultimately for their good), of them it is said, "Those who love Hashem are like the powerful rising sun." The sun is shamed, so to speak, when the moon rises during his reign, and yet does not take offense and continues to shine its light brightly. So too, when a person is insulted and does not reply, his greatness shines forth like the powerful rising sun.[133]

Biography

Rabban Shimon was the son of Rabban Gamliel, who was mentioned in the previous mishnah.

He used to participate personally in the simchas beis hasho'eivah celebration in the Beis Hamikdash, juggling eight burning torches.[134]

Rabban Shimon ben Gamliel worked to improve the social welfare of the nation. There was a time when evil merchants conspired to raise the price of doves for korbanos, making them extremely expensive. To combat this, Rabban Shimon made a temporary ruling making fewer bird korbanos necessary, lowering the demand, and forcing the prices to return to normal levels.[135]

Rabban Shimon was one of the Asarah Harugei Malchus—the famous group of ten Tzaddikim ruthlessly murdered by the Romans—and was killed alongside his friend Rabi Yishmael Kohen Gadol. While being led to their execution, each one begged to be killed first, so that he would be spared witnessing the torture and death of his friend. Rabi Yishmael claimed that as Kohen Gadol, he was entitled to die first, and Rabban Shimon argued that being Nassi gave him the right. Lots were drawn, and Rabban Shimon was executed first.

When Rabi Akiva heard about the death of Rabban Shimon and Rabi Yishmael, he rose, put on sackcloth, tore his garments in mourning and told his students, "Be prepared for punishment, for Hashem has taken these two Tzaddikim from the world so that they shouldn't experience it."[136] Rabban Shimon was killed on the 25th of Sivan and is buried in K'far Kanna.

Behind the Quote

Rabban Shimon says that all his life—including after he became Nassi—he grew up among Chachamim, because he continued learning from them. He teaches us that only when one is silent and listens humbly to the words of others does one's knowledge and character continue to grow. To emphasize his great humility, the mishnah refers to him simply as Shimon, without the title Rabban as he is usually called.[138]

Did You Know?

Louder than Words Actions speak louder than words. If you want to influence someone in a positive way, you can try to talk to him, but he may not be impressed. However, when you act a certain way, you are that much more likely to affect the person who sees it. He knows now that it's not just talk, but that you really mean it.[139]

Sheepishly Great

A newly appointed rav in a certain city realized that the people there were not careful to fulfill practical mitzvos such as netilas yadayim, tefillin, birkas hamazon, and tzitzis. When he brought it up to them, they replied, "The main thing is to have a good heart, and we all have good hearts; we don't steal, we don't fight, and we don't hurt anyone. That's what really counts!"

The rav realized he needed to teach them a lesson. One morning, he announced that a great Tzaddik had passed away. The rav cried bitterly and spoke of the Tzaddik who treated others very well, never stole, never hurt anyone, and never spoke lashon hara. Everyone mourned the loss of such a great individual and followed him to the cemetery to participate in the burial. To their shock, when they arrived, they saw a dead sheep being prepared for burial.

They complained to the rav, "Why did you make a joke out of us?"

The rav replied, "I don't understand. You told me that the main thing is a good heart, so what difference is there between a person and a sheep? In fact, the sheep must truly be a Tzaddik because he never did anything wrong."

The townspeople understood their mistake and started being careful in their performance of mitzvos.[137]

Rabban Shimon ben Gamliel says: The world continues to exist and function civilly because of three things: because of justice, because of truth, and because of peace. As it says in Zechariah: Judge with truth and try to negotiate a compromise—which leads to a peaceful judgment—within your gates.

רַבָּן שִׁמְעוֹן בֶּן גַּמְלִיאֵל אוֹמֵר, עַל שְׁלֹשָׁה דְבָרִים הָעוֹלָם קַיָּם: עַל הַדִּין, וְעַל הָאֱמֶת, וְעַל הַשָּׁלוֹם, שֶׁנֶּאֱמַר: אֱמֶת וּמִשְׁפַּט שָׁלוֹם שִׁפְטוּ בְּשַׁעֲרֵיכֶם.

Play Nicely, My Children

Just as parents love nothing more than to see their children getting along and caring for each other, Hashem takes great pleasure when we live in peace with one another. The three virtues mentioned in our mishnah are the keys to leading a peaceful life. Peace is attained when there is justice, which brings the truth to light. When a rav or Beis Din resolves an issue correctly, in accordance with the Torah, it brings to true peace.

 Did You Know?

Function Civilly The second mishnah of this perek talks about the three things upon which the world stands. This mishnah lists the three things that enable the world to exist. What is the difference between the two?

The three things for which the world was initially created—Torah, service of Hashem, and acts of kindness—are the foundation of the world, upon which it "stands." Once the world was created already, it needs justice, truth, and peace to continue to function, as explained in this mishnah.[140]

Compromise The passuk quoted in this mishnah, "אֱמֶת וּמִשְׁפַּט שָׁלוֹם שִׁפְטוּ בְּשַׁעֲרֵיכֶם—Truth and peaceful judgment…." refers to a compromise between two parties. Even though a compromise means that neither of the people receives what he would have if he had won the case, it is nevertheless the preferred way, since it enables peace between all those involved.[141]

 Word Power

וְעַל הָאֱמֶת In the holy script used for a Sefer Torah, called Ksav Ashuri, all the letters that make up the word שֶׁקֶר—falsehood, stand on only one foot. The letters of אֱמֶת—truth, on the other hand, have two feet that help them stand upright on their own.

In the end, lies will fall apart and truth will always remain standing.[142]

Biography

Rabban Shimon ben Gamliel of this mishnah is the grandson of Rabban Shimon ben Gamliel quoted in the previous mishnah. He was the father of Rabi Yehudah Hanassi. He was known for his humility, even referring to himself as a fox in comparison to Rabi Shimon bar Yochai.

Rabban Shimon worked very hard to strengthen the prestige and power of the office of the Nassi, not for his own honor but for the honor of the Torah. He is so greatly respected that wherever his opinion is brought down in the mishnah, in fact over 100 times, the halachah follows his opinion, with the exception of only three cases.

His son, Rabi Yehudah Hanassi, once said, "There are three people in history who were truly humble: Yehonasan ben Shaul Hamelech, the B'nei Beseirah, and my father."[143]

Sparks

Personal Pillars The three pillars of this mishnah can also refer to the three faculties of thought, speech, and action, the pillars that hold up each person's private world. Justice refers to action—treating your fellow in a fair manner. Truth refers to speech—speaking only the truth. Peace refers to thought—even in the privacy of your own mind, you should be at peace with everyone.[144]

Behind the Quote

Rabban Shimon was known for emphasizing the importance of justice. Rabi Tarfon and Rabi Akiva once said that if they had been part of the Sanhedrin when it still had the power to use the death penalty, they would ensure that no one would ever receive the death penalty by confusing the witnesses with questions they couldn't possibly answer. About this Rabban Shimon commented: "This would increase the number of murderers among B'nei Yisrael," because people would lose their fear of punishment.[145]

Rabban Shimon was also known to stress the importance of peace. He said about Yosef's brothers: "How great is peace, as we see how the shevatim lied to Yosef, telling him that their father had requested that he forgive them, just for the sake of bringing peace."[146]

Peace is Worth More

On Erev Pesach, many tzedakah collectors would come to the house of the Apter Rav, known as the אוֹהֵב יִשְׂרָאֵל because of his great love for his fellow Jews. One Erev Pesach, when the Apter Rav's attendant was giving matzos to the collectors, as was customary, he accidentally gave the special matzos that had been baked with additional stringencies especially for the Rav to use at the seder. When his wife realized the mistake, she took regular matzos and placed them where the special seder matzos had been. That night at the seder, all went well and nothing of the incident was mentioned.

After Pesach a quarreling couple came to the Rav. The husband explained that he wished to divorce his wife because she refused to maintain separate non-gebroks dishes for him on Pesach.

The Rav called in his wife and asked her, "What matzos did I use for the seder?" Seeing her hesitation, he continued, "Have no fear, just tell us what happened."

She recounted the mistake and how she had replaced the special matzos with regular ones. The Rav then turned to the unhappy husband and said, "At my seder, I fulfilled the mitzvah of eating matzah on simple matzos instead of the specially prepared matzos, but I didn't mention anything, only to keep peace in the home, and you want to divorce your wife because she won't give you separate dishes?"[147]

Say this mishnah upon completing each perek:

Rabi Chananya ben Akashya says:

The Holy One, blessed be He, wanted to make B'nei **Yisrael** have many **merits.**

He therefore gave them an abundance of Torah and mitzvos, so that they would have many opportunities to connect to Him.

As it says in Yeshayah: **Hashem wanted, for the sake of** increasing B'nei Yisrael's **righteousness, that the Torah be made great and glorious.**

רַבִּי חֲנַנְיָא בֶּן עֲקַשְׁיָא אוֹמֵר:
רָצָה הַקָּדוֹשׁ בָּרוּךְ הוּא
לְזַכּוֹת אֶת יִשְׂרָאֵל
לְפִיכָךְ הִרְבָּה לָהֶם
תּוֹרָה וּמִצְוֹת
שֶׁנֶּאֱמַר: יְיָ חָפֵץ לְמַעַן
צִדְקוֹ יַגְדִּיל תּוֹרָה וְיַאְדִּיר.

Endnotes

1. הקדמת הרמב"ם לספר היד
2. ברכות לג, א
3. מעשה אבות
4. רע"ב
5. בבא מציעא פה, ב
6. ביאורים
7. ר' בחיי
8. ביאורים
9. יומא לט, א
10. סוטה לג, א. מגילת תענית - עשרים ושנים בשבט
11. מדרש שמואל
12. נדרים ט, ב. יומא לט, א. ביאורים
13. יומא סט, א
14. לקו"ש ח"כ ע' 50
15. ירושלמי ב"מ פ"ב ה"ה
16. פיה"מ להרמב"ם
17. ביאורים ע' 47
18. תוספות יו"ט
19. הפלאה
20. דברים כח, י
21. ספורי חסידים - מועדים, שבועות
22. סוכה כא, ב
23. עבודה זרה יט, ב ברש"י ד"ה שיחת חולין
24. מלכים ב' ג, יא
25. חגיגה פ"ב מ"ז
26. חגיגה טז, א וברש"י שם
27. ביאורים
28. מדרש שמואל
29. ביאורים
30. כתובות קיא, ב
31. ראש השנה יח, ב. דרשות הר"ן דרוש ח'
32. ר' אברהם אחי הגר"א. פעולת צדיק לחיים (לר' חיים פלאג'י)
33. חגיגה ג, א
34. מדרש שמואל
35. תמורה טו, ב וברש"י שם
36. אלשיך
37. מדרש שמואל
38. רש"י. ר' בחיי
39. מסכת אבות ע"פ יינה של תורה עמ' 17
40. שמחת תורה תרצ"א
41. כתונת פסים
42. מהר"ש שי"ק
43. ביאורים
44. סוטה מז, א
45. סוטה מז, א
46. ביאורים
47. כתובות סז, א
48. היום יום י"ד מנחם אב
49. משפחות רבנים אין אונגארין חלק ב' ע' שט"ו
50. מדרש שמואל
51. מדרש שמואל
52. מדרש שמואל
53. מדרש שמואל
54. מהר"ל
55. מדרש שמואל
56. ספורי חסידים - תורה, בראשית
57. חיד"א בפתח עינים
58. חגיגה טז, ב
59. ירושלמי חגיגה פ"ב ה"ב
60. סוטה מז, א
61. ירושלמי כתובות פ"ח הי"א
62. סנהדרין מה, ב
63. מעשי אבות
64. רבינו יונה
65. ר"י חיון (רבו של האברבנאל)
66. ירושלמי ב"מ פ"ב ה"ה
67. רמב"ם
68. רבינו יונה
69. מדרש שמואל
70. ביאורים
71. גיטין נז, ב
72. רע"ב
73. מדרש שמואל
74. מדרש שמואל בשם הריטב"א
75. נדרים מט, ב
76. שבת יב, ב
77. תפארת ישראל
78. מילי דאבות לר' יוסף בן
79. ראה מדרש שמואל, תפארת ישראל ועוד
80. אמרי שפר ע' 119
81. ראה שבת לא, א
82. אבות דרבי נתן פרק י"ב משנה ג'
83. יומא לה, א
84. מדרש שמואל, תפארת ישראל, לקו"א פרק ל"ב
85. ספרי דברים לד, ז (פיסקא שנז)
86. סוטה כא, א
87. גיטין לד, ב
88. ביאורים
89. שה"ש רבה, סדרה תנינא י"ט
90. דברים א, ד וברש"י שם
91. הר' יוסף יעבץ
92. ירושלמי סוטה פ"א ה"ד
93. כסף משנה הל' תלמוד תורה פ"ג ה"י
94. רש"י, ספורנו, תפארת ישראל
95. סוטה כב, א
96. שבת לא, א
97. סוכה כח, א
98. ראה שבת לא, א
99. פסחים סו, א
100. ביאורים
101. מדרש שמואל
102. נדרים סב, א
103. דברים נחמדים
104. מדרש שמואל
105. דרך חיים להמהר"ל
106. מדרש שמואל
107. הר' ז' שושן, הובא במדרש שמואל
108. כתובות סז, א
109. סוטה מח, ב
110. תפארת ישראל
111. מדרש שמואל
112. רבינו יונה, רמב"ם
113. סיפורי חסידים - תורה, פ' וארא
114. רמב"ם, מבבא מציעא פז, א
115. חסדי אבות להחיד"א
116. ביצה טז, א
117. שבת לא, א
118. מילי דאבות לה"ר יחיאל מיכאל מושקין
119. מדרש שמואל
120. מבוא התלמוד לר' שמואל הנגיד
121. מקדש מלך, פ' בראשית יז, ב
122. מסכת אבות ע"פ יינה של תורה ע' 43
123. סנהדרין ז, ב. וראה הוריות ג, ב בשינוי קצת
124. תפארת ישראל
125. ירושלמי מו"ק פ"א ה"י
126. כנסת ישראל לה"ר ישראל גאלדמאנן
127. עבודה זרה ח, ב
128. מועד קטן כז, ב
129. מדרש שמואל
130. סנהדרין לט, א
131. שמן המשחה ע' 120
132. מילי דאבות לה"ר ישראל מרדכי בן זאב יוסף
133. פתח עינים להחיד"א
134. סוכה נג, א
135. כריתות פ"ו מ"ז
136. שמחות פ"ח ה"ח
137. מעשה אבות ע' 252
138. מדרש שמואל, ביאורים
139. מילי דאבות לה"ר יוסף חיון
140. ר' יונה, מאירי, תוספות יו"ט
141. ספורנו
142. שבת קד, א, הובא במגן אבות להרשב"ץ
143. בבא מציעא פד, ב
144. תפארת ישראל. וראה שבת קכז, ב
145. מכות ז, א
146. מסכת דרך ארץ זוטא, פרק השלום
147. ספורי חסידים - מועדים, פסח

44

Chapter Two

Kol Yisrael

Say this mishnah before beginning each new perek:

All B'nei **Yisrael have a portion in the World to Come.**

As it says in Yeshayah regarding B'nei Yisrael upon Moshiach's arrival: **Your people are all tzaddikim,** and **they will all inherit Eretz** Yisrael **forever**—they will never be exiled from it again.

All will recognize that they are **the branch of My planting and the work of My hands,** in which I, Hashem, **take pride.**

כָּל יִשְׂרָאֵל יֵשׁ לָהֶם
חֵלֶק לְעוֹלָם הַבָּא,
שֶׁנֶּאֱמַר: וְעַמֵּךְ כֻּלָּם צַדִּיקִים,
לְעוֹלָם יִירְשׁוּ אָרֶץ,
נֵצֶר מַטָּעַי מַעֲשֵׂה
יָדַי לְהִתְפָּאֵר.

PART 1

Rabi Yehudah Hanassi says:
Which is the proper path in life that a person should choose for himself?
Any path that is honorable and beneficial for himself as well as to other people.

Be careful with what seems to be an unimportant mitzvah just as with one that seems very important, because you do not know what reward is given for each of the mitzvos, or how important each one is to Hashem.

Compare the expenses or loss of money that a mitzvah might cause to the reward that you will receive for doing it, and compare the temporary physical gain from an aveirah with the loss that it will bring about.

רַבִּי אוֹמֵר: אֵיזוֹ הִיא דֶרֶךְ יְשָׁרָה שֶׁיָּבוֹר לוֹ הָאָדָם, כָּל שֶׁהִיא תִפְאֶרֶת לְעֹשֶׂיהָ וְתִפְאֶרֶת לוֹ מִן הָאָדָם, וֶהֱוֵי זָהִיר בְּמִצְוָה קַלָּה כְּבַחֲמוּרָה, שֶׁאֵין אַתָּה יוֹדֵעַ מַתַּן שְׂכָרָן שֶׁל מִצְוֹת, וֶהֱוֵי מְחַשֵּׁב הֶפְסֵד מִצְוָה כְּנֶגֶד שְׂכָרָהּ, וּשְׂכַר עֲבֵרָה כְּנֶגֶד הֶפְסֵדָהּ.

No Small Matter

When it is particularly hard to fulfill a specific mitzvah, the yetzer hara may try to discourage you and say, "Why work so hard to fulfill such a small mitzvah?" The mishnah tells us how to respond, "Be as careful with a small mitzvah as with a major one." Each mitzvah you fulfill connects you to Hashem, especially when you have to work hard.

Never underestimate the importance of a single mitzvah. The Rambam rules that one must view the entire world as balanced equally between good and bad. Just one good deed can tip the scales for good and bring about salvation for oneself and for the entire world![1]

Biography

Rabi Yehudah Hanassi Rabi Yehudah Hanassi, known also as Rebbi (teacher) or Rabbeinu Hakadosh (our holy teacher), was the son of Rabban Shimon ben Gamliel from the last mishnah of the previous perek. He was born on the day that Rabi Akiva was murdered by the Romans.[2]

Rebbi lived a long life and served as Nassi for many years. Rebbi is most famous for compiling the Mishnah. He realized that people were forgetting Torah Sheb'al Peh, so he brought all of the Chachamim together to resolve disputes and record all the halachos in a single system. He finished compiling the Mishnah in the year 3948, 120 years after the destruction of the second Beis Hamikdash.

Before his passing, Rebbi assured his family that he would return home every Friday night and asked them to prepare the candles, table, and his bed as before. So it was, even after his passing, Rebbi came home each week to make Kiddush for his family. This continued until it happened that a neighbor was visiting, and bore witness to the amazing scene. After that Rebbi did not return, out of concern that other Tzaddikim—who did not share the privilege of returning to their homes after their passing—shouldn't seem less righteous.[3]

Sparks

When You Can Choose We shouldn't differentiate or choose between big and small **mitzvos**. Therefore, the choice referred to in this mishnah is in regards to character traits that a person chooses to adopt.[4]

Do Unto Others The first part of the mishnah can also be read as a question and answer: "What is the proper path of treating someone else? Whatever you would choose for yourself!"

Before doing or saying something to another, stop and think: "Would I want this done for me?"[5]

Word Power

תִּפְאֶרֶת לוֹ מִן הָאָדָם People naturally love themselves and cannot judge themselves honestly. This mishnah can mean that when analyzing your actions and character, think how you would look at it if it were someone else. If you still think it is "beautiful" from the other person's perspective, then you can know that it is indeed correct.[6]

אֵיזוֹ הִיא דֶּרֶךְ יְשָׁרָה The Torah is the only guide for our way of life, so why does the Tanna ask which path we should choose for ourselves?

When a servant, child, or student obeys his superior, sometimes it's with resentment. When doing something by choice, however, it's usually done with a measure of enthusiasm.

This mishnah teaches us that even though mitzvos are commanded to us, we should fulfill them with the same enthusiasm as if it were our choice.[7]

This mishnah teaches the importance of balancing one's own needs with the needs of others. This balance was especially important for Rabi Yehudah Hanassi, who was the leader of his generation. A leader must be willing to forgo his own personal benefit in order to assist others.[8]

First Chance

There was once a man who was imprisoned. He obviously could not go to shul and had no access to the things he needed to fulfill the mitzvos, such as tefillin, a shofar, and the like. After pleading with his captors, he was finally permitted one day off when he could leave prison. But which day should he choose? Yom Kippur? Rosh Hashanah? Perhaps a day of Sukkos so that he could eat in a sukkah and shake the lulav and esrog?

Unable to decide, he wrote to the Radvaz, a leading Rav at the time, asking for guidance. The Radvaz answered: Choose the earliest day that you can so that you will be able to fulfill mitzvos that much sooner.

We never know which mitzvos are dearest to Hashem, so we should always take the first opportunity.[9]

PART 2

Consider the three things listed below and you will not come to do an aveirah; know what exists above you in heaven:

There is an eye that sees everything,

there is an ear that hears everything,

and all your deeds are written and recorded in a book.

הִסְתַּכֵּל בִּשְׁלֹשָׁה דְבָרִים,

וְאֵין אַתָּה בָא לִידֵי עֲבֵרָה.

דַּע מַה לְמַעְלָה מִמָּךְ,

עַיִן רוֹאָה,

וְאֹזֶן שׁוֹמַעַת,

וְכָל מַעֲשֶׂיךָ בְּסֵפֶר נִכְתָּבִים.

Living Lessons

Global Surveilance

The concept of an eye watching, ear listening, and hand recording is now easier than ever to relate to. With the aid of modern technology, people today can easily watch and listen to happenings on the other end of the world. Certainly Hashem, Who created the universe and directs everything within it, is constantly aware of everything that happens in it. As Dovid Hamelech says in Tehillim, הֲנֹטַע אֹזֶן הֲלֹא יִשְׁמָע אִם יֹצֵר עַיִן הֲלֹא יַבִּיט – Surely the One Who created the ear can hear, and the One Who formed the eye can see.

People act differently when they know that others are watching. We must always bear in mind that Hashem sees everything, and before every action, we must consider whether or not Hashem will be proud of it.

 Sparks

Humble as Yaakov Avinu Rebbi was known for his humility. Once, he asked Rabi Afos to write a letter for him to the king, Antoninus. Rabi Afos began to write as follows: "From Yehudah Hanassi to our master King Antoninus." Rebbi immediately tore it up and dictated to him as follows: "From Yehudah, your servant, to our master King Antoninus." When Rabi Afos asked why he was forgoing his honor, Rebbi answered him, "Am I better than my grandfather Yaakov? When he sent a messenger to his brother Eisav he said, 'So you shall say to my master Eisav… so has said your servant Yaakov.'"[10]

 **Word Power**

דַּע מַה לְמַעְלָה מִמְּךָ These words can also be read as follows: דַּע—You should know that מַה לְמַעְלָה—that which happens above in the spiritual worlds מִמְּךָ—is from you, and dependent upon your actions! For example, when you act mercifully, Hashem's attribute of mercy is aroused above.[11]

לִידֵי עֲבֵרָה These words can also mean "the handles of an aveirah." At first, the yetzer hara tries to lead us to do things that aren't actual aveiros, but like a handle that opens a door and brings you closer to them. Through these small permissible acts, he slowly introduces you to sin, starting small but eventually taking you very far off.

Keeping this mishnah in mind will help you avoid these little handles, and certainly real aveiros.[12]

 Connections

The two parts of this mishnah are related. Keeping in mind that Hashem is always watching makes it easier to do each mitzvah, big or small, with greater care. We know that Hashem is watching with delight as we fulfill His Will.[13]

 Did You Know?

It's the Action That Counts The mishnah says that a person's actions—but not his thoughts—are recorded in a book. This is because even if someone thinks about or plans to do an aveirah, but doesn't actually do it, it is not held against him.[14]

 **Story**

He's Watching

Two friends were traveling in a wagon. The driver saw a beautiful orchard with delicious fruit trees and wanted to take some fruit. He asked his friend to stand guard while he climbed the fence to take some fruit. Suddenly, as he began climbing the fence, his friend screamed, "Someone's watching!" The driver ran back to the wagon and they sped off. Once they were a safe distance away, he turned around to see who had been watching but saw no one. Bewildered, he asked his friend, "Who was watching?"

"Hashem was watching," answered the friend. "Hashem is the Eye that sees, in all places and at all times."[15]

רַבָּן גַּמְלִיאֵל בְּנוֹ שֶׁל רַבִּי יְהוּדָה הַנָּשִׂיא אוֹמֵר: יָפֶה תַלְמוּד תּוֹרָה עִם דֶּרֶךְ אֶרֶץ, שֶׁיְּגִיעַת שְׁנֵיהֶם מַשְׁכַּחַת עָוֹן, וְכָל תּוֹרָה שֶׁאֵין עִמָּהּ מְלָאכָה סוֹפָהּ בְּטֵלָה וְגוֹרֶרֶת עָוֹן,

וְכָל הָעוֹסְקִים עִם הַצִּבּוּר יִהְיוּ עוֹסְקִים עִמָּהֶם לְשֵׁם שָׁמַיִם, שֶׁזְּכוּת אֲבוֹתָם מְסַיַּעְתָּם, וְצִדְקָתָם עוֹמֶדֶת לָעַד,

וְאַתֶּם, מַעֲלֶה אֲנִי עֲלֵיכֶם שָׂכָר הַרְבֵּה כְּאִלּוּ עֲשִׂיתֶם.

Rabban Gamliel the son of Rabi Yehudah Hanassi says: Torah learning goes well with having a job, because working hard at both of them will keep you away from aveiros. Any Torah learning that is not accompanied by work will eventually end, and that will cause a person to do aveiros.

Whoever works in communal affairs should do so for the sake of Heaven and not for personal honor, because it is really the merit of the community's ancestors and their righteousness, which lasts forever, that helps them and gives them success in their affairs. Although their success is not merely due to their efforts, still Hashem says: I will give you great reward as if you had accomplished it alone.

Living Lessons

Find Him Everywhere

Learning Torah trains a person to see Hashem's hand directing everything in the world. Being involved in business gives a person opportunities to use that training and actually see Hashem's constant הַשְׁגָּחָה פְּרָטִית. In business it becomes very clear how Hashem orchestrates everything, and that a person's efforts are merely the vessel to receive Hashem's blessing. This awareness leads a person to a great level of trust in

Hashem. For if one is aware that Hashem is the One pulling the strings, then even in the direst of situations there is nothing to fear, for His salvation can come at any time.[16]

 Connections

The previous mishnah teaches three things one should consider to keep away from doing an aveirah. This mishnah adds that a combination of Torah learning and hard work will further empower the person to מַשְׁכַּחַת עָוֹן—forget sin; he will not even **think** about doing an aveirah.

 Word Power

שֶׁאֵין עִמָּהּ מְלָאכָה Another explanation of the word מְלָאכָה in this mishnah refers to the work of teaching Torah to others. For the Torah learning of one who learns for himself but not with others will not last. In fact, only when he does aid others will he merit to understand the true interpretation of Torah.[17]

Biography

Rabban Gamliel was Rebbi's oldest son, who took over the position of Nassi after his father's passing.

He is considered the last of the Tanna'im. He was chosen from among his brothers to be Nassi because of his great fear of sin, although his brother Shimon was superior to him in wisdom.[18] He was exceptionally careful with mitzvos. For example, although only holy foods such as terumah or korbanos had to be eaten in a state of taharah, he would not eat anything tamei.[19]

Rabban Gamliel had two sons, Rabi Yehudah Nesiah and Hillel. He is buried in Beis She'arim near his father.

Sparks

You Won't Lose Out One who dedicates his time to teaching Torah or bringing others closer to Torah and mitzvos may feel that it causes him to lose out on his own advancement in Torah learning or performance of mitzvos. Therefore, Hashem assures those who helps others for His sake, rather than for his personal benefit, "There is no need to worry. מַעֲלֶה אֲנִי—I consider it כְּאִלּוּ עֲשִׂיתֶם—as if you have performed mitzvos in the best possible way and שָׂכָר הַרְבֵּה—I will give you great reward!"[20]

Behind the Quote

The previous mishnah was taught by Rebbi, Rabban Gamliel's father. In his times, fear of Hashem and the desire for Torah was so great that Torah study alone could keep a person from sin.[21] Rabban Gamliel's generation was on a lower spiritual level, so they also needed to be busy with hard work to keep from sin.[22]

Story

Remember Your Place

R' Simchah Bunim of Pshischa would often visit the Danzig marketplace to seek out assimilated German Jews and bring them closer to Torah and mitzvos. After returning from one of these trips, he came to his Rebbe, the Chozeh of Lublin. Upon his arrival, instead of the warm greeting he usually received from his Rebbe, he was totally ignored. R' Simchah began to think, "What have I done wrong? Why is my Rebbe displeased with me?" He then realized that after these trips he tended to feel very good about himself and his accomplishments. It was after he came to this realization that his Rebbe finally welcomed him warmly.

The Chozeh explained to R' Simchah, "Don't be haughty, thinking that Hashem's help and blessings for your success comes to you because of your great merits. It's simply that in such a low place like the Danzig marketplace, Hashem has nowhere to rest, so if someone there has even the slightest merit, Hashem joins him."[23]

Beware of those in power, because they befriend a person only for their own needs. They appear to be a close friend as long as they have what to gain from him, but they will not stand by a person to help him in his time of need.

הֱווּ זְהִירִין בָּרָשׁוּת, שֶׁאֵין מְקָרְבִין לוֹ לְאָדָם אֶלָּא לְצֹרֶךְ עַצְמָן. נִרְאִין כְּאוֹהֲבִין בִּשְׁעַת הַנָּאָתָן, וְאֵין עוֹמְדִין לוֹ לְאָדָם בִּשְׁעַת דָּחֳקוֹ.

Living Lessons

Don't Rely on Them

The only One a person must put his trust in is, of course, Hashem. We shouldn't think that because an important government official is on our side, we are in safe hands. Our safety and salvation comes only from Hashem! So, when we see difficult times and we are in need of help, we must first increase our Torah learning, add in our performance of mitzvos with care, and call out to Hashem. Only once we've done all that should we turn to our friends in government for aid.[24]

We learn this from the story of Purim. When Mordechai heard of the evil decree against the Jewish people, his first step was to walk the streets in sackcloth and ashes to provoke the Jews to do teshuvah. He also gathered 22,000 children and learned Torah with them. Only afterward did he go to the palace to enlist Esther to plead with the king on behalf of her people. In the same way, Esther asked that all Jews fast on her behalf for three days, and only after would she go to Achashveirosh, the "friend" in government.

Connections

This mishnah continues from the previous mishnah in guiding the person involved in communal affairs. Even though they often need to be involved with government officials to service their communities, the mishnah warns them to bear in mind that contrary to how it may appear, these people act only for their personal interests.[25]

Word Power

הֱווּ זְהִירִין בָּרָשׁוּת Hashem commanded us to do mitzvos and stay far from aveiros. There are many things, however, that are neither mitzvos nor aveiros. These are referred to as דִּבְרֵי רְשׁוּת—permissible things. They include eating, drinking, sleeping, playing, and other neutral activities. About these the mishnah teaches: הֱווּ זְהִירִין בָּרָשׁוּת—be wary of permissible things. It is not enough to stay away from doing what's forbidden; a Jew must also keep himself from indulging in permissible worldly pleasures. For while these pleasures may appear as a "friend," and offer an enjoyable experience, they do not stand by him at his time of need—they do not help a person in the things that really matter, in his service of Hashem.[26]

Behind the Quote

Rabi Yehudah Hanassi appointed his son Rabban Gamliel to replace him as leader after his passing. Since Rabban Gamliel had to associate with government officials in his job as leader, he said this statement from his personal experience, warning against placing too much trust in these officials.

Sparks

Friendly Enemy "Beware of those in power" can also refer to the yetzer hara, who likes to be in charge. He presents an aveirah as a "friend," an enticing and enjoyable thing, when in fact, it yields only very short-lived pleasure. In fact, a short while later one usually regrets his mistake, and in the long run, the "friend" causes only trouble for the person, both in this world and in the next.[27]

Friend or Enemy?

The Malbim once had to travel to Paris to meet with government officials regarding a communal matter. He asked the mayor of his hometown, Bucharest, to write a letter of recommendation for him to present to the official. He thought that having such a reference would give him a better chance at succeeding with the officials he was going to see. Agreeably, the mayor wrote him the letter, sealed it, and sent him off.

While he was traveling, it occurred to him that it was likely that the mayor did not have the Malbim's best interest in mind at all, as he knew that such officials do things only for their own benefit. He decided against using the letter, tore it up, and placed his trust purely in Hashem.

One of the students who accompanied him was curious as to the contents of the letter, and so he quietly collected the shreds and painstakingly pieced them back together. He was shocked to discover that indeed, the mayor had written negatively of the Malbim, going so far as to suggest that the officials in Paris send the Malbim away without even hearing him out![28]

Rabban Gamliel **would** often **say: Make Hashem's will your will,** so that He will **make your will His will. Nullify your will before** Hashem's **will** so that He will **nullify the will of others before your will.**

Hillel says: **Do not separate yourself from the community** by ignoring their troubles.

Stay on guard and **do not be confident in your** ability to withstand temptation **until the day you die**.

Do not judge your friend until you are in his place and can fully understand what he is going through.

Do not say something that is not easily **understood,** assuming **that it will** eventually **be understood** after more thought, because it might be misinterpreted.

Do not say, "When I have **free** time **I will learn** Torah," **because you may never** have **free** time.

הוּא הָיָה אוֹמֵר: עֲשֵׂה רְצוֹנוֹ כִרְצוֹנְךָ, כְּדֵי שֶׁיַּעֲשֶׂה רְצוֹנְךָ כִרְצוֹנוֹ, בַּטֵּל רְצוֹנְךָ מִפְּנֵי רְצוֹנוֹ כְּדֵי שֶׁיְּבַטֵּל רְצוֹן אֲחֵרִים מִפְּנֵי רְצוֹנֶךָ.

הִלֵּל אוֹמֵר:
אַל תִּפְרוֹשׁ מִן הַצִּבּוּר,

וְאַל תַּאֲמִין בְּעַצְמְךָ עַד יוֹם מוֹתָךְ,

וְאַל תָּדִין אֶת חֲבֵרְךָ עַד שֶׁתַּגִּיעַ לִמְקוֹמוֹ,

וְאַל תֹּאמַר דָּבָר שֶׁאִי אֶפְשָׁר לִשְׁמוֹעַ שֶׁסּוֹפוֹ לְהִשָּׁמַע,

וְאַל תֹּאמַר לִכְשֶׁאֶפָּנֶה אֶשְׁנֶה, שֶׁמָּא לֹא תִפָּנֶה.

Don't Judge

Once, the idolatrous king Menasheh appeared to Rav Ashi in a dream. He challenged Rav Ashi with a difficult halachic question to which Rav Ashi had no answer. Rav Ashi pleaded with Menasheh to reveal the answer to him, promising to teach it in the name of Menasheh.

Menasheh agreed, and shared his answer. Impressed, Rav Ashi challenged him back, "So if you are indeed so wise, how did you come to worship idols?"

"Had you lived in my generation," Menasheh responded, "you would have personally lifted the hem of your cloak and sped after me [to worship avodah zarah]."[29] Rav Ashi understood that in Menasheh's times, the temptation to worship avodah zarah was so strong, that even the greatest men could not resist it.

When you see someone do wrong, don't rush to judge him. You likely do not understand what is motivating him to act that way. Ask yourself, "If I were in his situation, with his upbringing, his nature, and his yetzer hara, would I be any better?"

Sparks

Don't Be Different Being part of a community protects us from many of the yetzer hara's schemes. When the community holds certain standards, taking a good thing beyond its halachic requirement or refraining from going to certain places, one must abide by the community norms. (Of course, the requirement to follow community norms doesn't apply in a case where many in the community are doing something wrong.) Chazal say very strong things about one who disregards his community's boundaries, even with an act that is otherwise not wrong. Just breaking away from community standards will lead him to disregard more and more, and eventually even basic halachos.[30]

Everyone Counts The word צִבּוּר is an acronym for צַדִּיקִים בֵּינוֹנִים וּרְשָׁעִים—the righteous, intermediate, and wicked. A combination of all of these types of people is what forms a community.[31]

 **Did You Know?**

What We Really Want A Jew naturally wants to do the will of Hashem; it's merely that sometimes the yetzer hara covers over his true desire.[32] This mishnah can be read to say that you should fulfill His will, because that's what you truly want. Similarly, Hashem really wants to provide us with all we wish for, yet sometimes we aren't deserving of it. If we do Hashem's will (which is, in fact, our true will), then Hashem will fulfill our desires (which is what Hashem really wants).[32]

 **Story**

Understand His Pain

As a young man, R' Yechiel Michel of Zlotchov would sit all day in the local shul and learn Torah.

One day, a village wagon driver came to the Rav of the town, clearly distressed. He had accidentally done a melachah on Shabbos and was seeking a tikkun—a way to correct his wrongdoing. The Rav instructed him to donate candles to the shul to be used in honor of Shabbos.

Young R' Michel overheard the exchange, and was surprised by the Rav's approach. "A pound of candles to atone for violating Shabbos?" he thought to himself. "Does the Rav not realize the seriousness of the matter? Why is he treating it so lightly?"

That Friday, the wagon driver brought the candles to the shul and left them on the table. As soon as he left, a stray dog carried off the candles and ate them. When the wagon driver found out, he was devastated. "My repentance has been rejected in Heaven!" he wept. The next week he tried again, bringing more candles, but when they were lit, they inexplicably melted down very quickly, so that by the time Shabbos began nothing was left of them. Every week there was another strange problem, until, in desperation, the wagon driver went to seek the advice of the Ba'al Shem Tov.

The Ba'al Shem Tov heard him out, and replied, "It seems that a certain young scholar in your town finds fault with the path to teshuvah that the Rav has prescribed for you, and this is causing these strange events. Please ask R' Michel to come visit me."

Sure enough, R' Michel set out to see the Ba'al Shem Tov. On the way, the coachman took a wrong turn, and it seemed that R' Michel might not make it in time for Shabbos. He was greatly distressed by the thought that he might be forced to violate Shabbos for the first time in his life. When indeed they made it to Mezhibush just before Shabbos began, his relief was immense.

The Ba'al Shem Tov told him, "Until now, you had never tasted sin, so you could not comprehend the remorse a Jew feels at having transgressed the will of his Father in Heaven. Now that you understand something of the agony felt by the wagon driver, you know that his deep remorse alone more than atoned for his unwitting transgression."[33]

Hillel **would** often **say:**

A boor (an ignorant, rough, and uncivilized person) **cannot be one who fears sin.**

An unlearned person cannot be a **chassid**—one who is extra careful with Torah and mitzvos.

One who is too **shy** to ask questions **cannot learn.**

A person who is easily angered cannot teach.

And neither can all who spend much time on **business matters become wise** in Torah knowledge.

In a place where there are no leaders, try hard to be a leader yourself.

הוּא הָיָה אוֹמֵר:
אֵין בּוּר יְרֵא חֵטְא,

וְלֹא עַם הָאָרֶץ חָסִיד,

וְלֹא הַבַּיְשָׁן לָמֵד,
וְלֹא הַקַּפְּדָן מְלַמֵּד,
וְלֹא כָל הַמַּרְבֶּה
בִּסְחוֹרָה מַחְכִּים,
וּבְמָקוֹם שֶׁאֵין אֲנָשִׁים,
הִשְׁתַּדֵּל לִהְיוֹת אִישׁ.

Ask, or Remain Ignorant

Sometimes people are too shy to ask a question regarding what they are learning. One might be embarrassed to ask the teacher to repeat an idea or to explain it more simply, thinking that his classmates will mock him for not understanding, or that the teacher will be annoyed at having to explain it again. This mishnah gives us very important advice: Don't be shy to ask. One who is bashful and doesn't ask when he has a question will never end up understanding. One who does ask, with a sincere desire to understand, will gain much wisdom.

Step Up

This mishnah encourages us to "try to be a leader" even if we may not see ourselves as being a perfect example to lead. For when there is a need, you must step up in whatever way possible; you'll be surprised at what you can achieve.[34]

Did You Know?

Can't Teach Why can't an impatient person teach?

- His students will be afraid to ask questions.
- Anger causes a person to forget his knowledge.
- People don't readily accept what they hear from a short-tempered person.³⁵

Phew! Thank You! There is an opinion in the Gemara that one must make a brachah every day "שֶׁלֹּא עָשַׂנִי בּוּר," thanking Hashem for not making him an empty person.³⁶

 **Behind the Quote**

Hillel was known to be extremely patient and tolerant. Even when someone once came to Hillel's house at a very hectic time and repeatedly harassed him, Hillel would not become angry. (See 1:12)

In this mishnah Hillel mentions the importance of keeping one's cool and not being easily angered.³⁹

 Word Power

לִפְנִים מִשּׁוּרַת הַדִּין In this mishnah, the chassid refers to one who serves Hashem beyond the letter of the law. An example of how a chassid does things differently is described in the Gemara: A righteous person buries his nail clippings so that they should not harm someone, while a Chassid burns them, making it impossible for anyone to come in contact with them.

An עַם הָאָרֶץ doesn't know the details of halachah, so how could he possibly know enough to go beyond the letter of the law?³⁷

 Sparks

A Smart Boor A boor isn't necessarily unlearned. It is possible for a person to have much Torah knowledge, but if he doesn't allow it to refine his character, he cannot have true fear of Hashem.⁴⁰

 **Story**

Can You Please Repeat That?

Rabi Preida had a student who had such difficulty learning that he needed to hear every lesson explained 400 times before he understood it properly. Once while he was teaching him, Rabi Preida was approached to help out with a certain mitzvah. Rabi Preidah refused, explaining that he was busy teaching, and returned to his student. This time, however, after 400 times, the student still hadn't understood the lesson. Rabi Preidah asked him, "What is the matter today?" The student explained, "From the moment you were asked to go, I was unable to concentrate."

Rabi Preida patiently taught it to him another 400 times, until the student had finally mastered it. A heavenly voice was then heard offering a reward for Rabi Preida. He chose that his entire generation would merit great reward in Olam Haba.³⁸

ו
6

Hillel **also** once **saw a skull floating on the water. He said to** the skull: Hashem always brings justice in the end. **Because you drowned others, you were drowned, and those who drowned you will eventually be drowned** as well, in retribution for drowning you.

אַף הוּא רָאָה גֻלְגֹּלֶת אַחַת שֶׁצָּפָה עַל פְּנֵי הַמַּיִם, אָמַר לָהּ: עַל דְּאֲטֵפְתְּ אַטְפוּךְ, וְסוֹף מְטִיפַיִךְ יְטוּפוּן.

Living Lessons

Reap What You Sow

Hashem deals with a person middah k'neged middah—in the manner that the person deals with others. Yosef Hatzaddik personally took care of his father's body after his passing so that it would be done by the most honorable person of that time. In return, he merited that same care by an even greater person—Moshe Rabbeinu. In turn, because Moshe Rabbeinu gave Yosef's body the great honor of being tended by the greatest man of the time, he merited that his body was taken care of by someone even greater—Hashem Himself![41]

Sparks

Eventually, Oppressors Will Drown The second half of Hillel's statement, "ultimately, those who drowned you will drown," could be understood to be addressing B'nei Yisrael. "Just as Paraoh, who oppressed you in Mitzrayim, was drowned, know that ultimately, all the nations of the world who persecute you throughout the generations will come to the same sorry end."[42]

Sparks

Guilty of Bad Choice One might ask, if Hashem himself decreed that this person be killed for murdering others, why should the ones who kill the murderer also be punished? Aren't they fulfilling Hashem's decree?

Although Hashem has decreed that the murderer be punished, He has many messengers and endless ways of carrying out His decrees. Since Hashem didn't ask the second murderer to kill, rather he did it by choice, he therefore deserves his just punishment.[43]

 Word Power

וְסוֹף Don't despair when you see the righteous go unrewarded. Just as punishment eventually comes, ultimately every person receives his due reward.[45]

 **Behind the Quote**

Some say that the floating skull came from Paraoh, the very king who had decreed that all newborn baby boys be drowned in Mitzrayim. Hillel's neshamah had a spark of Moshe Rabbeinu. Hillel was extraordinarily humble just like Moshe, and lived the same lifespan of 120 years. In this mishnah, we see how he confronts Paraoh just as Moshe Rabbeinu confronted Paraoh in Mitzrayim.[44]

 **Story**

You Get What You Give

There was once an elderly man whose son did not care for him properly, but left him instead to live with the poor people of the city. One cold, winter day the old man was sitting with his poor friends when his grandson passed by. He pleaded with his grandson to ask his father to send him warm clothing to protect him from the freezing weather. When the grandson relayed the request, his father said, "Go up to the attic where you'll see a coat hanging on a hook. Take it and bring it to your grandfather."

The son climbed up to the attic where he found an old, worn-out garment already full of holes. Greatly disturbed by the way his father was treating his grandfather, he tore the garment in half. When he came down carrying half a garment, his father asked, "What is this? Why did you cut it in half?"

The son answered, "I'm saving the other half for you, when you'll be an old man and I'll send you to live on the street."

The father recognized his terrible mistake and ran to his father to beg him forgiveness and bring him back home.[46]

Hillel **would** often **say:** Do not indulge in too much eating, because **the more flesh** a person has on his body, **the more** there will be for the **worms** to eat in the grave.

The more possessions one has, **the more** he has **to worry about**.

The more wives one has, **the more** jealousy he creates among them, which may lead them to practice **witchcraft** in order to gain their husband's attention.

The more maids one has, **the more immorality** there is in the house. **The more servants** one has, **the more theft** there is in the house.

However, **the more Torah** one learns, **the more life** he has. **The more** one **sits** and learns, **the more wisdom** he has. **The more advice** one receives from Chachamim, **the more** he **understands** things on his own.

The more tzedakah one gives, **the more** blessings of **peace** he brings about.

One who **has acquired a good reputation has acquired** something good **for himself,** but only in this world. One who has **acquired for himself Torah** knowledge **has acquired for himself** everlasting **life in the World to Come.**

הוּא הָיָה אוֹמֵר:
מַרְבֶּה בָשָׂר מַרְבֶּה רִמָּה,

מַרְבֶּה נְכָסִים מַרְבֶּה דְאָגָה,

מַרְבֶּה נָשִׁים מַרְבֶּה כְשָׁפִים,

מַרְבֶּה שְׁפָחוֹת מַרְבֶּה זִמָּה,
מַרְבֶּה עֲבָדִים מַרְבֶּה גָזֵל.

מַרְבֶּה תוֹרָה מַרְבֶּה חַיִּים,
מַרְבֶּה יְשִׁיבָה מַרְבֶּה חָכְמָה,
מַרְבֶּה עֵצָה מַרְבֶּה תְבוּנָה,

מַרְבֶּה צְדָקָה מַרְבֶּה שָׁלוֹם.

קָנָה שֵׁם טוֹב קָנָה לְעַצְמוֹ, קָנָה לוֹ דִבְרֵי תוֹרָה קָנָה לוֹ חַיֵּי הָעוֹלָם הַבָּא.

Just a Spoonful

The word מַרְבֶּה means an abundance. Some things, like medicine or vitamins, are beneficial in small amounts, but harmful in large amounts. The things listed in the first part of this mishnah fall into that category. Although they may seem very satisfactory at first, having too much of them will eventually bring harm and pain. Learning Torah and doing mitzvos are the path to a truly happy and fulfilled life.[47]

Sparks

Doesn't Last Material gains are temporary, fated to be lost sooner or later. Spiritual gains, however, such as refined character traits, can never be taken away. So the mishnah says that one who acquires a good name—a result of his fine character—truly "acquires it for himself." Unlike the other possessions mentioned in this mishnah, that is a worthwhile investment!⁴⁸

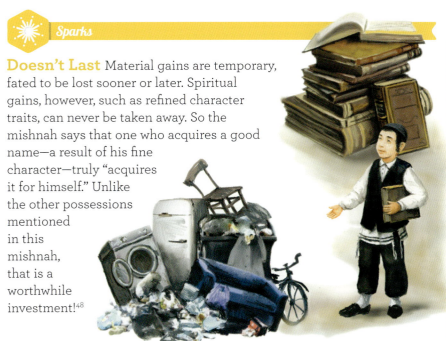

Did You Know?

Everlasting Teaching Torah doesn't just add life to one's physical lifetime, but it continues to give life even after one's passing. Chazal say that when a Torah thought is taught in the name of its original teacher who has passed on, the teacher's lips move in the grave. The more Torah he learns and teaches during his lifetime, the more life it gives him even after his passing.⁴⁹

Peace Between the Soul and its Creator When a person sins, his neshamah is held captive by his yetzer hara and prevented from expressing its love for Hashem and fulfilling His wishes. When that person gives tzedakah to a pauper, redeeming him from his misery, the person's neshamah is freed from its own captivity and is able once again to connect to Hashem. In this way, tzedakah brings peace between the giver and Hashem, enabling them to connect to each other without any interference—as the mishnah says, the more tzedakah one gives, the more blessings of peace he brings about.⁵⁰

Sparks

Scattered Soul A certain man used to daven that Hashem save him from having a "scattered soul." When asked to explain, he said, "I daven that I shouldn't own many assets in many places. For if I will, my soul will constantly be scattered about, worrying about them." The more possessions one has, the more worries he owns.⁵¹

Word Power

מַרְבֶּה עֵצָה מַרְבֶּה תְבוּנָה
The more advice, the more understanding. When one spends time considering how to advise another, one gains much understanding for oneself.

Story

Happy With Nothing

There was once a wealthy prince who became depressed. His doctor suggested that if he wore the shirt of a truly happy man who had no worries, he would be cured. His servants set out to find the man, visiting the richest people in town in hopes of finding one without worries. They went from one wealthy man to another, searching for someone truly happy, but each confessed of his numerous worries related to his business dealings.

Finally they came upon a simple, poor man, wearing patched rags. They asked him if he was happy and if he had any worries. He said: "Worries? I don't know what they are!"

Elated at having found their man, they asked him to lend them his shirt, only to discover it wasn't to be, as he replied: "I don't have one, because if I did, I would be worried about losing it! So why do I need a shirt? To make me worry? I have nothing, so I worry about nothing!"

They reported back to the prince, and he realized why he was depressed!⁵²

רַבָּן יוֹחָנָן בֶּן זַכַּאי קִבֵּל מֵהִלֵּל וּמִשַּׁמַּאי. הוּא הָיָה אוֹמֵר: אִם לָמַדְתָּ תּוֹרָה הַרְבֵּה, אַל תַּחֲזִיק טוֹבָה לְעַצְמָךְ, כִּי לְכָךְ נוֹצָרְתָּ.

Rabban Yochanan ben Zakkai received and learned Torah from Hillel and Shammai.

He would often say: If you have learned a lot of Torah, do not take credit for yourself, because this is what you were created for.

Just Doing My Job

Perhaps you have a very strong memory and understand your lessons more quickly than your friends. Maybe you can sing beautifully, or perhaps you are very sensitive and know just the right thing to say in order to cheer someone up. Whatever your talents are, remember that they are gifts from Hashem, and that using them to serve Him is not just a nice thing. In fact, it is for that purpose that Hashem gave them to you at all!

Don't Be Selfish

The mishnah says that if you have learned much Torah, "אַל תַּחֲזִיק טוֹבָה לְעַצְמָךְ." Literally, these words mean "don't hold the good for yourself." Don't keep your wonderful Torah knowledge to yourself—share it with others![54]

 Did You Know?

The Condition When Hashem created the world, he did so conditionally: If B'nei Yisrael would accept the Torah, it would continue to exist. If not, it would all return to nothingness. The purpose of the creation of the world was only that B'nei Yisrael would fulfill the Torah[53]

 Word Power

אַל תַּחֲזִיק טוֹבָה לְעַצְמָךְ These words can also mean that one shouldn't hold onto his pleasure in physical things. We were created to overcome our physical desires, not to indulge in them.[55]

 Sparks

Endless Sea However much Torah you learn, you are still always at the beginning, for Hashem's Torah is infinite, just as He is.[56]

Biography

Rabban Yochanan ben Zakkai lived through the destruction of the second Beis Hamikdash. As leader of B'nei Yisrael in that difficult time, he instituted many decrees to preserve the Torah way of life. He was the youngest student of Hillel, but considered one of the greatest.[57] He served as Av Beis Din, and like his teacher Hillel, lived for 120 years.[58]

Rabban Yochanan ben Zakkai was always the first to arrive at the Beis Medrash and the last to leave. He was knowledgeable in every area of Torah—Tanach, Mishnah, commentary on Mishnah, halachah, aggadah, tiny details and subtle points learned from the words of the Torah, astronomical cycles, and more. He was even familiar with the language of the malachim.[59] Nevertheless he said, "If the entire sky were parchment, all the trees were quills, and the oceans filled with ink, it would still be impossible to write all I have learned from my teachers. Yet all I have learned is still only but a drop in the vast ocean of their knowledge."[60]

He was always first to greet everyone, Jew and non-Jew alike.[61]

While on his deathbed, he told his students, "I see two paths before me, one leading to Gan Eden and the other to Gehinom. I don't know down which path I will be taken."[62] He was too busy learning, teaching, and helping the community that he did not have a spare minute to evaluate his personal service of Hashem.

Story

Just Fulfilling an Obligation

The Chafetz Chaim was once overheard saying the following, "Dear Father in Heaven, what have You done for me, and what have I done for You? You decided that the world needs the Mishnah Berurah, Shmiras Halashon, Tzipisa Liyeshua, etc. (the Chafetz Chaim's works). You gave me the great merit of fulfilling Your wishes and I have no words to thank You for that. But what have I done for You? Nothing! Please, dear Father, give me an opportunity to do something for You!"[63]

Rabban Yochanan ben Zakkai had five special students. They were: Rabi Eliezer ben Horkenus, Rabi Yehoshua ben Chananya, Rabi Yosei Hakohen, Rabi Shimon ben Nesanel, and Rabi Elazar ben Arach.

He used to list their praiseworthy qualities as follows:

Rabi Eliezer ben Horkenus is like a cement tank that does not lose a drop of water, because he does not forget anything he learns.

Rabi Yehoshua ben Chananya—Fortunate is his mother, who gave birth to such a son.

Rabi Yosei Hakohen is a chassid—he does more than the law requires.

Rabi Shimon ben Nesanel is a person who fears aveiros.

Rabi Elazar ben Arach is like a fountain that flows with ever-increasing strength, because he constantly adds to his wisdom.

Rabban Yochanan would often say: If all the knowledge of B'nei Yisrael's Chachamim would be on one side of a scale, and the knowledge of Rabi Eliezer ben Horkenus would be on the other side, his knowledge would outweigh all of theirs, for he had an exceptional memory.

Abba Shaul says a different version of this statement in Rabban Yochanan's name: If all of the wisdom of B'nei Yisrael's Chachamim would be on one side of a scale, including even the wisdom of Rabi Eliezer ben Horkenus, and the sharp wisdom of Rabi Elazar ben Arach would be on the other side, his wisdom would outweigh all of theirs, for he was exceptionally wise.

חֲמִשָּׁה תַלְמִידִים הָיוּ לוֹ לְרַבָּן יוֹחָנָן בֶּן זַכַּאי, וְאֵלּוּ הֵן: רַבִּי אֱלִיעֶזֶר בֶּן הוֹרְקְנוֹס, וְרַבִּי יְהוֹשֻׁעַ בֶּן חֲנַנְיָא, וְרַבִּי יוֹסֵי הַכֹּהֵן, וְרַבִּי שִׁמְעוֹן בֶּן נְתַנְאֵל, וְרַבִּי אֶלְעָזָר בֶּן עֲרָךְ. הוּא הָיָה מוֹנֶה שְׁבָחָם: רַבִּי אֱלִיעֶזֶר בֶּן הוֹרְקְנוֹס בּוֹר סוּד שֶׁאֵינוֹ מְאַבֵּד טִפָּה,

רַבִּי יְהוֹשֻׁעַ בֶּן חֲנַנְיָא אַשְׁרֵי יוֹלַדְתּוֹ,

רַבִּי יוֹסֵי הַכֹּהֵן חָסִיד,

רַבִּי שִׁמְעוֹן בֶּן נְתַנְאֵל יְרֵא חֵטְא,

וְרַבִּי אֶלְעָזָר בֶּן עֲרָךְ כְּמַעְיָן הַמִּתְגַּבֵּר.

הוּא הָיָה אוֹמֵר: אִם יִהְיוּ כָל חַכְמֵי יִשְׂרָאֵל בְּכַף מֹאזְנַיִם וֶאֱלִיעֶזֶר בֶּן הוֹרְקְנוֹס בְּכַף שְׁנִיָּה, מַכְרִיעַ אֶת כֻּלָּם.

אַבָּא שָׁאוּל אוֹמֵר מִשְּׁמוֹ: אִם יִהְיוּ כָל חַכְמֵי יִשְׂרָאֵל בְּכַף מֹאזְנַיִם וֶאֱלִיעֶזֶר בֶּן הוֹרְקְנוֹס אַף עִמָּהֶם, וְאֶלְעָזָר בֶּן עֲרָךְ בְּכַף שְׁנִיָּה, מַכְרִיעַ אֶת כֻּלָּם.

What's Your Talent?

There are basics that are expected from everyone. Beyond that, there are many specific areas in which different individuals excel. It is important to identify and develop your natural gifts so you can use them to serve Hashem.[64]

Biography

Abba Shaul was a student of Rabi Akiva. Very little is known about his life, except that he worked in a burial society. The Gemara says that he was very tall, so tall that Rabi Tarfon, who was also tall, only reached his shoulders.[65] The term Abba is a term of respect, similar to the title Rabi.

Behind the Quote

The praiseworthy quality of Rabi Eliezer was his tremendous memory. As a leader addressing the needs of the general community, Rabban Yochanan felt that it was most important to have a leader who remembered all the halachos and could properly guide the people. This is why Rabban Yochanan said that Rabi Eliezer's quality outweighed the specialties of all the others.[68]

Did You Know?

Go Beyond Abba Shaul was known for his outstanding memory, similar to the greatness of Rabi Eliezer. Yet, he said in the name of Rabban Yochanan that Rabi Elazar ben Arach, whose greatness was his ability to analyze deeply and come to a new and deeper understanding, outweighed the others. Abba Shaul was teaching us not to be satisfied with what comes naturally. Work hard to develop skills that are more challenging.[69]

Word Power

יְרֵא חֵטְא The true meaning of "one who fears sin" is one who fears the aveirah itself. When a person does an aveirah, he is separating himself from Hashem. Rabi Shimon didn't want to separate himself from Hashem even for a brief moment. The separation itself was what he feared, not the punishment that came as a result.[66]

Connections

In the previous mishnah, Rabban Yochanan warns against taking credit for one's Torah learning, since in fact that is the purpose of our creation. To illustrate this point, he enumerates the special traits his students had. Each one had his own unique quality that he used for Torah study.[67]

Sparks

Scared Away People stay far away from things that might lead to danger, out of fear that they will be hurt. So must be our fear of aveiros—so real and so strong that it keeps us far away from things that might not necessarily be forbidden, but have the potential to lead us to sin.[70]

Impress Hashem

When arriving in a city, R' Nachum of Chernobyl would check the shochet's knife before eating meat. One day, a shochet was sharpening his knife to make sure it was perfect for that day's shechitah. He was a G-d-fearing shochet who understood very well that the slightest nick or imperfection on the shechitah knife would render the animal non-kosher, so he carefully sharpened and checked his knife every day. Just as he finished, R' Nachum walked in and requested to inspect the knife. The shochet was about to recheck the knife to ensure it was perfect before handing it over, but then he had second thoughts. "I already checked the knife and it was perfectly sharp," he said to himself, "and I would shecht for anyone else without checking it again. If it truly was good enough for Hashem, then it's good enough for R' Nachum too." Without missing a beat, he confidently handed the knife over R' Nachum. Upon receiving it, R' Nachum thought for a moment and returned it without inspection. He explained, "If it is good enough for Hashem, then it is definitely good for me. Go ahead and shecht with it."[71]

PART I · 10

Rabban Yochanan ben Zakkai **said to** his students: **Go out and see which path is good for a person to follow**—Which good quality should a person strive most to acquire? The students came back with various answers.	אָמַר לָהֶם: צְאוּ וּרְאוּ אֵיזוֹ הִיא דֶּרֶךְ טוֹבָה שֶׁיִּדְבַּק בָּהּ הָאָדָם.
Rabi Eliezer says: Looking at everything with **a good eye**—with generosity and happiness in others' good fortune.	רַבִּי אֱלִיעֶזֶר אוֹמֵר: עַיִן טוֹבָה.
Rabi Yehoshua says: Being **a good friend** who helps and advises people.	רַבִּי יְהוֹשֻׁעַ אוֹמֵר: חָבֵר טוֹב.
Rabi Yosei says: Being **a good neighbor** who positively influences his surroundings.	רַבִּי יוֹסֵי אוֹמֵר: שָׁכֵן טוֹב.
Rabi Shimon says: Seeing and anticipating **the outcome of** one's own positive or negative **actions** before they occur.	רַבִּי שִׁמְעוֹן אוֹמֵר: הָרוֹאֶה אֶת הַנּוֹלָד.
Rabi Elazar says: Having **a good heart**—having kind and positive feelings toward others.	רַבִּי אֶלְעָזָר אוֹמֵר: לֵב טוֹב.
Rabban Yochanan ben Zakkai then **said to them: I prefer the words of Elazar ben Arach to** all of **your words, because his words**—having a good heart—**include** all of **your words.** A good heart leads to the rest of the qualities mentioned.	אָמַר לָהֶם: רוֹאֶה אֲנִי אֶת דִּבְרֵי אֶלְעָזָר בֶּן עֲרָךְ מִדִּבְרֵיכֶם, שֶׁבִּכְלָל דְּבָרָיו דִּבְרֵיכֶם.
He also **said to them: Go out and see which path is bad, from which a person should distance himself.**	אָמַר לָהֶם: צְאוּ וּרְאוּ אֵיזוֹ הִיא דֶּרֶךְ רָעָה שֶׁיִּתְרַחֵק מִמֶּנָּה הָאָדָם.
Rabi Eliezer says: Looking at everything with **a bad eye**—being stingy and jealous of others.	רַבִּי אֱלִיעֶזֶר אוֹמֵר: עַיִן רָעָה.
Rabi Yehoshua says: Being **a bad friend.**	רַבִּי יְהוֹשֻׁעַ אוֹמֵר: חָבֵר רַע.
Rabi Yosei says: Being **a bad neighbor.**	רַבִּי יוֹסֵי אוֹמֵר: שָׁכֵן רַע.
Rabi Shimon says: One who borrows but does not pay back. One who borrows from another person is like one who borrows from Hashem, **as it says** in Tehillim: **A wicked person borrows and does not pay back, but** Hashem, **the righteous One, acts graciously and returns** to the lender his money. Then the borrower owes it to Hashem.	רַבִּי שִׁמְעוֹן אוֹמֵר: הַלֹּוֶה וְאֵינוֹ מְשַׁלֵּם, אֶחָד הַלֹּוֶה מִן הָאָדָם כְּלֹוֶה מִן הַמָּקוֹם, שֶׁנֶּאֱמַר: לֹוֶה רָשָׁע וְלֹא יְשַׁלֵּם, וְצַדִּיק חוֹנֵן וְנוֹתֵן.
Rabi Elazar says: Having **a bad heart**—holding onto negative feelings toward others.	רַבִּי אֶלְעָזָר אוֹמֵר: לֵב רָע.
Rabban Yochanan ben Zakkai then **said to them: I prefer the words of Elazar ben Arach to** all of **your words, because his words**—having a bad heart—**include** all of **your words.** A bad heart leads to the rest of the things that were mentioned.	אָמַר לָהֶם: רוֹאֶה אֲנִי אֶת דִּבְרֵי אֶלְעָזָר בֶּן עֲרָךְ מִדִּבְרֵיכֶם, שֶׁבִּכְלָל דְּבָרָיו דִּבְרֵיכֶם.

Living Lessons

Will You Be My Friend?

A true good friend is one who really cares for you. Such a friend will tell you off when you act improperly. Because you understand that your friend only cares to help you improve, you will hear his point and use it to help you grow.[72]

Behind the Quote

According to Rabi Eliezer, the most important quality is a good eye—seeing the good in everyone and everything. Rabi Eliezer possessed this quality, and because people naturally remember positive things, he never forgot a thing he learned, as it says about him in the previous mishnah when describing his best trait.[73]

Rabi Yehoshua had amazing potential from birth because his mother brought him to the Beis Medrash as a baby.[74] He therefore says that a good friend—which can also refer to a good wife—is crucial, because a woman's actions will determine her children's future.

Rabi Yosei was called a chassid, someone who does more than what he is required to do by law. Such dedication to mitzvos is most apparent when one is at home. A bad neighbor might see this, and mock the extra care in performance of mitzvos, saying things like "since when are you so holy?" Therefore, Rabi Yosei advises us as to the importance of being good neighbors.

Rabi Shimon was known for his great fear of sin. Thinking about the potential results of your actions, and realizing that aveiros cause separation from Hashem, enables you to overcome the yetzer hara and stay away from sin.[75]

Rabi Elazar was known as a gushing fountain of wisdom. Being good-hearted brings joy, and joyfulness sharpens the mind. So if you want to be wise, have a good heart![76]

Did You Know?

It Leads to All Else Rabban Yochanan ben Zakkai preferred Rabi Elazar's choice, "a good heart" as most important because a good heart leads to the other four positive qualities. A good-hearted person also has a good eye, finding the positive in everything, and doesn't envy others, making him a good friend and neighbor to have. Having this positive outlook will also enable him to calmly weigh the consequences of his actions and judge whether they are favorable or not.[77]

Word Power

כְּלֹוֶה מִן הַמָּקוֹם The mishnah says that one who borrows money is considered to have borrowed from Hashem. How is this so?

In the case that the borrower is wicked and does not repay the loan (לֹוֶה רָשָׁע וְלֹא יְשַׁלֵּם), Hashem, Who is righteous, acts graciously and arranges for the lender to receive the money he is owed from another place (וְצַדִּיק חוֹנֵן וְנוֹתֵן). As a result, besides owing payment to the person from whom he borrowed, the borrower now also owes payment to Hashem![78]

Sparks

Two Sides of the Same Coin
After describing the proper path, isn't it obvious that its opposite is the bad path? Why did Rabban Yochanan ask his students from which path one should keep a distance?

Rabban Yochanan is teaching that your aversion to evil and your passion for doing good must be of equal measure. If someone loves doing good but doesn't dislike evil, or hates evil but isn't so passionate about doing good, his motives may not be pure for either.[79]

Be Happy for Him

A poor Jew once complained to the Tzaddik R' Moshe of Kobrin: "Why must I struggle to support my family, earning only a few coins a day, while my neighbor, who is in the same business as I, is very successful?"

The Tzaddik replied: "If you will not be jealous when your friend's store is bursting with customers but instead be happy for his success, you too will be successful. At first it will be hard for you to look at your friend's success with a good eye, but with time it will become natural. And when you thank Hashem for someone else's success, Hashem will make you successful as well."[80]

Each of these five Chachamim **said three things.**	הֵם אָמְרוּ שְׁלֹשָׁה דְבָרִים.
Rabi Eliezer says: Your friend's honor should be as dear to you as your own honor, so that even when he does something wrong, just as you would be patient with yourself, **you will not be angered easily.**	רַבִּי אֱלִיעֶזֶר אוֹמֵר: יְהִי כְבוֹד חֲבֵרְךָ חָבִיב עָלֶיךָ כְּשֶׁלָּךְ, וְאַל תְּהִי נוֹחַ לִכְעוֹס.
Do teshuvah one day before your death. Since you do not know which day will be your last, do teshuvah every day.	וְשׁוּב יוֹם אֶחָד לִפְנֵי מִיתָתְךָ.
Warm yourself next to the fire of Chachamim—keep in close contact with them—but **be careful not to** become too casual and friendly with them, because you might act disrespectfully and **be "burned by their coals"**—be punished; **because their bite is** like **the bite of a fox, their sting is** like **the sting of a scorpion, their hiss is** like **the hiss of a snake, and all their words are like fiery coals.**	וֶהֱוֵי מִתְחַמֵּם כְּנֶגֶד אוּרָן שֶׁל חֲכָמִים, וֶהֱוֵי זָהִיר בְּגַחַלְתָּן שֶׁלֹּא תִכָּוֶה, שֶׁנְּשִׁיכָתָן נְשִׁיכַת שׁוּעָל, וַעֲקִיצָתָן עֲקִיצַת עַקְרָב, וּלְחִישָׁתָן לְחִישַׁת שָׂרָף, וְכָל דִּבְרֵיהֶם כְּגַחֲלֵי אֵשׁ.

Every Day is Critical

Often, people push off doing good things they want to do in favor of less important pursuits, thinking that they will have plenty of time to catch up on the important things. Rabi Eliezer teaches us to cherish each moment as if it were your last. Put first things first: learn Torah, do mitzvos, and leave the other things for later, if there is time.[81]

Anger = Avodah Zarah

Everything that happens is by Hashem's decree,[82] even an act that appears to be a person's independent decision. Not only does Hashem decide everything that happens, but he does so only for our benefit.[83] Sometimes we see the benefit, but often we do not. Keeping this in mind can stop a person from feeling anger when another treats him badly.

Anger comes from blaming a specific person for the harm that was caused. In fact, this actually demonstrates a belief in a power other than Hashem—in this case the offending person. This is why Chazal say, "כָּל הַכּוֹעֵס כְּאִלּוּ עוֹבֵד עֲבוֹדָה זָרָה — Whoever gets angry is considered as if he worships avodah zarah."[84] One must realize that the person was merely a messenger of Hashem, fulfilling His decree, which is certainly good.

So the next time someone does something wrong to you, try to show him the right way to act, but don't become angry!

Biography

Rabi Eliezer ben Horkenus is also known as Rabi Eliezer Hagadol or simply Rabi Eliezer. When he was young, he worked for his wealthy father and had no interest in learning Torah. One day in his twenties, he was suddenly overcome by a desire to learn Torah and ran away from home to study with Rabban Yochanan ben Zakkai in Yerushalayim. There, despite having no money, he studied diligently until he became one of the greatest Chachamim of his time,[85] and wrote the famous compilation of Midrashim called Pirkei d'Rabi Eliezer. In fact, Rabban Shimon ben Gamliel was so impressed with Rabi Eliezer that he chose him as a son-in-law.

Rabi Yehoshua once kissed the stone that Rabi Eliezer would sit on in the Beis Medrash and said: "This stone is like Har Sinai, and the one who sat upon it is like the holy Aron."[86]

It is told that when Moshe Rabbeinu went up to Har Sinai, he found Hashem teaching a halachah in the name of Rabi Eliezer. He asked Hashem: "Please see to it that Rabi Eliezer be from my descendants." Hashem answered, "Indeed he will be."[87]

While on his deathbed he was asked a number of halachic questions including the following: If a new shoe that has not yet been removed from the shoe-press comes into contact with tumah—is it considered a finished product, and thus able to become tamei, or is it tahor? "Tahor!" he answered. And with that pure word on his lips, his soul departed.[88]

Story

The Honorable Butler

There was once a wealthy man who had a poor butler. Being a kind man, he trained the young butler and gave him money to start his own business, and eventually the butler became wealthy.

A while later, the employer lost his money, and with no other option, went to his former butler to ask for help getting back on his feet. To his dismay, the newly rich man gave his old boss the cold shoulder, refusing to give him a thing!

As soon as he left, however, the former butler sent a messenger dressed as a beggar to his former employer, to sell a precious diamond for one small coin. A few days later he sent another messenger dressed as a businessman, to "buy" the diamond for a huge sum of money.

The former butler's family, watching this strange sequence of events unfold, asked him to explain.

"I owe that man my entire fortune, and any honor I receive as a wealthy man is really his. How embarrassing it would have been for him to accept money from his former butler! As a result of this "business deal," however, he not only has the means to build up his wealth again, but more importantly, he still has his dignity!"[92]

Sparks

Not Too Far, Not Too Close Torah scholars are compared to fire. When you sit at a distance from a fire you can enjoy its light, but cannot feel its heat. The mishnah tells us to be warmed by the fire of Chachamim, meaning to develop a **close** relationship, and not just to listen to their teachings from afar. However, getting too close to a fire increases the risk of burns. When together with Chachamim, don't forget that you're not on their level. You must still be careful to treat them with the utmost respect.[89]

Did You Know?

Delayed Reaction The mishnah compares the power of Chachamim to that of foxes, scorpions, and snakes. The real impact of these animals' bites is not always apparent right away. The same is true with regard to the punishment for disrespecting Chachamim—it may not be immediate, but it is certain to come.[90]

Behind the Quote

Earlier in this mishnah we learned that Rabi Eliezer considered having a good eye the most important quality. Now he says that one should not anger easily. A good eye, seeing the positive in everything, results in being difficult to anger.[91]

Rabi Yehoshua says: Having **a bad**—stingy and jealous—**eye**, fulfilling the temptations of the **yetzer hara, and hating people** for no reason, can destroy **a person's** life and **drive** him **from the world.**

רַבִּי יְהוֹשֻׁעַ אוֹמֵר:
עַיִן הָרָע, וְיֵצֶר הָרָע,
וְשִׂנְאַת הַבְּרִיּוֹת, מוֹצִיאִין
אֶת הָאָדָם מִן הָעוֹלָם.

Living Lessons

I'm Happy if You're Happy

The three things listed by Rabi Yehoshua are very closely connected. When a person sees his friend's good fortune, the yetzer hara tries to get him to look at his friend with a "bad eye." He tries to arouse feelings of jealousy. And if the yetzer hara succeeds in this, then this person ends up hating all those who have been fortunate. This can literally drive a person from this world; he will have neither peace nor joy in his life.

When you see a friend receive something special, win a competition, or have anything good happen to him, ignore the yetzer hara and be happy for your friend. Not only is it good for your friend, it is good for you, because if you want to have a happy life— be happy for other people's good fortune!

 Connections

In the previous mishnah, we learned that Rabi Yehoshua considered being a good friend the most important quality. A person who has the bad qualities that he speaks of in this mishnah could not possibly be a good friend, since he is always full of envy and hatred.[93]

 Did You Know?

Rebuild The second Beis Hamikdash was destroyed due to שִׂנְאַת חִנָּם—senseless hatred toward fellow Jews.[94] Since the cause of its destruction was sinas chinam, its opposite, אַהֲבַת חִנָּם—unconditional love—will hasten the rebuilding of the third Beis Hamikdash![95]

 Sparks

Who Loses? A person who is hateful toward others won't be able to find a friend nor a mentor, because he always sees the flaws in people. With neither friend nor mentor one cannot lead a peaceful, satisfying life.[96]

Biography

Rabi Yehoshua ben Chananya was one of the great students of Rabban Yochanan ben Zakkai. His mother would bring him as a baby to the Beis Medrash to hear the words of Torah.⁹⁷

Rabi Yehoshua was a Levi and sang in the Beis Hamikdash. Although he was one of the great Chachamim of his time, he earned his living as a blacksmith. After the passing of Rabban Yochanan ben Zakkai, Rabi Yehoshua became the Av Beis Din. He was very knowledgeable—fluent in seventy languages and well-versed in witchcraft, making him well-suited to debating heretics. Rabi Yehoshua, together with Rabi Eliezer, were the primary teachers of Rabi Akiva.

Rabi Yehoshua was not a good-looking person. The story is told that when the emperor's daughter met him, she commented, "Such great wisdom in such an ugly vessel!"

Rabi Yehoshua replied, "Doesn't your father keep wine in an earthenware vessel?"

"In what sort of vessel shall he keep it?" she asked.

"You, who are nobles, should keep it in gold and silver vessels." She told this to her father, the emperor, and he had the wine put into vessels of gold and silver. After a few short days, the wine turned sour. The emperor had Rabi Yehoshua summoned before him and asked him, "Why did you give my daughter such advice?" He replied, "I answered her according to the way she spoke to me." After further conversation, Rabi Yehoshua explained that, like wine, wisdom is best preserved in simple and humble vessels.⁹⁸

Behind the Quote

Rabi Yehoshua was famous for his pleasant demeanor, harboring no ill feelings toward others. People loved him, praising his mother for the wonderful child she raised. In this mishnah Rabi Yehoshua emphasizes how one should have positive feelings for other people, by staying away from jealousy and hatred.⁹⁹

Jealous of Your Own Reflection

A man once complained to R' Meir of Premishlan that a certain person was preventing him from earning a livelihood.

"I'm sure that you noticed," replied R' Meir, "that when a horse drinks from the river it kicks at the water. While drinking, the horse sees his reflection in the water and thinks that another horse is also drinking from the same water. The envy makes him angry; he can't bear seeing another horse drink so much, so he stamps at the other horse so that it shouldn't drink up his water. But you, my friend, are no horse, and surely you realize that there is enough water in the river for everyone! No one can take anything away from the livelihood that has been predetermined for his fellow."¹⁰⁰

Rabi Yosei says: Your friend's money should be as dear to you as your own money.

Be prepared to work very hard for Torah learning, because it is not like an inheritance—it does not come to you easily and automatically.

All your actions, including mundane activities such as eating and sleeping, should be done for the sake of being able to serve Hashem.

רַבִּי יוֹסֵי אוֹמֵר: יְהִי מָמוֹן חֲבֵרְךָ חָבִיב עָלֶיךָ כְּשֶׁלָּךְ.

וְהַתְקֵן עַצְמְךָ לִלְמוֹד תּוֹרָה, שֶׁאֵינָהּ יְרֻשָּׁה לָךְ.

וְכָל מַעֲשֶׂיךָ יִהְיוּ לְשֵׁם שָׁמָיִם.

Available to All

Money and material possessions are things that can be inherited, sometimes so much that one does not need to work at all. However, although the Torah itself is an inheritance to every Jew, knowledge of Torah is not inherited; even the son of a great Torah scholar does not inherit his father's knowledge. To know Torah, one must study Torah!

Also, the fact that Torah is not an inheritance is encouraging to a person whose parents were not great Torah scholars. He should not think that there is no hope for him; even a simple Jew has the capability to learn Torah. Torah knowledge is available to any Jew who makes the effort to learn. All that's needed is determination.[101]

For the Sake of Heaven

Serving Hashem is not limited to the mitzvos we do. A royal chauffeur does not serve the king only by personally driving him from place to place. Part of his job is to clean and fix the car, so it will always be in perfect condition for the king. So it is when a person tends to his physical needs with the intention of keeping the body healthy to learn Torah, daven, and do mitzvos. When a person has that intention, then all of the mundane activities also become part of his service of Hashem.

 Word Power

שֶׁאֵינָהּ יְרֻשָּׁה לָךְ The mishnah says about Torah knowledge, "it does not come to you as an inheritance." This also means that Torah wasn't given exclusively to you. Just as Torah was given to you, it was given to the rest of B'nei Yisrael, and everyone has something to contribute within it.[102]

 Sparks

Clear Mind What kind of preparation is the mishnah referring to? Before beginning to study, a person should clear his mind of all matters not relevant to his Torah study. This way, while learning, he will feel as if all his affairs are already taken care of.[86]

Biography

Rabi Yosei was one of the five great students of Rabban Yochanan ben Zakkai.

A woman convert once asked Rabban Gamliel about a contradiction between pessukim: One passuk says, אֲשֶׁר לֹא יִשָּׂא פָנִים – (Hashem) does not show favor (forgive), and another says יִשָּׂא ה' פָּנָיו אֵלֶיךָ – May Hashem lift His countenance to you (forgive the sinner). Rabi Yosei joined the conversation and answered her with a parable. A man lent his friend money, fixing a time for payment, and the recipient swore by the life of the king to pay him. The date passed and the money was not returned. The borrower came before the king to beg forgiveness for swearing falsely by his life. The king, however, said to him, "I will forgive the wrong you have done to me, but you must obtain forgiveness from your friend (the lender)." So too, in one passuk, Hashem says that He will forgive transgressions against Him, but the aveiros that one does against another person Hashem does not forgive unless one obtains forgiveness from the person he wronged.103

Who's the Lucky One Here?

Someone came to the Tzemach Tzedek of Lubavitch and complained: "What should I do? I simply don't enjoy learning." The Tzemach Tzedek answered: "When one works very hard to learn, breaking his desire to be busy with other activities, he merits to reach great heights in Torah knowledge. So my question is, what should I do about the fact that I do enjoy learning?"109

Did You Know?

Acquired Three Ways

There are three ways that we receive Torah:

1. Inheritance: "תּוֹרָה צִוָּה לָנוּ מֹשֶׁה מוֹרָשָׁה קְהִלַּת יַעֲקֹב"104—The Torah, which Moshe commanded us, is an inheritance to the congregation of Yaakov." Every Jew inherits a connection to the Torah just by being a Jew.

2. Acquisition: A deep understanding of Torah can only be acquired through hard work. This is what Rabi Yosei is referring to in this mishnah.105

3. As a Gift: After trying your best to learn, Hashem gives you extra understanding, as a gift.106

Behind the Quote

Rabi Yosei teaches that just as you would do whatever you could to increase your own wealth, so should you do whatever you can to help someone else increase his wealth.107

Going so far is not something that is required by halachah. It is therefore fitting that Rabi Yosei, who was called a chassid—one who does more than required by halachah—is the one who tells us to cherish another person's financial wellbeing as if it were one's own.108

Sparks

Try, Try, and Try Again

יָגַעְתִּי וְלֹא מָצָאתִי, אַל תַּאֲמִין. לֹא יָגַעְתִּי וּמָצָאתִי, אַל תַּאֲמִין. יָגַעְתִּי וּמָצָאתִי, תַּאֲמִין.

If someone tells you, "I have worked very hard [in Torah study] but I did not succeed," don't believe him.

If he tells you, "I didn't work hard at all yet I succeeded," don't believe him either.

If he tells you, "I worked hard and I succeeded," then you can believe him.84

Rabi Shimon says: Be very careful about saying Krias Shema and davening at the proper time.	רַבִּי שִׁמְעוֹן אוֹמֵר: הֱוֵי זָהִיר בִּקְרִיאַת שְׁמַע וּבִתְפִלָּה.
When you daven, do not make your davening something you do out of habit, but a heartfelt plea and a request for mercy before Hashem, Who is merciful and kind.	וּכְשֶׁאַתָּה מִתְפַּלֵּל, אַל תַּעַשׂ תְּפִלָּתְךָ קֶבַע, אֶלָּא רַחֲמִים וְתַחֲנוּנִים לִפְנֵי הַמָּקוֹם, שֶׁנֶּאֱמַר: כִּי חַנּוּן
As it says in Sefer Yoel: Hashem is gracious and merciful; He is slow to anger, has much kindness, and rejects bad decrees.	וְרַחוּם הוּא, אֶרֶךְ אַפַּיִם וְרַב חֶסֶד, וְנִחָם עַל הָרָעָה.
Do not consider yourself to be a rasha, which can cause depression or apathy.	וְאַל תְּהִי רָשָׁע בִּפְנֵי עַצְמֶךָ.

Davening Tips

Since davening is so important, the yetzer hara tries very hard to disturb and distract you from doing it properly. In fact, when you try to concentrate, the yetzer hara works even harder to distract you. Here are some tips from our Chachamim to keep your davening focused and meaningful:

• Before davening, think for a few moments about Hashem and the great miracles He has done—miracles we learn about in Torah and miracles you have personally experienced or heard about.[110]

• Throughout davening, keep reminding yourself that you are standing before the King of all kings.[111]

• Even if you know the words of davening by heart, read them from inside the siddur. It's easier for the mind to wander when you're not looking inside.[112]

 Word Power

וְאַל תְּהִי רָשָׁע בִּפְנֵי עַצְמֶךָ These words can also be translated as "Don't be a rasha on your own." A person might say, "If I choose to do something wrong, it's my own business!" That is incorrect. We are responsible for one another, since each action done by one Jew affects all others.

Also, if you see someone doing something wrong, don't just stand there. Try to find a way to help rectify the situation, because it **is** your business![113]

Biography

Rabi Shimon ben Nesanel was one of Rabban Yochanan ben Zakkai's five great students. He was versed in the secret, mystical parts of the Torah (kabbalah) to the level of Rabi Shimon bar Yochai, author of the Zohar.

Rabi Shimon learned so diligently that he had the halachic status of "Toraso Umanaso"—Torah was his only pursuit. Therefore he was not obligated to interrupt his learning to daven each day and stopped only to recite Krias Shema.

Rabban Gamliel Hazaken's daughter married a man named Shimon ben Nesanel who was also a kohen, but different details seem to indicate that it was another man who happened to bear the same name.

Behind the Quote

Rabi Shimon's great quality was his fear of sin. In this mishnah he teaches us how to acquire this noble trait: by concentrating during krias shema and davening. Thinking about Hashem's greatness naturally leads to yiras Shamayim.[114]

Sparks

Righteous Tricks One of the tactics the yetzer hara uses to interfere with your service of Hashem is to convince you that you are a rasha. This can lead to one or more of the following scenarios:

- Depression, which prevents serving Hashem with joy.
- Indifference to your low status.
- Thoughts like, "If I'm already a rasha, what does it matter if I do another misdeed?"[115]

Don't fall for the tricks of the yetzer hara. Even when you make mistakes, remember that Hashem forgives those who sincerely regret their sins and are determined not to do them again. Move on, and return to being the great Jew that you truly are!

Purest Prayers

The Arizal would daven with extraordinary intensity on Rosh Hashanah and Yom Kippur. One year, it was revealed to him that the Rosh Hashanah davening of a certain Jew from a particular city had reached even higher than his. Amazed, the Arizal traveled to that city and asked the man: "Please tell me with what special kavanos did you daven? What were your thoughts and intentions? I was told that your davening reached an extremely high level."

The man replied, "There must be some mistake. In fact, I don't even know how to read all the alef-beis! All I only know are the first ten letters, from alef until yud."

"There is no mistake," said the Arizal, "You must have done something special. Please describe your davening to me."

Embarrassed of his ignorance and simplicity, the man hesitantly described what had happened. "When I came to shul and saw everyone praying

with such fervor, it broke my heart that I don't know how to daven properly. So I decided I would at least do what I can, so I said the letters that I know with all of my heart, 'alef, beis, gimmel, daled, hey, vav, zayin, ches, tes, yud.' Then I said to Hashem, 'Dear Father in Heaven, that is all that I know. Please, Hashem, combine these letters into words in the way that You see fit, and may they be acceptable in Your eyes.' And I continued, with a broken heart and with all my strength, saying: alef, beis, gimmel…"

The Arizal understood that this simple man's deeply heartfelt words had a tremendous effect in heaven, reaching the loftiest levels.[116]

Rabi Elazar says:

Be diligent in Torah learning and review it frequently.

Know what to answer an apikoros—someone who mocks or denies the Jewish beliefs.

Know before Whom you toil,
and Who your Master is Who will pay you the reward for your work.

רַבִּי אֶלְעָזָר אוֹמֵר:

הֱוֵי שָׁקוּד לִלְמוֹד תּוֹרָה.

וְדַע מַה שֶּׁתָּשִׁיב לְאֶפִּיקוֹרוֹס.

וְדַע לִפְנֵי מִי אַתָּה עָמֵל,
וּמִי הוּא בַּעַל מְלַאכְתֶּךָ
שֶׁיְּשַׁלֶּם לְךָ שְׂכַר פְּעֻלָּתֶךָ.

Keep at it!

Diligence and constant review is of utmost importance when learning. The best way to remember something is by reviewing it many times. Additionally, when you review a particular concept multiple times, it becomes increasingly clear in your mind.

Connections

The first two statements in the mishnah are connected: In order to know what to answer to an apikoros, all you need is to study Torah diligently. Do not think that you need to read their heretical books or become familiar with their ways—Torah has all the answers.[117]

Word Power

הֱוֵי שָׁקוּד לִלְמוֹד תּוֹרָה The word זכר—remember—has a gematria of 227, and שכח—forget—has a gematria of 328. The difference between them is 101. The difference between forgetting and remembering is to review your learning 101 times![118]

Biography

Rabi Elazar ben Arach was one of the five great students of Rabban Yochanan ben Zakkai.

When Rabban Yochanan ben Zakkai lost his son at a young age, he was inconsolable. Nothing anybody said brought him any comfort, until Rabi Elazar sat down before Rabban Yochanan and said, "A man who is entrusted by the king with a precious object is constantly anxious about his responsibility to guard it and keep it from harm, waiting for the day that he can return it. Your son learned Torah and left this world free of sin. You have returned him in the perfect condition that he was entrusted to you. Be comforted that you have successfully fulfilled your task." With these words, Rabban Yochanan was finally comforted.[119]

After Rabban Yochanan passed away, Rabi Elazar ben Arach moved to a city called Diyomsis under pressure from his wife, who was attracted to the city's beautiful gardens and rivers. Over time, Rabi Elazar forgot all his Torah learning. When Rabi Elazar returned to his former city and was honored with the reading of the Torah, he read the words הַחוֹדֶשׁ הַזֶּה לָכֶם as הַחֵרֵשׁ הָיָה לִבָּם. His friends and students realized that he had forgotten his learning. They davened for him and Eliyahu Hanavi retaught him everything that he had learned.[120]

Behind the Quote

Rabi Elazar's outstanding quality was his ability to expound on what he learned from his teachers. So it was especially important for him to review their teachings thoroughly, so he could be sure that when he built on them, the foundation would be solid and strong.

Additionally, since Rabi Elazar himself came to forget his Torah knowledge in his lifetime, he warns that to avoid forgetting, you must review your learning regularly.[121]

Did You Know?

It's the Effort that Counts
The mishnah teaches us that Hashem repays according to the effort you put in, not just what you accomplished. If you try your best, Hashem will reward you for your work—even if someone else achieved more through an equal amount of effort.[122]

Sparks

It's Not about You When learning Torah, and especially when answering an apikoros, bear in mind that the goal isn't to show off your knowledge. Remember that you are working for Hashem's sake and not for your own reputation.[123]

Word Power

וְדַע מַה שֶּׁתָּשִׁיב Although Torah has all of the answers to an apikoros' questions, you must not seek debate with him. Only if he might approach you, you must know what to **answer**.[124]

Fully Involved

R' Shlomoh Zalman from Volozhin would learn Torah constantly. Even when he was traveling, his lips never ceased from speaking words of Torah. Once, he was caught in a huge snowstorm. R' Shlomoh Zalman was riding on the back of a sled, covered in blankets to protect him from the freezing cold, while the driver sat up ahead, leading the horses. Throughout the journey, R' Shlomoh Zalman recited words of Torah by heart.

At one point during the trip the driver realized suddenly that the sled felt much lighter and was moving a lot quicker. He turned around and was shocked to see the back of the sled completely empty! He stopped the horses and rushed back to look for R' Shlomoh Zalman. After searching for a while he finally found him lying in the snow. R' Shlomoh Zalman was still reviewing Torah by heart, completely oblivious that he had fallen off the sled![125]

Rabi Tarfon says: **The day is short,** and time is very limited—there is **a lot of work** to be done in Torah learning and serving Hashem. **The workers are lazy** and could achieve more if they put in more effort. **The reward** for this work **is great, and** Hashem, **the Master, is pressuring the workers** to accomplish more.

רַבִּי טַרְפוֹן אוֹמֵר: הַיּוֹם קָצֵר, וְהַמְּלָאכָה מְרֻבָּה, וְהַפּוֹעֲלִים עֲצֵלִים, וְהַשָּׂכָר הַרְבֵּה, וּבַעַל הַבַּיִת דּוֹחֵק.

No Time to Waste!

For the forty days that Moshe was on Har Sinai, he didn't sleep at all. The Midrash[126] compares this to a king who gave his servant twenty-four hours to collect as much gold and silver as he wanted from the royal treasury. Of course, the servant would not waste even a minute of the precious time to take a break, for during that time he could be collecting more treasures.

So it is with each one of us. The day is short; we have been given a limited amount of time, and there is a lot of work—so much Torah to be learned and mitzvos to be performed. We must not waste our precious time!

Before Rabban Yochanan ben Zakkai passed away, he said "I don't know in which direction I will be taken (whether to Gan Eden or the opposite)."[128] He said this is because all throughout his life, he was so busy doing what needed to be done that he never felt it right to take time to make an accounting of his personal standing and accomplishments in his lifetime.

You Can Do Better When a parent punishes a child, he certainly doesn't mean to hurt him. On the contrary, he is disciplining him out of great love and care, so the child will grow up knowing the right way and reach his full potential! Similarly, Hashem urges us to keep doing more out of His tremendous love toward us; He knows our potential and wants us to put in the effort it takes to reach it.[127]

In the previous mishnah Rabi Elazar ben Arach tells us that we should remember who gives reward for diligence in Torah learning. This teaching of Rabi Tarfon's is brought now for it, too, stresses the great reward for Torah study.[129]

הַיּוֹם קָצֵר The mishnah says the day is short, rather than saying "time" is short. Day is a time of light and clarity, as opposed to night, which is a time of darkness. In this mishnah, "day" refers to youth, when one can learn Torah with a clear mind, free of major responsibilities. Night is when a person grows up and has other responsibilities. The mishnah tells us to remember that the "daytime" in a person's life is short and must be used to its fullest.[130]

Biography

Rabi Tarfon was a student of Rabi Eliezer ben Horkenus. A kohen, he even merited to hear the Kohen Gadol say Hashem's full name, the Sheim Hameforash, in the Beis Hamikdash.[131] He was a close friend (and at one point also a teacher) of Rabi Akiva, although they often differed in halachic matters.

Rabi Yehudah Hanassi compared Rabi Tarfon to a heap of walnuts—if you remove one walnut, the whole pile follows it. Similarly, when a student would ask Rabi Tarfon about a specific issue, he would answer with a stream of pessukim, mishnayos, halachos, and midrashim.[132]

Rabi Tarfon was very wealthy. Nevertheless, he was known for the extraordinary way in which he honored his elderly mother. For example, whenever she needed to get on or off of her bed, he would kneel beside the bed so that she could step onto his back. When Rabi Tarfon fell ill, his mother asked the Chachamim to daven that he should be healed in the merit of the great honor he gave her. She recounted that one Shabbos, while she was taking a stroll in her yard, her sandal broke. Rabi Tarfon placed his hands under his mother's feet so she could walk without dirtying her feet. The Chachamim replied, "Even if he were to do a million times more he would still not have reached the level of honoring one's parents mandated in the Torah."[133]

Once Rabi Akiva met Rabi Tarfon and said to him: "Would you like me to buy a city or two for you?" Rabi Tarfon agreed and gave him 4,000 gold dinars. Rabi Akiva took the money and distributed it all to poor Torah scholars. Later, when Rabi Tarfon inquired about the cities, Rabi Akiva brought him to the Beis Medrash, took a Tehillim and read the following passuk:[134] "פִּזַּר נָתַן לָאֶבְיוֹנִים צִדְקָתוֹ עוֹמֶדֶת לָעַד – He scattered [his wealth] by giving the poor. His righteousness endures forever." Pointing to the many people studying Torah supported by Rabi Tarfon's donation, Rabi Akiva said, "This is the city I have bought for you!"

Rabi Tarfon kissed Rabi Akiva and exclaimed: "You are my teacher and master; my teacher in Torah and master in conduct." He immediately gave more money to distribute to tzedakah.[135]

He is buried between the cities of Tzfas and Meron.

Once-in-a-Lifetime Guest

When R' Dov Ber from Radshitz would stay in Lublin, he would wake everyone at dawn saying, "Wake up! A guest has arrived whom you have never seen, and you'll never see again."

"Who is this guest?" the people would ask.

"Today!" he answered. "Today is here only once and it will never come again. What has to be done today cannot be done any other day, because each day has its special work."[136]

Rabi Tarfon **would** often **say:** Though indeed the day is short and there is much to be done, do not be discouraged, for **it is not your responsibility to complete** all **the work. However, you are not free to give up on** trying **to do it**; you are required to do as much as you possibly can.

If you have learned a lot of Torah, the Heavenly court **will give you a lot of reward. Your Master is trustworthy to pay you the reward for your work, but know that the reward for the righteous will be in the World to Come.**

הוּא הָיָה אוֹמֵר:
לֹא עָלֶיךָ הַמְּלָאכָה לִגְמוֹר,
וְלֹא אַתָּה בֶן חוֹרִין
לְהִבָּטֵל מִמֶּנָּה,

אִם לָמַדְתָּ תּוֹרָה הַרְבֵּה,
נוֹתְנִין לְךָ שָׂכָר הַרְבֵּה,
וְנֶאֱמָן הוּא בַּעַל מְלַאכְתְּךָ
שֶׁיְּשַׁלֵּם לְךָ שְׂכַר פְּעֻלָּתֶךָ,
וְדַע שֶׁמַּתַּן שְׂכָרָן שֶׁל
צַדִּיקִים לֶעָתִיד לָבֹא.

Be the Best You

R' Zushe of Anipoli once said: "I am not afraid that when I arrive in the Heavenly court, they will ask me why I wasn't like our forefathers or Moshe Rabbeinu. I am afraid they will ask me why I wasn't Zushe."

Hashem doesn't expect you to be as great as any other person. What He does expect of you is to maximize your own potential. A person who has a deep mind or is a quick learner is expected to learn more Torah than those who don't. A person blessed with wealth is expected to give more tzedakah than those who have less. A person who is naturally influential has the responsibility to influence others for the better. Each person is expected to use the tools and talents that he was given to serve Hashem to the best of his ability.

 **Word Power**

נוֹתְנִין לְךָ שְׂכַר הַרְבֵּה Why does the mishnah use the word נוֹתְנִין—they give, rather than מַשְׁלְמִין—they pay? Are we not being paid for our effort?

The answer is that although you are certainly being paid what is due for your efforts, in fact you are given extra reward as a gift, in addition to what you may have earned.[137]

 Did You Know?

Millions of Drops The Torah is like water. Just as water comes together drop by drop until it becomes a stream, learning two halachos today and two halachos tomorrow will eventually turn into a flowing stream of Torah.[138]

 Sparks

Equally Pleasing The Torah uses the same expression—"רֵיחַ נִיחוֹחַ לה׳ – it is a pleasing fragrance to Hashem" in reference to both an expensive animal korban, and a simple, cheaper korban of flour, which was offered by a poor person. The Gemara learns from here that to Hashem they are equally precious, as long as one has the right intentions.

However, if a rich person were to offer the same, inexpensive, poor-man's korban, he would not have fulfilled his obligation.[139]

Do Your Part When Paraoh's daughter saw a basket with an infant floating in the river, the Midrash says that she stretched out her arm to grasp it, although it was far away. Miraculously, her arm lengthened and she was able to reach the basket.

If the basket was so far that it was impossible for her to reach it, why did she reach out for it in the first place? Her action shows that when something good needs to be done, we have to put in all the effort we can, and whatever is beyond that, Hashem will arrange.[140]

 Connections

After learning in the previous mishnah that הַמְּלָאכָה מְרוּבָּה—there is much work, וּבַעַל הַבַּיִת דּוֹחֵק—and the Master is pressing, one might despair. "What's the point of trying? I'll never finish it all anyway!" This mishnah responds: "It's not your obligation to complete all the work." Do whatever you can; more than that was never asked of you.[141]

Just Give a Hand

Rabi Chanina ben Dosah was a very poor man. He felt bad that he was not able to afford a korban, so he decided to go into the forest and see if he could find something that was special enough to bring to the Beis Hamikdash.

In the forest, Rabi Chanina found a large, heavy stone, which he cut, smoothed down, and carved with beautiful designs. When he finished, he wanted to bring the stone to Yerushalayim. However, the stone was so big and heavy, that Rabi Chanina could not possibly bring it such a great distance himself. He asked people to help, but they all wanted more money than Rabi Chanina could afford to pay. Rabi Chanina was about to give up, when suddenly noticed a group of five men standing next to him. "Rabbi," they said, "we can take the stone to Yerushalayim for you if you give us five silver pieces and help us carry the stone." Rabi Chanina, thrilled, accepted the offer. Together with the five men, he lifted the stone, but instead of straining to move it, they immediately found themselves in Yerushalayim!

Rabi Chanina recovered from the shock of his sudden trip and turned around to pay his miraculous movers, but they had vanished!

Hashem had sent malachim to help bring the stone to the Beis Hamikdash. All Rabi Chanina had to do was put in a little effort, and Hashem took care of the rest!

Say this mishnah upon completing each perek:

Rabi Chananya ben Akashya says:

The Holy One, blessed be He, wanted to make B'nei **Yisrael** have many **merits.**

He therefore gave them an abundance of Torah and mitzvos, so that they would have many opportunities to connect to Him.

As it says in Yeshayah: **Hashem wanted, for the sake of** increasing B'nei Yisrael's **righteousness, that the Torah be made great and glorious.**

רַבִּי חֲנַנְיָא בֶּן עֲקַשְׁיָא אוֹמֵר:

רָצָה הַקָּדוֹשׁ בָּרוּךְ הוּא לְזַכּוֹת אֶת יִשְׂרָאֵל לְפִיכָךְ הִרְבָּה לָהֶם תּוֹרָה וּמִצְוֹת

שֶׁנֶּאֱמַר: יְיָ חָפֵץ לְמַעַן צִדְקוֹ יַגְדִּיל תּוֹרָה וְיַאְדִּיר.

Endnotes

1. רמב"ם הלכות תשובה פ"ג ה"ד. דרך אבות
2. קידושין עב, ב
3. כתובות קג, א
4. מרכבת המשנה
5. מרכבת המשנה
6. מדרש שמואל
7. הר' יוסף יעב"ץ
8. ביאורים
9. שו"ת רדב"ז ח"ג ס' יג
10. בראשית רבה עה, ה
11. כתר שם טוב ס' קמ"ה
12. מדרש שמואל
13. לקוטי בתר לקוטי בשם השל"ה
14. קידושין מ, א
15. מסכת אבות ע"פ יינה של תורה ע' 43
16. דורש לפרקים
17. דורש לפרקים
18. כתובות קג, ב
19. חולין קו, א
20. רמב"ם. רבינו יונה. וראה שו"ת שואל ונשאל יו"ד ח"ד סימן ס"ט
21. ראה סוטה מט, א
22. הר' יוסף יעב"ץ
23. ספורי חסידים - תורה, אחרי מות
24. מהר"ם שי"ק
25. רע"ב. הר' יוסף יעב"ץ
26. מדרש שמואל
27. לב אבות ששמע ממוהרי"ט, הובא במדרש שמואל
28. פרדס האבות ע' 173
29. סנהדרין קב, ב
30. דרך ארץ זוטא פ"ה
31. ככר לאדן להחיד"א, סימן ז
32. רמב"ם הלכות גירושין פ"ב ה"כ
33. ספורי חסידים - מועדים, עשרת ימי תשובה
34. מרכבת המשנה
35. תפארת ישראל
36. מנחות מג, ב
37. דברי שאול, הובא בלקוטי בתר לקוטי
38. עירובין נד, ב
39. שבת לא, א
40. מאמרי אדמו"ר הזקן הקצרים עמוד 305
41. פירוש המשניות להרמב"ם
42. אריז"ל בשער מאמרי רז"ל
43. רמב"ם שמונה פרקים פ"ח. הלכות תשובה סוף פ"ו
44. אריז"ל בשער מאמרי רז"ל, הובא גם במדרש דוד
45. הר' יוסף יעב"ץ
46. בן יהוידע - בבא מציעא לג, א
47. ספורנו
48. תפארת ישראל
49. אבות עולם
50. אגרת הקדש סימן ד
51. רע"ב
52. חיים שיש בהם על פרקי אבות ח"ב ע' תקס"ד. מעשי אבות ע' רל"ו
53. שבת פח, א
54. מדרש שמואל. מדרש דוד
55. קדושת לוי, ליקוטים לאבות
56. ר' יונה
57. ירושלמי נדרים פ"ה ה"ו
58. סנהדרין מא, א
59. סוכה כח, א
60. מס' סופרים פט"ז ה"ו
61. ברכות יז, ב
62. ברכות כח, ב
63. בים דרך ע' צד
64. כנסת ישראל. דרך החיים
65. נדה כד, ב
66. רוח חיים
67. ספורנו
68. לב אבות
69. ביאורים
70. מדרש שמואל
71. מסכת אבות ע"פ יינה של תורה ע' 239
72. תפארת ישראל
73. באר האבות
74. ירושלמי יבמות פ"א ה"ו
75. מדרש שמואל
76. תפארת ישראל
77. רמב"ם. רע"ב. תפארת ישראל
78. רש"י. רע"ב
79. הר' יוסף יעב"ץ
80. פרדס האבות ע' 169
81. מדרש שמואל
82. ברכות לג, ב
83. בראשית רבה נא, ג
84. שבת קה, ב. רמב"ם הלכות דעות פ"ב ה"ג
85. אבות דר' נתן פ"ו
86. שיר השירים רבה א, א
87. במדבר רבה יט, ז
88. סנהדרין סח, א
89. תפארת ישראל
90. בית הבחירה להמאירי
91. הר' יוסף יעב"ץ
92. מעיל צדקה סימן תנ"א בשם ס' העקידה
93. פרקי משה
94. יומא ט, ב
95. ביאורים
96. מדרש שמואל
97. ירושלמי יבמות פ"א ה"ו
98. תענית ז, א
99. ספורנו
100. ספורי חסידים - תורה, פרשת מקץ
101. מגן אבות לה"ר מאיר בן חליפה
102. מדרש שמואל
103. ראש השנה יז, ב
104. דברים לג, ד
105. שמות רבה לג, א
106. ברכות ה, א
107. תפארת ישראל
108. ספורנו
109. שיחות קודש תשכ"ט ב, פרשת חוקת-בלק
110. שו"ע או"ח ח"ס צ"ח
111. ראה תפארת ישראל
112. דרך חיים להמהר"ל
113. ספורנו
114. מדרש שמואל
115. לקו"א פרק א
116. ספורי חסידים - תורה, נח
117. זרוע ימין
118. כלי יקר
119. אבות דר' נתן פי"ד
120. שבת קמז, ב
121. ביאורים
122. מדרש שמואל
123. חתם סופר. וראה רבינו יונה
124. מדרש דוד
125. עטרת אבות ע' 150
126. שמות רבה מ"ז
127. מדרש שמואל. תפארת ישראל
128. ברכות כח, ב
129. מגן אבות להרשב"ץ
130. מדרש שמואל
131. קידושין עא, א
132. גיטין סז, א וברש"י שם
133. ירושלמי פאה פ"א ה"א
134. תהלים קיב, ט
135. מסכת כלה, א
136. מסכת אבות ע"פ יינה של תורה ע' 41
137. מדרש שמואל
138. שיר השירים רבה א, ב (י"ט) על "כי טובים"
139. ראה תוספות יו"ט
140. ר' מענדל מקאצק, הובא בספר אמת ואמונה (תרל"ו)
141. רבינו יונה. מגן אבות. תפארת ישראל

פֶּרֶק שְׁלִישִׁי

Chapter Three

Kol Yisrael

Say this mishnah before beginning each new perek:

All B'nei **Yisrael** have a portion in the World to Come.

As it says in Yeshayah regarding B'nei Yisrael upon Moshiach's arrival: **Your people are all tzaddikim,** and **they will all inherit Eretz** Yisrael **forever**—they will never be exiled from it again.

All will recognize that they are **the branch of My planting and the work of My hands,** in which I, Hashem, **take pride.**

כָּל יִשְׂרָאֵל יֵשׁ לָהֶם חֵלֶק לָעוֹלָם הַבָּא,

שֶׁנֶּאֱמַר: וְעַמֵּךְ כֻּלָּם צַדִּיקִים, לְעוֹלָם יִירְשׁוּ אָרֶץ,

נֵצֶר מַטָּעַי מַעֲשֵׂה יָדַי לְהִתְפָּאֵר.

עֲקַבְיָא בֶּן מַהֲלַלְאֵל אוֹמֵר: הִסְתַּכֵּל בִּשְׁלֹשָׁה דְבָרִים, וְאֵין אַתָּה בָא לִידֵי עֲבֵרָה. דַּע מֵאַיִן בָּאתָ, וּלְאָן אַתָּה הוֹלֵךְ, וְלִפְנֵי מִי אַתָּה עָתִיד לִתֵּן דִּין וְחֶשְׁבּוֹן.

Akavya ben Mahalalel says: **Look at** and consider these **three things** at all times, **and you will not come to** do **an aveirah:** Know from where you came, to where you are going, and before Whom you are going to have to **give justification and a detailed report** of everything you did during your lifetime.

מֵאַיִן בָּאתָ: מִטִּפָּה סְרוּחָה. וּלְאָן אַתָּה הוֹלֵךְ: לִמְקוֹם עָפָר רִמָּה וְתוֹלֵעָה. וְלִפְנֵי מִי אַתָּה עָתִיד לִתֵּן דִּין וְחֶשְׁבּוֹן: לִפְנֵי מֶלֶךְ מַלְכֵי הַמְּלָכִים הַקָּדוֹשׁ בָּרוּךְ הוּא.

The mishnah explains: **Where did you come from?** The body begins growing **from a spoiled drop** of fluid in the mother's womb. **Where are you going?** You will eventually die and go **to a** grave, a **place** full **of earth, worms, and maggots.** Before Whom will you give a detailed report? Before the supreme **King of** all **kings, the Holy One, blessed be He.**

Living Lessons

Long Lived

A person is made up of a neshamah and a body. But while the body will eventually die, the neshamah lasts forever. Physical pleasures too are only temporary, whereas the connection to Hashem earned through learning Torah or doing a mitzvah is eternal. Bearing this in mind helps us make wise choices and stay away from aveiros.

Biography

Akavya ben Mahalalel was a student of Yehudah ben Tabbai and Shimon ben Shatach, and a colleague of Shmayah and Avtalyon, in the era of the second Beis Hamikdash. Not much is known about him when he was young. Later in life he became very famous, so much so that he is one of the few Tannaim who does not carry a title such as Rebbi, since his name alone was known and respected by all.

There was once an argument between the majority of the Chachamim and Akavya regarding four specific halachos. Akavya held his opinion because he had heard it from the majority of Chachamim of the previous generation. Akavya was offered the position of Av Beis Din if he would retract his opinion. He refused, saying that he preferred to be considered a fool for the rest of his life for forgoing this opportunity, rather than cause a chilul Hashem by changing his mind to gain a position of honor.

Later on in his life, when he was on his deathbed, he told his son to go along with the Chachamim on that same issue, and explained, "I heard these halachos from the majority of the sages of the previous generation, and therefore I held that that was the halachah. You, however, heard these same halachos only from the minority—me, and therefore you must go along with the majority of the current leadership on this."

When his son asked him to put in a good word for him to the Chachamim, Akavya refused, saying that a person's own actions would determine how he would be perceived by others.[1]

Behind the Quote

Akavya ben Mahalalel lived in the era of the second Beis Hamikdash when B'nei Yisrael were financially prosperous.[2] He therefore warns that physical things eventually come to an end; one must remember to focus on spiritual things, which last forever.[3]

Sparks

Do You Know Who You Are? The first part of the mishnah can be interpreted as an empowering message:

Know from where you come: your neshamah originates from directly beneath Hashem's throne. It doesn't suit you to sin—you're so much greater than that!

Know that you are returning there to explain all your actions: Hashem values your actions and eagerly records every one. Don't let Him down![4]

Did You Know?

Humility Matzah, a flat bread, is symbolic of humility. Chametz, which rises, represents haughtiness. The difference in gematria between מַצָה and חָמֵץ is three. It is the awareness of the three things mentioned in this mishnah that can change a person from being in a lowly state of chametz to the refined state of matzah.[5]

Only Temporary

A wealthy man left two wills for his family, one to be opened upon his passing and the other at the end of the Shloshim, thirty days after his passing. When he passed away his family rushed to open the will and found instructions that left them confused: their father requested to be buried in a pair of socks. They rushed to the Chevra Kadisha with their request, but no amount of arguing could change the halachah that one may not be buried in anything other than simple tachrichim.

After the Shloshim, the family opened the second will. It read as follows: By now you certainly know that you couldn't bury me in my socks. This should be an important lesson for you: No matter how much money you make in this world, none of it can come with you to the World to Come; even a simple pair of socks cannot be taken. So, my dear children, when you divide my money don't fight about it, because the only thing that stays with you forever is Torah and mitzvos.[6]

Rabi Chanina, the chief assistant to the Kohen Gadol, says: Daven for the well-being and success of the government, because if not for fear of the government, people would swallow each other alive.

Rabi Chanina ben Teradyon says: If two people sit together and there are no words of Torah discussed between them, it is a gathering of fools who don't understand enough to appreciate the Torah's value, and a person should not sit with them. As it says in Tehillim: A righteous person does not sit among a gathering of fools.

But if two people sit together and words of Torah are discussed between them, the Shechinah rests among them, as it says in Malachi: Then those who fear Hashem spoke words of Torah one to another, and Hashem paid attention and heard, and their words were written in a book of remembrance before Him, to reward those who fear Hashem and think about His Name.

From this passuk we know only that the Shechinah rests among two people who discuss Torah. From where do we know that if even one person sits alone and occupies himself with Torah, the Holy One, blessed be He, sets a reward for him? From a passuk in Eichah, where it says: Let him sit alone and study Torah quietly, because for doing so he can take a reward for himself.

רַבִּי חֲנִינָא סְגַן הַכֹּהֲנִים אוֹמֵר: הֱוֵי מִתְפַּלֵּל בִּשְׁלוֹמָהּ שֶׁל מַלְכוּת, שֶׁאִלְמָלֵא מוֹרָאָהּ, אִישׁ אֶת רֵעֵהוּ חַיִּים בְּלָעוֹ.

רַבִּי חֲנִינָא בֶּן תְּרַדְיוֹן אוֹמֵר: שְׁנַיִם שֶׁיּוֹשְׁבִין וְאֵין בֵּינֵיהֶם דִּבְרֵי תוֹרָה, הֲרֵי זֶה מוֹשַׁב לֵצִים, שֶׁנֶּאֱמַר: וּבְמוֹשַׁב לֵצִים לֹא יָשָׁב.

אֲבָל שְׁנַיִם שֶׁיּוֹשְׁבִין וְיֵשׁ בֵּינֵיהֶם דִּבְרֵי תוֹרָה, שְׁכִינָה שְׁרוּיָה בֵּינֵיהֶם, שֶׁנֶּאֱמַר: אָז נִדְבְּרוּ יִרְאֵי יְיָ אִישׁ אֶל רֵעֵהוּ וַיַּקְשֵׁב יְיָ וַיִּשְׁמָע, וַיִּכָּתֵב סֵפֶר זִכָּרוֹן לְפָנָיו לְיִרְאֵי יְיָ וּלְחוֹשְׁבֵי שְׁמוֹ.

אֵין לִי אֶלָּא שְׁנַיִם, מִנַּיִן אֲפִילּוּ אֶחָד שֶׁיּוֹשֵׁב וְעוֹסֵק בַּתּוֹרָה שֶׁהַקָּדוֹשׁ בָּרוּךְ הוּא קוֹבֵעַ לוֹ שָׂכָר, שֶׁנֶּאֱמַר: יֵשֵׁב בָּדָד וְיִדֹּם כִּי נָטַל עָלָיו.

What a Partner!

There is a famous saying that two heads are better than one. This mishnah tells us that although learning Torah alone is valuable, it still doesn't come close to the value of learning with a partner. There are so many benefits when two people learn together; you understand what you learn much better, and remember it for longer than when you learn alone.

This mishnah highlights another major advantage: when you learn with other people, Hashem joins in the learning. Just imagine, you are learning together with Hashem Himself!

Biography

Rabi Chanina Sgan Hakohanim lived through the destruction of the second Beis Hamikdash and later recounted many of the practices he saw there. He is called Sgan Hakohanim in the plural form because in his times, wealthy kohanim who were not worthy bought the position of Kohen Gadol. Being that they were not worthy, they died on Yom Kippur when entering the Kodesh Hakadashim, and so Rabi Chanina served as the deputy to many Kohanim Gedolim.

Rabi Chanina was killed by the Romans on the 25th of Sivan, the same date that Rabi Yishmael Kohen Gadol and Rabban Shimon ben Gamliel were killed, and is buried in Kfar Chananya.

Rabi Chanina ben Tradyon lived in Sichnin in the Lower Galil, and headed the court there. He was a student of Rabi Akiva, and was known as a most trustworthy tzedakah collector. He had a son and two daughters, one of them Bruriah wife of Rabi Meir, a unique, scholarly woman, who is often mentioned in the Gemara.

Rabi Chanina ben Tradyon was one of the Asarah Harugei Malchus—the ten martyrs brutally killed by the Romans. He was killed for teaching Torah publicly after the Roman government had outlawed this practice. The Romans wrapped him in a Torah scroll together with bundles of twigs and set them on fire. They maliciously put wet material on his chest to prolong his suffering. Seeing this, his daughter cried out, "Must I see father suffer in this way?" To which Rabi Chanina answered, "If I had been burned to death alone, I would have worried, but with the Sefer Torah I know that He who will avenge the Torah will avenge me as well."[7] He was killed on the 27th of Sivan and is buried in Sichnin.

Word Power

שְׁלוֹמָהּ שֶׁל מַלְכוּת These words can also mean that you should daven for the government to be peaceful. Not all governments are righteous and just. If a government is corrupt and wicked, we must daven that they change and promote peaceful and civil behavior.[8]

שְׁנַיִם שֶׁיּוֹשְׁבִין The mishnah says that people who are (already) sitting together must be sure to exchange words of Torah. This shows that although they did not necessarily sit down for the purpose of learning, but for another purpose, they nevertheless must be sure to share words of Torah.

Torah is not like other subjects that are learned only at specific times before they are put away. Torah is part of everything we do, and words of Torah should be brought into every conversation.[9]

Behind the Quote

Rabi Chanina Sgan Hakohanim was assistant to the Kohen Gadol for many years, and technically should have been promoted to become Kohen Gadol himself.[10] However, that didn't happen because he lived in a time of corruption, during which wealthy kohanim bribed the Romans for the unearned privilege of being the Kohen Gadol. Although Rabi Chanina had valid reason to resent the government, he tells us that we still must respect and even daven for them.[11]

In Rabi Chanina ben Tradyon's times, the government outlawed public study of Torah. He therefore emphasizes that Hashem cherishes all Torah study, even when it is done in private.[12]

Make Room

The Kotzker Rebbe once said to his chassidim, "Do you know where Hashem is found? I'll tell you. Hashem is found wherever man allows Him to enter!"

If a person is full of himself and thinks he is so important, then there is no room for Hashem there. However, when a person removes his feeling of "me," he makes room for Hashem to enter. That's where Hashem can be found.[13]

Rabi Shimon says: If three people ate together at one table and did not speak words of Torah over it, it is as if they ate from sacrifices offered to idols that are made of lifeless, physical material. As it says in Yeshayah: If a meal consists only of physical indulgence, with no mention of Hashem, then in fact all the tables are filled with vomit and waste.

But if three people ate at the same table and spoke words of Torah over it, it is as if they ate from the table of Hashem, as it says in Yechezkel regarding the Shulchan in the Beis Hamikdash: "And he said to me, 'This is the table that is before Hashem.'"

רַבִּי שִׁמְעוֹן אוֹמֵר: שְׁלֹשָׁה שֶׁאָכְלוּ עַל שֻׁלְחָן אֶחָד וְלֹא אָמְרוּ עָלָיו דִּבְרֵי תוֹרָה, כְּאִלּוּ אָכְלוּ מִזִּבְחֵי מֵתִים, שֶׁנֶּאֱמַר: כִּי כָּל שֻׁלְחָנוֹת מָלְאוּ קִיא צֹאָה בְּלִי מָקוֹם,

אֲבָל שְׁלֹשָׁה שֶׁאָכְלוּ עַל שֻׁלְחָן אֶחָד וְאָמְרוּ עָלָיו דִּבְרֵי תוֹרָה, כְּאִלּוּ אָכְלוּ מִשֻּׁלְחָנוֹ שֶׁל מָקוֹם, שֶׁנֶּאֱמַר: וַיְדַבֵּר אֵלַי, זֶה הַשֻּׁלְחָן אֲשֶׁר לִפְנֵי יְיָ.

So Much More to Life

This mishnah teaches us that our eating should be imbued with holiness. Yes, our bodies need food and drink, but the purpose of eating is to give the body the energy that is required to learn Torah and do mitzvos. When one says words of Torah at a meal, showing that he is eating for a higher purpose than pure physical pleasure, the meal becomes filled with purpose and life. In contrast, a meal without any Torah learning lacks life and purpose, and is considered dead.[14]

This idea applies to all areas of our life. Some people eat, sleep, and work only so that they can eat, sleep, and work more! This is one of the meanings of the Gemara's words,[15] "Those Babylonians are fools because they eat their bread with bread." Foolish people eat so they have energy to work, only so they can earn enough to eat once again—they eat their bread only to produce more bread. A Jew, however, works in order to have food in order to have energy to serve Hashem. Everything we do is for the sake of serving Hashem![16]

 Did You Know?

Our Mizbeiach When one speaks words of Torah at a meal and eats with the right intentions, it is like shechting the yetzer hara, since it is being forced to do things for Hashem and not for its personal enjoyment. This is why a table where words of Torah are spoken is called a table of Hashem, a mizbeiach, for on it we shecht the yetzer hara.[17]

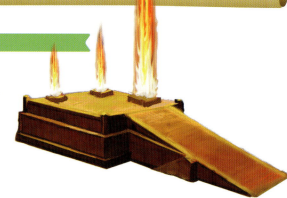

Biography

Rabi Shimon bar Yochai was born to his parents after many years of childlessness. When he was still a young boy, he was sent to learn in the cheder established by Rabban Gamliel in Yerushalayim, and later learned from Rabi Akiva for many years.

During the rule of the evil Romans over Eretz Yisroel, Rabi Shimon spoke out strongly against them, and as a result was persecuted by the government. Together with his son Rabi Elazar, he hid in a secluded cave where they learned Torah continuously. A carob tree and spring of fresh water miraculously appeared at the cave's entrance to sustain them. After thirteen long years, there was a change of government and they were finally able to come out of hiding.[18]

Rabi Shimon learned with so much devotion that he had the status of Toraso Umnaso—Torah learning was his only occupation. This meant that he was exempt from most mitzvos so as not to interrupt his learning. He established a yeshivah in the city of Takoa and taught many students there. He wrote the midrashim called Sifri and Mechilta of Rabi Shimon bar Yochai, as well as the holy Zohar, containing mystical interpretations of the Torah. In fact, in almost every case where a mishnah quotes something in the name of Rabi Shimon, it is referring to Rabi Shimon bar Yochai.

Rabi Shimon passed away on the 18th of Iyar, Lag Ba'omer, and is buried in Meron, a village near Tzfas. Before he passed away, Rabi Shimon requested that people spend the day of his passing in joyous celebration, and till today, many people visit his resting place on Lag Ba'omer to daven and celebrate.

Behind the Quote

Rabi Shimon spent thirteen years of his life learning alone in a cave with his son.[19] He emphasizes the importance of learning in groups of three or more, something he missed out on for so long.

Connections

The previous mishnah says to learn whenever possible. This mishnah adds that when it's not possible to be learning new things, such as while eating, you should discuss that which you have previously learned.[20]

Word Power

שֶׁאָכְלוּ The word שֶׁאָכְלוּ—who ate—is in past tense because one must speak only after finishing to swallow the food. Speaking while eating is dangerous because you might choke.[21]

The Difference

As a young child, R' Sholom Dovber of Lubavitch was discussing the specialness of a Jew with his brother, R' Zalman Aharon. Their father R' Shmuel heard their discussions and summoned Bentzion, a helper in the Rebbe's home.

Bentzion was a simple Jew. Every day he would recite the entire book of Tehillim, and every evening he would participate in a shiur on Ein Yaakov in the local shul.

When he arrived, the Rebbe asked him: "Bentzion, did you eat today?"

"Yes," he replied.

"And why did you eat?" The Rebbe probed, to which Bentzion replied, "So that I may live."

"But why live?" inquired the Rebbe. With a heartfelt sigh, expressing a deep longing to be a better servant of Hashem, Bentzion replied, "To be a good Jew and do what Hashem wants."

"You may go. Please send me Ivan the coachman," said the Rebbe.

When the coachman arrived, the Rebbe asked him: "Did you eat today?"

"Yes," he replied.

"And why did you eat?"

"So that I may live."

"But why live?" inquired the Rebbe. "To take a swig of vodka and have a bite to eat," replied the coachman.

"You may go," said the Rebbe.[22]

Rabi Chanina ben Chachinai says: One who stays awake at night or travels alone on a road and turns his heart to worthless things, instead of thinking about Torah, is responsible for anything bad that happens to him, because studying Torah would have helped protect him from danger.

רַבִּי חֲנִינָא בֶּן חֲכִינַאי אוֹמֵר: הַנֵּעוֹר בַּלַּיְלָה, וְהַמְהַלֵּךְ בַּדֶּרֶךְ יְחִידִי, וּמְפַנֶּה לִבּוֹ לְבַטָּלָה, הֲרֵי זֶה מִתְחַיֵּב בְּנַפְשׁוֹ.

It Never Returns

This mishnah reminds us that every second is a precious gift given to us by Hashem. In fact, a person should care more about his time than his money, because while lost money can be acquired again, lost time can never be regained! Just as you would care for a precious diamond, be smart and cherish every minute of your time, utilizing it to the very last second!

A great Talmid Chacham once said that it took him just two minutes to gain his tremendous knowledge—all of those "two spare minutes" that he had, he used for learning![24]

Don't Go It Alone

The words of this mishnah can also mean that if someone chooses to travel alone on his own spiritual path and does not seek to help others, it is as if he is guilty of murder. All Jews are responsible for one another, both spiritually and physically.[25]

 Connections

The previous mishnah discusses learning Torah at convenient times. This mishnah adds that even when it is inconvenient, such as while traveling, one should still learn Torah.[23]

 Sparks

Study to Stay Safe Living in good company helps a person stay on the proper path. When one is alone, on the other hand, there is a greater risk that he might stray. This mishnah emphasizes that at such times, it is especially important to learn Torah. Staying connected in this way will ensure that he continue to follow Hashem's ways.[26]

Biography

Rabi Chanina ben Chachinai was a student of Rabi Akiva and studied in his yeshivah together with Rabi Shimon bar Yochai.

He fasted every day from when he turned twelve years old, eating only a small meal after nightfall. Rabi Chanina left his wife and family to learn from Rabi Akiva for thirteen years. When he returned, his wife passed away just as he walked through the door. Rabi Chanina cried out to Hashem, "How can this be her 'reward' after waiting for me for thirteen years while I learned Torah?" Miraculously, she immediately came back to life![27]

When he was very old, he was killed by the Romans together with the other Asarah Harugei Malchus. It was a Friday, and while being led to his death, he started reciting Kiddush. Upon reaching the word "וַיְקַדֵּשׁ—and He made it holy," he was killed. At that moment, a voice from Heaven was heard saying, "Happy are you, Rabi Chanina ben Chachinai, that you were holy, and your soul left you in holiness."

He is buried in Tzfas.

 Behind the Quote

This mishnah calls for a great diligence and love for Torah learning, which leads one to learn at every opportunity. Rabi Chanina himself exhibited a great thirst for Torah throughout his life. At one point, Rabi Shimon and Rabi Chanina had decided to travel to study with their teacher. However, Rabi Shimon was just finishing the days of sheva brachos after his wedding, and he pleaded with Rabi Chanina to wait for his sheva brachos to conclude so they could travel together. However, Rabi Chanina's desire to learn Torah was so great that he didn't want to delay at all, and instead he traveled alone.[28]

Rabi Chanina lived at a time when public Torah learning was forbidden and it was especially dangerous to learn in groups. He therefore emphasizes that when a person is alone, and it is thus safer to learn, he must seize the opportunity and not waste the time on empty thoughts.[29]

 **Story**

I'll Sleep Later

When the Chafetz Chaim was old, he would often fall asleep while learning at the table. His family urged him, "Why don't you go to bed and sleep properly?"

He answered, "You want me to sleep now? Very soon I'll have plenty of time to rest! Now that I'm still in this world, let me use my time for things that can only be done in this world."[30]

 Did You Know?

Night is for Torah Hashem created nighttime, when people cannot work, so there would be time to learn without distractions. He created the moon so that there would be enough light at night to be able to learn.[31]

Rabi Nechunya ben Hakanah says: Whoever accepts upon himself the burden of learning Torah, Hashem removes the burden and oppression of government and the burden and stress of worldly affairs from him.

Whoever removes the burden of Torah from himself, Hashem places the burden of government and the burden of worldly affairs upon him.

רַבִּי נְחוּנְיָא בֶּן הַקָּנָה אוֹמֵר: כָּל הַמְקַבֵּל עָלָיו עוֹל תּוֹרָה, מַעֲבִירִין מִמֶּנּוּ עוֹל מַלְכוּת וְעוֹל דֶּרֶךְ אֶרֶץ, וְכָל הַפּוֹרֵק מִמֶּנּוּ עוֹל תּוֹרָה, נוֹתְנִין עָלָיו עוֹל מַלְכוּת וְעוֹל דֶּרֶךְ אֶרֶץ.

Torah First

There is so much that needs to be done! Rabi Nechunya teaches that if we accept upon ourselves the responsibility of learning Torah and consider it our first and foremost responsibility, everything else won't feel like a burden and it will be easier to get everything done.

Not For the Fun of It

Rabi Nechunya says to accept the "burden" of Torah. This teaches us that while learning Torah can be very enjoyable, we shouldn't learn only for enjoyment, but because Hashem commanded us to. The same goes for all mitzvos: we should fulfill them because Hashem told us to, and not because they are enjoyable or make sense.[32]

Lucky Responsibility Why is Torah referred to as an עוֹל—burden?

- If you encounter parts of Torah that you don't understand, don't just leave them and move on. Your obligation is to keep trying, and in the end Hashem will help you understand.[33]
- When Torah doesn't appeal to you but instead feels like a yoke, strengthen your resolve and learn anyway.[34]
  - Just as an ox can't remove a yoke placed upon it, the Torah is always a part of us, and not something that can be sometimes removed.[35]
  - Someone who is not always able to learn must still accept the responsibility of Torah study by supporting others who do learn.[36]

Biography

Rabi Nechunya ben Hakanah was a colleague of Rabban Yochanan ben Zakkai. Some say that he passed away before the churban. He is known as a master of kabbalah and authored the Sefer Habahir, one of the first books of kabbalah. Though a great Talmid Chacham, he would ask Hashem every morning that no mistakes should be made in halachah because of him, and at the end of the day he would thank Hashem for fulfilling his request.37

He lived to a very old age and is buried in Tzfas. When his students once asked him why he had merited such a long life he explained: he would never rejoice in another's embarrassment, he would never go to sleep before forgiving anyone who had aggravated him that day, and he was generous with his money.38

 **Behind the Quote**

Rabi Nechunya ben Hakanah lived at a time when the Romans prohibited the public study of Torah. Therefore, he emphasized the importance of Torah study by assuring us that it has the power to remove any pressure from the government.39

Rabi Nechunya was a greatly accomplished Talmid Chacham, recognized by his peers as superior to them. Obviously, he enjoyed learning Torah and it was certainly no burden for him. Yet he reminds us that we do not learn for the great pleasure that it brings us but for the holy obligation that we must fulfill.40

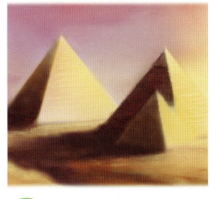

 **Did You Know?**

Not Enslaved The lesson of this mishnah was clearly seen when B'nei Yisrael were in Egypt. Shevet Levi, who held firm to Torah and mitzvos, weren't subjected to the forced physical labor that the other shevatim suffered at the hands of the Egyptians.41

Hashem Provides

Every morning after davening, R' Zushe of Anipoli would pray: "Hashem, Zushe wants to eat, please give me food." When the shamash would hear him say that, he knew it was time to bring in breakfast for the Tzaddik.

One day it occured to the shamash, "Is it really Hashem Who prepares the breakfast, or is it me?"

He decided to teach R' Zushe a lesson, and resolved that the following day he would not bring in the food when R' Zushe said his daily prayer. He hoped R' Zushe would realize whom it really was that he should be thanking.

The next day as usual, R' Zushe finished davening and said "Hashem, Zushe wants to eat, please give me food." The shamash, however, did not bring in the food as he usually would, but instead stood quietly at the side and waited to see what would happen. Just then, the door burst open and a man came in with a tray bearing an entire prepared breakfast. The shamash was shocked. Who was this man and how did he know to come now?

The man explained, "Yesterday I was walking on the narrow bridge over the river and someone was coming toward me. There wasn't enough room for both of us so I pushed him to the side, and he fell. Later, to my horror, I found out that it was the Tzaddik R' Zushe whom I pushed! I am coming now with this humble present to beg forgiveness for my terrible act."

The shamash realized that Hashem provides for those who serve Him truthfully, and that he, the shamash was the lucky witness to this daily miracle.42

Rabi Chalafta ben Dosa of Kfar Chananya says: If **ten** people sit together and are involved in **Torah** learning, **the Shechinah rests among them, as it says** in Tehillim: **Hashem stands in the congregation of God.** The Shechinah rests in a congregation—a group of ten people—when they learn Torah.

רַבִּי חֲלַפְתָּא בֶּן דּוֹסָא אִישׁ כְּפַר חֲנַנְיָא אוֹמֵר: עֲשָׂרָה שֶׁיּוֹשְׁבִין וְעוֹסְקִין בַּתּוֹרָה שְׁכִינָה שְׁרוּיָה בֵּינֵיהֶם, שֶׁנֶּאֱמַר: אֱלֹהִים נִצָּב בַּעֲדַת אֵל.

From where do we know that the Shechinah rests **even** among **five** people who learn Torah together? From a passuk in Amos, where **it says:** Hashem **established His bundle on the earth** and He rests upon it. A bundle is carried with the five fingers of the hand, symbolizing five people who learn Torah together.

וּמִנַּיִן אֲפִילוּ חֲמִשָּׁה, שֶׁנֶּאֱמַר: וַאֲגֻדָּתוֹ עַל אֶרֶץ יְסָדָהּ.

From where do we know that the Shechinah rests **even** among **three** people who learn Torah together? From a passuk in Tehillim, where **it says:** Hashem sits **among** the three **judges** of a Beis Din and **makes** His own **judgment.**

וּמִנַּיִן אֲפִילוּ שְׁלֹשָׁה, שֶׁנֶּאֱמַר: בְּקֶרֶב אֱלֹהִים יִשְׁפֹּט.

From where do we know that the Shechinah rests **even** among **two** people who learn Torah together? From a passuk in Malachi, where **it says: Then the people who fear Hashem spoke to each other, and Hashem paid attention and heard.**

וּמִנַּיִן אֲפִילוּ שְׁנַיִם, שֶׁנֶּאֱמַר: אָז נִדְבְּרוּ יִרְאֵי יְיָ אִישׁ אֶל רֵעֵהוּ, וַיַּקְשֵׁב יְיָ וַיִּשְׁמָע.

From where do we know that the Shechinah rests upon **even one** person who learns Torah? From the Torah, where **it says: In any place where I** have permitted you to **mention My name**—if you mention it, **I will come to you and bless you.**

וּמִנַּיִן אֲפִילוּ אֶחָד, שֶׁנֶּאֱמַר: בְּכָל הַמָּקוֹם אֲשֶׁר אַזְכִּיר אֶת שְׁמִי אָבֹא אֵלֶיךָ וּבֵרַכְתִּיךָ.

Learn Together

Even if a person learns Torah alone, Hashem joins him. However, it is better to study Torah in a group, since learning with a group has tremendous benefits. The first and foremost of those benefits is that a very high level of Hashem's Shechinah rests with a group, and the larger the group the more Shechinah present!

So while this should make you excited to learn in a group, you must also remember to be sure to conduct yourself properly, in a way that is fitting for the presence of the King of kings!

Biography

Rabi Chalafta ben Dosa of Kfar Chananya was a student of Rabi Meir. He is not to be confused with the father of Rabi Yosei ben Chalafta, who had the same name. Not much is recorded about his life. He is buried in Kfar Chananya, a small city near Tzfas in northern Eretz Yisrael.

Sparks

Five Alive

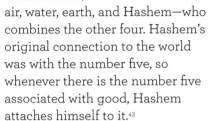

The world is made from five elements: fire, air, water, earth, and Hashem—who combines the other four. Hashem's original connection to the world was with the number five, so whenever there is the number five associated with good, Hashem attaches himself to it.[43]

Word Power

שֶׁנֶּאֱמַר The mishnah brings a passuk to support the statements that Hashem rests with each size group, which are learned as follows:

- **Ten** – The word עֵדָה is used in reference to the spies who reported negative information about Eretz Yisrael. There were twelve spies in total, but since Yehoshua and Kalev did not give a negative report, there were only ten negative reporters. From there we learn that the word עֵדָה means ten people.[44]

- **Five** – An agudah means a bundle, which is held by the five fingers of the hand. Hashem's Shechinah, described in the beginning of this passuk as "dwelling in the Heavens," comes down to rest in this world when there are five people learning together.

- **Three** – The passuk uses the word judgment, and the minimum requirement for a Beis Din is three judges.[45]

- **Two** – The second mishnah of this perek says that if two people sit together without exchanging words of Torah, it is a gathering of fools. So we understand that if two people who fear Hashem—not fools—are talking together, they are certainly speaking words of Torah, and so the passuk must refer to them when it says that Hashem pays attention and hears.[46]

- **One** – It says in singular form, "I will come to **you** and bless you." So even when one is learning alone we know that Hashem joins him.

Story

Hashem is With You

Young Yisrolik loved to learn Torah. In fact, he quickly mastered all that his teachers had to offer him, and instead spent his time learning alone in the town shul, often till late at night.

Worried that his son would get sick from lack of sleep, his father R' Shabse gave Yisrolik a curfew. But when Yisrolik sat down to learn, he forgot about everything else, and completely lost track of time. R' Shabse came up with an idea: after supper, before Yisrolik returned to the shul to learn, he gave him a candle that would burn for one hour. This way, when the candle would burn out, Yisrolik would realize that it was time to go home to sleep.

That evening, Yisrolik returned to shul as usual, carrying his candle. More than an hour passed and Yisrolik had not yet come home. R' Shabse became worried. When another hour passed and Yisrolik was still not back, R' Shabse hurried to the shul. As he approached, he was surprised to see a light in the window. He entered and found Yisrolik sitting and learning, completely unaware that his father had arrived.

"Yisrolik! Why did you not keep your word?" R' Shabse blurted out.

Startled, Yisrolik looked up from his sefer in surprise, and immediately, the candle went out. "The candle burned, so I continued learning," he said tearfully.

It became clear to R' Shabse that when Yisrolik learned with such purity and love, the Shechinah came down and rested there, keeping the candle burning so he could continue to learn. That was why as soon as he stopped, the candle went out.

From then on, R' Shabse never stopped his son from learning. Sure enough Yisrolik grew up to be the famous Maggid of Kozhnitz.[47]

Rabi Elazar of Bartosa says: When you serve Hashem, **give Him from what** you have received from **Him.** For example, spend your money on mitzvos or give generously to tzedakah, **because you, and** everything **that you own,** really **belong to Him**. That is what Dovid Hamelech **says: Everything comes from You,** Hashem, **and** everything that **we give You is** originally **from Your hand.**

Rabi Yaakov says: Someone who walks on the street studying Torah and interrupts his study, even to admire Hashem's beautiful world and say, "How beautiful is this tree! How beautiful is this plowed field!" is considered by the Torah as if he is taking his life into his own hands and is in danger, for he no longer has the power of Torah to protect him.

רַבִּי אֶלְעָזָר אִישׁ בַּרְתּוֹתָא אוֹמֵר: תֶּן לוֹ מִשֶּׁלּוֹ, שֶׁאַתָּה וְשֶׁלָּךְ שֶׁלּוֹ. וְכֵן בְּדָוִד הוּא אוֹמֵר: כִּי מִמְּךָ הַכֹּל וּמִיָּדְךָ נָתַנּוּ לָךְ.

רַבִּי יַעֲקֹב אוֹמֵר: הַמְהַלֵּךְ בַּדֶּרֶךְ וְשׁוֹנֶה, וּמַפְסִיק מִמִּשְׁנָתוֹ וְאוֹמֵר: מַה נָּאֶה אִילָן זֶה, מַה נָּאֶה נִיר זֶה, מַעֲלֶה עָלָיו הַכָּתוּב כְּאִלּוּ מִתְחַיֵּב בְּנַפְשׁוֹ.

Just Doing My Job

The common translation for tzedakah is charity. The correct translation, however, is justice or righteousness. Giving tzedakah is really only what's expected and right. Think about it: If someone gives you money to be delivered to another, when you give it to the rightful recipient you are not being kind, you are simply doing what's right by giving the money to its rightful owner.

In the same way, Hashem gives you money so that part of it goes to others in need. By giving it to worthy causes, you are merely doing what is right. A person who recognizes this is giving real tzedakah.

In fact, this mishnah doesn't actually mention money, but talks about giving from everything you have. Think about what qualities you have. Are you smart? Are you able to sing nicely? Can you build a sukkah really quickly, or draw great pictures?

Hashem gave each person different qualities as a gift that he can use in whichever way he chooses. Be a worthy custodian of His gifts—share them with others and use them for the service of Hashem.

Biography

Rabi Elazar ben Yehudah of Bartosa was a colleague of Rabi Akiva and a student of Rabi Yehoshua ben Chananya. He was known for giving much tzedakah. One day, while he was in the marketplace buying wedding needs for his daughter, he found people collecting tzedakah for the wedding of two orphans. Rabi Elazar took all he had on him and gave it to them, and was left with only one zuz. With it, he bought some wheat, which he carried home and deposited in the granary. When he returned to the granary a short while later, the grain had miraculously become so abundant that the granary was bursting and the door could not be opened![48]

Rabi Yaakov was the teacher of Rabi Yehudah Hanassi (Rebbi). It happened once that he used that position to save Rabban Shimon ben Gamliel, Rebbi's father, from a plot. Some people weren't convinced of Rabban Shimon's greatness, and Rabi Yaakov heard that they were going to challenge him publicly on an obscure halachic topic. He hinted to Rabban Shimon to familiarize himself with that topic, saving him from great embarrassment.[49]

Sparks

Don't Interrupt Another way to understand Rabi Yaakov's teaching is as follows: someone who is traveling the path of serving Hashem, and stops to marvel at his great accomplishments in learning Torah, thinking to himself, "How beautiful is my explanation!" Such a person is unfortunately using his learning to interrupt his connection with Hashem, since one can only be connected to Hashem if he remains humble.[50]

Behind the Quote

Rabi Elazar was known for his extreme generosity in giving tzedakah. It came to such a point that when charity collectors would see him, they would run and hide, because they knew he would give them everything he had.[51] Appropriately, he tells us the importance of seeing tzedakah as a righteous obligation and giving generously.

Rabi Yaakov was involved in business and knew how easy it was to be distracted from learning. He therefore tells us to ignore distractions and learn with complete concentration.[52]

See Others

There once was a man who loved to give tzedakah, but as he wasn't very rich, he didn't have much to give. One day, R' Yechiel Michel of Zlotchov passed through his town and took note of how much this man loved giving tzedakah. R' Michel blessed him with riches, so that he would be able to help many others. Somehow, however, once the man became wealthy, he changed completely and became a miser. He even hired a guard at his door to stop any beggar from entering. "Let them find work and earn a living instead of collecting tzedakah the whole day," he would say.

When R' Michel heard what had happened he traveled to visit the man. Upon entering the mansion, he asked the rich man to look into the mirror and describe what he saw. The miser answered that he saw himself and his beautiful furniture. R' Michel continued, "Now look out the window. What do you see there?"

The rich man answered, "I see people walking, children playing, birds eating…"

R' Michel interrupted and asked, "If both the mirror and the window are made of glass, why from the window do you see the whole world, yet from the mirror you see only yourself?

"I'll tell you why—because the mirror has a layer of silver coating it, which prevents you from seeing anyone but yourself. If we were to remove the silver, perhaps you would once again see the needs of others."

The rich man understood the hint, and began once again helping needy people with his traditional vigor.[53]

רַבִּי דוֹסְתָּאִי בְּרַבִּי יַנַּאי מִשּׁוּם רַבִּי מֵאִיר אוֹמֵר: כָּל הַשּׁוֹכֵחַ דָּבָר אֶחָד מִמִּשְׁנָתוֹ, מַעֲלֶה עָלָיו הַכָּתוּב כְּאִלּוּ מִתְחַיֵּב בְּנַפְשׁוֹ, שֶׁנֶּאֱמַר: רַק הִשָּׁמֶר לְךָ וּשְׁמֹר נַפְשְׁךָ מְאֹד פֶּן תִּשְׁכַּח אֶת הַדְּבָרִים אֲשֶׁר רָאוּ עֵינֶיךָ. יָכוֹל אֲפִילוּ תָּקְפָה עָלָיו מִשְׁנָתוֹ, תַּלְמוּד לוֹמַר: וּפֶן יָסוּרוּ מִלְּבָבְךָ כֹּל יְמֵי חַיֶּיךָ, הָא אֵינוֹ מִתְחַיֵּב בְּנַפְשׁוֹ עַד שֶׁיֵּשֵׁב וִיסִירֵם מִלִּבּוֹ.

Rabi Dostai bar Rabi Yannai said in the name of Rabi Meir: Whoever forgets even one thing of his Torah learning because he did not review it is considered by the Torah as if he has done an aveirah for which he would lose his life, as it says in the Torah: But be careful and guard your life very much in case you forget what your eyes saw at Har Sinai, namely, the giving of the Torah.

You could think that this applies even if he forgot what he learned because it was too difficult for him to remember, so the Torah says: "In case the words of Torah are removed from your heart throughout all the days of your life." This teaches us that he is not considered to have done an aveirah for which he would lose his life unless he knowingly removes what he learned from his mind by sitting around and not reviewing.

Don't Forget

Our Chachamim teach many tips to help us remember what we learn. Some of them include:

- אִם עֲרוּכָה בְּרַמַ״ח אֵבָרִים שֶׁלְּךָ מִשְׁתַּמֶּרֶת וְאִם לָאו אֵינָהּ מִשְׁתַּמֶּרֶת. If Torah is learned with all of your body it will be protected and remain with you, and if not, it is not protected, and you might forget it.[54]

  When you learn by just reading the text silently, only your mind and eyes are involved. When you say the words aloud and with great energy, much more of you is involved in the learning, and your ability to remember increases greatly.

- Review what you learn many times. The more you review it, the longer you will remember it.

- Make yourself hints and reminders. Here's an example of an interesting one: the number of pessukim in the longest parshah in the Torah (Parshas Nasso), the longest perek in Tanach (Perek 119 of Tehillim), and the number of pages in the longest mesechta of Gemara (Bava Basra) are all 176. How can you remember this? Remind yourself that Torah is good—טוב, which has the gematria of 17. Now, the difference between 1 and 7 is 6, so place a 6 at the end of the number and you get 176!

  Reminders, even quirky ones like these, help you remember things for much longer.

Biography

Rabi Dostai the son of Rabi Yannai Very little is known about Rabi Dostai, as he is mentioned only twice in all of the Mishnah—once here, and again in a mishnah in Maseches Eruvin. In both places, Rabi Dostai quotes from Rabi Meir, who was his primary teacher.

 **Connections**

In the previous mishnah, Rabi Yaakov stressed the importance of uninterrupted learning. In this mishnah Rabi Dostai warns about not forgetting what you learn. In the following mishnah, Rabi Chanina will tell you what trait helps you be successful at both: fear of sin.⁵⁵

 **Story**

Life

Someone once came to the Chidushei Harim, the first Gerrer Rebbe, and complained that he keeps forgetting his learning.

"Do you forget to eat?" asked the Rebbe.

"Of course not," the man replied.

"Why not?" asked the Rebbe.

"Because I need to eat in order to live; how can I forget such an important thing?"

"And the Torah?" asked the Rebbe. "Your life is also dependent on it, as it says in Tehillim, 'I will never forget Your commandments, because it is my life.' How can you forget it if it's your life?"⁶⁰

 Did You Know?

Different Thought Process Before leaving Bavel to learn in Eretz Yisrael, Rabi Zeira fasted 100 fasts to forget the learning style of Bavel, so he would able to grasp the style and learning methods of Eretz Yisrael.⁵⁶ How could he have chosen to forget his learning?

One answer lies in the passuk quoted in the mishnah: "…in case you forget what your eyes saw at **Har Sinai**," meaning that it is only strictly forbidden to forget the Written Torah.⁵⁷ The mishnah here is adding a stringency not to forget anything of Torah at all. Rabi Zeira therefore was able to forgo that stringency for the purpose of reaching even greater heights in Torah learning.

 Word Power

הַשּׁוֹכֵחַ דָּבָר אֶחָד Although the passuk says the word דְּבָרִים in the plural, the mishnah still uses it as a source that if one willfully forgets even one thing he is liable. This is because every individual part of Torah in fact contains in it many ideas and lessons.⁵⁸ Rabi Akiva would teach many halachos from not only the words and letters of the Torah, but even from the little crowns on top of the letters!⁵⁹

 Sparks

Don't Forget the One and Only The mishnah says, "Whoever forgets even one thing of his Torah learning," which can also be interpreted as "whoever forgets the One of his Torah learning," referring to the One who gave us the Torah—Hashem. One who forgets that, is indeed guilty of a sin punishable by death!⁶¹

One of the reasons stated as to why the Beis Hamikdash was destroyed is that לֹא בֵרְכוּ בַּתּוֹרָה תְּחִילָּה—the people did not say the brachos on Torah before learning.⁶² This is saying that they did indeed learn Torah, but just without acknowledging the Giver of the Torah, Hashem. Their learning was purely an intellectual activity instead of a holy one.⁶³

Rabi Chanina ben Dosa says: Anyone whose fear of aveiros takes priority over his wisdom—his wisdom will last. But anyone whose wisdom takes priority over his fear of aveiros—his wisdom will not last.

רַבִּי חֲנִינָא בֶּן דּוֹסָא אוֹמֵר: כֹּל שֶׁיִּרְאַת חֶטְאוֹ קוֹדֶמֶת לְחָכְמָתוֹ, חָכְמָתוֹ מִתְקַיֶּמֶת. וְכֹל שֶׁחָכְמָתוֹ קוֹדֶמֶת לְיִרְאַת חֶטְאוֹ, אֵין חָכְמָתוֹ מִתְקַיֶּמֶת.

Living Lessons

Eternal Truth

Just as a soldier follows his General's decree, whether he understands it or not, a Jew must follow what Hashem says. If each person only did what made sense to him, everyone would be doing different things based on how he understands the world. Not only that, but each person's actions would keep changing as his ideas change. But when someone acts out of yiras Shamayim—awe and fear of Hashem and His commandments—his way will never change and he will always do what's right.[65]

Practice is Perfect

A person may have learned all about a specific mitzvah, but if he never actually performs that mitzvah, he has missed the point. This mishnah reminds us that the goal of learning Torah is to make us better servants of Hashem, who do more mitzvos and serve Him better.

 Connections

The previous mishnah warns against forgetting one's learning. It is natural for people to forget, and so they need Hashem's help to remember things well. This mishnah adds that someone whose fear of sin precedes his studying is worthy of Hashem's help with remembering what he learns.[64]

 Sparks

Already Wise It says in Sefer Daniel that Hashem gives wisdom to the wise. But how does one become wise in the first place? The passuk says "רֵאשִׁית חָכְמָה יִרְאַת ה׳—the beginning of wisdom is the fear of Hashem." Once a person has the foundation of fear of Hashem, he merits Hashem's gift of wisdom.[66]

 Word Power

קוֹדֶמֶת The word קוֹדֶמֶת—precedes—is in the present tense to show that yiras Shamayim must come before wisdom at all times, on a regular basis. Not only do you need to have a basis of fear of Hashem before you start to learn, but the fear of Hashem must always guide you in your learning itself.[67]

Biography

Rabi Chanina ben Dosa was a student of Rabban Yochanan ben Zakkai who lived at the end of the era of the second Beis Hamikdash. He was known as a miracle worker and was sought out by many people to daven for them. He once commented that he knew whether his tefillos would be accepted based on how smoothly the words flowed from his mouth.[68]

Rabi Chanina and his family were very poor. In fact, a Heavenly voice once proclaimed, "The entire world is sustained in the merit of my son Chanina, yet Chanina himself is sustained on just a small amount of carob from one Erev Shabbos to the next."

It came to such a point that one day Rabi Chanina's wife begged him to daven that Hashem relieve their extreme poverty. Rabi Chanina agreed, and a golden table-leg miraculously appeared. That night his wife had a dream. She saw many Tzaddikim eating in Gan Eden, each seated at a three-legged table, while her husband's table had only two legs. She realized what the dream was telling her—that wealth in this world can take away from the reward in the World to Come. Immediately, she asked that he daven for Hashem to take back the treasure. Rabi Chanina did so, and the golden leg disappeared.

One Friday, Rabi Chanina's daughter accidentally poured vinegar into the oil lamp instead of oil. To comfort her, Rabi Chanina said, "Don't worry—the One who determined that oil should burn can decide that vinegar should burn too." A miracle happened, and the lamp burned the entire Shabbos![69]

Behind the Quote

There are many stories recorded about Rabi Chanina ben Dosa, but this mishnah is the only mention of his teaching. This is because he lived by his statement that fear of sin (which is achieved through tefillah) is a prerequisite to everything, and he spent most of his time davening, not teaching.[70]

Story

Divine Bakery

Embarrassed that they had no food to cook for Shabbos, Rabi Chanina ben Dosa's wife placed twigs in her oven to make smoke so her neighbors would think that they were cooking.

She had an evil neighbor, however, who thought to herself, "I know that she has nothing to cook, so what is making all that smoke?" and she went to investigate. When she knocked on the door, Rabi Chanina's wife, in her embarrassment, ran out of the kitchen and into another room. The neighbor walked into the kitchen and lo and behold, the oven was filled with loaves of bread, and the kneading-bowl full of dough.

The neighbor quickly called out to Rabi Chanina's wife, "Hurry and take your bread out of the oven before it burns!"

The pious woman, elated at the miracle that had occurred, came out with her bread shovel and they had plenty of bread for Shabbos.[71]

הוּא הָיָה אוֹמֵר: כֹּל שֶׁמַּעֲשָׂיו מְרֻבִּין מֵחָכְמָתוֹ, חָכְמָתוֹ מִתְקַיֶּמֶת. וְכֹל שֶׁחָכְמָתוֹ מְרֻבָּה מִמַּעֲשָׂיו, אֵין חָכְמָתוֹ מִתְקַיֶּמֶת.

הוּא הָיָה אוֹמֵר: כֹּל שֶׁרוּחַ הַבְּרִיּוֹת נוֹחָה הֵימֶנּוּ, רוּחַ הַמָּקוֹם נוֹחָה הֵימֶנּוּ. וְכֹל שֶׁאֵין רוּחַ הַבְּרִיּוֹת נוֹחָה הֵימֶנּוּ, אֵין רוּחַ הַמָּקוֹם נוֹחָה הֵימֶנּוּ.

רַבִּי דוֹסָא בֶּן הָרְכִּינַס אוֹמֵר: שֵׁנָה שֶׁל שַׁחֲרִית, וְיַיִן שֶׁל צָהֳרַיִם, וְשִׂיחַת הַיְלָדִים, וִישִׁיבַת בָּתֵּי כְנֵסִיּוֹת שֶׁל עַמֵּי הָאָרֶץ, מוֹצִיאִין אֶת הָאָדָם מִן הָעוֹלָם.

Rabi Chanina ben Dosa would often say: Anyone whose good deeds exceed his wisdom, his wisdom will last. But anyone whose wisdom exceeds his good deeds, his wisdom will not last.

Rabi Chanina ben Dosa would often say: Anyone who acts with love toward his fellow so people find him to be pleasant, Hashem also finds pleasant, because that person has treated Hashem's children well. But anyone whom people do not find pleasant, Hashem does not find pleasant either, because he has mistreated His children.

Rabi Dosa ben Harkinas says: Sleeping late in the morning, drinking wine in the middle of the day, having childish conversations, and sitting in places where ignorant people gather—all these remove a person from having a fulfilled life in the world.

Be Nice to My Children

דְּרָכֶיהָ דַרְכֵי נֹעַם וְכָל נְתִיבוֹתֶיהָ שָׁלוֹם – To live in the ways of Torah, you must be pleasant and peaceful. Not only is ahavas Yisrael a crucial mitzvah, but it is the surest way to find favor in the eyes of Hashem. The greatest cause of satisfaction for parents is when they see their children getting along, and all of us are called Hashem's children.[72]

Trust Me, It's Good for You

Torah is not a history book or an interesting novel. Torah is the guidebook by which we lead our lives, with directives for all areas of our life. From our very beginning as a nation we said נַעֲשֶׂה וְנִשְׁמָע – first and foremost we do; then we learn and try to understand.

When a doctor prescribes a medication, you take it unquestioningly, even though you don't understand exactly how or why it works. In the same way, you must not say "I will wait until I know everything about the mitzvah and then I will start doing it." You must fulfill every mitzvah and halachah, even if you don't understand the reason.[73]

Biography

Rabi Dosa ben Horkinas was a student of Hillel and Shammai, and a friend and colleague of Rabban Yochanan ben Zakkai and Rabi Azaryah. In his old age, no longer able to see well, he was unable to go to the Beis Medrash. Instead, the Chachamim of Yavneh would come to his house to ask him questions in halachah.[74]

He was very wealthy and lived a very long life, passing away a few years after the destruction of the second Beis Hamikdash. He is buried in Tzfas.

Behind the Quote

People commonly think that sleeping a lot, eating and drinking well, taking it easy, and having a good time cause a person to live a long life. Because Rabi Dosa ben Horkinas lived a very long life, he speaks from experience that the opposite is true—these things drive a person from this world, while hard work and toiling in Torah give a person long life.[75]

Sparks

Hands First When putting on tefillin, the tefillin shel yad is placed first, and then the tefillin shel rosh. When removing the tefillin, first the shel rosh is removed, and then the shel yad. This results in the tefillin shel yad being worn for longer than the tefillin shel rosh, showing that a person's actions must be more numerous than his wisdom.[76]

Connections

In the previous mishnah, Rabi Chanina spoke of the importance of combining one's wisdom with fear of aveiros—negative commandments. In this mishnah Rabi Chanina explains that wisdom must also be combined with the fulfillment of mitzvos asei—positive commandments.[77]

Word Power

וְכֹל שֶׁאֵין רוּחַ הַבְּרִיּוֹת נוֹחָה הֵימֶנּוּ

The mishnah states that someone who is pleasant to people is pleasant to Hashem. What is added by saying the inverse, that "whoever is not pleasant to people is not pleasant to Hashem?"

From the first statement, one might think that being pleasant to people is one way to be pleasing to Hashem, though there may be other ways too. So the mishnah adds the second part, to emphasize that it is the **only** way—if someone is unpleasant to people, he cannot please Hashem![78]

No Guests? No Visitors!

R' Pinchas of Koretz was a well-known tzaddik, and many people would come to him for advice and brachos. It began taking up so much of his schedule that one day, he davened that he shouldn't be so popular, so he would have more time to learn alone. The plan worked, and, for the time being, he was glad.

When Sukkos arrived he sat in the sukkah alone, and began to sing the traditional invitation to the first of the Ushpizin. He looked up and saw Avraham Avinu standing just outside the door of the sukkah, but not entering.

"What's wrong?" R' Pinchas asked him, "Why won't you enter my sukkah?"

Avraham Avinu replied, "It is not my custom to enter a place where there are no guests."

R' Pinchas understood that isolating himself was not a good thing, especially when people needed his guidance. He immediately asked Hashem to undo his previous request.[79]

Rabi Elazar of Modi'in says: Someone who **disgraces holy things**, someone who **disrespects the Yamim Tovim**, someone who **embarrasses his friend in public**, someone who **nullifies the Bris of Avraham Avinu** by not having a bris milah, **and** someone **who explains Torah not according to** its **correct meaning**—

even if that person **has** learned much **Torah and** performed many **good deeds, he has no part in the World to Come** unless he does great teshuvah for his actions.

רַבִּי אֶלְעָזָר הַמּוֹדָעִי אוֹמֵר: הַמְחַלֵּל אֶת הַקֳּדָשִׁים, וְהַמְבַזֶּה אֶת הַמּוֹעֲדוֹת, וְהַמַּלְבִּין פְּנֵי חֲבֵרוֹ בָּרַבִּים, וְהַמֵּפֵר בְּרִיתוֹ שֶׁל אַבְרָהָם אָבִינוּ, וְהַמְגַלֶּה פָנִים בַּתּוֹרָה שֶׁלֹּא כַהֲלָכָה,

אַף עַל פִּי שֶׁיֵּשׁ בְּיָדוֹ תּוֹרָה וּמַעֲשִׂים טוֹבִים, אֵין לוֹ חֵלֶק לָעוֹלָם הַבָּא.

Rather Die

Think about the most embarrassing moment in your life. Did you think of Korach and wish the ground would swallow you up so you would disappear? That's how it can feel when you're embarrassed. It can even make a person wish that he was no longer alive!

Chazal say that embarrassing someone in public is just like killing him. Just as we must be prepared to be killed rather than to kill someone else, we must also be prepared to be killed rather than to embarrass someone else in public.[80]

 Did You Know?

Be Like Yosef When Yosef Hatzaddik revealed himself to his brothers, he ordered everybody out of the room in order to avoid embarrassing them. Though they had acted terribly toward him in the past, he was still very careful not to shame them in front of other people.[81]

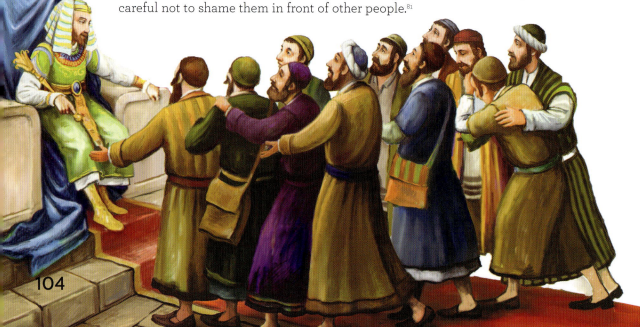

Biography

Rabi Elazar Hamoda'i was a student of Rabban Yochanan ben Zakkai and lived in Modi'in during the end of the era of the second Beis Hamikdash. He was known as such a great master of Aggadah—alternative explanations of pessukim—that when discussions on Aggadah arose in the Beis Medrash, Rabban Gamliel would say, "We still need to hear the interpretation of the Moda'i."[82]

Rabi Elazar was an uncle of Bar Kochba, and supported his revolt against the Romans, davening all day that Hashem protect B'nei Yisrael. However, in the confusion of those difficult and dangerous times, Rabi Elazar was falsely accused of aiding the other side and was put to death by members of his own party. Since B'nei Yisrael were protected in his merit, shortly after his passing the war was lost and many Jews were killed.[83] He lived to an old age, and is buried in Moshav Dalton, near Tzfas.

Word Power

וְהַמַּלְבִּין פְּנֵי חֲבֵרוֹ בָּרַבִּים
The word used in this mishnah for embarrassing someone literally means making his face white, because when somebody is embarrassed, at first the blood rushes to his face and then the color leaves and it turns pale.

The same word can also mean "to clean," which teaches us that a person who is embarrassed is cleansed from the "stains" of his aveiros on his neshamah—which are then transferred to the one who embarrassed him! So if it does happen to you that you are embarrassed, take comfort and remember that you have just been cleansed of all your aveiros. And be sure that you never embarrass another, or you will receive the stains of all his aveiros![87]

הַמְחַלֵּל The mishnah is written in the present tense, because it refers to someone who continues to sin. Someone who has done teshuvah for his misdeeds indeed receives a portion in Olam Haba.[88]

Behind the Quote

The Gemara calls Modi'in a city that was "a fair distance from Yerushalayim."[84] This was true not only physically, but in a spiritual way too—the level of the people there was far from that of Yerushalayim, the center of holiness. Being that Rabi Elazar was from Modi'in, he was qualified to make a statement about someone who sins and the reasons why he might do so.[85]

Sparks

You Won't Get It Torah and mitzvos are meant to refine and elevate a person, thereby enabling him to enjoy the great spiritual delight of Olam Haba. However, if it happens that a person has a great accumulation of Torah and mitzvos, but still remains unrefined and thus capable of doing terrible aveiros, he is simply unable to appreciate Olam Haba.[86]

Story

Sensitivity Saves Lives

Shmuel, the great Amora, was sitting with Ablat, a non-Jewish scholar and stargazer, and observed a group of workers pass them on their way to chop wood. Ablat pointed to one of the men and said to Shmuel, "That man is going but will not return, for a snake will bite him and he will die."

"If he is a Jew," replied Shmuel "he will go and return."

Indeed, the man later returned. Ablat arose and threw off the man's knapsack, discovering a dead snake cut in two pieces; the man had unknowingly killed the snake when he was chopping wood.

Said Shmuel to him, "What did you do special today to be saved from death?"

The man replied: "Every day everyone puts their lunch in one basket and then we eat it. Today I realized that one of the workers had nothing to put in the basket, and he was ashamed. So I told everyone, 'I will collect the bread.' When I came to him, I pretended to take bread from him so that he should not be embarrassed but instead just gave of my own."

Based on this story, Shmuel taught his students: "Charity saves from death!"[89]

Rabi Yishmael says:
Be agreeable to a great person, and be pleasant to a younger person without lowering yourself to act immaturely.
And greet every person cheerfully.

רַבִּי יִשְׁמָעֵאל אוֹמֵר:
הֱוֵי קַל לְרֹאשׁ, וְנוֹחַ לְתִשְׁחוֹרֶת,
וֶהֱוֵי מְקַבֵּל אֶת כָּל הָאָדָם בְּשִׂמְחָה.

Everyone Enjoys a Smile

Different positions in life call for different behaviors. A leader needs to be respected, while a young person needs to be treated in a warm and pleasant way. Everyone, however, needs to be greeted with a smile!

Connections

The first two directives in the mishnah say to be respectful to all people—both those of lower and higher standing to yourself. So what is the third directive adding?

The first two parts of the mishnah are saying how you should **act** toward others. The last part adds that you should also **feel** happy when seeing other people, and thus greet them with genuine cheer.[90]

Word Power

הֱוֵי קַל לְרֹאשׁ... בְּשִׂמְחָה This mishnah can also be explained as follows: הֱוֵי קַל לְרֹאשׁ—Give in easily to the desires and wishes of the Neshamah, which is like one's head, וְנוֹחַ לְתִשְׁחוֹרֶת—and be less relenting to the body, only giving in to the bare minimum. וֶהֱוֵי מְקַבֵּל אֶת כָּל הָאָדָם בְּשִׂמְחָה—Accept happily all the tests of materialism that you encounter, because they are the reason you are in this world: to refine the physical things you encounter and use them for the service of Hashem.[91]

הֱוֵי קַל לְרֹאשׁ, וְנוֹחַ לְתִשְׁחוֹרֶת The word תִּשְׁחוֹרֶת can also mean an old person, who typically has darkened skin, and has the root שָׁחוֹר, which means black. The mishnah can be understood to mean as follows: הֱוֵי קַל לְרֹאשׁ—Be swift to do mitzvos at the beginning of your life, וְנוֹחַ לְתִשְׁחוֹרֶת—and that will make it easier to continue on that path when you're older.[92]

Biography

Rabi Yishmael was a colleague of Rabi Akiva, who served together with him in the high court of Rabban Gamliel, along with Rabi Tarfon, Rabi Elazar ben Azaryah, among others.

When he was a young boy, Rabi Yishmael was taken captive by the Romans. Rabi Yehoshua ben Chananya realized that he was destined to be a great leader, and worked very hard to free him.[93]

Rabi Yishmael's sharp wisdom earned him the title עוֹקֵר הָרִים—uprooter of mountains, because with his sharp intellect he would pull apart a topic in Torah and analyze it with great depth and brilliance. Once, when his nephew wanted to study Greek philosophy, having already learned the entire Torah, Rabi Yishmael quoted the passuk וְהָגִיתָ בּוֹ יוֹמָם וָלַיְלָה—and you should toil in [Torah] day and night—and told him that when he found a time that's neither day nor night, that's when he should learn the Greek philosophy.[94]

He headed a great yeshivah that is often quoted in the Gemara, and has many midrashim attributed to it. Rabi Yishmael is most famous for listing the thirteen rules by which the Torah may be interpreted.

Rabi Yishmael had a great love for the Jewish people. He said once that he was willing to personally be their kaparah.

Behind the Quote

Rabi Yishmael was a kohen, and according to some opinions, a Kohen Gadol. He teaches us that even someone who is on a high level of serving Hashem must treat everyone pleasantly, regardless of their age or status.[95]

Bribery Really Works

A man once came to Rabi Yishmael, who was a kohen, and offered him his רֵאשִׁית הַגֵּז—the first shearing of his sheep that must be given to a kohen. Upon hearing that the man lived quite far from him, Rabi Yishmael asked, surprised, "Are there no kohanim in your area to whom you can give the gifts?"

The man replied, "I have a court case coming up for which I'd like you to serve as judge. I figured that since I was coming anyway, I'd bring you the wool."

Rabi Yishmael, realizing accepting the gift would take away from the local kohen's portion, immediately refused the gift and disqualified himself from judging the case, arranging instead for two other Chachamim to preside over it.

While listening to the case from the sidelines, Rabi Yishmael found himself thinking of arguments to bolster the man's case. He suddenly stopped, realized what had transpired, and said, "Look how bribery can twist the mind: If I was affected even after I **refused** a gift that I was allowed to accept, how much more so would it affect a person who actually takes a bribe!"[96]

Rabi Akiva says:

Laughter and silliness accustom a person to immorality.

Our **tradition**—the Torah Sheb'al Peh—**is a fence** around the **Torah** Shebichsav—the written Torah, protecting it from misinterpretation.

The various types of **ma'aser** that we are commanded to give **are a fence for riches** because they increase and protect a person's wealth.

Vows to refrain from certain permitted things can **be a fence to separate** ourselves from forbidden things.

The fence for wisdom is silence because it allows us to listen and gain wisdom from others.

רַבִּי עֲקִיבָא אוֹמֵר:
שְׂחוֹק וְקַלּוּת רֹאשׁ,
מַרְגִּילִין אֶת הָאָדָם לְעֶרְוָה.

מָסֹרֶת סְיָג לַתּוֹרָה,

מַעַשְׂרוֹת סְיָג לָעֹשֶׁר,

נְדָרִים סְיָג לַפְּרִישׁוּת,

סְיָג לַחָכְמָה שְׁתִיקָה.

Living Lessons

Fine with Fences

Many times parents give rules that might feel overbearing and unnecessary. Sometimes it seems that they're just trying to take away the fun. But the mishnah teaches us that adding extra precautions is beneficial. Nobody intentionally drowns in a pool, but it can happen much more easily when "annoying" safety precautions are not followed. Have you ever noticed the extra effort it takes to open a pill box? Protective measures may seem a nuisance, but they are there for a reason. Boundaries are good, warning signs are helpful, and tricks for how to get things done are gifts.

The same is true with Torah and mitzvos. Of course, we don't intentionally disregard

them, but situations arise and habits kick in, sometimes stronger than our will to do what's right, and cause us to do the wrong thing. We must realize this and appreciate the extra rules that keep us from physical and spiritual harm.

Connections

The previous mishnah spoke of the importance of having an accepting, easygoing, and happy manner. Here, Rabi Akiva counters that this too must be within sensible limits, because exuberant displays of laughter and silliness lead a person to aveiros.[97]

Biography

Rabi Akiva lived during the end of the time of the Second Beis Hamikdash and through its destruction. He started learning Torah very late in his life; in fact, when he was forty he was still ignorant. He married a very righteous woman named Rochel, who encouraged him to leave home and learn Torah. After twenty-four years he had become the leading Torah scholar of his time with 24,000 students. He once told one of his students that because it was his wife who had pushed him to learn, "All the Torah that you and I have is really hers!"[98]

Rabi Akiva's 24,000 students all died during his lifetime, during the period between Pesach and Shavuos. After losing all his students, he began anew, and taught five outstanding students who would go on to revitalize Torah among B'nei Yisrael—Rabi Meir, Rabi Yehudah, Rabi Yosei, Rabi Shimon bar Yochai, and Rabi Elazar ben Shamua.[99]

Rabi Akiva's love for Torah knew no bounds, and when the Romans outlawed Torah learning, he disregarded the decree. He explained with a parable: When there are fishermen's nets cast in the water, it is indeed dangerous for the fish. But if they were to abandon the water and jump onto dry land, they would certainly die! The same is true with B'nei Yisrael. Although it is dangerous to learn Torah, for fear of being caught by the Romans, abandoning Torah would mean certain death!

Rabi Akiva lived a very long life, until he was eventually imprisoned by the Romans for learning and teaching Torah. He was cruelly killed at the age of 120. As he was being tortured, he was joyously reciting Shema. His student asked him how he could do so, and he replied, "My whole life I awaited the time when I could give my life for Hashem, and now it is finally possible!"[100]

 **Behind the Quote**

Rabi Akiva was a descendant of geirim.[101] It can be very challenging for geirim to stay on the path of Torah and mitzvos, and aveiros can be especially tempting. Rabi Akiva, a descendant of geirim, understood the need for preventive barriers to protect from doing aveiros.[102]

Sparks

Another Tenth The preventive measures mentioned in the mishnah here are additional acts that go beyond the letter of the law. How does ma'aser, which is a clear obligation from the Torah, fit into this list?

One explanation is that the ma'aser referred to here is actually in addition to the tenth that the Torah commands a person to give of his earnings. It is a suggestion that goes beyond the basic fulfillment of the mitzvah, when one voluntarily gives a full fifth of his earnings to tzedakah instead of only the required tenth.[103]

 **Story**

Without Tradition There's Nothing

A non-Jew once came to Shammai and said that he wanted to convert, but that he only wanted to learn the written Torah. Shammai rebuked the man and sent him away, because the law is that a convert must accept everything in Torah.

The man then went to Hillel with the same request, who agreed on condition that he would learn the written Torah only from Hillel himself.

When the man arrived to learn, Hillel began by teaching him the first four Hebrew letters: alef, beis, gimmel, and daled. The following day when the man arrived for his study session, Hillel showed him a taf, shin, reish, and kuf, and said that these are actually alef, beis, gimmel, daled. Confused, the prospective convert asked, "But yesterday you did not teach them to me like this! Then you showed me different letter forms!"

Hillel replied: "How do you know which letters are alef, beis, gimmel, and daled? You relied upon me to teach you? So you see, the only way you can know the written Torah is if it is accompanied by oral tradition. Then rely upon me with respect to the rest of the Oral Torah too!"[104]

Rabi Akiva **would** often **say**: The fact **that man was created in the image** of Hashem shows that he **is beloved** to Him. The fact that it was **made known to man that he was created in the image of** Hashem shows an even **greater love**. It was made known to man **as it says** in the Torah: **Because in the image of Hashem He** (Hashem) **created man.**

The fact **that** B'nei **Yisrael are called children of Hashem** shows that they **are beloved** to Him. The fact that it was **made known to them that they are called children of Hashem** shows an even **greater love**. It was made known to them, **as it says** in the Torah: **You are children of Hashem your God.**

The fact **that a precious item**, the Torah, **was given to** B'nei **Yisrael** shows that they **are beloved** to Hashem. The fact that it was **made known to them that a precious item was given to them** shows an even **greater love**. It was made known to them **as it says** in Mishlei: **I have given you a good teaching; do not turn away from My Torah.**

הוּא הָיָה אוֹמֵר: חָבִיב אָדָם שֶׁנִּבְרָא בְּצֶלֶם, חִבָּה יְתֵרָה נוֹדַעַת לוֹ שֶׁנִּבְרָא בְּצֶלֶם, שֶׁנֶּאֱמַר: כִּי בְּצֶלֶם אֱלֹהִים עָשָׂה אֶת הָאָדָם.

חֲבִיבִין יִשְׂרָאֵל שֶׁנִּקְרְאוּ בָנִים לַמָּקוֹם, חִבָּה יְתֵרָה נוֹדַעַת לָהֶם שֶׁנִּקְרְאוּ בָנִים לַמָּקוֹם, שֶׁנֶּאֱמַר: בָּנִים אַתֶּם לַייָ אֱלֹהֵיכֶם.

חֲבִיבִין יִשְׂרָאֵל שֶׁנִּתַּן לָהֶם כְּלִי חֶמְדָּה, חִבָּה יְתֵרָה נוֹדַעַת לָהֶם שֶׁנִּתַּן לָהֶם כְּלִי חֶמְדָּה, שֶׁנֶּאֱמַר: כִּי לֶקַח טוֹב נָתַתִּי לָכֶם, תּוֹרָתִי אַל תַּעֲזֹבוּ.

Living Lessons

Real Self-Esteem

Being arrogant is terrible. Yet the other extreme, feeling small and unimportant is also a problem. So how should you feel about yourself?

This mishnah describes the proper way to see yourself. Your value is not based on what you **do**. It is based on who you **are**—your entire being represents Hashem, you are Hashem's child, and you possess His holy Torah! For these reasons you are extremely important!

Viewing yourself in this way will make you feel humble and small, and important and powerful all at the same time. You will feel humbled because it wasn't your actions that earned you these things—they were simply given to you. You will also realize that since you have these great attributes, you have such a great potential and responsibility that has yet to be fulfilled.

At the same time, you will also feel important and powerful. Just think—Hashem created you in His image, loves you like a child, and gave you a special mission. You really count!

Biography

Rabi Akiva The Gemara relates that when Moshe Rabbeinu went up to heaven, he saw Hashem weaving crowns for the letters of the Torah. Moshe asked Hashem why He was doing so, to which Hashem said that one day there will be a man by the name of Akiva ben Yosef who will teach countless halachos based on the crowns of these letters.

"Show me this man," requested Moshe.

"Turn around," said Hashem.

Suddenly Moshe found himself in the yeshivah of Rabi Akiva. After listening for some time, he became distraught when he did not recognize much of what he was hearing. Later, someone asked Rabi Akiva for the source of a particular halachah, to which Rabi Akiva replied "This is הֲלָכָה לְמֹשֶׁה מִסִּינַי—a halachah that Moshe received from Hashem on Har Sinai." Upon hearing that, Moshe Rabbeinu was comforted.

Moshe returned and asked Hashem, "So if You have someone as great as Rabi Akiva, why was the Torah given through me?"

Hashem responded, "Silence! This is what I have decided."[105]

 **Story**

Save My Son

There was an evil Roman official named Turnusrufus who loved to pester Rabi Akiva with heretical questions when he was imprisoned by the Romans. The official once asked, "If your G-d loves the poor, why doesn't He feed them?"

Rabi Akiva answered him: "So that we should be saved from punishment in the merit of the tzedakah we give."

"On the contrary," Turnusrufus argued, "for this you deserve to be punished! Imagine a king who became angry at his slave and locked him away in a dungeon, commanding that he not be given food or drink. If a person fed him anyway, would the king not be angry at him?"

Rabi Akiva replied, "I'll give you a different analogy. Imagine a king who became angry at his son and locked him away in a dungeon, commanding that he not be given food or drink. If a person fed him anyway, would the king not be thankful to that person for saving his son's life?"[108]

Behind the Quote

Rabi Akiva mentions the privileges in the order that he learned to appreciate them. Being a descendant of geirim, the first thing he appreciated was being human. As he grew up, he came to appreciate being Jewish. When he was forty years old and began learning Torah, he appreciated the value of Torah.[106]

 Sparks

Powerful Tool Chazal often refer to the Torah as Hashem's כְּלִי—His tool. A tool is used to make a change in something. This tells us that Torah is not just something to learn, but a powerful and precious tool with which we can change and improve ourselves and the world. We are so fortunate to receive this precious tool; let's make sure to use it![91]

 Connections

The three statements in this mishnah are three reasons why every Jew has the ability to succeed in his or her mission in this world.

1. You were created in the image of Hashem and therefore have tremendous abilities.
2. You are called the child of Hashem. Parents want their child to succeed. If he should fail, the parents do not think to replace him, but instead give him additional guidance and resources to help him get back on track to succeed.
3. Hashem has given you the ultimate tool with which to succeed—the Torah![107]

 Word Power

בָּנִים לַמָּקוֹם Just as a son is similar to his father, so should we try to be just like Hashem. We should model our character traits after Hashem's, acting with kindness and mercy.[109]

Rabi Akiva said: **Everything** that happens in the world **is foreseen** by Hashem, yet **the choice** to do good or bad **is given** to people.

The world is judged by Hashem **in a good** and kind manner, **and everything is according to the many** good **deeds**—the more mitzvos and good deeds one does, the more kindly he will be judged by Hashem.

הַכֹּל צָפוּי,
וְהָרְשׁוּת נְתוּנָה,

וּבְטוֹב הָעוֹלָם
נִדּוֹן, וְהַכֹּל לְפִי
רוֹב הַמַּעֲשֶׂה.

He Knows the Truth

People are always quick to blame others. The first man, Adam, blamed Chavah for his eating from the Eitz Hada'as, and Chavah in turn blamed the nachash!

This mishnah reminds us that Hashem knows the truth of what really happens. He sees everything, even when no one else is around. Hashem is always watching![111]

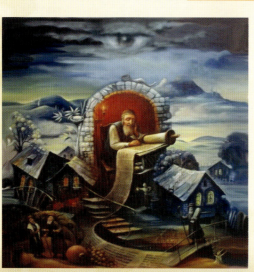

Master Plan Everything that happens is foreseen and arranged by Hashem. When Rabi Yochanan would see a hawk flying to catch its next prey, he would say the passuk מִשְׁפָּטֶיךָ תְּהוֹם רַבָּה—Your judgment is in the great depths—with great awe. Hashem coordinates every little thing that happens, down to which bird catches which fish in the ocean.[110]

Biography

Rabi Akiva A stargazer once told Rabi Akiva, "I see that on your daughter's wedding day, she will be bitten by a snake and die."

On the night of her wedding, as she was preparing for sleep, his daughter removed a golden hairpin and stuck it in the wall for the night. The next morning, as she removed it from the wall, she was horrified to find a poisonous snake stuck on it. Her pin had killed the snake! When she told her father what had happened, Rabi Akiva said, "Tell me, what could you have done yesterday to deserve this miracle?"

"Well," she replied. "Just hours before, a poor man came to the door, but everyone was busy and there was no one to attend to him, so I took my portion from the wedding-feast and gave it to him."

"Tzedakah saves from death!" Rabi Akiva exclaimed.[112]

 Behind the Quote

Like the previous one, this mishnah is authored by Rabi Akiva. As a descendant of geirim, he appreciated those who **choose** to accept and fulfill Torah and mitzvos, and highlights the importance of making good choices.[113]

 Word Power

בְּטוֹב הָעוֹלָם נִדּוֹן These words can also mean that whenever the world is judged it is always for its own good. No matter how the judgment may manifest itself, it is always for the purpose of purifying and elevating the world.[114]

 Did You Know?

You've Already Chosen If Hashem foresees everything, how can we possibly have free choice?

There are many answers to this question. One of them: Hashem is not limited by time, and to Him, past, present, and future are all the same. Therefore, Hashem knows what you are going to do because, as Hashem sees it, you have already done it![115]

 Sparks

Do Good. Repeat. The words רֹב הַמַּעֲשֶׂה can also mean that everything goes according to the majority of action. When a person acts a certain way many times, it affects him much more than doing even a very dramatic act once. Repeating kind acts ingrains a kind nature in a person, and the same with other traits.[116]

The same is also true about the world as a whole—each mitzvah brings more kedushah into the world. For this reason it's better to give a small sum of tzedakah every weekday, rather than to give a large sum once a week or month.[117]

 **Story**

See the Whole Picture

Yeshayah Hanavi says of Mashiach's coming, "אוֹדְךָ ה' כִּי אָנַפְתָּ בִּי יָשֹׁב אַפְּךָ וּתְנַחֲמֵנִי—I will thank You Hashem, because You were angry with me, Your anger turns away, and You will comfort me."

Why would we thank Hashem for being angry at us?

The Chachamim explain with a story. Two men once set out together on a business trip, but a short while into the trip, one got a thorn in his foot and was unable to continue. At first, the injured man was terribly upset. Not long after, however, he heard that his friend's ship had sunk at sea. He understood now that his injury had saved him from sharing the same fate, and thanked Hashem for showing him His "anger."

We see only a tiny part of the world and know very little of the bigger picture. The injured man in the story was lucky to see the end, and understood that it was for the best. Usually though, we don't see the big picture. So when something appears to be bad, remember this story, and that somehow, everything Hashem does is only good![118]

Rabi Akiva **would** often **say: Everything** that a person owns **is given** to him by Hashem **on condition** that it will be used for its correct purpose.	**הוּא** הָיָה אוֹמֵר: הַכֹּל נָתוּן בְּעֵרָבוֹן,
A net is spread over all living things—they are unable to escape Hashem's judgment.	וּמְצוּדָה פְרוּסָה עַל כָּל הַחַיִּים,
The world is like a **shop** that **is open** for anyone to take what he wants. **The Shopkeeper**—Hashem— **offers credit** and is willing to wait for people to repay Him with teshuvah.	הֶחָנוּת פְּתוּחָה, וְהַחֶנְוָנִי מַקִּיף,
The record book is open to record everyone's actions, **and the hand writes** everything that happens. **Whoever wants to borrow** from Hashem and owe Him teshuvah is free to **borrow**, but every debt must eventually be repaid through teshuvah.	וְהַפִּנְקָס פָּתוּחַ, וְהַיָּד כּוֹתֶבֶת, וְכָל הָרוֹצֶה לִלְווֹת יָבֹא וְיִלְוֶה,
The collectors go around often each day, collecting payment **from** each **person** for his debts in many ways, whether the person **realizes** it or **not. The** collectors **have something to rely on**—the record book that records everyone's actions.	וְהַגַּבָּאִין מַחֲזִירִין תָּדִיר בְּכָל יוֹם, וְנִפְרָעִין מִן הָאָדָם מִדַּעְתּוֹ וְשֶׁלֹא מִדַּעְתּוֹ, וְיֵשׁ לָהֶם עַל מַה שֶּׁיִּסְמוֹכוּ,
The judgment is a judgment of truth, and Hashem judges people fairly.	וְהַדִּין דִּין אֱמֶת,
Everything is prepared for the feast of Olam Haba, when all people will receive what they deserve.	וְהַכֹּל מְתֻקָּן לַסְעוּדָה.

Talent on Loan

Hashem gave you specific qualities, abilities, and possessions. They are meant for you to use during your stay in this world, but eventually, you will have to justify how you used them. Did you use your mind to study Torah? Did you use your mouth to teach Torah or say nice things about your friend? Did you use the abilities to hear, see, walk, and talk to serve Hashem?

Each morning, when you wake up, Hashem loans you many things, and you repay the loan by using them to serve Him!

Biography

Rabi Akiva was one of the four Tzaddikim who entered Pardes, the spiritual chamber that holds the deepest secrets of the Torah. He was the only one whose mind was able to handle it and returned from it unharmed.[119]

Word Power

וְיֵשׁ לָהֶם עַל מַה שֶּׁיִּסְמֹכוּ—They have on what to rely. These words can also refer to every Jew. Even when someone does an aveirah, there is always something that he can count on if he wants to return to Hashem—the power of teshuvah. Teshuvah is always there, no matter how far a person goes.[120]

Sparks

Whether He Realizes It Or Not Before Hashem judges a person for something he did wrong, He arranges that he come across another person making the same mistake. He then watches to see how the person judges his fellow Jew, and Hashem then applies that judgment to him. So in fact the person has judged himself knowingly—he consciously passed judgment on the action, but unknowingly at the same time—he was unaware that the judgment was really on himself![121]

Behind the Quote

The word מִדַּעְתּוֹ can also mean with a person's permission. Rabi Akiva is the author of this mishnah, and he hints here that when tortured to death by the Romans,[122] he had in fact accepted the pain wholeheartedly. In fact, he did not cry out to Hashem to save him from the pain. Instead, he accepted the suffering, saying, "The judgment is a judgment of truth."[123]

Hashem Tallies Every Act

There was once a Jewish farmer who was honest and righteous, but extremely poor. Hashem decided to reward him. Eliyahu Hanavi, disguised as an Arab, came to the man while he was working in the field and said, "G-d wants to bless you with great wealth for six years. Would you like to become rich now, or later on?" The first two times that the Arab came to the Jew, he did not take it seriously. But when the Arab came a third time, he consulted with his wife, and then replied: "We would like it now."

"Good," said the Arab. "When you return home, you will find that G-d has blessed you."

Sure enough, the farmer's children had found a chest full of coins buried under their home! After praising Hashem for His kindness, his wife said: "We will use the money only for our basic needs, such as food and clothing. The rest will be for tzedakah." Every day, the woman recorded in a notebook how they spent every penny.

Six years later, the Arab—Eliyahu Hanavi—returned. "Six years are up," he said. "The time has come for you to return the money Hashem gave you."

The woman said to her husband, "Show him our notebook, and tell him, 'If there are people who will use the money better, give it to them!'" Hashem was so pleased with the way they had used the money that He blessed them with wealth and prosperity for the rest of their lives.[124]

רַבִּי אֶלְעָזָר בֶּן עֲזַרְיָה אוֹמֵר:
אִם אֵין תּוֹרָה אֵין דֶּרֶךְ אֶרֶץ,
אִם אֵין דֶּרֶךְ אֶרֶץ אֵין תּוֹרָה,

אִם אֵין חָכְמָה אֵין יִרְאָה,
אִם אֵין יִרְאָה אֵין חָכְמָה,

אִם אֵין דַּעַת אֵין בִּינָה,
אִם אֵין בִּינָה אֵין דַּעַת,

אִם אֵין קֶמַח אֵין תּוֹרָה,
אִם אֵין תּוֹרָה אֵין קֶמַח.

הוּא הָיָה אוֹמֵר: כֹּל שֶׁחָכְמָתוֹ מְרֻבָּה מִמַּעֲשָׂיו, לְמָה הוּא דוֹמֶה: לְאִילָן שֶׁעֲנָפָיו מְרֻבִּין וְשָׁרָשָׁיו מוּעָטִין, וְהָרוּחַ בָּאָה וְעוֹקַרְתּוֹ וְהוֹפַכְתּוֹ עַל פָּנָיו, שֶׁנֶּאֱמַר: וְהָיָה כְּעַרְעָר בָּעֲרָבָה, וְלֹא יִרְאֶה כִּי יָבֹא טוֹב, וְשָׁכַן חֲרֵרִים בַּמִּדְבָּר, אֶרֶץ מְלֵחָה וְלֹא תֵשֵׁב.

אֲבָל, כֹּל שֶׁמַּעֲשָׂיו מְרֻבִּין מֵחָכְמָתוֹ, לְמָה הוּא דוֹמֶה: לְאִילָן שֶׁעֲנָפָיו מוּעָטִין וְשָׁרָשָׁיו מְרֻבִּין, שֶׁאֲפִלּוּ כָּל הָרוּחוֹת שֶׁבָּעוֹלָם בָּאוֹת וְנוֹשְׁבוֹת בּוֹ, אֵין מְזִיזִין אוֹתוֹ מִמְּקוֹמוֹ, שֶׁנֶּאֱמַר: וְהָיָה כְּעֵץ שָׁתוּל עַל מַיִם, וְעַל יוּבַל יְשַׁלַּח שָׁרָשָׁיו, וְלֹא יִרְאֶה כִּי יָבֹא חֹם, וְהָיָה עָלֵהוּ רַעֲנָן, וּבִשְׁנַת בַּצֹּרֶת לֹא יִדְאָג, וְלֹא יָמִישׁ מֵעֲשׂוֹת פֶּרִי.

Rabi Elazar ben Azaryah says: If a person does **not** learn **Torah,** he **cannot** have proper **derech eretz,** because proper derech eretz is learned from the Torah. **If** a person has **no derech eretz,** the **Torah** he learns **cannot** be properly absorbed.

If a person has **no wisdom,** he **cannot** have true **fear** of Hashem. **If** a person does **not fear** Hashem, his **wisdom** will **not** last.

If a person has **no knowledge,** he **cannot** have deep **understanding.** If a person has **no** deep **understanding,** he **cannot** gain a lot of **knowledge.**

If a person has **no flour** (food to eat), he **cannot** study **Torah.** If he does **not** study **Torah, there is no** point in having **flour** (food).

Rabi Elazar ben Azaryah would often **say:** Anyone whose **wisdom** exceeds his **good deeds,** to **what is he compared? To** a tree that has many branches but only a **few roots:** a wind comes and uproots it, and turns it upside down. **As it says** in Yirmiyahu: **He will** be like a lone tree on dry, windy **land, and will not** survive to **see the good** rain **when it comes;** it will dwell dried out in the desert, on a **salty land** where **nobody lives.**

But anyone whose **good** deeds exceed his **wisdom,** to what is he compared? To a tree that has only a **few branches** but **many roots:** even **if** all the winds in the world come and blow against it, they do not move it from its place.

As it says in Yirmiyahu: He **will** be like a tree **planted next to water,** which **will** spread its **roots** toward **the stream;** it **will not** notice when the heat comes, and its leaves will always **be fresh.** In a year of drought it will not worry, for it will not stop producing fruits.

Living Lessons

Strong Roots

You might find that sometimes you don't have a feeling for a certain mitzvah and have a hard time appreciating its value. Don't despair! The Sefer Hachinuch writes: "אַחֲרֵי הַפְּעוּלוֹת נִמְשָׁכִים הַלְּבָבוֹת – A person's emotions follow his actions."[125] The things that you do have a greater effect on your mind and heart than anything you learn. So teach yourself good habits, and they will stay with you for life.

Biography

Rabi Elazar ben Azaryah was born a few years before the second Beis Hamikdash was destroyed. He was a kohen, a tenth generation descendant from Ezra Hasofer, and a very wealthy man. In fact, he was so rich that every year, the ma'aser of his animals was 1,200 calves![126]

When he was just eighteen, he was chosen to be the Nassi. Concerned that he looked too young for people to respect, he miraculously grew eighteen rows of white hair overnight. As Nassi, he instituted a major change in yeshivas. Until that point, only select students were allowed to attend yeshivah. Rabi Elazar decreed that anyone should be allowed attend. On the day that this change took effect, hundreds of benches were added to the study hall to accommodate the flood of new students.[127]

Rabi Yehudah Hanassi compared Rabi Elazar to a fully-stocked spice merchant, since one could ask him a question in any area of the Torah and get a good answer.[128]

He is buried in Kfar Almah in the upper Galil.

Behind the Quote

Because Rabi Elazar ben Azarya decreed that anyone can attend yeshivah, including those with less than desirable personalities,[129] he saw it necessary to encourage working on one's character by saying אִם אֵין דֶּרֶךְ אֶרֶץ אֵין תּוֹרָה—Torah study requires a refined personality.[130]

Sparks

Strong Foundations A tree's roots grow before its branches and support the entire tree. If a tree has more branches than roots, the branches endanger the tree because the force of the wind could cause the tree to topple.

The same is true with one's service of Hashem. Torah study, like the tree's branches, must be founded on kabbalas ol malchus Shamayim—accepting Hashem's commands unconditionally. With that foundation, questions or doubts will not threaten the person's service of Hashem, rather he will have the strength to stand firmly until they are resolved. On the other hand, if one's life is not based on kabbalas ol malchus Shamayim, more knowledge merely increases the risk of falling from the foreign winds of questions and doubts.[131]

Did You Know?

What's the Point? When Moshe went up to Heaven to receive the Torah, the malachim challenged why humans deserve the Torah. Moshe responded, "Do you have parents whom you could honor? Do you work, that you need to rest on Shabbos? Do you have a yetzer hara?" Moshe was explaining to the malachim that Torah can only be fulfilled with physical things. Without "derech eretz—the way of the land," we would not have received the Torah, for without a world to purify and refine, Torah could not fulfill its purpose.[132]

Pay Up!

Someone who has truly learned from Torah will be extra careful in his interpersonal dealings.

R' Zushe of Anipoli was very poor. His wife really wanted a new dress, so they saved up money, purchased fine material, and brought it to the tailor.

The tailor's daughter was soon to be married and her chasan happened to notice the beautiful dress in the house. When he learned that the dress was for R' Zushe's wife, he was disappointed, and the poor tailor was filled with guilt. R' Zushe's wife, witnessing the scene, immediately gave the dress to the bride as a wedding gift.

When she told her husband what had happened, R' Zushe asked, "So did you pay the tailor?"

"Pay him?" she exclaimed, "But I gave him the whole gown! Why should I pay him?"

"Giving the gown was a beautiful act of tzedakah," he replied, "but you hired the tailor to work for several days, and he expected to be paid so that he can feed his family. Is it his fault that you decided to give his daughter a gift? He must be paid."[133]

Word Power

אִם אֵין תּוֹרָה The word אֵין in this mishnah can also be read as אַיִן—nothing. If one does not study Torah, אַיִן קֶמַח—his food becomes nothing. If the energy produced from the food is not used to study Torah, the food does not fulfill its purpose and is as worthless as dirt.[134]

Rabi Eliezer (the son of) Chisma says: The mathematical calculations to determine what to do when **bird offerings** become mixed up and unidentifiable, and mathematical calculations to determine when **a niddah will begin** being tamei **are actually halachos** of the Torah. However, the mathematical calculations of **astronomy and gematria** only add **flavor to** a person's **wisdom** and should be treated as secondary to Torah knowledge.

רַבִּי אֱלִיעֶזֶר (בֶּן) חִסְמָא אוֹמֵר: קִנִּין וּפִתְחֵי נִדָּה, הֵן הֵן גּוּפֵי הֲלָכוֹת. תְּקוּפוֹת וְגִמַטְרִיָּאוֹת, פַּרְפְּרָאוֹת לַחָכְמָה.

The Good Guide

A person can possibly know much philosophy about right or wrong without the knowledge affecting his actions. The root of halachah is ה.ל.כ., which means "go." Torah is the path that leads to a good and meaningful life. Other intellectual pursuits, brilliant and enjoyable as they may be, do not guide a person's behavior as the Torah does.[135]

Biography

Rabi Eliezer (ben) Chisma

was a student of Rabi Yehoshua, and Rabi Akiva. Some say that he received the name Chisma from the following episode that occurred before he became a scholar: He was once asked to lead the davening, but did not know how. Overcome by embarrassment at his ignorance, he decided to go learn Torah. When he returned, people said that he had become stronger—אִיתְחַסָּם, and the name stuck.[136]

Rabi Eliezer was very poor. Rabban Gamliel offered him a position at the yeshivah, but he refused until Rabban Gamliel convinced him that it was not a position of honor because he would become a servant to the public. Upon hearing this, Rabi Eliezer accepted.[137]

Story

Don't Remain the Same

Torah must influence the way a person lives. There is a legend told about the Greek philosopher Aristotle who was once found by his students doing something immoral. His students asked him, "You teach such profound morals and ethics. How could you do such a low act?"

Aristotle answered: "When I am teaching, I am Aristotle the philosopher. Now I am just plain Aristotle."

Behind the Quote

Rabi Eliezer ben Chisma was a genius in mathematics. The Gemara[138] says that he had a formula that could calculate the number of drops in the ocean. Yet even he, who was so fluent in these subjects, compared mathematics and science to flavoring agents. They can only add flavor to Torah, but cannot replace the main body of Torah.[139]

Connections

The previous mishnah states that action is what counts the most. Continuing that thought, this mishnah emphasizes learning the parts of Torah that are relevant to action, namely halachah.[141]

Word Power

פַּרְפְּרָאוֹת Why does the mishnah say that astronomy "only adds flavor," when in fact it is crucial to the Jewish calendar?

Some of the many answers to this question are as follows:

1. Our mishnah refers specifically to the study of the nature of the sun, stars, and planets, which have no bearing on halachah.
2. It refers to the study of the weather patterns.
3. It refers to the study of mazalos—the constellations.[140]

Sparks

Uncommon Yet Dear Rabi Eliezer lived after the destruction of the Beis Hamikdash, a time when the complicated laws of bird sacrifices were no longer applicable. Indeed, most of the halachos of kinim and pischei niddah are so uncommon that they were rarely relevant even when the Beis Hamikdash stood. Nevertheless, the mishnah tells us, even these halachos, dealing with situations that will never arise during one's lifetime, are still part of the primary body of Torah.[142]

Say this mishnah upon completing each perek:

Rabi Chananya ben Akashya says:

The Holy One, blessed be He, wanted to make B'nei **Yisrael** have many **merits.**

He therefore gave them an abundance of Torah and mitzvos, so that they would have many opportunities to connect to Him.

As it says in Yeshayah: **Hashem wanted, for the sake of** increasing B'nei Yisrael's **righteousness, that the Torah be made great and glorious.**

רַבִּי חֲנַנְיָא בֶּן עֲקַשְׁיָא אוֹמֵר:

רָצָה הַקָּדוֹשׁ בָּרוּךְ הוּא לְזַכּוֹת אֶת יִשְׂרָאֵל לְפִיכָךְ הִרְבָּה לָהֶם תּוֹרָה וּמִצְוֹת

שֶׁנֶּאֱמַר: יְיָ חָפֵץ לְמַעַן צִדְקוֹ יַגְדִּיל תּוֹרָה וְיַאְדִּיר.

Endnotes

1. עדיות פ"ה מ"ו-ז
2. עדיות פרק ג
3. תולדות יהושע. דרך אבות
4. מדרש שמואל
5. בן איש חי הובא בבן איש חיל, דרוש ב' לשבת הגדול
6. פניני דברי יאשיהו ע' ריח
7. עבודה זרה י"ח, א
8. קיצורו של אברבנאל
9. הובא במדרש שמואל
10. רמב"ם הלכות כלי המקדש פ"ד הי"ט
11. ספר היובל למהר"ם שפירא מלובלין
12. דרך אבות
13. באר יצחק, ימים נוראים - יצחק ברנר - ע' קד
14. כנסת ישראל. ביאורים
15. ביצה ט"ז, א
16. מילי דאבות ליחיאל מיכל מושקין
17. מדרש דוד לרבינו דוד הנגיד נכדו של הרמב"ם
18. שבת ל"ג, ב
19. שבת ל"ג, ב
20. מדרש שמואל
21. תענית ה, ב
22. אגרות קודש, אדמו"ר מוהריי"צ - ח"ז ע' עב
23. ביאורים
24. רבינו יונה
25. מדרש שמואל
26. ילקוט יהודה
27. כתובות ס"ב, ב. ויקרא רבה כ"א, ח
28. כתובות ס"ב, ב
29. מוסר אבות
30. חיים שיש בהם, על פרקי אבות - ח"א ע' רפז
31. עירובין ס"ה, א
32. מדרש שמואל
33. מדרש שמואל. מגילה ו, ב
34. ביאורים
35. חפץ חיים בספרו שמירת הלשון שער התורה פ"ג
36. בית אבות
37. ברכות כ"ח, ב
38. מגילה כ"ח, א
39. מוסר אבות
40. ביאורים
41. מדרש שמואל
42. אור יקרות ע' כד
43. תפארת ישראל
44. מגילה כ"ג, ב
45. מדרש שמואל. תפארת ישראל
46. אברבנאל. ספורנו
47. ספורי חסידים, מועדים - חנוכה
48. תענית כ"ד, א
49. הוריות י"ג, ב
50. רמזי תורה תמ"ב. לקוטי בתר לקוטי בשם עבודת ישראל
51. תענית כ"ד, א
52. ביאורים
53. מחניים ל"ג ע' 107 בשם ר' מאיר שפירא
54. עירובין נ"ד, א
55. נחלת אבות
56. בבא מציעא פ"ה, א
57. רמב"ן בהשמטות לספר המצוות מצות לא תעשה ב
58. מדרש שמואל
59. מנחות כ"ט, ב
60. מסכת אבות ע"פ יינה של תורה ע' קמה
61. ידות אפרים
62. ירמי' ט, י"א. ב"מ פ"ה, ב.
63. ב"ח או"ח סי' מז ד"ה ומ"ש דאמר רב יהודה. רבינו יונה הובא בר"ן
64. מדרש שמואל
65. ספורנו
66. רוח חיים פרק ד' משנה א'
67. מדרש שמואל
68. ברכות ל"ד, ב
69. תענית כ"ד, ב-כ"ה, א
70. צדקת הצדיק אות רי
71. תענית כ"ד, ב-כ"ה, א
72. דברים י"ד, א
73. רבינו יונה
74. יבמות ט"ז, א
75. דרך אבות
76. לקוטי בתר לקוטי
77. רע"ב
78. מדרש שמואל
79. סיפורי חסידים, מועדים - סוכות אשפיזין
80. שערי תשובה לר' יונה שער ג
81. מדרש תנחומא, ויגש
82. שבת נ"ה, ב
83. ירושלמי תענית פ"ד ה"ה
84. פסחים צ"ג, ב
85. ביאורים
86. ביאורים
87. כנסת ישראל
88. מדרש שמואל
89. שבת קנ"ו, ב
90. מדרש שמואל
91. מגן אבות
92. רבינו עובדיה (הובא במדרש שמואל)
93. גיטין נ"ח, א
94. מנחות צ"ט, ב
95. ביאורים
96. כתובות ק"ה, ב
97. ביאורים
98. כתובות ס"ב, ב
99. יבמות ס"ב, ב
100. ברכות ס"א, ב
101. רבינו נסים גאון ברכות כ"ז, ב
102. ביאורים
103. פרי חיים
104. שבת ל"א, א
105. מנחות כ"ט, ב
106. ביאורים
107. חסדי אבות
108. בבא בתרא י', א
109. רבינו יוסף בן שושן
110. חולין ס"ג, א
111. רש"י
112. שבת קנ"ו, ב
113. ביאורים
114. תפארת ישראל הובא בלקו"ט בתר לקוטי
115. מדרש שמואל בשם רבי משה אלמושנינו
116. רמב"ם
117. אגרת הקודש כא
118. נדה ל"א, א
119. ירושלמי חגיגה פ"ב ה"א
120. מאירי
121. הוספות לכתר שם טוב ספ"ח
122. ברכות ס"א, ב
123. ביאורים
124. ילקוט שמעוני - רות, תרז
125. חינוך מצוה טז
126. שבת נ"ד, ב
127. ברכות כ"ז, ב
128. אבות דר' נתן פי"ח
129. ברכות כ"ח, א
130. פתח עינים לרב משה יקר אשכנזי
131. מגן אבות, מהר"ל ע"פ יומא ע"ב, ב. מדרש שמואל
132. הר' יוסף יעב"ץ
133. סיפורי חסידים - תורה, קדושים
134. מדרש שמואל
135. ילקוט לקח טוב - חיים של תורה - ע' קצא, קונטרס וגם לשמונה עמוד ז', ובכ"מ
136. ויקרא רבה כ"ג, ד
137. הוריות י', א
138. הוריות י', א
139. תוספות יו"ט
140. רשב"ץ. תוספות יו"ט
141. יוסף עליו (מיוסף מונטקיו)
142. מדרש שמואל

פֶּרֶק רְבִיעִי

Chapter Four

Kol Yisrael

Say this mishnah before beginning each new perek:

All B'nei **Yisrael have a portion in the World to Come.**

As it says in Yeshayah regarding B'nei Yisrael upon Moshiach's arrival: **Your people are all tzaddikim,** and **they will all inherit Eretz** Yisrael **forever**—they will never be exiled from it again.

All will recognize that they are **the branch of My planting and the work of My hands,** in which I, Hashem, **take pride.**

כָּל יִשְׂרָאֵל יֵשׁ לָהֶם חֵלֶק לְעוֹלָם הַבָּא,

שֶׁנֶּאֱמַר: וְעַמֵּךְ כֻּלָּם צַדִּיקִים, לְעוֹלָם יִירְשׁוּ אָרֶץ,

נֵצֶר מַטָּעַי מַעֲשֵׂה יָדַי לְהִתְפָּאֵר.

Ben Zoma says: Who is truly wise?
Someone who learns from every person.

As it says in Tehillim: I have gained wisdom from all my teachers, whoever they may be, because Hashem's testimonies, written in the Torah, are my only concern and conversation—so I will put aside my pride and learn from anyone who can teach me something.

Who is truly strong?
Someone who conquers his yetzer hara. As it says in Mishlei: Someone who can control himself and is slow to anger is better than someone who is physically strong, and someone who controls his feelings is better than someone who conquers a city.

Who is truly rich?
Someone who is happy with his portion. As it says in Tehillim: When you are satisfied that you can buy food and eat from money earned by the work of your hands, and don't seek more than you have, you are fortunate and it will be good for you. The words "you are fortunate" refer to good fortune in this world, and the words "it will be good for you" refer to goodness in the World to Come.

Who is truly honorable?
Someone who honors other people. As Hashem says: To those who honor Me by honoring My creations, I will bring honor. And those who ridicule Me by disrespecting My creations will be shamed.

בֶּן זוֹמָא אוֹמֵר:
אֵיזֶהוּ חָכָם, הַלּוֹמֵד מִכָּל אָדָם, שֶׁנֶּאֱמַר:
מִכָּל מְלַמְּדַי הִשְׂכַּלְתִּי, כִּי עֵדְוֹתֶיךָ שִׂיחָה לִי.

אֵיזֶהוּ גִבּוֹר, הַכּוֹבֵשׁ אֶת יִצְרוֹ, שֶׁנֶּאֱמַר:
טוֹב אֶרֶךְ אַפַּיִם מִגִּבּוֹר, וּמוֹשֵׁל בְּרוּחוֹ מִלֹּכֵד עִיר.

אֵיזֶהוּ עָשִׁיר, הַשָּׂמֵחַ בְּחֶלְקוֹ, שֶׁנֶּאֱמַר: יְגִיעַ כַּפֶּיךָ כִּי תֹאכֵל, אַשְׁרֶיךָ וְטוֹב לָךְ, אַשְׁרֶיךָ בָּעוֹלָם הַזֶּה, וְטוֹב לָךְ לָעוֹלָם הַבָּא.

אֵיזֶהוּ מְכֻבָּד, הַמְכַבֵּד אֶת הַבְּרִיּוֹת, שֶׁנֶּאֱמַר:
כִּי מְכַבְּדַי אֲכַבֵּד וּבֹזַי יֵקָלּוּ.

Your Gift to the World

Everyone in the world has something unique and special to share that no one else has. That means you, too! Realizing this will also give you confidence and enthusiasm to help others, since indeed, you have a certain quality to share that nobody else has.

Biography

Ben Zoma lived around the time of the destruction of the second Beis Hamikdash, and was a student of Rabi Yehoshua ben Chananya. He was one of the four Tannaim who entered Pardes, the spiritual chamber of the deepest secrets of the Torah.[1]

There are a couple of explanations as to why he was called ben Zoma, instead of by his full name, Shimon ben Zoma. For one, he became famous for his learning when he was very young, when he had hardly established his identity, and so was simply called "Zoma's son." Also, there were four Tannaim who were colleagues with the same first name, Shimon. To differentiate between them, some were called after the name of their fathers, like ben Zoma, ben Azzai, and ben Nanas, while Shimon Hataimani was called after his place of origin.

Behind the Quote

Ben Zoma served Hashem on a very high level, as is evident from the fact that he was one of the four Tannaim who had the privilege to enter Pardes[2] and learn the most hidden secrets of the Torah. The Gemara says that when he passed away, there were no longer any Chachamim with the ability to uncover alternative explanations of the words of the Torah.[3]

Despite his great level, even ben Zoma found it important to learn from everyone, recognizing that each person has something unique to share.[4]

Did You Know?

Torah Truth Being rich or poor is not defined by how much money or possessions one has. In fact, the more belongings one has, the more one seems to need.[5] A person who is unsatisfied is never happy, so while he may own a lot, he can hardly be called rich. By contrast, one who is happy with whatever Hashem has blessed him is indeed rich, for such a person is truly satisfied, and that is something that money cannot buy.

Sparks

Fighting Shadows It can be more difficult to conquer your yetzer hara than to conquer a city. Usually it is obvious when an enemy is threatening you, but the yetzer hara is different. Often he comes in disguise, and may even convince you to do things that seem holy just to trap you!

The key is to remember the rule: anything that will serve to distract you from learning more Torah or doing a mitzvah is coming from the yetzer hara.[6]

Where to Look When it comes to physical matters, one should always be happy with what he has. However, in matters of serving Hashem it's exactly the opposite—one must never feel satisfied with his current level but should constantly strive higher. This is hinted to in the passuk —"בַּשָּׁמַיִם מִמַּעַל וְעַל הָאָרֶץ מִתָּחַת"—in matters of heaven always look to someone who is above you and work toward their level, while in earthly matters think of those who are less fortunate than you and be happy with your lot.[7]

Story

Precious Dissatisfaction

R' Shalom of Belz was once in the shul of his Rebbe, the Chozeh of Lublin, and overheard a simple man sighing to his friend, "I traveled so far and at such great expense to learn from and be inspired by the Chozeh. Now it's already time to return home and I have not used my time here well enough. I could have gained so much more!" and he sighed again.

R' Shalom told the man: "The heavenly court was once evaluating all the mitzvos of the Jews, and whatever Malach Michoel would present about the Jews, the Satan showed that gentiles did the same: the Jews gave tzedakah, brought in guests, and helped poor brides—the gentiles did the same. Finally, Malach Michoel presented the Jews' broken hearts about their spiritual standing, and for that, the Satan couldn't find a match!"

Regarding physical things we should always be content with what we have. Regarding our spiritual status, however, we must never be satisfied, and always seek to accomplish more.[8]

בֶּן עַזַּאי אוֹמֵר: הֱוֵי רָץ לְמִצְוָה קַלָּה, וּבוֹרֵחַ מִן הָעֲבֵרָה, שֶׁמִּצְוָה גּוֹרֶרֶת מִצְוָה, וַעֲבֵרָה גּוֹרֶרֶת עֲבֵרָה, שֶׁשְּׂכַר מִצְוָה מִצְוָה, וּשְׂכַר עֲבֵרָה עֲבֵרָה.

Ben Azzai says: Run to do even an easy, small mitzvah and away from any aveirah, because one mitzvah, no matter how small, brings about another mitzvah, and one aveirah brings about another aveirah. For the reward for a mitzvah is the opportunity to do another mitzvah, and the result of an aveirah is the possibility of doing another aveirah.

Living Lessons

I'm Running

When you enjoy doing something, you do it with great enthusiasm. Nobody is lazy when doing something he likes. Mitzvos should be so special to us that we do them with all our energy as soon as we can. In fact, we even ask Hashem for help with this in davening, at the end of every Shmoneh Esreh when we say "וּבְמִצְוֹתֶיךָ תִּרְדֹּף נַפְשִׁי"—and may I chase after Your mitzvos."

It's Never Just One Time

A person should never think that helping another Jew fulfill one mitzvah is a small thing. Besides for what he achieves through that single mitzvah, it will also bring him to fulfill more and more mitzvos.

Sparks

Commandments = Connections The word מִצְוָה can be translated as connection, from the word צַוְותָא.[9] This is because mitzvos are not only commandments from Hashem, but a way to connect to Him. With every mitzvah that we do, our connection with Hashem grows stronger and closer.

This means that the greatest reward for a mitzvah is actually the mitzvah itself: the opportunity to fulfill Hashem's desire and thereby strengthen our connection to Him. The opposite applies with aveiros. There is no worse punishment than having done the aveirah itself, and thereby putting something in the way of our connection to Hashem.[10]

Word Power

שֶׁשְּׂכַר מִצְוָה מִצְוָה There is a system of letter substitution called א"ת ב"ש (at-bash) where the first letter of the Alef Beis (א) is exchanged with the last (ת), the second (ב) with the second to last (ש), the third (ג) with the third to last (ר), and so on. Using this system for the first two letters of the word מִצְוָה results in a י and a ה, and it then spells Hashem's name![11]

Biography

Ben Azzai's full name was Shimon ben Azzai. This mishnah was stated before he received semichah, so he was still called by his father's name.

He was one of the smartest Tannaim of his time, second only to Rabi Akiva himself. Ben Azzai was so devoted to his learning that he did not want to marry so as not to be distracted. He was one of the four Tannaim who entered Pardes.

The Gemara says that if someone sees ben Azzai in a dream, he should expect success in his efforts to become righteous.[12]

Connections

Working to conquer the yetzer hara may seem overwhelming and difficult, especially since, as ben Zoma taught in the previous mishnah, it takes more strength than it would to conquer a city. Ben Azzai therefore advises that a person run enthusiastically toward doing a mitzvah, which will start a trend of doing more mitzvos, as one mitzvah brings about the next. You just need to start enthusiastically![13]

Behind the Quote

Ben Azzai was on a very high spiritual level. His intense devotion to serving Hashem led him to teach about running toward doing a mitzvah. Mitzvos are so precious that you cannot even walk normally toward them, rather you must run in excitement.[14]

Did You Know?

Increased Opportunities

Chazal tell us that the reward for giving ma'aser is greater wealth. This means that the mitzvah of ma'aser enables us to give even more ma'aser from our newly acquired wealth!

In this case it is clear how one mitzvah brings on the opportunity to perform more mitzvos![15]

Snowball Acts

The Ba'al Shem Tov was once traveling with his students when he approached a stranger and told him something privately. When the students later asked the man what he was told, he responded with the following story:

"I have a very good friend whom I know from when we were little children. We love each other like brothers and hide nothing from each other. We now both have families and live near each other.

"A little while ago my friend came back from a long business trip during which he invested a lot of borrowed money and had made a nice profit for his investors. I went into his house to welcome him back home, and noticed that he had left all his earnings from the past few months right out in the open. I was upset at how careless he was with his money, so I decided to teach him a lesson not to leave money lying around. I took the money and left the house, planning on returning it in an hour or so.

"However, when my friend realized the money was gone, he fainted, and it became a big commotion in town. I ran to his house to return the money but when I saw all the people gathered, I was scared to publicly admit what I had done, and decided to wait it out until everyone left and when I'd be alone with my friend I would return it. However, the more I waited the more embarrassed I became.

"Eventually, I decided to invest the money, since it was just lying in my house, and to find a way to return it to my friend later. I was now on my way, and the Ba'al Shem Tov, who had never seen me before, stopped me and said I should go back and return the money immediately. He promised to come to testify that I didn't have bad intentions. I now feel confident to return the money and everything will work out as your Rebbe said. I just regret all the pain and suffering that grew out of my silly little prank!"[16]

Ben Azzai **would** often **say:**

Do not treat anyone with disrespect, and do not reject anything as valueless, **because every man has his hour** when he is needed, **and every thing has its** valuable **place** and purpose in the world.

הוּא הָיָה אוֹמֵר:

אַל תְּהִי בָז לְכָל אָדָם וְאַל תְּהִי מַפְלִיג לְכָל דָּבָר, שֶׁאֵין לְךָ אָדָם שֶׁאֵין לוֹ שָׁעָה, וְאֵין לְךָ דָבָר שֶׁאֵין לוֹ מָקוֹם.

Living Lessons

Part of the Plan

Everything has a purpose. Even a leaf blowing in the wind is part of Hashem's master plan.[17] Dovid Hamelech once wondered about why Hashem made spiders. Later, his life was saved by one!

Certainly every person, and especially every Jew, has a place in Hashem's master plan. If you are tempted to minimize someone's importance, remember that Hashem gave him an important job to do and thinks he is very important.

Connections

In this mishnah, ben Azzai elaborates on ben Zoma's message in mishnah 1 to honor all creations. If every creation is precious in Hashem's eyes, how could you even think of insulting any of them?[18]

Word Power

לְכָל אָדָם The words לְכָל אָדָם can also mean "the whole person." When Yaakov Avinu reprimanded Shimon and Levi, he cursed their anger, not them.[19] This shows us that even when someone's behavior warrants rebuke, one must not confuse his behavior with who he truly is.

מַפְלִיג לְכָל דָּבָר These words can also mean "do not discount (the power of) any word." Words are powerful, and even a single word can have a tremendous effect.[20]

Sparks

River Secrets Rabi Pinchas ben Yair was once on his way to yeshivah when he came upon a river blocking his path. "Why are you stopping me from going to yeshivah?" he asked. Miraculously, the river split, and he passed through on dry land.

When his students asked him if he thought they could do the same, he replied that only one who is confident that he has never shamed another could demand that nature give way before him.[21]

Biography

Ben Azzai didn't have a title Rabi. Some say that this was because he didn't manage to receive semichah before passing away at a young age.[22] In his short life, he was known for his brilliance. In fact, he soon became the symbol of insight, so that it became common among the Chachamim to say when feeling insightful, "I feel ready to teach just like ben Azzai!"[23]

It is told that when he learned, flames surrounded him, just as at Mattan Torah itself.[24]

 **Behind the Quote**

Ben Azzai was of the opinion that the mitzvah in Torah וְאָהַבְתָּ לְרֵעֲךָ כָּמוֹךְ (Love your fellow as yourself) does not exclude one who is not "your fellow," but applies to every single creation.[28] In this mishnah he stresses that point again.[29]

 Sparks

Judging Favorably Every person is affected by his surroundings. Every man has his hour of temptation, when his test is particularly tough, and every thing has its place where it serves as a challenge, since no one is completely immune to his environment. You cannot judge people for a mistake they might make, because who knows what temptations or influences lead them to do that act![25]

Turn to Teshuvah The word שָׁעָה can also mean to turn.[26] This mishnah is also telling us that every Jew will have a time when he will want to turn back to Hashem and do teshuvah. One must not look down at a person who is behaving wrongly, but instead help and encourage him to repent.[27]

 Did You Know?

Fathers and Sons Ben Azzai and ben Zoma were so smart that even when they were young, they would debate halachah with Chachamim. At that point they were called "Azzai's son" and "Zoma's son," because of their youth. When they grew older, the names they received as boys stuck.[30]

You Never Know

Rabi Elazar ben Shamua was once walking along the beach when he noticed a sorry-looking man who was soon discovered to be the lone survivor of a shipwreck. The man had lost all his clothes and was begging the passersby for help. "I am a descendant of Eisav, your great-uncle. Please give me some clothing." But his plea fell on deaf ears.

"May your entire nation suffer your fate!" the Jews shouted at him. Only Rabi Elazar ben Shamua hurried to the man's aid. He gave him his own coat, brought him home and gave him food, drink, and some money. He even accompanied him for some of his return journey. The man vowed never to forget the episode.

Years later, that same man became king. He made a decree that all Jewish men should be killed and the women taken as captives. Terrified and stunned, the Jews put together a present to appease the king's anger and begged Rabi Elazar ben Shamua to bring it to the king and beg for mercy. When Rabi Elazar entered the throne room, the king immediately recognized him as his benefactor from so many years before.

"Please have mercy on my brothers," Rabi Elazar begged.

"They deserve to be killed!" the king angrily replied. "They transgressed the commandments in the Torah regarding helping people in need."

After more pleading from Rabi Elazar, and in gratitude for Rabi Elazar's kind act many years earlier, the king agreed to rescind the decree. He told Rabi Elazar to keep the gift for himself and to choose seventy pieces of clothing from his treasury.[31]

Rabi Levitas of Yavneh says: Be very, very humble, because while a person's neshamah lives forever, his body, the source of arrogance, will ultimately end up in the grave, eaten by worms.

Rabi Yochanan ben Berokah says: Whoever desecrates and brings dishonor to Hashem's Name, even in a private, small group, will be punished for it in public.

When it comes to desecrating Hashem's Name, it makes no difference whether it was done by mistake or on purpose, because in any case Hashem's Name was dishonored.

רַבִּי לְוִיטַס אִישׁ יַבְנֶה אוֹמֵר: מְאֹד מְאֹד הֱוֵי שְׁפַל רוּחַ, שֶׁתִּקְוַת אֱנוֹשׁ רִמָּה.

רַבִּי יוֹחָנָן בֶּן בְּרוֹקָה אוֹמֵר: כָּל הַמְחַלֵּל שֵׁם שָׁמַיִם בַּסֵּתֶר, נִפְרָעִין מִמֶּנּוּ בַּגָּלוּי,

אֶחָד שׁוֹגֵג וְאֶחָד מֵזִיד בְּחִלּוּל הַשֵּׁם.

Watch My Step

The term "chilul Hashem" usually means giving Hashem a bad name. However, it can also mean cheapening the value of Hashem's mitzvos. If someone sees you doing something against the Torah and thinks that is acceptable, that is a chilul Hashem, because you have made Hashem's mitzvos less important in that person's eyes.

Rav said that he never bought anything if he couldn't pay for it fully on the spot. He didn't want anyone to see him walk out of the store without paying and think that stealing is acceptable behavior.[32]

Everything we do has the power to affect someone else's attitude toward mitzvos, so be sure that all your actions will teach only positive lessons.

 Did You Know?

Follow the Leader When a person is in a position of leadership, he must be especially careful to monitor his actions. Even something that is really permitted and merely **appears** wrong may lead those watching to assume that wrong action is acceptable.[33]

 Connections

Rabi Levitas continues ben Azzai's message from the previous mishnah. Not only should we respect each person, we must feel humble in their presence as well![34]

The mishnah continues with the teaching of Rabi Yochanan ben Berokah, which hints that one who does not make himself humble before another person is in fact desecrating Hashem's name.[35]

Biography

Rabi Levitas This is the only time Rabi Levitas' name appears in all of the Mishnah. He is called the "man of Yavneh" because he was the most influential person there. His name לְוִיטָס hints that he was one of the seventy members of the Sanhedrin. Levi, his original name, counts as one, and the added "טס" adds a numerical value of sixty-nine to his name, for the other sixty-nine members. He is buried in Yavneh.

Rabi Yochanan ben Brokah studied under Rabi Yehoshua together with Rabi Eliezer ben Chisma and was a colleague of Rabi Akiva and Rabi Yishmael. His son Rabi Yishmael was also a great tanna. It is written that he merited to learn from Eliyahu Hanavi.

 ### Sparks

Humble Pride Pride can be terrible, but it's necessary to feel some pride in order to stand up for what's right. Such pride will not interfere with humility because it's not self-pride, but pride in being Hashem's servant![36]

Holy and Humble The Gemara says that Hashem cannot stay with a haughty person.[37] To be close to Hashem, one must put aside his own feelings and desires and make space for the Will of Hashem.[38]

Everything in Moderation, Including Moderation One must not spend too much money, but nor should one be stingy. Being angry is harmful, but so is being cold and uncaring.[39] When it comes to pride, however, we need to go to the opposite extreme, and be very, very humble.[40]

 ### Behind the Quote

As the most respected man in Yavneh, Rabi Levitas taught the importance of humility, especially while in a position of leadership.[41]

Word Power

הַמְחַלֵּל In its essence, the whole world is filled with Hashem's light. When one does a mitzvah it enables that light to shine. An aveirah, on the other hand, prevents Hashem's light from shining through, leaving that part of the world empty of Hashem's revealed presence.[42] That is why it is called a חִלּוּל הַשֵּׁם, because חִלּוּל comes from the word חָלָל—an empty space. An aveirah creates a hole where Hashem's presence could have been revealed.

 ### Story

Hidden Treasure

Rabi Akiva once went to the marketplace with a diamond to sell. He was approached by an unfortunate-looking man who offered to pay full price for the gem. Recognizing him from his place with the beggars in shul, Rabi Akiva was doubtful that he would have the money to buy such an expensive gem, but the man insisted that Rabi Akiva follow him home. As they neared his house, Rabi Akiva was surprised to see servants rushing to wash the man's feet and seat him in a golden chair. Upon his signal, the servants brought in the sum of money, which the man gave to a bewildered Rabi Akiva. The "poor man" then invited Rabi Akiva and his students to a feast. After they finished eating, Rabi Akiva asked him why he pretended to be poor if in truth, he was wealthy.

"For three important reasons," the man replied.

"Firstly, I know that one day I will return to dust and my wealth will mean nothing to me, so I don't take pride in it. Secondly, I know that wealth comes and goes, and so I sit with the beggars because this way if I lose my money, I will already have a group of accepting friends. And finally, I believe that every person is equally a creation of Hashem, regardless of his financial status. Hashem hates when people place themselves above others and think they are better."

Rabi Akiva was very pleased with his answer.[43]

Rabi Yishmael bar Rabi Yosei says: Someone who learns Torah in order to teach it to others is given the opportunity both to learn it and to teach it.	רַבִּי יִשְׁמָעֵאל בַּר רַבִּי יוֹסֵי אוֹמֵר: הַלּוֹמֵד תּוֹרָה עַל מְנָת לְלַמֵּד, מַסְפִּיקִין בְּיָדוֹ לִלְמוֹד וּלְלַמֵּד,
Someone who learns Torah in order to practice what he has learned is given the opportunity to learn Torah, teach it, guard himself from aveiros, and fulfill mitzvos.	וְהַלּוֹמֵד עַל מְנָת לַעֲשׂוֹת, מַסְפִּיקִין בְּיָדוֹ לִלְמוֹד וּלְלַמֵּד לִשְׁמוֹר וְלַעֲשׂוֹת.
Rabi Tzadok says: Do not separate yourself from the community. If you are judging a case, do not act as a lawyer by advising those being judged.	רַבִּי צָדוֹק אוֹמֵר: אַל תִּפְרוֹשׁ מִן הַצִּבּוּר, וְאַל תַּעַשׂ עַצְמְךָ כְּעוֹרְכֵי הַדַּיָּנִין,
Do not make the Torah as a crown to make yourself great, and do not use it to earn money as a woodchopper earns his living by chopping wood with his axe.	וְאַל תַּעֲשֶׂהָ עֲטָרָה לְהִתְגַּדֵּל בָּהּ, וְלֹא קַרְדּוֹם לַחְתָּךְ בָּהּ,
This is what Hillel would often say: Someone who uses the crown of Torah for personal benefit will be destroyed.	וְכָךְ הָיָה הִלֵּל אוֹמֵר: וּדְאִשְׁתַּמֵּשׁ בְּתַגָּא חֳלָף,
You have learned from these words of Hillel that whoever seeks personal benefit from the words of Torah removes his life of reward from the World to Come.	הָא לָמַדְתָּ, כָּל הַנֶּהֱנֶה מִדִּבְרֵי תוֹרָה, נוֹטֵל חַיָּיו מִן הָעוֹלָם.

Living Lessons

Mutual Benefit

Sometimes you might feel that helping someone learn will take away from time that could have been used better for your own learning. The mishnah teaches that the opposite is true! Learning with the intention of helping others benefits everyone.[44]

   Connections

Rabi Yishmael teaches the correct attitude toward Torah study. Rabi Tzadok warns against selfish reasons for learning Torah that will lead one away from a true Torah life.[45]

   Did You Know?

Hourly Rate To avoid using Torah for personal gain, a teacher gets paid for the time he spends teaching, not the actual Torah he taught.[46]

Biography

Rabi Tzadok lived during the time of the destruction of the second Beis Hamikdash. Foreseeing that the Beis Hamikdash would be destroyed, Rabi Tzadok fasted for forty years, eating only a small amount of food at night. After some time he became so weak that all his body could tolerate was fig juice.⁴⁷

Rabban Yochanan ben Zakkai held him in such high esteem that he proclaimed "had there been one more Tzaddik like Rabi Tzadok, the Beis Hamikdash would not have been destroyed."⁴⁸ During the siege of Yerushalayim, when Rabban Yochanan ben Zakkai met with the newly-appointed Caesar Vespasian to plead for the Jews, one of the few requests he was granted was for a doctor to heal Rabi Tzadok. The doctor prescribed a special system of eating and Rabi Tzadok was healed.⁴⁹

Rabi Tzadok established his own yeshivah in Tevi'im, but was often called to Yavneh to teach halachos he remembered from the Beis Hamikdash.

 Sparks

Learn to Do Chazal teach that maaseh—action—is the most important thing. Torah is taught for us to fulfill it. In fact, if you are learning Torah and are presented with an opportunity to do a mitzvah that no one else can do, you must stop learning and perform the mitzvah.⁵⁰

Reward in Itself Rabi Tzadok teaches not to use the Torah as a crown. This refers to the reward that Tzaddikim receive in Gan Eden, where they sit wearing crowns of glory.⁵¹ Although one who learns Torah will ultimately merit this reward, his learning should be for the sake of connecting to Hashem and not to earn the crown, even though it is a holy spiritual reward.⁵²

Lishmah—For the Right Reason Chazal teach that one should always learn Torah, even if it's initially with improper intentions, since eventually the proper intention will come.⁵³ However, since Pirkei Avos talks to one who goes beyond the letter of the law, Rabi Tzadok stresses the importance of learning lishmah.⁵⁴

 Word Power

כָּל הַנֶּהֱנֶה The last line of the mishnah can be translated to mean, "Whoever derives pleasure from learning Torah takes away his life from the world"—he will no longer have a desire for worldly indulgences. The more one is involved with holy things, the less interest one will have in physical gratification!⁵⁵

עַל מְנָת לַעֲשׂוֹת There are people who have yiras Shamayim and refined middos but aren't so knowledgeable in Torah. This mishnah teaches that הַלּוֹמֵד עַל מְנָת לַעֲשׂוֹת – one who spends time learning from these people how to behave has not wasted his time, but ultimately מַסְפִּיקִין בְּיָדוֹ לִלְמוֹד וּלְלַמֵּד לִשְׁמוֹר וְלַעֲשׂוֹת – he will have the opportunity to succeed in all areas.⁵⁶

 **Behind the Quote**

There is a discussion in the Gemara between Rabi Shimon bar Yochai and Rabi Yishmael about occupying oneself with Torah. Rabi Shimon says that one should be busy only with Torah and rely on Hashem to provide for a living. Rabi Yishmael says that one must also have a job to earn a living.⁵⁷ However, in this mishnah, Rabi Yishamel admits that, though it is not for everyone, if one chooses to live as Rabi Shimon says, Hashem will help him to succeed.⁵⁸

 **Story**

Why They Come

Witnessing the hordes of people coming to the Chozeh of Lublin for guidance, a great gaon once asked him, "Why do people flock to you, while no one comes to me? I am an even greater Talmid Chacham than you!" The Chozeh couldn't agree more. "I have the same question! I know who I am—I am a nothing. I don't understand why people ask me for guidance in avodas Hashem when I myself have so much to work on. It would make more sense for them to go to you, a distinguished and famous Talmid Chacham.

"Although," the Chozeh continued softly, "perhaps the question itself is the answer. They come to me because I wonder why they come; they don't come to you because you wonder why they don't."⁵⁹

Rabi Yosei says:

Whoever brings honor to the Torah is in turn **honored by** other **people.**

Whoever brings disgrace to the Torah is **disgraced by** other **people.**

רַבִּי יוֹסֵי אוֹמֵר:
כָּל הַמְכַבֵּד אֶת הַתּוֹרָה,
גּוּפוֹ מְכֻבָּד עַל הַבְּרִיּוֹת,
וְכָל הַמְחַלֵּל אֶת הַתּוֹרָה,
גּוּפוֹ מְחֻלָּל עַל הַבְּרִיּוֹת.

Respect the Book

Part of honoring Torah is honoring books containing words of Torah. When carrying sefarim, carry them differently than you would carry regular books. Honor the sefarim by ensuring they look presentable and repairing torn or broken sefarim.[62]

 Connections

Despite the warning in the previous mishnah not to use the Torah to earn a living, a Talmid Chacham might think that it would be disrespectful for him to work at menial tasks, and perhaps it would be better for him to earn a living through Torah instead. In this mishnah, Rabi Yosei says that the opposite is true: if a person honors the Torah by **not** using it for his livelihood and instead works for a living, people will honor him for doing so.[60] In fact, Rabi Yosei himself worked as a tanner so he would not have to rely on earning money from his Torah knowledge.[61]

 Word Power

גּוּפוֹ This mishnah can also be read: Whoever honors the Torah through his body—by making sure to look tidy and presentable—brings extra honor to the Torah. And the opposite: Whoever desecrates the Torah through his body—by looking messy and unclean—brings desecration upon the Torah.[63]

 Sparks

Respect and Beyond Honoring the Torah and Talmidei Chachamim is a halachah in Shulchan Aruch.[64] This mishnah is encouraging further measures of respecting Torah that go beyond the letter of the law, such as recognizing that every detail of Torah is precise,[65] and making sure to learn Torah in a clean environment and with clean hands.[66]

Biography

Rabi Yosei ben Chalafta was a descendant of Yisro,⁶⁷ and one of the five students whom Rabi Akiva taught later in life.⁶⁸ Although a tanner by trade, Rabi Yosei ben Chalafta was a great Talmid Chacham, who received semichah from Rabi Yehudah ben Bava. He was exiled to Tzipori when he was caught speaking out against the Romans.⁶⁹ While there, he received regular visits from Eliyahu Hanavi and authored a sefer called Seder Olam, a record of generations from creation until his time.

Rabi Yosei used his great wisdom to bring others closer to Hashem by explaining the Torah to all people, including non-Jews. A Roman noblewoman once asked him what Hashem does all day. Rabi Yosei replied, "He makes shiduchim, which is as difficult as krias yam suf." Hearing this, she replied, "Difficult? I can do it quite easily." That night she matched up a thousand of her servants to a thousand of her maids. The next morning they reported to her that not a single one of them was happy with their new spouse! Immediately she called for Rabi Yosei and said, "I see that it is indeed difficult and your G-d is indeed very great."⁷⁰

His halachic positions are always accepted since he brings logical explanations for his rulings. In fact, whenever the mishnah writes Rabi Yosei without specifying which one, it refers to Rabi Yosei ben Chalafta. Whenever anyone would challenge Rabi Yosei's teachings, Rabi Yehudah Hanassi would say, "The distance between Rabi Yosei's generation and ours is like the difference between the Kodesh Hakadashim and the most mundane."⁷¹

After his brother died childless, he married the widow (a yevamah) and had five sons, all of whom became great Torah scholars.⁷²

 Sparks

Dig Deeper Honoring Torah includes recognizing each word in Torah has a deeper meaning in addition to its simple meaning. Torah is comprised of four parts, which make up the פַּרְדֵּ"ס: פְּשָׁט – the simple meaning, רֶמֶז – hints to deeper lessons or insights, דְּרוּשׁ – alternative meanings of the words, and סוֹד – the secrets of the deepest, most esoteric part of Torah. This is why the mishnah says that גופו – his body will be honored. By realizing that Torah's body, or simple meaning, also has a soul, a deeper meaning, one merits that his body be honored as well.⁷³

 **Story**

Saved by Faith

Rabi Abba bar Zamina was a Talmid Chacham who worked as a tailor. Once, while working in the home of a Roman, the owner came in with a plate of non-kosher meat and demanded that Rabi Abba eat it. Rabi Abba categorically refused.

The Roman then told him, "I was testing you, and if you would have eaten the meat, I would have killed you. If you are a Jew, be a Jew all the way; if you are a Roman, be a Roman all the way."

Because Rabi Abba respected the Torah and its mitzvos, the Roman respected him, and his life was spared.⁷⁴

 Behind the Quote

Rabi Yosei was known for explaining Torah in a very logical way.⁷⁵ He went out of his way to explain Torah to non-Jews.⁷⁶ All of this was to show the beauty of Torah and bring more honor to it—ideals that he emphasizes in this mishnah.

Rabi Yishmael the son of Rabi Yosei says: A judge who avoids making a judgment and instead works out a compromise between two parties removes hatred from himself because he satisfies both sides, avoids accidentally causing theft through an incorrect ruling, and prevents an unnecessary or false promise that might have been made had it proceeded to court.

Someone who is too self-confident in issuing a ruling is a fool and a wicked, arrogant person.

רַבִּי יִשְׁמָעֵאל בְּנוֹ אוֹמֵר: הֶחָשֵׁךְ עַצְמוֹ מִן הַדִּין, פּוֹרֵק מִמֶּנּוּ אֵיבָה וְגָזֵל וּשְׁבוּעַת שָׁוְא,

וְהַגַּס לִבּוֹ בְּהוֹרָאָה, שׁוֹטֶה רָשָׁע וְגַס רוּחַ.

Rabi Yishmael would often say: Do not judge alone, because there is none who can judge alone besides Hashem, the one God.

Even if you consider yourself greater than the other judges, do not say to them, "Accept my opinion." They are the majority, so they are allowed to say that to you, but you may not say that to them.

הוּא הָיָה אוֹמֵר: אַל תְּהִי דָן יְחִידִי, שֶׁאֵין דָּן יְחִידִי אֶלָּא אֶחָד,

וְאַל תֹּאמַר קַבְּלוּ דַעְתִּי, שֶׁהֵן רַשָּׁאִין וְלֹא אָתָּה.

The Perfect Compromise

Even if you are sure that you are right, it's better to quietly come to a peaceful compromise than to argue. In the heat of an argument, people often get upset and say things they wouldn't have said if they were calm. They don't think logically anymore and aren't capable of judging objectively who is correct. When faced with a conflict, always strive for compromise.[77]

Friend or Judge?

Although this mishnah is advising judges in a courtroom, we can take the lesson for our daily lives as well. Don't be quick to judge your friends. You never know what influenced them or what they may be going through. By allowing yourself to be open and accepting, you will earn others' respect.[78]

Agree to Disagree

Arrogant people usually have fewer friends because it's hard to find someone who will always agree with them. This mishnah teaches not to force your opinions on others. Instead, discuss it with them, hear their opinion, and come to a mutual understanding.[79]

Don't Judge Yourself by Yourself

When the mishnah says not to judge alone, it is referring not only to judging others, but to evaluating yourself as well. People are naturally biased toward themselves and will excuse themselves time and time again for whatever they do. If you want an honest evaluation of yourself, appoint someone else to review and advise you accordingly.[80]

Biography

Rabi Yishmael succeeded his father's position as Rav of Tzipori. He greatly respected Rabi Yehudah Hanassi (Rebbi), even though Rebbi was younger than him, and participated in Rebbi's efforts to compile Torah Sheb'al Peh into the Mishnah. In turn, Rebbi respected him as well.

Behind the Quote

Rabi Yishmael was well known for being extra particular about judging fairly.

As a partial owner of a field, he had a sharecropper who would bring his portion of crops every Friday. One week, the man came with the crops a day early, on Thursday. When Rabi Yishmael asked him why that was, the man told him he had a case that day he wanted Rabi Yishmael to judge. Immediately, Rabi Yishmael disqualified himself, afraid that the gesture would influence his judgment.

Indeed, while listening to the case from the sidelines, Rabi Yishmael found himself thinking of arguments to help the man win his case. "I see how harmful accepting bribes can be," he exclaimed. "I was given something that was rightfully mine and even then my mind was affected. How much more so will a real gift affect one's judgment!"[81]

In this mishnah, he stresses the care a judge must take in deliberating before ruling.[82]

Sparks

Err on the Side of Caution R' Yonasan Eibishetz, a great rav and Talmid Chacham, always read his ruling from the sefer when dealing with a complex response.[83] Although he knew many sefarim by heart, he wanted to make sure that he wouldn't make a mistake.

Word Power

הַחְשֵׁךְ עַצְמוֹ When the mishnah says to "hold yourself back from judgment," it is teaching that a judge must not let his "self" become involved in the case. If he feels personally involved, he will not be able to make a fair and impartial decision.[84]

Did You Know?

Just a Splinter Before Rav Huna would make a ruling, he would gather ten of his students to judge with him. He explained that in case a mistaken judgment was made, he would receive "only a splinter from the beam"—only part of the blame since they all shared responsibility for the decision.[85]

Who is Really Deserving?

R' Zushe of Anipoli had a wealthy chassid who supported him. The chassid knew that he only earned his wealth because he supported a Tzaddik, and he happily gave R' Zushe money. Once, he came for a visit, only to be told that R' Zushe had gone to visit his Rebbe, the Maggid of Mezritch. "Well," the chassid thought. "If I became so wealthy from supporting my Rebbe, I will probably become even wealthier if I support my Rebbe's Rebbe!"

From then on, the chassid traveled only to Mezritch and stopped visiting R' Zushe. Shortly thereafter, the chassid lost all his money. Immediately, he traveled to R' Zushe and asked for an explanation. "Where did I go wrong?" he asked.

R' Zushe explained: "When you gave me money, Hashem knew I didn't deserve it because I'm not a real Tzaddik. But because he saw that you gave to me even though I didn't deserve it, Hashem did the same for you although you didn't deserve it. But then you gave money to the Maggid who is a real Tzaddik and truly deserving. Hashem then judged to see whether you truly deserved your money..."[86]

135

Rabi Yonasan says:

Whoever **fulfills the Torah** by learning it even as a **poor** man will **end** up **fulfilling** it as a **rich** man.

But **whoever neglects Torah** learning as a **rich** man will **end** up neglecting it as a **poor** man.

רַבִּי יוֹנָתָן אוֹמֵר:
כָּל הַמְקַיֵּם אֶת הַתּוֹרָה מֵעֹנִי,
סוֹפוֹ לְקַיְּמָהּ מֵעֹשֶׁר,
וְכָל הַמְבַטֵּל אֶת הַתּוֹרָה
מֵעֹשֶׁר, סוֹפוֹ לְבַטְּלָהּ מֵעֹנִי.

Excuses, Excuses, Excuses

Some people can come up with an excuse for anything. While excuses may get you out of doing homework, they do not help you grow or accomplish anything!

Poor Grasp

The mishnah refers not only to one's financial status, but also to one's intellectual status. When one begins learning Torah with a weak understanding, he is guaranteed that one day, he will learn Torah with the rich and deep understanding he has earned through his effort.[87]

It's natural to get discouraged when you look around and see your friends understanding the teacher without a problem while you're struggling to keep up. It seems unfair that after studying for hours, you get an 84% while another who barely studied got a 98%. This mishnah teaches that even when learning seems hard or even impossible, don't give up. Hashem sees your efforts, appreciates them, and will reward you.

 Sparks

Future Vision The Torah is Hashem's wisdom and far beyond the scope of human understanding. If so, what is the point of learning Torah when we'll never be able to fully understand its depth?

Think of a child born on a faraway island, isolated from civilization. His parents try to teach him about the world by drawing pictures of the wonders they remember. While he may not fully comprehend what the drawings are, when he finally reaches civilization, things will be familiar to him and he will understand exactly what his parents were trying to show him.

The same thing applies to learning Torah. By studying Torah now, even without fully comprehending what we're learning, when Mashiach comes and G-dliness is fully revealed, we will look back and say, "Oh! That's what it really means!"[88]

Biography

Rabi Yonasan bar Yosef was a student of Rabi Yishmael.

He was known for his piety and for his kindness to widows and orphans. He would maintain good ties with visiting officials in the hope that they would be more benevolent toward him if he needed a favor on behalf of a widow or orphan.[89]

He was also very careful about judging honestly. Once, a woman whom he was meant to judge brought him a case of figs as a gift. He requested that she take them with her in exactly the way she brought them in so that it would be clear that he did not accept even a part of it.[90]

Following the fall of Beitar, Rabi Yonasan ran away to the city of Hutzal, Bavel, where his friend Rabi Yoshiya was the rav, and lived there for much of the rest of his life. There, the two of them worked together to finalize the Mechilta, which was written by their Rebbe, Rabi Yishmael.

He lived a long life and some say that in his later years he was the teacher of the amora, Rabi Shmuel bar Nachmeini.

Did You Know?

Once This is the only reference to Rabi Yonasan in all of the Mishnah but he is often quoted in the Mechilta. The Mechilta was written by Rabi Yishmael, Rabi Yonasan's teacher, who quoted him often.

From Rags to Riches

The famous Rabi Akiva wasn't always famous. He began as a simple shepherd for the rich Kalba Savua. When Kalba Savua found out that his precious daughter Rochel had married this ignorant shepherd, he vowed never to give them any money at all. Akiva and Rochel were now terribly poor, and forced to sleep on straw. As he picked out the straw from his wife's hair each morning, he promised that one day she would wear a gold crown with an image of Yerushalayim engraved on it. He worked hard the whole day, gathering bundles of wood, half of which he sold and the other half he brought home to use for warmth and to light a fire so he could learn. Eventually, he went off to yeshivah for twenty-four years. When he returned, he was a learned and respected rabbi, and Kalba Savua deeply regretted the hasty vow he had made. He nullified his vow and gave Rabi Akiva and Rochel half of his money. Rabi Akiva also received large sums of money a number of times from different wealthy people. Rabi Akiva bought Rochel the gold crown he had promised her so long ago. His tables were made of silver and gold and he climbed up golden steps to get to his bed at night. Rochel was bedecked in jewelry and expensive clothing. Rabi Akiva declared that she deserved it all, because her sacrifice to live a difficult life of poverty allowed him to learn Torah and become the great scholar he was.[91]

Rabi Meir says: **Minimize** your **business activities and occupy** yourself **with Torah** learning.

Be humble before every person.

If you neglect Torah learning due to stress from business matters, **you will have** even less success in your business, giving you **many** more excuses to **neglect** Torah learning. Whereas **if you work very hard** to learn **Torah** despite any difficulties, **there is much reward for you.**

רַבִּי מֵאִיר אוֹמֵר: הֱוֵי מְמַעֵט בְּעֵסֶק וַעֲסוֹק בַּתּוֹרָה,

וֶהֱוֵי שְׁפַל רוּחַ בִּפְנֵי כָל אָדָם,

וְאִם בָּטַלְתָּ מִן הַתּוֹרָה, יֶשׁ לְךָ בְטֵלִים הַרְבֵּה כְּנֶגְדָּךְ,

וְאִם עָמַלְתָּ בַתּוֹרָה הַרְבֵּה, יֵשׁ שָׂכָר הַרְבֵּה לִתֶּן לָךְ.

The Greatest is Humility

How can a person honestly feel humble before everyone, even people who are clearly on a much lower level than him?

Realize that you can never know what factors exist in his life to make him act the way he does. You don't know how strong his yetzer hara is, what his family or work life is like, or other circumstances that influence him. If you were given his yetzer hara, upbringing, and circumstances, who knows how you would have performed! And if he was put in the exact situation as you, perhaps he would accomplish even more than you have![92]

A Greater Whole It's easier to feel humble when you remember that all Jews are compared to parts of one body. Just as every limb serves its important function, every single Jew is needed for the nation to be complete.

Not a Nine-to-Five Job
According to halachah, one who works all day can fulfill his obligation to learn Torah by designating time to learn before and after work. In this mishnah, Rabi Meir urges to go beyond the letter of the law and even take extra time from work to study Torah.

The two topics of the mishnah—minimizing your business dealings to make time for Torah, and feeling humble—seem entirely unconnected. In truth, however, the two are closely linked. Sincerely committing to the study of Torah makes one humble.[93] It is also a warning that even after achieving in Torah one must not become arrogant.[94]

וַעֲסוֹק בַּתּוֹרָה - The wording used in the mishnah is "וַעֲסוֹק בַּתּוֹרָה, involve yourself in Torah," which has the same root as the word עֵסֶק, meaning business. To be עוֹסֵק בַּתּוֹרָה means to be concerned with Torah learning at all times, constantly seeking ways to expand your knowledge just as a businessman constantly thinks about growing his business.[95]

Biography

Rabi Meir was one of the five greatest students of Rabi Akiva, and also a student of Rabi Yishmael and Elisha ben Avuyah.

A descendant of geirim, he became a great Talmid Chacham. He was one of Rebbi's great teachers, and in fact any halachah mentioned in Mishnayos without a name is from Rabi Meir. He married Bruriah, the daughter of Rabi Chanina ben Tradyon.

During the times of the Roman persecution following the fall of Beitar, Bruriah's parents were killed and her sister was taken captive. Wanting to save his sister-in-law, Rabi Meir disguised himself as a Roman horseman and tried to bribe the prison guard with a bag of gold to let her free. The guard didn't want to accept it because he knew he would be punished severely when the girl was found to be missing.

"Take half the money for yourself and use the other half to bribe your superiors," Rabi Meir advised.

"And what happens when the money is used up?" the guard retorted.

"Call out, 'אֱלָקָא דְמֵאִיר עֲנֵנִי (G-d of Meir, help me!)' and you will be saved," Rabi Meir answered. Seeing that the guard was not convinced, Rabi Meir strode over to the pack of vicious dogs stationed nearby. Excited at their new prey, they jumped to tear him apart, until Rabi Meir called out, "אֱלָקָא דְמֵאִיר עֲנֵנִי!" and the dogs miraculously retreated. Finally impressed, the guard set Rabi Meir's sister-in-law free.

In short order the guard was caught for his deed and sentenced to be hanged. As the rope was being tightened around his neck, he called out the phrase Rabi Meir had taught him and the rope broke. It was from this story that Rabi Meir earned the title "Rabi Meir Ba'al Haness."[96]

Rabi Meir passed away in Turkey while visiting there, and is buried in Teveriah.[97]

Behind the Quote

Rabi Meir was known for his sharp wisdom. It is said about him that "It is clear to the Creator that there is nobody equal in greatness and sharpness to Rabi Meir in his generation."[98] His love for Torah was so strong that even after his teacher, Acher, left the path of Torah and mitzvos, Rabi Meir continued to learn from him. In this mishnah, Rabi Meir extols the virtues of learning Torah.

Story

In the Lion's Den

The Ohr Hachaim was not only a brilliant Talmid Chacham but a talented goldsmith as well. However, he only worked until he had exactly the money he needed, and then sat and learned Torah, refusing to take any other orders until his money ran out.

One day he received a request from the king to make all the jewelry for his daughter's upcoming wedding. The Ohr Hachaim could not refuse the king's request, but since he had enough money, he continued learning and delayed the job. As the wedding drew closer, the king sent a messenger to pick up the jewelry, but the Ohr Hachaim had not even begun working on it! When the king heard this, he was furious, and decreed that the Ohr Hachaim be thrown into the lion's den.

The Ohr Hachaim calmly accepted the decree. He took along his tefillin and some sefarim, and was thrown into the den. Three days later, the guard returned to the lion's den, expecting to clean up a corpse. Instead he was shocked to find the Ohr Hachaim sitting and learning while the lions sat peacefully around him.

Upon hearing what happened, the king realized that he was dealing with a great and holy man, and ordered the guards to free the Ohr Hachaim immediately. He fell on his knees, begging forgiveness, and sent the Ohr Hachaim home with many gifts and deepest apologies.[99]

Rabi Eliezer ben Yaakov says: A person who does one mitzvah acquires one supporting angel **for himself,** who will defend him to the Heavenly Court, **and one who transgresses one aveirah acquires one accusing** angel **for himself,** who will tell Hashem about his aveirah. **Teshuvah and good deeds protect against punishment**.

Rabi Yochanan Hasandlar says: Any gathering that is held **for the sake of Heaven will** have a **lasting** effect, but any gathering **that is not** held **for the sake of Heaven will not** have a **lasting** effect.

רַבִּי אֱלִיעֶזֶר בֶּן יַעֲקֹב אוֹמֵר: הָעוֹשֶׂה מִצְוָה אַחַת, קוֹנֶה לוֹ פְּרַקְלִיט אֶחָד, וְהָעוֹבֵר עֲבֵרָה אַחַת, קוֹנֶה לוֹ קַטֵּגוֹר אֶחָד, תְּשׁוּבָה וּמַעֲשִׂים טוֹבִים כִּתְרִיס בִּפְנֵי הַפּוּרְעָנוּת.

רַבִּי יוֹחָנָן הַסַּנְדְּלָר אוֹמֵר: כָּל כְּנֵסִיָּה שֶׁהִיא לְשֵׁם שָׁמַיִם סוֹפָהּ לְהִתְקַיֵּם, וְשֶׁאֵינָהּ לְשֵׁם שָׁמַיִם אֵין סוֹפָהּ לְהִתְקַיֵּם.

Every Action Counts

Every action, no matter how big or small, has consequences. Don't pass up doing a good thing because it seems small, because every good action creates a defending angel.[100] The Rambam writes, "Think of the world as a perfectly balanced scale, so that any single action you do tips the scales one way or another!"[101]

Never Too Late

This mishnah teaches that despite negative behavior in the past, one always has a chance to do teshuvah and reach the greatest heights.[102] The Gemara tells about Rabi Elazar ben Durdaya, who left the path of Torah and transgressed every possible aveirah. After a while, he regretted his mistakes and cried bitter tears of teshuvah until his neshamah left his body. A Heavenly voice proclaimed that Rabi Elazar ben Durdaya would receive a portion in Olam Haba. When Rabi Yehudah Hanassi heard this, he cried out, "See how a person can earn his entire world in one moment!"[103]

Higher Purpose

Disagreements are natural because all people are different. A higher purpose like Torah keeps peace, because the individual opinions don't matter as much anymore when compared to the greater goal.[104]

 Word Power

פְּרַקְלִיט The word פְּרַקְלִיט can be split into two Aramaic words: פְּרַק לִיט – remove the curse. When we do a good deed, we succeed in removing negativity from ourselves.[105]

Biography

Rabi Eliezer ben Yaakov was a student of Rabi Akiva and a colleague of Rabi Meir, and was known as an expert in the halachos of the Beis Hamikdash. He had a student who was a great Talmid Chacham but became sick and forgot all his learning. Rabi Eliezer ben Yaakov davened for him and his memory returned.[106]

Rabi Yochanan Hasandlar was a student of Rabi Akiva and is considered one of the greatest authorities on his teachings.[107] He is called "Hasandlar" since he was a shoemaker by trade, and also because he came from the city of Alexandria (אֲלֶכְּסַנְדְּרִיָא), which sounds similar.

Once, a discussion came up whether chalitzah done without witnesses was kosher. The students wanted to ask Rabi Akiva, but he was already imprisoned by the Romans. Rabi Yochanan dressed up as a peddler and stood outside the prison selling needles and pipes. Amid his calls, he disguised the question. "Who wants needles? Who wants pipes? If chalitzah is done just between him and her, what is its status? Who wants needles? Who wants pipes?" Hearing the peddler's calls and understanding the question, Rabi Akiva asked, "Do you have kushin (skewers)? Do you have kosher?" Since the two words sounded so similar, Rabi Akiva's answer was safely disguised.[108]

Behind the Quote

Rabi Eliezer ben Yaakov once saw a blind stranger in town and noticed that no one was helping him. Rabi Eliezer sat down next to him, and just as he hoped, people assumed the blind man was an important person and gave him money and food. The blind man was happily surprised and asked the people why they were being so generous. "Because we saw Rabi Eliezer sitting next to you," they replied. The blind man sought out Rabi Eliezer and blessed him, "Just as you were kind to one who is seen but cannot see, may Hashem, Who sees but cannot be seen, show kindness to you."[109] In this mishnah, Rabi Eliezer teaches that every mitzvah creates a supportive angel for you.

Story

Mitzvos Protect

There was once a chassid of the Rebbe Rashab, the fifth Lubavitcher Rebbe, who would always seek the Rebbe's brachah before embarking on a business trip. Once, he was scheduled to travel over Chanukah. "Make sure to take extra-long candles with you," the Rebbe advised. The chassid was puzzled but did as the Rebbe requested. His journey took him through dark forests that presented danger at every turn. Night was falling and the chassid urged his horse through the trees, hoping to make it to an inn before it became too dark. Suddenly, four armed men appeared from the darkness and ordered him to stop. The frightened chassid silently complied, and to his horror, they rummaged through his belongings and took all his valuables. "Now we're going to kill you," they informed him carelessly. The chassid begged for mercy, to no avail.

"At least allow me one favor before I die, and let me light my candles" he pleaded. The robbers reluctantly agreed.

He lit his extra-long candles and began to chant the brachos. He sang by the light of the menorah with tears streaming down his face. The thieves were so busy counting their pickings, they were oblivious to the sound of hoof beats steadily approaching. A few minutes later, the surprised ruffians were arrested by the local police and the chassid was set free. The captain handed him a large sack of money and told him, "We've been trying to catch this gang for years. We were finally able to get them thanks to your lights. The reward money rightfully belongs to you." The chassid immediately traveled back to the Rebbe and thanked him for his life-saving advice.

Rabi Elazar ben Shamua says: Your student's honor should be as dear to you as your own honor, **your friend's honor** as important **as the awe** and respect you have **for your teacher, and** the **awe** and respect you have **for your teacher** should be **as** great as the **awe** and respect you have for Hashem in **heaven**.

רַבִּי אֶלְעָזָר בֶּן שַׁמּוּעַ אוֹמֵר: יְהִי כְבוֹד תַּלְמִידְךָ חָבִיב עָלֶיךָ כְּשֶׁלָּךְ, וּכְבוֹד חֲבֵרְךָ כְּמוֹרָא רַבָּךְ, וּמוֹרָא רַבָּךְ כְּמוֹרָא שָׁמָיִם.

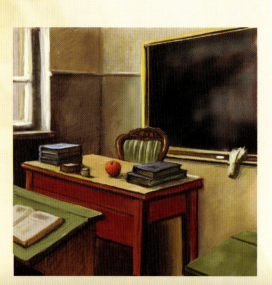

Due: Respect

There are many halachos describing the honor due to a teacher of Torah. One may not argue with them and must speak and act respectfully when learning with them. One may not call a teacher by his first name or sit in his seat.

When the passuk says "אֶת ה' אֱלֹקֶיךָ תִּירָא" - You should fear Hashem your G-d," the word "אֶת" is there to add that teachers must be revered as well. The fact that it comes from a command to fear Hashem shows us that our respect for teachers should be similar to our respect for Hashem!

Did You Know?

Like Yehoshua and Moshe We can learn respect for a student from the way Moshe treated Yehoshua. When preparing to fight Amalek, he told Yehoshua, "Let's choose men for ourselves," rather than "choose men for me," addressing Yehoshua as an equal.

We can learn how to respect a teacher from the way Yehoshua respected Moshe. When Eldad and Meidad spoke against Moshe, Yehoshua asked Moshe to destroy them, as if they had spoken against Hashem.[110]

Word Power

מוֹרָא רַבָּךְ כְּמוֹרָא שָׁמָיִם Arguing with a teacher of Torah is like arguing with Hashem. Becoming angry at a teacher is like becoming angry at Hashem, and doubting a teacher is like doubting Hashem.[111]

Biography

Rabi Elazar ben Shamua was a student of Rabi Akiva and one of five talmidim to receive semichah from Rabi Yehudah ben Bava. Whenever the Mishnah quotes Rabi Elazar without specifying which one, it refers to Rabi Elazar ben Shamua. He was one of the main teachers of Rebbi, who quotes many things in his name.

Once, he decided to travel to learn Torah from the great Rabi Yehudah ben Beseirah, who lived outside of Eretz Yisrael. When he reached Tzidon, however, the pain of leaving Eretz Yisrael was too strong for him to bear. He tore his clothes and cried out, "Living in Eretz Yisrael is equivalent to keeping all the mitzvos!" and he turned back.[112]

He was such a great teacher that each amah of the Beis Medrash was occupied by six people squeezed together, each determined not to miss a word of his lecture.[113]

He passed away at the age of 105 and never said an unkind word to anyone in all those years. He also fasted for 80 years. When asked what he did to deserve such a long life, he replied that it was in the merit of three things: he never used the Beis Medrash as a shortcut, he came early or sat outside to avoid having to step over students' heads to reach the front, and he never gave birkas kohanim (he was a kohen) without saying a brachah first.[114]

He was one of the Asarah Harugei Malchus. It was Erev Shabbos when the order of his execution was given. He was in middle of Kiddush, and reached the words "asher bara Elokim" and with the word Elokim on his lips, he was brutally killed. A bas kol rang out, "Fortunate are you, Elazar, who resembled Hashem in his life and whose soul departed with Hashem's name on his lips."

 Sparks

Revere My Officers The Midrash says that revering Talmidei Chachamim brings a person to have more yiras Shamayim, a feeling of awe and respect for Hashem Himself.[115]

 **Behind the Quote**

Rabi Elazar was one of the five survivors of the plague that wiped out Rabi Akiva's students.[116] Having seen the devastating results of disrespecting people, Rabi Elazar teaches about the importance of properly honoring your colleague.[117]

 **Story**

Mystery Husband

A woman once came to Rabi Meir with a terrible dilemma. One of Rabi Meir's students had betrothed her in a way that was halachically problematic, but she didn't know who it was. Now she couldn't marry anyone else, since she was betrothed and needed a get, but she had no idea from whom to demand it from. Rabi Meir wanted to help her, but he also didn't want to embarrass any of his students. Instead, he came up with an amazing strategy to free her. He wrote out a get for her in his own name and, of course, all his students followed suit. Among the many that she received was one from her real betrothed, who was able to divorce her according to halachah, without revealing his identity.[118]

Rabi Yehudah says: Be careful to learn and teach Torah correctly, because if your incorrect learning causes the unintentional transgression of an aveirah, it will be considered intentional.

Rabi Shimon says: Respect those who possess any of these three crowns: the crown of Torah, possessed by Talmidei Chachamim, the crown of kehunah, possessed by kohanim, and the crown of kingship, possessed by kings.

However, there is another crown of respect—the crown of having a good name and reputation—which is higher and greater than the other three.

רַבִּי יְהוּדָה אוֹמֵר: הֱוֵי זָהִיר בְּתַלְמוּד, שֶׁשִּׁגְגַת תַּלְמוּד עוֹלָה זָדוֹן.

רַבִּי שִׁמְעוֹן אוֹמֵר, שְׁלֹשָׁה כְתָרִים הֵן: כֶּתֶר תּוֹרָה, וְכֶתֶר כְּהֻנָּה, וְכֶתֶר מַלְכוּת,

וְכֶתֶר שֵׁם טוֹב עוֹלֶה עַל גַּבֵּיהֶן.

Blinding Oneself

A man was once warned not to walk on a certain path because of the many pits and dangers there. After thinking for a moment, the man asked for a cloth to cover his eyes. "This way, if I fall into a hole, no one can blame me because my eyes were covered!" he explained.

"Fool!" the others told him. "You have eyes. Why would you place yourself in danger by covering them?"

The yetzer hara tries to trick us into doing the same thing. He tells us to "tie a cloth" over our eyes and remain ignorant about what the Torah commands us. He reasons that this way, if we fall and sin we won't be held responsible since we didn't know. Of course, that idea is all wrong, because ignorance is no excuse for one who had the opportunity to learn.[119]

 Connections

Another version of this mishnah reads, "An innocent error by a student is counted as an intentional sin (by the teacher)." The previous mishnah spoke about treating students with respect. This mishnah adds that treating a student with respect shouldn't interfere with discipline or high expectations. A teacher who does is held accountable for the student's mistake.[120]

 Word Power

זָהִיר The word הֱוֵי זָהִיר בְּתַלְמוּד also means to shine. This mishnah is also saying that a teacher should make sure his lesson shines clear and bright, without room for misunderstanding.[121]

Biography

Rabi Yehudah bar Ilai was a student of Rabi Tarfon and Rabi Akiva and received semichah from Rabi Yehudah ben Bava. He is the most frequently mentioned tanna in the entire Mishnayos, often referred to simply as Rabi Yehudah (a name that refers to him unless stated otherwise). Whenever the mishnah tells of a chassid without specifying who it is, it refers to either Rabi Yehudah bar Ilai or Rabi Yehudah ben Bava.[122] Although he was such a great and respeced teacher, it did not prevent him from dancing in front of kallahs with a myrtle branch and praising their beauty at their weddings.[123]

He once spoke favorably about the wicked Roman government and in appreciation, the Romans established a law that he should be the first to speak at all Jewish gatherings.[124]

One Shabbos, while walking through his vineyard, he noticed a breach in the fence, which caused him to speculate about fixing it during the week. Immediately he regretted thinking about mundane actions on Shabbos and committed to never patch the hole, as an atonement for what was considered a transgression for someone on his level. Hashem was pleased with his actions, and a tree with valuable produce began to grow in that very location. It filled the breach and at the same time supplied a livelihood for Rabi Yehudah for the remainder of his life.[125]

Story
You Gotta Know

R' Chaim of Sanz once heard about a man in a certain city who had a very hard life with no one to help him. He contacted the rav of that town and asked him why he had done nothing to help the man.

"I had no idea how terrible his circumstances were," the rav said.

"That's no excuse!" R' Chaim rebuked him. "A rav needs to know the situation of everyone in his city! Not knowing is in itself a sin!"[129]

Behind the Quote

Rabi Shimon bar Yochai had a spark of Moshe Rabbeinu's neshamah. For this reason Rabi Shimon speaks of three great qualities, or crowns, which Moshe Rabbeinu possessed: He was king over the Jewish people, he served as a kohen during the dedication of the mishkan, and the Torah was given through him. Of course, he also had the crown of a good name.[126]

Did You Know?

Tough Talmud The mishnah gives an extra warning not to make a mistake when learning Gemara (Talmud). Since it requires more independent thought than Chumash and Mishnah, extra care is required.[127]

Three Crowns The three crowns of Rabi Shimon are three things that warrant value and respect. A Talmid Chacham—one who has acquired the crown of Torah—should be treated as though he is wearing a physical crown. The same applies to a kohen and a king. Someone with a "good name" deserves the most honor of all.[128]

Sparks
Actually, Four Crowns

The mishnah actually lists four crowns when a good name is included, so why does it begin with the statement that there are three crowns?

One of the reasons given is that this fourth crown cannot be acquired on its own. The crown of a good name depends on having one of the first three crowns. This is learned from the wording in the mishnah, which says עוֹלָה עַל גַּבֵּיהֶן, literally meaning "rises on their backs." The crown of a good name is only acquired along with another crown.[130] In order to acquire a good name, a person must either study Torah, be like a kohen who is meticulous in his service of Hashem, or be as a king who rules fairly.[131]

Rabi Nehora'i says: If there are no other Torah students where you live, **exile** yourself **to a place** of **Torah** learning. **Do not say that** you will remain and wait for other Torah students to **follow you, because** it is vital to have **fellow** Torah students nearby with whom to discuss your studies, as only they **will establish** Torah **within you.**

Do not rely on your own **understanding.**

רַבִּי נְהוֹרַאי אוֹמֵר: הֱוֵי גוֹלֶה לִמְקוֹם תּוֹרָה, וְאַל תֹּאמַר שֶׁהִיא תָבוֹא אַחֲרֶיךָ, שֶׁחֲבֵרֶיךָ יְקַיְּמוּהָ בְיָדֶךָ, וְאֶל בִּינָתְךָ אַל תִּשָּׁעֵן.

Environmentally Friendly

People are affected greatly by where they are and whom they are around. Being around a happy and cheerful person makes you feel refreshed and happy, while meeting an angry person might make you feel upset and angry.

We all want friends. But sometimes, we need to stop and think: Who are the people I want to be friends with? Will it be good for me if I become friends with this person? Will I learn from their good ways, or will I end up worse off? Will I be warmed by their middos and kindness, or will I be hurt by their arrogance and selfishness?

Imagine yourself in the sun. Its light and warmth are working their magic on you, and you feel great. This is what good people are like. Their goodness shines out of them, giving strength to others. Choosing your friends is like choosing between being in the warm sun or in the cold night. Our good friends bring out the best in us, and in the light of their wisdom and goodness, we are able to grow.

Connections

Torah was the first crown listed in the previous mishnah. This mishnah follows that theme by emphasizing the importance of Torah and urging everyone to occupy themselves with Torah, even if it means traveling to a distant city.[132]

Word Power

הֱוֵי גוֹלֶה The word used in this mishnah is גוֹלֶה – exile, which is the same term used when a person accidentally kills another and has to flee to an Ir Miklat. Just as the accidental killer flees immediately to save himself from the victim's avengers, so must one feel the urgent need to exile oneself for the sake of Torah.[133]

Biography

Rabi Nehora'i is called by this name because Nehora'i in Aramaic means light, and he was famous for enlightening the eyes of the Chachamim with his teachings of halachah. In fact, Eliyahu Hanavi would often come to his Beis Medrash to learn Torah with him.[134] However, his true identity is highly disputed. Some say he is Rabi Meir Ba'al Haness, some say it is Rabi Nechemiah, student of Rabi Akiva, and others say it is Rabi Elazar ben Arach.[135]

Sparks

Why Exile? The term exile is usually associated with a negative experience. Why does the mishnah use this word to describe going to a place of Torah?

One reason for this is that Torah learning doesn't require a place with all physical comforts like at home. In fact, exiling yourself to a place with limited physical comfort will help you succeed in learning Torah.[136]

Using this term also teaches that if necessary, one must wander from place to place like a person in exile, until he finds an appropriate place of Torah.[137]

Learn from Talmidei Chachamim One might think that exiling yourself to a place of Torah means to isolate yourself. The mishnah therefore continues with a warning against this: don't wait for Torah to follow you, or be tempted to rely on your own understanding. Rather, go to a place of Talmidei Chachamim and seek guidance from them.[138]

Behind the Quote

Rabi Elazar ben Arach lived in a city where people regularly indulged in whatever they desired. Influenced by this attitude, he followed them until he forgot all his learning. According to the opinion that Rabi Elazar ben Aruch is Rabi Nehora'i (see Biography), that is why he advises exiling yourself to a place of Torah so that you will be positively influenced by your surroundings.[139]

Although Rabi Nehora'i was a great and famous teacher, he understood the dangers of relying on one's own wisdom and cautions us about it as well.[140]

Did You Know?

Sharpener When metal rubs against metal, it becomes sharper. When two people discuss a topic together, their understanding becomes clearer and sharper.[141]

Alone it Doesn't Last

Rabi Elazar ben Arach was known as a flowing spring of Torah learning in Yavneh. His wife wanted to move to the cities of Diyumeses and Perugaysa, which were beautiful and known for their excellent wine and clear waters. Once there, Rabi Elazar hoped that some of his friends would follow him so they could continue to learn together. As time passed and none of his colleagues came, Rabi Elazar suggested moving back to Yavneh. "Tell me," his wife asked him, "do you need them or do they need you?" "They need me," Rabi Elazar admitted. "When you have a mouse and a container of food," she continued, "the mouse obviously goes to the food. If they need you, they'll come to you. You don't need to go to them." Rabi Elazar listened to her and they continued living there. Over time, Rabi Elazar forgot all his learning. When they finally returned to Yavneh, he was given an Aliyah at the Torah. Instead of reading "הַחוֹדֶשׁ הַזֶּה לָכֶם," he read "הַחֵרֵשׁ הָיָה לִבָּם—their hearts were deaf." Seeing his great embarrassment at his inability to read, his colleagues davened for him and he remembered his learning.[142]

Rabi Yannai says: **We are unable** to understand **neither** the reason why **wicked people** have **peace nor** the reason for **the suffering of righteous people**.

Rabi Masya ben Charash says: Be the **first to greet everyone**, and do not wait for them to greet you.

Better **be a tail**—a humble follower—**of lions**—great people, **and do not be a leader of foxes**—low people.

רַבִּי יַנַּאי אוֹמֵר: אֵין בְּיָדֵינוּ לֹא מִשַּׁלְוַת הָרְשָׁעִים, וְאַף לֹא מִיִּסּוּרֵי הַצַּדִּיקִים.

רַבִּי מַתְיָא בֶּן חָרָשׁ אוֹמֵר: הֱוֵי מַקְדִּים בִּשְׁלוֹם כָּל אָדָם,

וֶהֱוֵי זָנָב לָאֲרָיוֹת, וְאַל תְּהִי רֹאשׁ לַשּׁוּעָלִים.

Living Lessons

Follow the Leader …or Not

Being popular among friends is very tempting, but the mishnah warns us that leadership is not always a good thing. It's still always better to be a "tail of lions," a simple follower of good people who are doing the right thing, than even to be a "head of the foxes," lowly people who will follow you blindly.[143]

 Connections

The two teachings of Rabi Masya in this mishnah are actually connected. Although in general it is proper to greet others first, when it comes to the lions, the Chachamim, one should be like the tail, and wait respectfully for them to greet us before starting a conversation.[144]

 Sparks

Walk With the Wise Shlomoh Hamelech teaches, "הוֹלֵךְ אֶת חֲכָמִים יֶחְכָּם, וְרֹעֶה כְסִילִים יֵרוֹעַ – One who walks with the wise will grow wise, but one who accompanies fools will become broken." Our mishnah teaches the same lesson: it is better to spend time with Chachamim than with fools. Even if we are insignificant compared to the Chachamim, we stand to gain from their wisdom.[145]

Strong as a Lion The lion is the king of the jungle. A fox, on the other hand, is a sly creature that uses trickery to accomplish its goals. These animals represent two approaches to learning Torah. The mishnah advises us to be like a lion and put in all our effort, even if we fall short and reach only the level of its tail, rather than mastering the skills of the fox, finding shortcuts and excuses for inadequate accomplishments.[146]

Biography

Rabi Yannai is mentioned only once in the Mishnah. He was a student of Rebbi, later becoming a member of his Beis Din, and helped to finalize the Mishnah, and was a teacher of Rav and Rabi Yochanan.

Rabi Yannai heard of a certain merchant who offered a lifesaving potion. Eager to acquire it for himself, he requested that the merchant come to him. "Where is the potion?" Rabi Yannai asked.

"מִי הָאִישׁ הֶחָפֵץ חַיִּים – Who is the man who desires life with goodness?" the merchant quoted from Tehillim. "נְצֹר לְשׁוֹנְךָ מֵרָע וּשְׂפָתֶיךָ מִדַּבֵּר מִרְמָה – Guard your tongue from speaking evil and your lips from telling lies."

"I say that passuk every day," Rabi Yannai exclaimed, "but I never understood it at this basic level until now."[147]

Rabi Masya ben Charash was a student of Rabi Yishmael and opened the biggest yeshivah of his time in Rome. He always guarded his eyes from seeing immodest things, and as a reward, his face shone like an angel. The Satan once tried to test him and appeared before him in the form of a beautiful woman. Rabi Masya looked away but the Satan confronted him again. He asked his students for some nails and blinded himself. The malach Refael wanted to heal him immediately but Rabi Masya refused until he was promised that he would be free from the temptations of the yetzer hara.[148]

Behind the Quote

Rabi Yannai was one of the last of the Tannaim and lived after the destruction of the second Beis Hamikdash.[149] The Romans were in control and they mercilessly persecuted Jews, including many Tzaddikim. This may be the reason he ponders the treatment of reshaim and Tzaddikim.

Did You Know?

Don't Look Back The fox is known as an animal that's always looking back. "Do not be a head to foxes" means not to look down upon those who are behind you when it comes to their service of Hashem. Every fellow Jew should be treated with equal respect.[150]

We See But Through a Keyhole

Rabi Yehoshua ben Levi begged Eliyahu Hanavi to let him accompany him on his journeys. "You won't be able to handle it," Eliyahu tried to dissuade him, "since you won't understand why I do certain things." But Rabi Yehoshua ben Levi insisted, so Eliyahu Hanavi reluctantly agreed.

"Just don't ask me why I do what I do," Eliyahu warned him, "for if you ask, I will tell you, but you won't be able to continue on with me."

Their first stop was at the home of a poor but kind and hospitable couple. They owned nothing much of value other than a single cow, which they used for its milk. As they left, Eliyahu Hanavi davened that the cow should die, and it instantly dropped dead.

That night, they met a stingy, snobby rich man who didn't as much as offer them anything to eat or drink. A wall on his property had fallen and was waiting to be repaired. Eliyahu Hanavi davened that it be rebuilt, and so it was.

Rabi Yehoshua contained himself with difficulty at these strange occurrences. Soon they approached another city whose residents were arrogant and unwelcoming. Eliyahu Hanavi blessed them that they all become leaders. The next city they came to was filled with pious, generous citizens and Eliyahu Hanavi blessed them to have but one great leader.

By now, Rabi Yehoshua's bewilderment was too much and he burst out, "Please explain your actions."

"Very well," Eliyahu Hanavi replied. "The poor woman of the first house was slated to die that day, so I prayed that Hashem kill the cow instead and spare the good woman's life. The rich man who treated us so rudely had a large treasure buried under that wall that he would have discovered had he fixed the wall himself."

"And what about your strange brachos?" Rabi Yehoshua persisted.

"Having many leaders is really a curse," Eliyahu Hanavi explained, "since everyone's opinions and egos cause arguments. Having just one leader whose opinion is accepted by everyone brings peace and harmony to the city."[151]

Rabi Yaakov says: This world is like the entrance hall to the World to Come. Prepare yourself in this world, the entrance hall, by doing mitzvos, so that you may enter the main banquet hall—the World to Come.

רַבִּי יַעֲקֹב אוֹמֵר: הָעוֹלָם הַזֶּה דּוֹמֶה לִפְרוֹזְדוֹר בִּפְנֵי הָעוֹלָם הַבָּא, הַתְקֵן עַצְמְךָ בִּפְרוֹזְדוֹר כְּדֵי שֶׁתִּכָּנֵס לִטְרַקְלִין.

Living Lessons

Waiting for the Banquet

This world is compared to a foyer, or entrance hall, of Olam Haba, the banquet hall. Some of the reasons for this include:

1. A banquet hall is larger than its foyer, just as Olam Haba is bigger than this world.[152]
2. The pleasures of a foyer are really minor compared to a banquet hall, similar to the pleasures of this world, which pale in comparison to Olam Haba.[153]
3. The time spent in the foyer is shorter than the time in the banquet hall. So too, our time in this world is short, relative to the eternity of Olam Haba.[154]
4. The decor in the foyer is simple compared to the banquet hall. So is the beauty of this world incomparable to the beauty of Olam Haba.[155]
5. Much more time and resources are invested in the hall, rather than in the foyer. In the same way there is so much more value in concentrating on amassing the treasures of Olam Haba than in the empty values of this world.[156]
6. The foyer is but one step from the street and therefore receives all the incoming dirt, while the banquet hall itself remains pristine. So is Olam Haba untainted by the physicality of this world.[157]
7. The foyer is never the ultimate destination. So too, this world is not an end to itself, but merely a stop on the way to Olam Haba, our true purpose.[158]

Connections

This is the same Rabi Yaakov who is quoted earlier in the previous perek. The reason this mishnah is quoted here, rather than together with his other sayings, is because it is connected to the theme of the previous mishnah. The previous mishnah discusses how the hardships of Tzaddikim in this world may not seem fair, and this mishnah reminds us that it is because in truth it's only a preparation for their true reward in Olam Haba.[159]

Word Power

הַתְקֵן עַצְמְךָ The word הַתְקֵן comes from the word תִּיקוּן, which means correction. At times, when a person does an aveirah, his yetzer hara might try to convince him that since now he has lost his Olam Haba anyway, he may as well continue doing aveiros. This mishnah tells us otherwise: הַתְקֵן עַצְמְךָ בִּפְרוֹזְדּוֹר—Correct yourself in the entrance hall so that you may indeed enter Olam Haba. It is never too late to earn your portion of Olam Haba by doing teshuvah and correcting your ways.[160]

Did You Know?

The Future is Yet to Come The term עוֹלָם הַבָּא literally means the world to come. It can either refer to Gan Eden or to the future era of Mashiach, after techias hameisim.[161]

Sparks

Construction Our mission in this world is to transform it into a more permanent banquet hall for Hashem to reside. We accomplish this by learning Torah and doing mitzvos.

Erev Shabbos Erev Shabbos is a busy time because we are preparing for Shabbos. Just as every minute of Erev Shabbos is used to the utmost to prepare for Shabbos, every minute in this world should be spent energetically preparing for Olam Haba.[162]

On a Journey

The Ba'al Shem Tov once asked one of his chassidim to stop in Mezritch on his way home to give regards to one of his closest disciples, R' Dov Ber. When the chassid arrived in Mezritch, he was directed to a small, rickety hut in the poorest section of town. Upon entering, he found the house practically bare, save for a plank of wood on wooden blocks that served as a table. When he arrived, R' Dov Ber was glad to see him, but asked him to return after he had finished teaching his students. When the chassid returned, he saw that the makeshift table had now been converted into beds for R' Dov Ber's children.

This sight troubled the chassid greatly, and he burst out, "Listen, I may not be a rich man, but at least I have furnishings in my house! How do you live like this?"

"And where is your furniture now?" R' Dov Ber asked gently.

"I'm traveling!" the chassid protested. "I don't bring my furniture along with me on a journey!"

"I too am on a journey," R' Dov Ber explained. "This world is only a stop on the way to Olam Haba."[163]

Rabi Yaakov would often say: One hour of teshuvah and good deeds in this world is superior to all of life in the World to Come, because once there, one cannot do teshuvah and good deeds.

Yet one hour of pleasure in the World to Come is better than all the life of this world, because one cannot enjoy Hashem's presence in this world as one can in the World to Come.

הוּא הָיָה אוֹמֵר: יָפָה שָׁעָה אַחַת בִּתְשׁוּבָה וּמַעֲשִׂים טוֹבִים בָּעוֹלָם הַזֶּה, מִכָּל חַיֵּי הָעוֹלָם הַבָּא, וְיָפָה שָׁעָה אַחַת שֶׁל קוֹרַת רוּחַ בָּעוֹלָם הַבָּא, מִכָּל חַיֵּי הָעוֹלָם הַזֶּה.

Don't Underestimate

This mishnah seems to contradict itself, on one hand saying this world is better, but right away saying the same about the next world. The answer is that each world has an advantage over the other, which is explained by the different terms used to describe each world's advantage. The opportunity to connect to Hashem exists only in this world, through performing mitzvos. Even a single moment of teshuvah and good deeds forges a connection to Hashem on a deeper level than an entire life in Olam Haba.

Once there, however, we are able to enjoy the reward of our actions, a far greater satisfaction than any pleasures this world can offer. So, while this world has more *opportunity* to connect to Hashem, the actual *enjoyment* of that connection is far greater in the next world.[164]

It is told that when Mashiach comes, or in Gan Eden, we will yearn for the chance to fulfill Hashem's mitzvos as we did at the time of galus, and bemoan every second we wasted while we had the chance. Let's seize every opportunity now to do mitzvos and acquire benefits in both worlds: a bond with Hashem in this world, and the reward for that connection in the World to Come.

Did You Know?

Teshuvah is for Everyone Teshuvah is often thought of as something that is done only when one fails to fulfill a mitzvah, yet here the mishnah lists it first. This is because teshuvah, which means to return, also refers to our neshama's desire to return to Hashem. Arousing this yearning is an avodah that applies to everyone, even Tzaddikim who have never sinned. This thirst to be close to Him is even more precious to Hashem than just doing good deeds, and is therefore mentioned first.[165]

No Presents?

R' Moshe Leib of Sassov once returned home from a long journey. His children started pestering him for presents but R' Moshe Leib had not brought back any. "Tatte, when you go on a long journey, you're supposed to come back with something! Why didn't you bring anything?" Hearing their entreaties, R' Moshe Leib fainted.

When he awoke, his wife asked him, "Why did you faint? Have you never before heard children ask for something?"

"I heard the deeper message of their question," R' Moshe Leib explained. "When I go up to heaven, they will also ask me, 'You've just returned from a long journey. Why didn't you bring back anything?' I'll have nothing to show them for all my years spent on earth. That is why I fainted."[167]

Connections

After learning in the previous mishnah that this world is merely an entranceway to the real world, one might assume that everything in this world is unimportant. Rabi Yaakov elaborates in this mishnah and advises us to spend our time in this world wisely, because we will no longer have the same opportunities in Olam Haba.[166]

Sparks

Pale Pleasures Though Hashem certainly rewards us for every mitzvah we do, this mishnah teaches that the reward is not the most important thing. All of the pleasures of Olam Haba are not as important as our main purpose in this world—to create a home for Hashem by doing teshuvah and good deeds.

Rabi Shimon ben Elazar says: **Do not** try to **calm your friend in the** heated **moment of his anger,** because you might only make him angrier. **Do not comfort him while his dead** relative is still **lying before him,** because he cannot be comforted at that time. **Do not ask him, as soon as he makes a promise,** if he will fulfill it without any conditions, because if he says yes, he will have to keep to his word and may later regret the decision. **Do not try to see him when he is disgraced,** because it will only embarrass him further.

רַבִּי שִׁמְעוֹן בֶּן אֶלְעָזָר אוֹמֵר: אַל תְּרַצֶּה אֶת חֲבֵרְךָ בְּשַׁעַת כַּעֲסוֹ, וְאַל תְּנַחֲמֶהוּ בְּשָׁעָה שֶׁמֵּתוֹ מֻטָּל לְפָנָיו, וְאַל תִּשְׁאַל לוֹ בְּשַׁעַת נִדְרוֹ, וְאַל תִּשְׁתַּדֵּל לִרְאוֹתוֹ בְּשַׁעַת קַלְקָלָתוֹ.

Stop, Think, Speak

Sometimes, even the best intentions can have a negative or hurtful effect. The mishnah gives four examples of good deeds that can result in the opposite of the intended effect if performed at the wrong time. Consoling someone who is grieving is a wonderful thing to do, but if you try to reassure him just after the sad event took place, he will feel that you don't truly understand what he is going through and your words of comfort won't help. Before you speak, try to think what would make the **other** person feel better at that moment, rather than what will feel good for you to say.[168]

 Connections

Some might take the lessons of the previous mishnayos too literally and rush to do any mitzvah they can think of in any way they can. Therefore Rabi Shimon warns us in this mishnah to be cautious because some mitzvos can be harmful if done too early.[169]

 Sparks

A Time and Place for Everything
Shlomoh Hamelech writes in Mishlei,[170] "שִׂמְחָה לָאִישׁ בְּמַעֲנֵה פִיו, וְדָבָר בְּעִתּוֹ מַה טּוֹב" – A man is gladdened through the reply of his mouth, and how good is a word in its time!" Words can be moving and powerful—if spoken at the right time.[171]

 **Did You Know?**

Doesn't Count When a person wrongs another, he is obligated to ask for forgiveness three times. After three attempts, however, even if he does not succeed in appeasing his friend, he is freed of his obligation. However, if any of the attempts were made while the other was angry, they are not counted, since speaking to another in his time of anger is futile.[172]

Biography

Rabi Shimon ben Elazar was one of the greatest students of Rabi Meir and a colleague of Rabi Yehudah Hanassi. The identity of his father is unknown, although some say that he was Rabi Elazar of Bartosa.

Another Tanna, Rabi Shimon the son of Rebbi, once had a halachic question that no one could answer, until Rabi Shimon ben Elazar came along with the solution. He explained that he knew the answer because he had served Rabi Meir when he was hiding from the Romans and witnessed him doing something similar.[173]

Rabi Shimon lived to such an old age that Rabi Shmuel bar Nachmeini, an Amora, remembered seeing him.[174]

Behind the Quote

Rabi Shimon learned the hard way how important it is to be sensitive to others' feelings. Once, on a return journey from yeshivah, he met a very ugly man who stopped to greet him. Instead of returning the greeting, Rabi Shimon asked him why he was so ugly. "Go ask the One who made me," the man replied. Rabi Shimon then realized what a terrible thing he had said and fell on his knees begging for forgiveness. Not only did the man refuse, he told all the people who had come to greet Rabi Shimon, "You think he is a great man? May there be no more great men like him!" and told them all what had happened. The people begged him to forgive Rabi Shimon, which he finally did. Rabi Shimon then delivered a lecture, exhorting the people to be kind and accepting of all others.[175]

Sparks

Private Avodah The mishnah advises us not to seek out a person in the time of his disgrace. When a person commits an aveirah, he is naturally filled with shame. This is part of the process of teshuvah. While it is a necessary and important step, it is a private matter, and others should not attempt to be present and embarrass him further.[176]

The mishnah specifies that we should not "seek him out," teaching us that while you must not try to be there, if you happen to be present in such a situation, it is for a reason. It would then be appropriate to take the opportunity to share kind words and make your friend feel better.[177]

Word Power

אַל תְּרַצֶּה The word תְּרַצֶּה – appease, is related to the word רָצוֹן – will. The mishnah can also be read, "Do not do the will of your friend when he is angry." If someone asks you to do something for him while he is angry, you should ignore his request. When he calms down and regains control of his emotions, he will likely regret what he wanted to do in his moment of rage and will thank you for not having fulfilled it.[178]

Speak Only If It Will Be Heard

R' Yisrael of Vizhnitz came to the home of a wealthy banker. R' Yisrael sat down, didn't say a word and after a while, stood up and prepared to leave. When his host asked him why he had decided to stop by, R' Yisrael replied: "As part of the mitzvah to give rebuke, Chazal say that it is important not to give rebuke when you know that it won't be heeded. Now, I have to tell you something to which I know you won't listen. So, I came to you so I can fulfill my obligation not to give rebuke, since I know that you certainly won't listen!"

His curiosity piqued, the banker assured him that he would listen to whatever R' Yisrael had to say. After some back and forth, R' Yisrael agreed.

"Very well," he said, "There is a penniless widow who is about to be evicted from her home because she owes a lot of money to your bank. My hope was that you, as the bank manager, would ignore her debt, but I was sure you wouldn't listen, so I have a mitzvah to remain quiet." The bank manager interrupted, "But I can't do anything! I don't own the bank, and she owes an enormous amount of money!"

"See! I knew you wouldn't listen!" The Rebbe sighed, arose once again, and left. The bank manager was so inspired that, after finding no other alternative, he paid up the poor widow's debt from his own money.[179]

Shmuel Hakatan says: Do not be glad when **your enemy falls** and do not rejoice in **your heart when he stumbles, in case Hashem sees** your joy **and it is bad in His eyes,** and He then **redirects His anger** from your enemy toward you.

שְׁמוּאֵל הַקָּטָן אוֹמֵר:
בִּנְפֹל אוֹיִבְךָ אַל תִּשְׂמָח,
וּבִכָּשְׁלוֹ אַל יָגֵל לִבֶּךָ,
פֶּן יִרְאֶה יְיָ וְרַע בְּעֵינָיו,
וְהֵשִׁיב מֵעָלָיו אַפּוֹ.

Living Lessons

He Takes No Joy in it
We should never rejoice in the misery of others, even the most wicked people. We must remember that Hashem Himself punishes only out of necessity, and hates to see the suffering of any of His creations, even the greatest reshaim! So how can we rejoice in their pain when Hashem Himself is unhappy?[180]

Another reason we must not celebrate another's downfall is that Hashem punishes a person in exact measure. Mocking them only adds to their punishment, which we have no permission to do. We can bless Hashem for executing a fair judgment, but we must never rejoice in another's pain.[181]

Connections

The previous mishnah speaks about being sensitive to a friend's feelings and needs when he goes through difficult times. This mishnah takes it one step further, and extends the same principle to our enemies.[182]

Sparks

Helpful Mirrors The Ba'al Shem Tov taught that everything we come across in our lives is for the purpose of teaching a lesson in serving Hashem. If you see a negative trait in another, it is a sign from Hashem that you bear at least a hint of that same bad trait, and you are being reminded to correct it.

Therefore, the mishnah warns, "Do not rejoice in the downfall of a wicked person." If you see someone punished for a bad trait he possesses, don't feel all smug—actually, you may have the same problem yourself! By rejoicing in the punishment of another, you may bring Hashem's attention to that same failing in yourself, and then you too might share the same fate.[183]

Biography

Shmuel Hakatan was one of the youngest students of Hillel Hazaken, and earned this title because of his extreme humility. A Heavenly voice once declared that there was but one man worthy of the presence of the Shechinah but the rest of his generation was undeserving. All the Chachamim looked toward Shmuel Hakatan as the man to whom the announcement referred.[184] He composed the tefillah וְלַמַּלְשִׁינִים in Shmoneh Esreh because he lived at a time when there were many informers who caused harm to B'nei Yisrael.[185]

He passed away a short time after the destruction of the second Beis Hamikdash. He had no children, and when he passed away, Rabban Gamliel and Rabi Elazar ben Azaryah eulogized him as follows, "It is worth crying and mourning over this, for while kings leave over their wealth to their children, Shmuel Hakatan took all the treasure in the world and has left us with no replacement."[186]

Behind the Quote

This mishnah refers not just to a physical downfall, but an intellectual one as well. When debating in Torah, one must aim to reach the truth, not to be proven right. This is an exercise in humility, which can clearly be learned by a great man who was famously called Hakatan—the Small One.[187]

Sparks

When It's You You may wonder why it is so terrible to be happy when wicked people suffer. Isn't it proper to be joyous when justice is served?

The mishnah reminds us that we should never wish on another what we would not wish on ourselves. Just as you would not appreciate being laughed at during your difficulties, you should extend the same courtesy to others.[188]

Did You Know?

Who Said It? Shmuel's statement is actually a direct quote from a passuk in Mishlei. However, he used to repeat it so often that it was considered his motto, and so the mishnah quotes it in his name.[189]

Story

Not Even a Tiny Grudge

R' Yisrael Salanter was once traveling by train. A young man entered the car and sat down next to him, unaware of his identity. Throughout the journey, the man was far from a courteous neighbor—he complained and bothered R' Yisrael at every opportunity.

When they finally reached their destination, the young man found out who his fellow traveler was. Filled with shame, he came to R' Yisrael and begged for forgiveness. R' Yisrael forgave him, and, when he found out the young man had come to get a shechitah certificate but had failed his test, he found someone to teach him the halachos, helped him get his accreditation, and even found him a position in another town!

As the story got around, people were amazed at R' Yisrael's behavior. They asked him, "Why did you help him so much? Didn't he make you miserable?"

"I forgave him wholeheartedly," R' Yisrael replied. "However, I was concerned that I may still have had a tiny grudge against him so I went out of my way to help him. In fact, that is the true test to see if you have fully forgiven someone."[190]

Elisha ben Avuyah says:

Someone who learns Torah as a child, to what is he compared? To ink written on fresh paper, which will not fade. So will the Torah he learned as a child stay sharp in his memory.

Whereas someone who only studies Torah as an old person, to what is he compared? To ink written on worn out paper, which fades easily. So does one more easily forget what he studies in old age.

Rabi Yosei bar Yehudah of Kfar Habavli says: Someone who learns Torah from young people, to what is he compared? To someone who eats unripe grapes and drinks wine straight from the press, before it has reached its potential. Learning from a young person is similar, since his mind is not fully developed.

Someone who learns Torah from old people—to what is he compared? To someone who eats ripe grapes and drinks aged wine, which has now developed to its full potential.

Rabi Meir says: However, do not judge wine by looking at its container—do not judge a teacher by his physical age. Rather, judge it by what is contained in it: there can be a new vessel filled with high-quality, aged wine—a young teacher with deep wisdom—and an old one that contains nothing, not even fresh, low-quality wine—an old teacher lacking wisdom altogether.

אֱלִישָׁע בֶּן אֲבוּיָה אוֹמֵר, הַלּוֹמֵד תּוֹרָה יֶלֶד לְמָה הוּא דוֹמֶה: לִדְיוֹ כְּתוּבָה עַל נְיָר חָדָשׁ,

וְהַלּוֹמֵד תּוֹרָה זָקֵן לְמָה הוּא דוֹמֶה: לִדְיוֹ כְּתוּבָה עַל נְיָר מָחוּק.

רַבִּי יוֹסֵי בַּר יְהוּדָה אִישׁ כְּפַר הַבַּבְלִי אוֹמֵר, הַלּוֹמֵד תּוֹרָה מִן הַקְּטַנִּים, לְמָה הוּא דוֹמֶה: לְאוֹכֵל עֲנָבִים קֵהוֹת וְשׁוֹתֶה יַיִן מִגִּתּוֹ,

וְהַלּוֹמֵד תּוֹרָה מִן הַזְּקֵנִים, לְמָה הוּא דוֹמֶה: לְאוֹכֵל עֲנָבִים בְּשׁוּלוֹת וְשׁוֹתֶה יַיִן יָשָׁן.

רַבִּי מֵאִיר אוֹמֵר: אַל תִּסְתַּכֵּל בַּקַּנְקַן, אֶלָּא בְּמַה שֶׁיֵּשׁ בּוֹ, יֵשׁ קַנְקַן חָדָשׁ מָלֵא יָשָׁן, וְיָשָׁן שֶׁאֲפִילוּ חָדָשׁ אֵין בּוֹ.

While You're Young

Young minds are quick to absorb new things, and are impressed so deeply with what they learn so that they retain it forever. The older you grow, the harder it becomes to remember things. Don't make the mistake of thinking that it's easier to learn Torah when you are older and wiser. Learn as much as you can as early as you can.[191]

Biography

Elisha ben Avuyah was a great Talmid Chacham and one of the four sages who entered Pardes. Unfortunately, the experience proved to be too much for him and, soon after, he left the way of Torah and mitzvos, earning himself the title "Acher—other." Despite this, his devoted student Rabi Meir continued learning from him, saying that he could "eat the fruit and discard the peel," meaning that he could take the correct teachings and disregard those that were not compatible with Torah.[192] Rabi Meir urged him to do teshuvah but Acher remained unmoved. When Acher fell ill, Rabi Meir rushed to his bedside and assured him that no matter how far he had strayed, his teshuvah would be accepted. Overcome, Acher began to weep in remorse and died a short time later, with thoughts of teshuvah on his mind.[193]

Rabi Yosei bar Yehudah Ish Kfar Habavli, was known by many names in order to avoid detection by the Romans. Some of his aliases were Rabi Yosei Habavli and Issi (the Aramaic version of Yosei) ben Yehudah (because he was from Shevet Yehudah). His real name, however, was Issi ben Akavya.[194] He was a student of both Rabi Yehudah bar Ilai and Rabi Elazar ben Shamua, and a colleague of Rebbi. He was very beloved by Rabi Elazar ben Shamua, who once cried tears of joy when he saw how happy Rabi Yosei had become from understanding a halachah.[195]

Behind the Quote

Even after Acher (Elisha ben Avuyah) left the Torah life, he retained the knowledge he had learned in previous years and continued teaching. He credited it to his childhood learning, comparing it to writing on fresh paper.[196]

Rabi Meir's decision to continue learning from Acher after his leaving the ways of Torah was because Rabi Meir was able to look beyond Acher's negative outward appearance and see the depth of Torah knowledge contained "inside the vessel."[197]

Did You Know?

Like a Child Children have humble, flexible minds that are open to new ideas. That is the best way to learn, while one who tries to fit Torah learning into his existing understanding will likely not understand it accurately.[198]

Older and Wiser The Torah says, "שְׁאַל אָבִיךָ וְיַגֵּדְךָ, זְקֵנֶיךָ וְיֹאמְרוּ לָךְ – Ask your father and he will tell you; inquire of your elders and they will say it to you." It is best to learn from an older, wiser person.[199]

The Power Within The statement, "Do not look at the container, but rather at what is inside," can also be referring to the body and the neshamah, telling us: keep your priorities straight. Don't focus on what the container—the body wants, but what the neshamah inside it desires.[200]

Look at the Inside

Rabi Yehoshua ben Chananya was a brilliant Talmid Chacham but was not so handsome. The story is told that when the emperor's daughter met him, she commented, "Such great wisdom in such an ugly vessel!"

Rabi Yehoshua replied, "Doesn't your father keep wine in an earthenware vessel?"

"In what sort of vessel shall he keep it?" she asked.

"You, who are nobles, should keep it in gold and silver vessels."

She told this to her father, the emperor, and he had the wine put into vessels of gold and silver. After a few short days, the wine turned sour.

The emperor had Rabi Yehoshua summoned before him and asked him, "Why did you give my daughter such advice?"

He replied, "I answered her according to the way she spoke to me." In further conversation, Rabi Yehoshua explained that, like wine, wisdom is best preserved in simple and humble vessels.[201]

Peel the Fruit In this mishnah, Rabi Meir is teaching us a very important lesson, similar to the English expression, "Don't judge a book by its cover." External appearances do not define the thing or person. It's the internal qualities that matter the most![202]

Rabi Elazar Hakapar says: Jealousy, desire for pleasure, **and** the pursuit of **honor** lead to no good, **removing a person from the World** to Come, and prevent him from enjoying his life in this world, because he will never feel satisfied.

רַבִּי אֶלְעָזָר הַקַּפָּר אוֹמֵר: הַקִּנְאָה וְהַתַּאֲוָה וְהַכָּבוֹד, מוֹצִיאִין אֶת הָאָדָם מִן הָעוֹלָם.

Nature vs. Nurture

The three things the mishnah discusses are all natural traits, yet can cause extensive damage. An instinctive response may feel good, but it is not necessarily the best thing. Hashem gave us the ability to improve ourselves and expects us to rid ourselves of any bad qualities.

 Connections

Each of the three bad characteristics of this mishnah can be a direct obstacle to fulfilling one of the messages of the previous mishnah, which is why this mishnah now advises one to avoid them all:

1. Jealousy can prevent one from learning from a younger person.
2. A focus on physical pleasures is to see only the external, while the proper attitude is to focus on what's deeper.
3. The pursuit of honor blinds people from seeing another's inner beauty.[203]

 Sparks

Transform to Good

This mishnah can also be explained in a positive light. These three middos can enable a person to remove himself from the physicality of this world and rise above to live on a higher level:

1. Jealousy of another's accomplishments in learning motivates one to learn more.
2. Seeking out spiritual pleasure motivates people to become closer to Hashem.
3. Giving honor to Talmidei Chachamim helps increase one's yiras Shamayim.

 Did You Know?

Not a Jealous Bone

Shlomoh Hamelech writes in Mishlei,[204] "Jealousy causes bones to rot." After a person passes away, the envy that he felt during his lifetime causes his bones to disintegrate, literally removing him from this world.[205]

Lost Two Worlds
The three traits in this mishnah remove a person both physically from this world, and spiritually from the world to come. Overindulgence in food and other pleasures can cause major health issues and early death. Jealousy and honor-seeking are the cause of most wars and thus responsible for countless deaths.[206] These three traits also lead to many aveiros, preventing one from benefiting from the spiritual rewards of Olam Haba.[207]

 Biography

Rabi Elazar Hakapar was given this title after his birthplace, Kafrisin. He is sometimes referred to as Rabi Elazar Hakapar Beribi, meaning great and important. He was one of the last Tannaim, a colleague of Rabi Yehudah Hanassi and the teacher of Rabi Yehoshua ben Levi.

Selfish Motives

R' Yonasan Eibeshitz once commented, "It's interesting to observe the different reactions a rav receives in response to a psak. When he is approached with a question about the kashrus of an animal, the owner will generally follow the psak calmly, even at times when it results in a great financial loss. However, when there is a quarrel between two people, even if it's for a much a lesser amount of money, the psak is rarely accepted peaceably by the losing party!

"It is human nature to be able to come to terms with a loss of money. But when one's personal loss means the gain of another, emotions get involved and suddenly people behave as they might never otherwise."[208]

Rabi Elazar Hakapar **would** often **say: Those who are born will** eventually **die, those who are dead will** eventually **be** be brought back **to life, and** all **those who live will be judged** by Hashem on the Day of Judgment.

This happens in order for people **to know**, to let others **know, and to make it known** throughout the world **that** Hashem **is God, He is the Maker** of the universe, **He is the Creator** of the universe, **He is the** One **Who understands** everything,

He is the Judge Who decides what happens in this world, **He is the Witness** to every action, **He is the Plaintiff** Who was wronged and demands the trial, and **He will judge in the future**, in the World to Come.

He is blessed, because there is no injustice before Him, there is **no forgetfulness, no favoritism, and no bribery,** so every verdict is correct and fair. **Know that all** of Hashem's rewards and punishments **are** given **according to the account** that He has kept.

Do not let your yetzer hara **assure you that** once you die, your **grave will be a safe haven for you** to avoid judgment, **because** just as **you were formed without your consent, born without your consent, and you are forced to live, and you will be forced to die** whenever Hashem decides, so too, **will you be forced to give justification and a detailed report** of everything you did during your life **to the supreme King of** all **kings, the Holy One, blessed be He.**

הוּא הָיָה אוֹמֵר: הַיִּלּוֹדִים לָמוּת, וְהַמֵּתִים לְחֲיוֹת, וְהַחַיִּים לִדּוֹן,

לֵידַע וּלְהוֹדִיעַ וּלְהִוָּדַע שֶׁהוּא אֵל, הוּא הַיּוֹצֵר, הוּא הַבּוֹרֵא, הוּא הַמֵּבִין,

הוּא הַדַּיָּן, הוּא הָעֵד, הוּא בַּעַל דִּין, הוּא עָתִיד לָדוֹן.

בָּרוּךְ הוּא, שֶׁאֵין לְפָנָיו לֹא עַוְלָה וְלֹא שִׁכְחָה, וְלֹא מַשּׂוֹא פָנִים, וְלֹא מִקַּח שֹׁחַד, וְדַע שֶׁהַכֹּל לְפִי הַחֶשְׁבּוֹן.

וְאַל יַבְטִיחֲךָ יִצְרְךָ שֶׁהַשְּׁאוֹל בֵּית מָנוֹס לָךְ, שֶׁעַל כָּרְחֲךָ אַתָּה נוֹצָר, וְעַל כָּרְחֲךָ אַתָּה נוֹלָד, וְעַל כָּרְחֲךָ אַתָּה חַי, וְעַל כָּרְחֲךָ אַתָּה מֵת, וְעַל כָּרְחֲךָ אַתָּה עָתִיד לִתֵּן דִּין וְחֶשְׁבּוֹן לִפְנֵי מֶלֶךְ מַלְכֵי הַמְּלָכִים, הַקָּדוֹשׁ בָּרוּךְ הוּא.

No Favorites

Hashem does not practice favoritism and, therefore, every person is under the same scrutiny. Tzaddikim and reshaim equally are judged for all their actions. This means that no matter how you behaved yesterday, Hashem is looking for you to do mitzvos today. Every person has an equal chance to connect to Hashem![209]

Bribery Unwanted

Hashem cannot be bribed to look away from our aveiros because of other mitzvos we have done. Each action is accounted for individually.[210] Only teshuvah erases aveiros. Instead of justifying aveiros with your usually good behavior, do teshuvah for what you did wrong and work on yourself to be better.[211]

Word Power

הוּא הַיּוֹצֵר הוּא הַבּוֹרֵא

The words בּוֹרֵא and יוֹצֵר both refer to Hashem as the Maker of the world, but there is a slight distinction between the two. בּוֹרֵא translates as creator, referring to the original creation when Hashem created the world from nothing. יוֹצֵר means fashioner, referring to how the world is like clay in Hashem's hands, whose form is constantly fashioned at His will.[212]

 Did You Know?

Tug-of-War Life is a seesaw of conflicting emotions. On the one hand, the neshamah is forced to live in this world against its will, for it yearns to be close to Hashem. On the other hand, the neshamah feels its purpose here, to serve Hashem. Therefore, it is against its will that it eventually dies.[213]

 Sparks

Against Our Will If we weren't given a choice to be born or not, how can we be held accountable for our actions?

Human nature is to cherish life. This in itself is proof that while we weren't given a choice to come, we are happy to be here. Therefore we are fully accountable for our actions.[214]

Personal Account A mitzvah that one person finds simple may prove challenging for another. When the mishnah says that "everything is according to the account," it is assuring us that Hashem judges not just the amount of mitzvos we do, but also how much effort we put into it. Even if two people have performed the same mitzvos, their personal accounts differ based on their respective efforts.[215]

 **Story**

Part of the Plan

The Ba'al Shem Tov once told his student the Maggid of Mezritch to go out to the forest to see the justice with which Hashem runs the world.

The Maggid settled near a stream to watch events unfold. An armed man on a horse soon appeared and rested by the stream for a while. He soon moved on, accidentally leaving his wallet behind. Shortly afterward, a rich man approached, saw the wallet, took it, and left. He was followed by a poor man a few minutes later who gratefully bent down to drink. At that moment, the armed man reappeared and demanded his wallet back from the poor man. The poor man protested his innocence, to no avail. Incensed, the armed man beat him and left him wounded by the stream.

The Maggid was completely perplexed by the strange sequence of events. He asked the Ba'al Shem Tov, "Why did the first man lose his money, the second receive it, and the poor man beaten without cause?"

The Ba'al Shem Tov explained that in a previous life, the armed man had borrowed money from the rich man but got out of his debt by bribing the judge, now reincarnated as the poor man. The armed man paid back the money he owed, the rich man received his rightful payment, and the judge received his just punishment for accepting a bribe and perverting justice.[216]

Say this mishnah upon completing each perek:

Rabbi Chananya ben Akashya says:

The Holy One, blessed be He, wanted to make B'nei **Yisrael** have many **merits.**

He therefore gave them an abundance of Torah and mitzvos, so that they would have many opportunities to connect to Him.

As it says in Yeshayah: **Hashem wanted, for the sake of** increasing B'nei Yisrael's **righteousness, that the Torah be made great and glorious.**

רַבִּי חֲנַנְיָא בֶּן עֲקַשְׁיָא אוֹמֵר:
רָצָה הַקָּדוֹשׁ בָּרוּךְ הוּא
לְזַכּוֹת אֶת יִשְׂרָאֵל
לְפִיכָךְ הִרְבָּה לָהֶם תּוֹרָה וּמִצְוֹת
שֶׁנֶּאֱמַר: יְיָ חָפֵץ לְמַעַן צִדְקוֹ
יַגְדִּיל תּוֹרָה וְיַאְדִּיר.

Endnotes

1. חגיגה יד, ב
2. חגיגה יד, ב
3. סוטה מט, א
4. ביאורים
5. קהלת רבה א, יג
6. היום יום ע׳ סד
7. חסדי אבות להחיד״א פ״ו מ״ה
8. מסכת אבות ע״פ יינה של תורה ע׳ שיח
9. מאור ושמש, פרשת חוקת
10. הר׳ יוסף יעב״ץ
11. מרכבת המשנה
12. ברכות נז, ב
13. מדרש שמואל
14. ביאורים
15. אמרי שפר (לר׳ שלמה קלוגער) דברים יד, כב
16. סיפורי חסידים - תורה, יתרו
17. דרך חיים להמהר״ל
18. מדרש שמואל בשם החסיד (הר׳ יוסף יעב״ץ)
19. מוסר אבות
20. רבינו יונה. מדרש שמואל
21. ירושלמי דמאי פ״א ה״ג
22. ע״פ רש״י חגיגה יד, ב ועוד
23. עירובין כט, ב. קידושין כ, א
24. ויקרא רבה טז, ד
25. מילי דאבות. תניא פרק ל׳
26. בראשית ד, ה
27. עבודת ישראל
28. ירושלמי נדרים פ״ט ה״ד
29. מוסר אבות
30. דרך חיים למהר״ל
31. קהלת רבה יא
32. יומא פו, א
33. מהר״ל
34. דרך חיים למהר״ל
35. מדרש שמואל בשם ר׳ מתתיהו היצהרי
36. ביאורים
37. סוטה ה, ב
38. אגרת הקודש סי׳ ב
39. רמב״ם הל׳ דעות פ״א ה״ד
40. רע״ב
41. מדרש שמואל
42. טעם זקנים
43. מנורת המאור נר ז כלל א - חלק א פרק ב
44. מדרש שמואל
45. תפארת ישראל
46. תוספות בכורות כט, א
47. ד״ה מה
48. גיטין נז, א
49. איכה רבה לה, לא
50. גיטין נז, ב
51. מו״ק ט, ב
52. ברכות יז, ב
53. פסחים נ, ב
54. מדרש שמואל
55. לקוטי בתר לקוטי בשם ליקוטי מוהר״ן
56. מדרש שמואל
57. ברכות לה, ב
58. רוח חיים
59. סיפורי חסידים, תורה - קרח
60. מדרש שמואל
61. שבת מט, ב
62. הר׳ יוסף יעב״ץ
63. אברבנאל
64. שו״ת יו״ד סי׳ רמ״ד ורפ״ב
65. רע״ב
66. הר׳ יוסף יעב״ץ
67. ירושלמי תענית פ״ד ה״ב ע״פ רש״י חגיגה יד, ב וע״פ ירמי׳ לה, ב
68. יבמות סב, ב
69. שבת לג, ב
70. בראשית רבה סח, ד
71. ירושלמי גיטין פ״ז ה״ז
72. ירושלמי יבמות פ״א ה״א
73. פתח עינים להחיד״א
74. ירושלמי שביעית פ״ד ה״ב. סנהדרין פ״ג ה״ה
75. גיטין סז, א
76. בראשית רבה סח, ד
77. מהר״ל
78. זכות אבות הובא במעם לועז
79. מהר״ל
80. ביאורים
81. כתובות קה, ב
82. מעשה אבות
83. תומים חו״מ סי׳ י
84. כנסת ישראל בשם החלק יעקב
85. סנהדרין ז, ב ובפירש״י שם
86. סיפורי חסידים - תורה, כי תשא
87. בשם ר׳ אברהם מסלונים הובא בספר מעיינות הנצח
88. חלק יעקב
89. ירושלמי שבת פ״א ה״ד
90. ירושלמי בבא בתרא פ״ב ה״א
91. כתובות סב, ב, נדרים נ, א
92. אבות דרבי נתן פ״ו
93. רבינו בחיי
94. רבינו יונה
95. ספרי חסידות
96. עבודה זרה יח, א
97. ירושלמי כלאים פ״ט ה״ג
98. עירובין יג, ב
99. פי׳ אה״ח עה״ת הוצאת א. בלום בתולדות המחבר
100. מאירי
101. רמב״ם הל׳ תשובה פ״ג ה״ד
102. מאירי
103. עבודה זרה יז, א
104. ביאורים
105. מדרש שמואל
106. עירובין נד, א
107. ירושלמי חגיגה פ״ג ה״א
108. ירושלמי יבמות פי״ב ה״א
109. ירושלמי פאה פ״ח ה״ח
110. אבות דרבי נתן רש״י
111. סנהדרין קי, א
112. ספרי דברים יב, כט (פיסקא פ׳)
113. עירובין נג, א
114. סוטה לט, א
115. במדבר רבה טו, יז
116. יבמות סב, ב
117. דרך אבות
118. סנהדרין יא, א
119. עטרת אבות ב׳ עמוד 74
120. מדרש שמואל
121. מנחת שבת
122. בבא קמא קג, ב
123. כתובות יז, א
124. שבת לג, ב
125. שבת קנז, ב
126. בן איש חי
127. ביאורים
128. רע״ב
129. מסכת אבות ע״פ יינה של תורה ע׳ רמא
130. ר׳ שמחה מויטרי
131. רש״י
132. אברבנאל
133. מדרש שמואל
134. ירושלמי ברכות פ״ט ה״ב
135. עירובין יג, ב
136. ר׳ יוסף בן שושן
137. החסיד הר׳ יוסף יעב״ץ
138. לב אבות
139. מפרשים - רבינו אפרים, מחזור ויטרי וכו׳
140. ביאורים
141. תענית ז, א
142. שבת קמז, ב. קהלת רבה ז, טו
143. בית אבות
144. מדרש שמואל
145. רש״י משלי יג, כ
146. מדרש שמואל
147. ויקרא רבה טז, ב
148. מדרש תנחומא חוקת הוספה א
149. רשב״ץ
150. מדרש שמואל
151. ספר מעשיות לרבינו ניסים גאון - בתחילתו
152. מילי דאבות
153. מילי דאבות
154. מילי דאבות
155. מילי דאבות
156. מאסף דרושי
157. מילי דאבות
158. הר׳ יוסף יעב״ץ
159. אברבנאל
160. חסד לאברהם
161. אברבנאל
162. מדרש משלי י, ו
163. סיפורי מופת - המגיד ממעזריטש ע׳ 29
164. המפרשים, מובא בביאורים
165. ביאורים
166. עטרת אבות
167. מסכת אבות ע״פ יינה של תורה ע׳ רנג
168. מדרש שמואל
169. החסיד
170. משלי טו, כג
171. מילי דאבות
172. מסכת אבות ע״פ יינה של תורה ע׳
173. ירושלמי מועד קטן פ״ג ה״א
174. בראשית רבה ט, ה
175. אבות דרבי נתן פמ״א
176. תענית כ, ב - כא, א
177. רע״ב. לחם שמים
178. ר׳ משה אלמושנינו
179. לב אבות
180. סיפורי חסידים - זון
181. רבינו יונה. מדרש שמואל
182. הר׳ יוסף יעב״ץ
183. עוגת אליהו
184. ביאורים
185. סנהדרין יא, א
186. ברכות כח, ב
187. שמחות פ״ח ה״ז
188. ביאורים
189. מן אבות
190. רמב״ם. רע״ב
191. במחיצת רבינו ע׳ סח, אור חדש (זייטשיק) בראשית ע׳ נב
192. מאירי
193. חגיגה טו, ב
194. ירושלמי חגיגה פ״א ה״א
195. פסחים קיג, ב ע״פ ספר יוחסין
196. מנחות יח, א
197. ביאורים
198. ביאורים
199. ביאורים
200. אברבנאל
201. מדרש שמואל
202. תענית ז, א
203. רש״י. רע״ב. מאירי
204. מדרש שמואל
205. משלי יד, ל
206. הר׳ יוסף יעב״ץ
207. הרשב״ץ
208. לחם יהודה
209. עטרת אבות ח״ב ע׳ 108
210. רמב״ם
211. רמב״ם
212. מדרש שמואל. תוס׳ יו״ט
213. רע״ב
214. ביאורים
215. לקוטי בתר לקוטי
216. הר׳ יוסף יעב״ץ
217. מוסף יוסף על התורה ומועדים ע׳ שכ״ח, וראה גם דגל מחנה אפרים פ׳ משפטים

Chapter Five

Kol Yisrael

Say this mishnah before beginning each new perek:

All B'nei **Yisrael have a portion in the World to Come.**

As it says in Yeshayah regarding B'nei Yisrael upon Moshiach's arrival: **Your people are all tzaddikim,** and **they will all inherit Eretz** Yisrael **forever**—they will never be exiled from it again.

All will recognize that they are **the branch of My planting and the work of My hands,** in which I, Hashem, **take pride.**

כָּל יִשְׂרָאֵל יֵשׁ לָהֶם חֵלֶק לָעוֹלָם הַבָּא,

שֶׁנֶּאֱמַר: וְעַמֵּךְ כֻּלָּם צַדִּיקִים, לְעוֹלָם יִירְשׁוּ אָרֶץ,

נֵצֶר מַטָּעַי מַעֲשֵׂה יָדַי לְהִתְפָּאֵר.

The world was created by Hashem uttering **ten statements** commanding everything to come into existence. **What** does this **teach** us? **Couldn't** the world **have been created with** just **one statement**?

The reason for this was so He could **demand** maximum **payment from the wicked, who destroy the** valuable **world that was created by** not one, but **ten statements,**

and to give the maximum **good reward to** Tzaddikim, who keep the valuable **world—that was created by** not one, but **ten statements**— in existence through their righteousness.

בַּעֲשָׂרָה מַאֲמָרוֹת נִבְרָא הָעוֹלָם, וּמַה תַּלְמוּד לוֹמַר, וַהֲלֹא בְמַאֲמָר אֶחָד יָכוֹל לְהִבָּרְאוֹת,

אֶלָּא לְהִפָּרַע מִן הָרְשָׁעִים שֶׁמְּאַבְּדִין אֶת הָעוֹלָם שֶׁנִּבְרָא בַּעֲשָׂרָה מַאֲמָרוֹת, וְלִתֵּן שָׂכָר טוֹב לַצַּדִּיקִים שֶׁמְּקַיְּמִין אֶת הָעוֹלָם שֶׁנִּבְרָא בַּעֲשָׂרָה מַאֲמָרוֹת.

True Purpose

Everything exists for one purpose only: for the service of Hashem. Yet Hashem gives people the freedom to choose how to use everything. Information technology, for example, can expose people to damaging sights and information, and can serve as a terrible distraction. At the same time, however, it gives constant access to shiurim and a tremendous amount of Torah knowledge. Modern communication can spread lashon hara around the world in a second, and yet also provides the means to fulfill the mitzvah of bikur cholim, face to face even with someone across the globe. Our mission is to utilize the tools around us for their intended purpose, the service of Hashem.

 Word Power

וּמַה תַּלְמוּד לוֹמַר The very question of this mishnah is there to teach us something: that every word in Torah bears an everlasting lesson. Reading about ten statements that created the world, we must immediately seek the lesson that can be learned from it.[1]

 Sparks

A Different Kind of Speech Hashem speaks and humans speak. Yet these are very different types of speech. A person's words cannot create anything, whereas Hashem's words create the world. When a person speaks, the spoken words take on an existence separate from him, whereas Hashem's words always remain a part of Him, just like everything else in His world.[2]

A Good Horse

A chassid of the Tzemach Tzedek was very pleased to have acquired a brilliant young prodigy as a son-in-law. He urged him to concentrate on his studies and promised to care for all his material needs. Things went fine until the young genius made some bad friends and fell into a lowly, sinful life. Devastated, the chassid poured out his woes to the Tzemach Tzedek.

"Bring him here," the Rebbe told him. It took a while, but the chassid was finally able to convince his son-in-law to visit the Tzemach Tzedek.

When he arrived, the Rebbe asked him, "Which is better, a young, healthy horse, or an old, frail one?"

"Why, the younger one, of course," replied the young man. "By the time the old horse walks five kilometers, the younger horse will have traveled twenty."

"But when the driver gets lost, the healthy horse will be deeper in unfamiliar territory," the Rebbe countered.

"That's true," the young man agreed. "In that case, the benefit of the better horse serves as a disadvantage."

"However," the Tzemach Tzedek continued softly, "once the mistake is realized, the younger horse can return to the proper path more speedily."

The young man understood the Rebbe's pointed message and eventually did teshuvah.[5]

One in Potential Hashem originally created the entire world in a partially spiritual form on the first day of Creation, and He spent the remaining six days bringing it into physicality. The mishnah here questions why that first spiritual form was not enough. Why did the world have to be physical?

The answer is that had the world been left in its partially spiritual form, there could be no real struggle between good and bad. That's why Hashem said the following nine statements—to create a physical world where people could make choices, and earn their just reward or punishment.[3]

Constant Creation The passuk says "לְעוֹלָם ה' דְּבָרְךָ נִצָּב בַּשָּׁמָיִם" – Your word, Hashem, stands forever in heaven." The Midrash explains that while the world was created once through the original ten statements, Hashem constantly repeats those words to keep the world in existence. If Hashem stopped saying them for even a moment, the world would cease to exist, and all would revert to the way it was before the six days of creation.[4]

The Ten Statements:

1. בְּרֵאשִׁית בָּרָא אֱלֹקִים – Hashem created everything in potential.
2. וַיֹּאמֶר אֱלֹקִים יְהִי אוֹר – Hashem said, "Let there be light."
3. וַיֹּאמֶר אֱלֹקִים יְהִי רָקִיעַ – Hashem said, "Let there be a sky."
4. וַיֹּאמֶר אֱלֹקִים יִקָּווּ הַמַּיִם – Hashem said, "Let the water gather and leave dry land."
5. וַיֹּאמֶר אֱלֹקִים תַּדְשֵׁא הָאָרֶץ דֶּשֶׁא – Hashem said, "Let the ground grow all kind of vegetation."
6. וַיֹּאמֶר אֱלֹקִים יְהִי מְאֹרֹת בִּרְקִיעַ הַשָּׁמַיִם – Hashem said, "Let there be luminaries in the sky."
7. וַיֹּאמֶר אֱלֹקִים יִשְׁרְצוּ הַמַּיִם... וְעוֹף יְעוֹפֵף – Hashem said, "Let there be fish in the water and birds flying in the sky."
8. וַיֹּאמֶר אֱלֹקִים תּוֹצֵא הָאָרֶץ נֶפֶשׁ חַיָּה – Hashem said, "Let there be animals on the dry land."
9. וַיֹּאמֶר אֱלֹקִים נַעֲשֶׂה אָדָם – Hashem said, "Let us make man."
10. וַיֹּאמֶר ה' אֱלֹקִים... אֶעֱשֶׂה לּוֹ עֵזֶר כְּנֶגְדּוֹ – Hashem said, "I will make him a helper—Chavah."

עֲשָׂרָה דורות מֵאָדָם וְעַד נֹחַ, לְהוֹדִיעַ כַּמָּה אֶרֶךְ אַפַּיִם לְפָנָיו, שֶׁכָּל הַדּוֹרוֹת הָיוּ מַכְעִיסִין וּבָאִין, עַד שֶׁהֵבִיא עֲלֵיהֶם אֶת מֵי הַמַּבּוּל.

There were **ten generations from Adam Harishon to Noach**. This **shows us how** great is Hashem's **patience**: each generation **made** Him **increasingly angry**, yet He waited ten generations **until He** finally **brought the waters of the Mabul upon them**.

עֲשָׂרָה דורות מִנֹּחַ וְעַד אַבְרָהָם, לְהוֹדִיעַ כַּמָּה אֶרֶךְ אַפַּיִם לְפָנָיו, שֶׁכָּל הַדּוֹרוֹת הָיוּ מַכְעִיסִין וּבָאִין, עַד שֶׁבָּא אַבְרָהָם אָבִינוּ וְקִבֵּל שְׂכַר כֻּלָּם.

There were **ten generations from Noach to Avraham** Avinu. This **also shows how** great is Hashem's **patience**: each of the generations **made** Him **increasingly angry**, yet He waited ten generations **until Avraham Avinu came and received the reward** that they **all** would have received had they not angered Hashem.

Standing up to Peer Pressure

What's right is not always popular, and what's popular is not always right. Although sometimes it may seem impossible to stand up for what's right, look to Noach and Avraham for inspiration. They weren't affected by the evil around them and dared to be different. Avraham was called אַבְרָהָם הָעִבְרִי – Avraham from the other side because the **entire world** stood on one side, while he stood alone on the other.

Noach had to endure ridicule for 120 years while building the teivah, predicting and preparing for what he knew was the truth.

You too can be like him. Even if the entire world says differently, stand strong in what you know to be true—Hashem's Torah and mitzvos.

Did You Know?

Twenty Generations Both sets of ten generations are listed in the Torah.

The ten generations from Adam to Noach: Adam, Shes, Enosh, Keinan, Mahalalel, Yered, Chanoch, Mesushelach, Lemech, and Noach.

The ten generations from Noach to Avraham: Shem, Arpachshad, Shelach, Ever, Peleg, Reu, Serug, Nachor, Terach, and Avraham.

Hashem's Patience Has a Limit In these final years of galus, it is comforting to realize that while Hashem is patient, He does not let evil flourish forever. Our enemies, who seem to be so successful, will ultimately receive retribution for their actions.[6]

Word Power

עֲשָׂרָה Ten is a significant number in Torah. There are ten levels of holiness and ten levels of impurity. Hashem waited ten generations and destroyed the world only once the people had descended to the tenth level of impurity.

עַד שֶׁהֵבִיא עֲלֵיהֶם At first glance, it seems unfair that the last generation had to suffer for all the mistakes of the previous generations. In truth, however, the souls that perished in the flood were the same souls of the previous ten generations. Hashem brought them down into the world time and again to allow them to rectify their mistakes. When they failed, Hashem finally brought the waters of the mabul down upon them. The plural word "them" includes the people of the previous ten generations.[7]

Sparks

Accumulated Reward The ten generations from Adam to Noach did not accumulate any reward for Noach to reap. The following ten generations, on the other hand, weren't as cruel toward each other and thus earned some reward. However, since they did not believe in Hashem, they themselves were unable to receive their reward and Avraham acquired it instead. He earned it through his efforts to reach out to those around him and to influence them to do teshuvah.[8]

Infinite Rewards

The first Gerrer Rebbe, R' Yitzchak Meir Alter, once met a non-frum Jew who challenged him, "Rebbe, I can prove your Torah is false. The second paragraph in Shema foretells terrible consequences for not listening to Hashem. I have committed every one of those transgressions and yet I am living a happy life with financial success, good health, and a beautiful family."

The Rebbe smiled in response. "You seem familiar with the Shema. I assume you must have read it at some point."

"Of course!" the man exclaimed. "Even a sinner like myself has visited shul once or twice."

"Now just imagine," the Rebbe replied, "the reward awaiting those who faithfully fulfill each of Hashem's commands if even you received such plentiful payment just for visiting a shul once or twice."[9]

Avraham Avinu was tested with ten trials to see if he would remain faithful to Hashem, **and he passed them all. This shows how** great Avraham Avinu's love for Hashem was.

עֲשָׂרָה נִסְיוֹנוֹת נִתְנַסָּה אַבְרָהָם אָבִינוּ, וְעָמַד בְּכֻלָּם, לְהוֹדִיעַ כַּמָּה חִבָּתוֹ שֶׁל אַבְרָהָם אָבִינוּ.

Yay! Another Test!

Although tests may not be fun, they are designed to keep you focused, challenged, and committed to learning.

The same applies to tests of character. When someone is trying your patience, use the opportunity to work on yourself and become a more patient person. When someone is disturbing you during davening, use that opportunity to concentrate more intensely on the words you're saying. Although we'd prefer to have it easy, when put into a trying situation, use it to become stronger. Challenges help you become a better person!

A Personal Lech Lecha
One of Avraham's tests was Hashem's command to leave everything that was comfortable and familiar to him and travel to a new place to influence people around him.

We face this challenge in our lives too. Our neshamah is forced to leave its comfortable home in heaven, where everything is familiar and holy, and confront this foreign world. Keeping Avraham's struggle in mind empowers the neshamah to pass the test and work to create a holy home for Hashem in this world.

Genetic Power
When your service of Hashem is being tested, you're not in it alone. The mishnah specifically mentions that Avraham was אָבִינוּ – our father, to teach us that since the Avos passed their tests, we inherit the strength to overcome ours.[10]

עֲשָׂרָה נִסְיוֹנוֹת Ten represents completion. Avraham's ten tests represent how every facet of his being was tested and he managed to prevail.[11]

This mishnah explains why Avraham was so deserving of all the reward described in the previous mishnah.[12]

 **Did You Know?**

Beyond a Doubt Avraham was attempting to introduce an entirely innovative idea to the world, namely belief in one G-d. In order to prove his faith in it beyond a shadow of a doubt, he needed to pass ten tests. Just one, or a few, could be explained as a coincidence or a fluke.[13]

And Even More Avraham had many more than ten difficult tests in his life. The mishnah is referring to the ten most difficult ones. Following are some of the bigger tests he went through:[14]

1. Hiding for thirteen years from Nimrod, who wanted to kill him.
2. Being thrown into a furnace after smashing his father's idols.
3. Being commanded by Hashem to leave his land, birth-place, and father's home.
4. The famine in the land of Canaan.
5. His wife, Sarah, being taken by Paraoh.
6. His nephew, Lot, being captured.
7. The war against the four kings who conquered Sedom.
8. Being told at the bris bein habesarim that his descendants would be slaves.
9. His wife, Sarah, being barren for many years.
10. Having to take Hagar as a wife.
11. Giving himself a bris at ninety-nine years old.
12. Sending away Hagar.
13. Sending away Yishmael.
14. Akeidas Yitzchak.
15. Even though he had been promised by Hashem that the whole Eretz Yisrael would be his, he was still forced to pay an enormous price to bury Sarah in Eretz Yisrael.

 **Story**

The Reward for Hospitality

There was a once a childless couple named Eliezer and Sarah. They were renowned for their hospitality, never turning away a guest. Once, an old, unkempt beggar asked to stay with them for Shabbos, and despite other guests' objections, they agreed. The old man didn't offer a word of gratitude and complained about everything. No matter what they gave him, he demanded more, and became angry when they couldn't fulfill his ridiculous requests. He stayed on after Shabbos, still bitterly criticizing everything. Eliezer and Sarah continued to treat him with patience and respect despite his rude behavior and went out of their way to make him as comfortable as possible.

Before he left, the beggar revealed himself as Eliyahu Hanavi, who was sent to test them. Since they passed their test admirably, they would be rewarded with a son who would light up the world with his Torah. A year later, they had a baby boy who grew up to become the famous Ba'al Shem Tov.[15]

Ten miracles were performed for our **ancestors in Egypt** to protect them from the ten plagues, **and ten** miracles were performed for them **at the Yam** Suf.

The Holy One, blessed be He, brought ten plagues upon the Egyptians in Egypt and **ten** additional punishments **at the Yam** Suf.

Our ancestors tested the patience of **the Holy One, blessed be He, with ten tests in the desert, as** Hashem **says** in the Torah: They have tested Me these ten times and they have not listened to My voice.

עֲשָׂרָה נִסִּים נַעֲשׂוּ לַאֲבוֹתֵינוּ בְּמִצְרַיִם, וַעֲשָׂרָה עַל הַיָּם.

עֶשֶׂר מַכּוֹת הֵבִיא הַקָּדוֹשׁ בָּרוּךְ הוּא עַל הַמִּצְרִיִּים בְּמִצְרַיִם, וְעֶשֶׂר עַל הַיָּם.

עֲשָׂרָה נִסְיוֹנוֹת נִסּוּ אֲבוֹתֵינוּ אֶת הַקָּדוֹשׁ בָּרוּךְ הוּא בַּמִּדְבָּר, שֶׁנֶּאֱמַר: וַיְנַסּוּ אֹתִי זֶה עֶשֶׂר פְּעָמִים, וְלֹא שָׁמְעוּ בְּקוֹלִי.

Appreciate the Good

It seems puzzling to read through the mishnah and discover that even after Hashem performed twenty miracles for B'nei Yisrael, their ungrateful response was to test Hashem. This teaches a valuable lesson about acknowledging and appreciating kindness. We have plenty to thank Hashem for. Have you ever considered what a gift it is to wake up in the morning? Do you think about that when you say Modeh Ani? How about walking, talking, seeing, hearing, feeling, touching, having clothes to wear and food to eat? Thank Hashem for these priceless treasures when you say the morning brachos. The same applies with appreciating people who do things for you. Say thank you to your teacher after class, when a classmate holds the door open for you, when your parent helps you with your homework, or when your sibling passes you the ketchup.

 Connections

In the merit of the ten tests that Avraham passed, B'nei Yisrael experienced the two sets of ten miracles listed in this mishnah—in Mitzrayim and at the Yam Suf. The tests also gave them the power to overcome their own ten tests in the desert.[16]

 Sparks

What Once Was Isn't Now Though the Avos passed many difficult tests and their trust in Hashem never faltered, their descendants didn't always live up to the same standard, testing Hashem many times.

Having great ancestors endows us with great potential. However, it is up to us to actualize that potential. A person might have an illustrious lineage, descending from giants in Torah and mitzvos who dedicated their lives to the service of Hashem. Yet if that person himself doesn't fulfill his potential, the lineage is practically worthless.[17]

Did You Know?

Ten and Ten

The ten miracles performed at the sea:

1. The waters split.
2. The waters formed an arch around B'nei Yisrael.
3. The ground dried and hardened.
4. That same ground was like wet cement when the Egyptians walked on it.
5. The waters split into twelve tunnels, one for each shevet.
6. The waters became hard like stone and injured the Egyptians.
7. The waters became like a beautiful wall for B'nei Yisrael.
8. The waters remained transparent so that each shevet could see its neighbor.
9. Sweet waters flowed from the walls, which B'nei Yisrael were able to drink.
10. The flowing waters that they did not drink hardened and did not spill onto the ground.[18]

The ten times B'nei Yisrael tested Hashem's patience in the desert:

1. When approaching the sea they said, "Are there no graves in Egypt that you took us to die in the desert?"
2. When they finished crossing the sea, they still feared that the Egyptians would follow them.
3. They complained about the water at Marah.
4. They cried about lack of water in Refidim.
5. They disobeyed the prohibition against collecting mann on Shabbos.
6. They ignored the prohibition against leaving over mann for the next day.
7-8. They complained twice regarding the quail.
9. They sinned with the Golden Calf.
10. They cried and made a great fuss about the negative report of the spies about Eretz Yisrael.[19]

Sparks

Empty Void The desert is a symbol of the unholy since it is an empty, barren place.[20] Anything that is devoid of holiness has the potential to be filled with the opposite.[21] The mishnah is excusing the Jews somewhat by stating that they tested Hashem in the midbar, implying that they sinned because they found themselves in a place empty of kedushah.[22]

Equal Chance Only the first part of the passuk quoted in the mishnah is needed to prove that B'nei Yisrael tested Hashem ten times. The second part is brought to teach us an important lesson. Although we may think that had we lived at a different time, such as in the times of the Beis Hamikdash, we would have behaved better than we do now, the Jews in the midbar witnessed countless miracles and still tested Hashem. Circumstances help, but ultimately the choice is up to us to heed the voice of Hashem.[23]

Refusing to See

There was once a man whose daughter was paralyzed. He visited many doctors, but no one was able to cure her. His friends urged him to seek the help of the Ba'al Shem Tov, whose fame as a holy miracle worker was starting to spread. The man refused, saying that he didn't believe that the Ba'al Shem Tov could perform miracles.

As time passed and his daughter's situation didn't improve, the man finally gave in to his friends' persistent urging. He placed his daughter up onto the wagon and drove to Mezhibuzh. Leaving his daughter in the wagon, he came into the Ba'al Shem Tov's room, threw a bag of coins on the desk, and barked, "Here is some money. Let's see if you can heal my daughter."

The Tzaddik threw the money out the open window and said, "Go in peace. I have no need for your money." The father glanced out the window, and to his shock, saw his (formerly) paralyzed daughter climb out of the carriage and eagerly collect the scattered coins. Still unable to change his beliefs even after witnessing a miracle with his own eyes, the man said to his driver, "Quick—let's leave here at once before people start claiming that the Ba'al Shem Tov has performed a miracle!"[24]

Ten miracles were done for our ancestors in the Beis Hamikdash:

1. **No woman miscarried because of** cravings caused by the smell of the **roasting** meat of the korbanos.
2. **The meat of the** korbanos **never spoiled.**
3. **Not a fly was seen in the** place where the korbanos were **cut up.**
4. **Never did the Kohen Gadol** become **impure on Yom Kippur.**
5. **The rains did not extinguish the fire of the woodpile** on the Mizbeiach.
6. **The wind did not succeed** in disrupting **the** upright **column of smoke** rising from the fire on the Mizbeiach.
7. **No disqualifying issues were ever found with the Omer** offering on the second day of Pesach, **with the two loaves** offered on Shavuos, **or with the Lechem Hapanim** baked each week.
8. When the people **stood** in the Beis Hamikdash, **they were packed tightly** together, yet when **they bowed,** they had **plenty of space.**
9. **No snake or scorpion caused harm in** Yerushalayim.
10. **No person said to his friend, "Yerushalayim is** too **crowded for me to stay overnight."**

עֲשָׂרָה נִסִּים נַעֲשׂוּ לַאֲבוֹתֵינוּ בְּבֵית הַמִּקְדָּשׁ: לֹא הִפִּילָה אִשָּׁה מֵרֵיחַ בְּשַׂר הַקֹּדֶשׁ, וְלֹא הִסְרִיחַ בְּשַׂר הַקֹּדֶשׁ מֵעוֹלָם, וְלֹא נִרְאָה זְבוּב בְּבֵית הַמִּטְבָּחַיִם, וְלֹא אֵירַע קֶרִי לְכֹהֵן גָּדוֹל בְּיוֹם הַכִּפּוּרִים, וְלֹא כִבּוּ הַגְּשָׁמִים אֵשׁ שֶׁל עֲצֵי הַמַּעֲרָכָה, וְלֹא נִצְּחָה הָרוּחַ אֶת עַמּוּד הֶעָשָׁן, וְלֹא נִמְצָא פְסוּל בָּעוֹמֶר וּבִשְׁתֵּי הַלֶּחֶם וּבְלֶחֶם הַפָּנִים, עוֹמְדִים צְפוּפִים וּמִשְׁתַּחֲוִים רְוָחִים, וְלֹא הִזִּיק נָחָשׁ וְעַקְרָב בִּירוּשָׁלַיִם, וְלֹא אָמַר אָדָם לַחֲבֵרוֹ: צַר לִי הַמָּקוֹם שֶׁאָלִין בִּירוּשָׁלָיִם.

Recognizing Miracles

Not all of the miracles listed in this mishnah were major, nature-defying miracles. Yet still we are sure to acknowledge them as the work of Hashem.

In our lives, we witness many daily wonders that we often take for granted. Waking up in the morning, enjoying the sunshine or the snow on the ground, hearing birds singing, being able to walk and talk, having friends to play with, and being able to run, talk, and play are all small miracles that happen to us every day. We must make an effort to recognize and thank Hashem even for these little kind acts He performs for us every day.

Sparks

Venomous Bite One of the miracles mentioned in the mishnah is the lack of bites from two creatures: a snake and a scorpion. A snake's bite releases a warm venom, burning the body with its lethal heat, while a scorpion's spreads cool venom throughout its victim.[25] These represent two poisonous mindsets to the service of Hashem: being overly passionate about worldly things, and being cool and unaffected by holy things. Yerushalayim was protected from these spiritual problems too, and no one there suffered from either of these conditions. Their heated enthusiasm was directed only toward the holy, and no one was indifferent to it.[26]

Continued Miracle After the Beis Hamikdash was destroyed, the miracles ceased. However, B'nei Yisrael still came to daven in the Great Shul in Yerushalayim and although it was crammed, none of them ever complained because they all felt a strong love and desire to be there.[27]

 Did You Know?

Just In Case Every Yom Kippur, there was a kohen prepared as a backup to take over the Kohen Gadol, should he become impure. However, out of respect and honor for the Kohen Gadol's position, Hashem never allowed that to occur. This teaches the importance of respecting another's dignity.[28]

 Word Power

עוֹמְדִים צְפוּפִים וּמִשְׁתַּחֲוִים רְוָחִים A student once complained to his teacher that he felt like everyone was stepping on him and treating him rudely in the Beis Medrash. His wise teacher responded, "You spread yourself and your ego out all over the Beis Medrash, no one has anywhere else to step, other than on you!"[29]

When a person stands strong and rigid, leaving no space for another's opinion or feelings, his life might feel crowded around others. One who chooses to "bow his head," allowing room for another's presence, will suddenly find that there is more than enough room for everyone.

צְפוּפִים The word צְפוּפִים literally means floating. When the people stood in the Beis Hamikdash, it was so packed that their feet didn't even reach the floor. They remained suspended in midair, supported by the crowds around them.[30]

 **Story**

Stay Put!

R' Chaim Brisker was disturbed to see bochurim walking around during davening. He called over one bochur and asked him, "The mishnah states that one of the miracles in the Beis Hamikdash was that the Jews stood crowded together, but when they bowed, they had plenty of space. Wouldn't it have been a greater miracle if they had plenty of space even while they stood?"

R' Chaim then went on, and answered his own question: "Perhaps, having the tight space while standing was also part of the miracle. In reality, there would have been enough space for all to stand comfortably. However, since it's disrespectful to Hashem to stroll around the room while talking to Him, there was a miracle that they stood so crowded, that even if someone wanted to walk around, it was impossible."[31]

Ten miraculous things were created on Erev Shabbos at twilight—at the end of the sixth day of creation. They are:

1. **The opening of the earth** that swallowed Korach and his followers,
2. **The opening of the well** that provided water for B'nei Yisrael in the desert,
3. **The mouth of** Bilam's talking **donkey**,
4. **The rainbow** that appeared after the Flood,
5. **The mann** that B'nei Yisrael ate in the desert,
6. **The stick** that Moshe Rabbeinu used to perform miracles,
7. **The shamir** worm that cut the stones used to build the Beis Hamikdash,
8. **The** written shape of the **letters** of the Alef-Beis,
9. **The** engraved **writing** of the Luchos,
10. **The** first set of **Luchos**.

Some say that also created then **were the grave of Moshe Rabbeinu and the ram that Avraham Avinu** offered at the Akeidah in place of Yitzchak. **Some say that also the destructive** spirits were created then, **and even** the first pair of **tongs to make** other **tongs**—Hashem created the first pair, so man could then create more.

עֲשָׂרָה דְבָרִים נִבְרְאוּ בְּעֶרֶב שַׁבָּת בֵּין הַשְּׁמָשׁוֹת, וְאֵלּוּ הֵן:

פִּי הָאָרֶץ, פִּי הַבְּאֵר, פִּי הָאָתוֹן, הַקֶּשֶׁת, וְהַמָּן, וְהַמַּטֶּה, וְהַשָּׁמִיר, הַכְּתָב, וְהַמִּכְתָּב, וְהַלֻּחוֹת.

וְיֵשׁ אוֹמְרִים: אַף קִבְרוֹ שֶׁל מֹשֶׁה רַבֵּנוּ, וְאֵילוֹ שֶׁל אַבְרָהָם אָבִינוּ.

וְיֵשׁ אוֹמְרִים: אַף הַמַּזִּיקִין, וְאַף צְבָת בִּצְבָת עֲשׂוּיָה.

Living Lessons

No Time to Waste

Hashem had just finished creating an entire world and only moments were left until Shabbos. Still these moments were utilized to their fullest to create additional things, so not a precious second would be wasted. Each minute we are given is an opportunity to do another positive action.

 Did You Know?

Better than Steel It is forbidden to use any metal instruments to cut the stones of the Beis Hamikdash, since metal is also used for weapons of destruction. To alleviate the challenge of cutting through the huge rocks without classic tools, Hashem created the shamir worm to cut them instead.[32]

 Word Power

וְאַף צְבָת בִּצְבָת עֲשׂוּיָה The first tongs had no intrinsic purpose but were created only to facilitate the fashioning of other tongs. Yet, they are included in the important additions of bein hashmashos to teach us that the preparations for a mitzvah should be as treasured as the actual deed.[33]

Sparks

Engraved in Your Heart When ink colors paper, the ink and paper remain separate entities that can be separated. When letters are engraved in stone, however, the two become inseparable.

Torah can be learned so that it's like ink on paper: the Torah doesn't truly become one with the person, but is like an additional part of his life. The better way is like engraving on stone, like the miraculous writing of the luchos, when the Torah is an inseparable part of his being.[34]

Created With a Purpose What seems to be a random list of items is really a master plan for the creation of the world; each item was created to serve a particular purpose. The same applies to all creations in this world, from ice cream to Mt. Everest. Everything was created with a specific intention and can be used to make this world a home for Hashem.

Story

Mysterious Burial

The Roman governor in the area of Beis Pe'or (modern day northwest Jordan, where Moshe Rabbeinu was buried) was once commanded by the Emperor to find the kever of Moshe Rabbeinu.

The governor immediately dispatched a battalion of troops there to search for it. They located the mountain where he was buried, but when they climbed to the top they found that the kever was actually at the bottom of the mountain. They immediately went down the mountain, but when they reached the bottom, the kever appeared to them to be at the top of the mountain. Determined to get to the bottom of it, they split into two groups, one posted at the bottom and the other sent up to the top. However, this didn't help them either, for the group at the top saw the kever at the bottom of the mountain and the group at the bottom saw it at the top!

Hashem made it appear to them that way because He did not want anyone to ever find Moshe Rabbeinu's kever.[35]

There are **seven things** that identify a **foolish person**, and **seven** that identify a **wise person**.

A wise person:

1. **does not speak before someone who is greater than him in wisdom or in years** of age,
2. **does not interrupt his friend** while he is **speaking**,
3. **does not rush to answer** a question, but thinks carefully first,
4. **asks** questions that are relevant to **the subject, and replies to the point**,
5. **speaks** in an organized manner, dealing with matters of **first** priority **first, and the less important matters last**,
6. says, **"I have not heard"** when people ask him about things he has not heard,
7. **acknowledges the truth** when he is wrong, and does not continue to justify his previous opinion.

A foolish person does the **opposite** of all these things.

שִׁבְעָה דְבָרִים בְּגוֹלֶם וְשִׁבְעָה בְחָכָם,

חָכָם: אֵינוֹ מְדַבֵּר לִפְנֵי מִי שֶׁגָּדוֹל מִמֶּנּוּ בְּחָכְמָה וּבְמִנְיָן, וְאֵינוֹ נִכְנָס לְתוֹךְ דִּבְרֵי חֲבֵרוֹ, וְאֵינוֹ נִבְהָל לְהָשִׁיב, שׁוֹאֵל כְּעִנְיָן וּמֵשִׁיב כַּהֲלָכָה, וְאוֹמֵר עַל רִאשׁוֹן רִאשׁוֹן וְעַל אַחֲרוֹן אַחֲרוֹן, וְעַל מַה שֶּׁלֹּא שָׁמַע אוֹמֵר לֹא שָׁמַעְתִּי, וּמוֹדֶה עַל הָאֱמֶת, וְחִלּוּפֵיהֶן בְּגוֹלֶם.

Student Handbook

Living the lessons of this mishnah will enhance your learning experience and allow you to gain more wisdom. Your teachers are older than you and have a lot of experience from which you can benefit. Your friends may be asking important questions that you didn't even think of, so listen carefully to what your friends say too. Recognizing that there is more for you to learn is the first step to learning something new.

 Sparks

Wise Sensitivity What is so wise about answering questions in order?

People don't always ask questions in order of their importance. It takes an intelligent person to realize which question is really first in importance, requiring a more immediate response.

A Positive Message Whenever possible, it is best to speak in positive terms. Therefore, the mishnah enumerated the seven constructive habits of a wise person clearly, and merely referenced the bad habits of a fool as being the opposite.[36]

 Did You Know?

Acknowledge the Truth It takes wisdom and honesty to recognize and thank someone who has helped you, rather than convincing yourself that you have accomplished everything on your own. This is another aspect of the seventh attribute of a wise person listed here, acknowledging the truth.[37]

Story

Answer Carefully

A chassid of the Ba'al Shem Tov, R' Zev Kitzes, came to seek his Rebbe's brachah before embarking on a journey to Eretz Yisrael.

After blessing him for his trip, the Ba'al Shem Tov added a cryptic warning: "Weigh each word you say and be sure to answer each question properly."

R' Zev didn't understand what the Rebbe meant, but he was sure that he would find out soon enough. A short while into the journey, the captain announced an unscheduled stop to restock supplies and invited the passengers to disembark in the meanwhile. R' Zev sat down on a nearby bench and became so deeply lost in thought that he missed the call to reboard the ship. When he realized that he had been left behind, he became distressed and wandered around the town forlornly. Suddenly, a kindly-looking old Jew greeted him joyfully, informed him that the island had a minyan and mikvah, and invited him to spend the next few days with him until another ship would dock. R' Zev gratefully accepted and spent a delightful Shabbos with his gracious host.

As R' Zev was boarding the new ship, the man asked him, "Tell me, how are the Jews in your country faring?"

"Baruch Hashem," R' Zev answered distractedly. "Hashem does not forsake His people."

The ship was well out of the harbor when he realized what had just happened. "I ignored the Ba'al Shem Tov's instructions!" he rebuked himself. "I should have thought carefully before answering and told him about all the terrible suffering we endure."

He disembarked at the very next stop and returned immediately to Mezhibuzh to tell the Ba'al Shem Tov what had happened.

"R' Zev," the Ba'al Shem Tov began sadly, "every day Avraham Avinu confronts Hashem and demands that the Yidden be redeemed from their suffering. Hashem replies that He does not forsake His children. You were chosen to be the spokesperson to prove our terrible suffering and Avraham Avinu himself was the one to ask you the question. Had you responded properly, Mashiach would have come."[38]

 Word Power

וְאוֹמֵר עַל רִאשׁוֹן רִאשׁוֹן These words can also mean acknowledging the first as first: recognizing that the people of previous generations were greater than we are today. Rabi Yochanan once said, "If the earlier generations were on the level of angels, then we are like regular people. If they were just people, then we are like the level of donkeys."[39]

Seven types of punishment strike the world because of seven types of aveiros:

1. If **some** people **give ma'aser and some do not, a famine strikes, caused by** disrupting events that prevent normal planting or harvesting, and **some** people **go hungry while some are satisfied.**

2. If **they** all **decide not to give ma'aser, a famine of drought strikes,** when there is not enough rain to water the crops.

3. If they also decide **not to separate challah** when baking bread, **a famine of destruction strikes,** when not only is there no rain, but even rivers and lakes dry up.

4. **Deadly plagues strike the world** when people do aveiros that require the **death penalty according to Torah** law but which **Beis Din was not given** the responsibility to carry out, **and** also for not following the halachos regarding **produce** grown during the **seventh** (shmittah) year.

5. The **sword** of war **strikes the world because of the agony** that judges cause when they delay announcing a **verdict, because of** judges issuing a **corrupt verdict, and because of** people **who** interpret and **teach Torah** matters **not in accordance with the halachah.**

שִׁבְעָה מִינֵי פּוּרְעָנִיּוֹת בָּאִין לְעוֹלָם, עַל שִׁבְעָה גּוּפֵי עֲבֵרָה:

מִקְצָתָן מְעַשְּׂרִין וּמִקְצָתָן אֵינָן מְעַשְּׂרִין, רָעָב שֶׁל מְהוּמָה בָּא, מִקְצָתָן רְעֵבִים וּמִקְצָתָן שְׂבֵעִים.

גָּמְרוּ שֶׁלֹּא לְעַשֵּׂר, רָעָב שֶׁל בַּצֹּרֶת בָּא.

וְשֶׁלֹּא לִטּוֹל אֶת הַחַלָּה, רָעָב שֶׁל כְּלָיָה בָּא.

דֶּבֶר בָּא לְעוֹלָם עַל מִיתוֹת הָאֲמוּרוֹת בַּתּוֹרָה שֶׁלֹּא נִמְסְרוּ לְבֵית דִּין, וְעַל פֵּרוֹת שְׁבִיעִית.

חֶרֶב בָּאָה לְעוֹלָם עַל עִנּוּי הַדִּין, וְעַל עִוּוּת הַדִּין, וְעַל הַמּוֹרִים בַּתּוֹרָה שֶׁלֹּא כַהֲלָכָה.

Repaying a Loan

The word פּוּרְעָנִיּוֹת is closely related to the word פֵּרָעוֹן, which means repayment. When a person does an aveirah, it is as if he has taken out a debt with Hashem that he must pay back. His punishment serves as the repayment, and so it will fit his debt exactly—measure for measure.[40]

A plague of wild animals is the punishment for making unnecessary promises, because just as these aveiros are done primarily with the mouth, wild animals attack people with their mouths.[41] Additionally, it is our power of speech that makes us uniquely superior to animals. Misusing our power of speech brings us down to their level, and Hashem therefore makes us susceptible to their physical attacks as well.[42]

Deadly plagues result from withholding gifts to the poor, since these gifts can be literally a matter of life and death for them, as it is their only source of sustenance. If B'nei Yisrael show disregard for the lives of poor people, they are punished with life-threatening plagues.[43]

The same idea holds true for mitzvos—the reward matches the mitzvah performed.

6. Wild beasts strike the world because of **unnecessary oaths** that people make **and because of** people **desecrating Hashem's Name**.

7. **Exile comes to the world because of idol-worship, immorality, murder, and for** not letting the **earth** rest during the **shmittah** year.

Deadly plagues increase at four periods during every seven-year shmittah cycle: **in the fourth** year, **in the seventh** year, **in** the year **after the seventh** year, **and every year after** the end of **the Yom Tov** of Sukkos.

The plagues increase at those specific periods for the following reasons: **In the fourth** year they increase **because of ma'aser** withheld from the **poor**, which is required **in the** preceding **third** year. **In the seventh** year they increase **because of ma'aser** withheld from the **poor**, which is required **in the** preceding **sixth** year. **In** the year **after the seventh** (shmittah) year they increase **because of** people not keeping the laws concerning **produce** of the **seventh** year, and **every year after the Yom Tov** of Sukkos, when the harvesting season has ended, they increase **because of** people **stealing** from the **poor** by withholding the harvest **gifts** that are due them.

חַיָּה רָעָה בָּאָה לְעוֹלָם עַל שְׁבוּעַת שָׁוְא וְעַל חִלּוּל הַשֵּׁם.

גָּלוּת בָּא לְעוֹלָם עַל עֲבוֹדָה זָרָה, וְעַל גִּלּוּי עֲרָיוֹת, וְעַל שְׁפִיכוּת דָּמִים, וְעַל שְׁמִטַּת הָאָרֶץ.

בְּאַרְבָּעָה פְרָקִים הַדֶּבֶר מִתְרַבֶּה, בָּרְבִיעִית, וּבַשְּׁבִיעִית, וּבְמוֹצָאֵי שְׁבִיעִית, וּבְמוֹצָאֵי הֶחָג שֶׁבְּכָל שָׁנָה וְשָׁנָה.

בָּרְבִיעִית, מִפְּנֵי מַעֲשַׂר עָנִי שֶׁבַּשְּׁלִישִׁית.

בַּשְּׁבִיעִית, מִפְּנֵי מַעֲשַׂר עָנִי שֶׁבַּשִּׁשִּׁית.

בְּמוֹצָאֵי שְׁבִיעִית, מִפְּנֵי פֵּרוֹת שְׁבִיעִית.

בְּמוֹצָאֵי הֶחָג שֶׁבְּכָל שָׁנָה וְשָׁנָה, מִפְּנֵי גֶזֶל מַתְּנוֹת עֲנִיִּים.

 Sparks

Withholding is Stealing

Shlomoh Hamelech teaches, "Do not steal from a poor person, because he is poor." A poor person doesn't actually have any possessions to steal; instead the passuk is teaching one to be careful to give the proper ma'aser to the poor, and not withhold that which is rightfully theirs.[44]

The Real Owner

There was once a wealthy man whose field yielded 1,000 kur (an ancient measure, each about 2,500 cubic meters) of produce yearly. He was always very careful to give ma'aser properly and before he died, he instructed his son to do the same. The first year, the son heeded his father's advice and faithfully gave 100 kur to a levi. The second year, however, he was unhappy to give away so much produce, so he decided not to give at all. The third year, the field yielded him only 100 kur of produce. His friends explained to him that in his first year, Hashem allowed him to keep 90% of the produce since he gave 10% to Hashem. However, when he failed to give ma'aser, the next year Hashem took 90% and left him with 10%![45]

There are four types among people:

אַרְבַּע מִדּוֹת בָּאָדָם:

1. **One who says,** "There should not be any private ownership; **my** property **is yours, and your** property **is mine,"** is an ignorant person.

הָאוֹמֵר שֶׁלִּי שֶׁלָּךְ וְשֶׁלָּךְ שֶׁלִּי, עַם הָאָרֶץ.

2. One who says, **"My** property **is mine and your** property **is yours."** This is a **normal** character. **Some say that it is the character of the city of Sedom,** where it was a crime to share things or give tzedakah.

שֶׁלִּי שֶׁלִּי וְשֶׁלָּךְ שֶׁלָּךְ, זוֹ מִדָּה בֵּינוֹנִית, וְיֵשׁ אוֹמְרִים זוֹ מִדַּת סְדוֹם.

3. One who says, **"My** property **is yours and your** property is also **yours,"** is a **chassid,** because he goes beyond what the law requires by giving without expecting anything in return.

שֶׁלִּי שֶׁלָּךְ וְשֶׁלָּךְ שֶׁלָּךְ, חָסִיד.

4. One who says, **"Your** property **is mine and my** property **is mine,"** is **wicked,** because he wants everything for himself without giving anything in return.

שֶׁלָּךְ שֶׁלִּי וְשֶׁלִּי שֶׁלִּי, רָשָׁע.

Yours and Not Yours

The main reason people don't share their possessions is because they feel that they are the owners and have no obligation to give to others. In reality, however, none of our possessions truly belong to us—everything we have is from Hashem. Hashem has given it to us on temporary loan, so we should extend the same courtesy to others.

 Did You Know?

Giving Happily The Torah tells us regarding a poor person, "You shall surely give him, and your heart shall not be upset when you give to him."[46] This passuk cures us of the stinginess of the residents of Sedom and Amorah. By giving tzedakah repeatedly, we will eventually be able to give it with a happy heart and not begrudgingly.[47]

 Word Power

שֶׁלִּי שֶׁלָּךְ וְשֶׁלָּךְ שֶׁלָּךְ A chassid says, "what's mine is Yours," proclaiming to Hashem that whatever he does, even when fulfilling his personal, physical needs, is really all to enhance his service of Hashem. And certainly "what's Yours is Yours,"—his Torah and mitzvos are only for the sake of Hashem.[48]

Connections

The previous mishnah enumerated the punishments for not giving ma'aser. Not giving ma'aser is effectively claiming others' property as your own, which is the theme discussed in this mishnah.[49]

Sparks

A Shifted Focus "What's mine" can also refer to a person's responsibility in life—namely, to improve himself spiritually—and "what's Yours" can refer to Hashem's responsibility—to provide for our physical needs. The person who focuses on his physical needs and leaves his spiritual improvement up to Hashem is like one who says "what's mine is Yours and what's Yours is mine,"—his mindset is backward. We must focus all our energies on improving ourselves spiritually. Our physical worries should be placed on Hashem's shoulders with our efforts focused merely on creating a vessel for His brachos.[50]

Story

An Old Custom

When R' Levi Yitzchak became rav of Berditchev, he made a condition that he would attend community meetings only when new resolutions were being decided. Once, the community leaders decided to abolish the custom of collecting tzedakah door to door. Instead, they instituted a new practice where each poor family would receive a set amount from the treasury. Before they passed the resolution, they invited R' Levi Yitzchak to review it.

"I told you to only call me for new decisions," he exclaimed when he heard the plan. "This custom existed years ago in the cities of Sedom and Amorah where they refused to give food to poor people." The leaders took the rebuke to heart and the idea was canceled.[51]

There are four types of temperaments:

1. One who is **easily angered and easily calmed—the benefit outweighs the loss** because his anger passes quickly.

2. One who is **hard to anger and hard to calm—his loss outweighs the gain** because once he is angered, it remains for a long time.

3. One who is **hard to anger and easily calmed is a chassid.**

4. One who is **easily angered and hard to calm is a wicked person.**

אַרְבַּע מִדּוֹת בְּדֵעוֹת:
נוֹחַ לִכְעוֹס וְנוֹחַ לֵרָצוֹת,
יָצָא הֶפְסֵדוֹ בִּשְׂכָרוֹ.

קָשֶׁה לִכְעוֹס וְקָשֶׁה לֵרָצוֹת,
יָצָא שְׂכָרוֹ בְּהֶפְסֵדוֹ.

קָשֶׁה לִכְעוֹס וְנוֹחַ לֵרָצוֹת, חָסִיד.

נוֹחַ לִכְעוֹס וְקָשֶׁה לֵרָצוֹת, רָשָׁע.

Pure Character

Allowing our anger to get the better of us is a clear violation of halachah, so that is obviously not what the mishnah is talking about. Pirkei Avos is about refining your character—in this case, working to eliminate even an angry streak in your character, even if you never act on it.

When something upsets you, count slowly to ten in your mind before reacting to it. Take a few seconds to remind yourself that Hashem is the One Who truly makes everything happen, and the person who wronged you is merely one of His messengers. Hashem loves you as a father loves his child and He obviously wouldn't want to hurt you. Think about the deeper message He might be sending you with this particular aggravation. Perhaps it is in place of something even worse that may have happened, which Hashem, in His kindness, changed to this mild occurrence. Or perhaps Hashem is giving you an opportunity to strengthen your character by improving your patience. Even if it was truly a terrible thing, it is possible that the suffering in this world will prevent you from greater suffering in the next.

Interestingly, although anger management is a מִדָּה, the mishnah uses the word דֵּעוֹת, which means opinions. This is because anger has more to do with mindset than character. Someone whose mind is settled and can think rationally will be less easily angered, while a confused mind flies into a rage at the slightest provocation.[53] When someone understands that everything is truly meant for his good, he won't have reason to be angry.

 Connections

The previous mishnah discussed different attitudes toward one's possessions. This mishnah continues with the idea of anger because financial concerns often lead to anger and arguments.[52]

 Did You Know?

Keep Calm and Enjoy Life Chazal list three types of people who do not allow themselves to enjoy life. One of them is a person who is easily angered. He is always in a bad mood, and even when he is momentarily happy, he is liable to fly into a rage at any moment. What kind of a life is that?[54]

Sparks

Like Avodah Zarah Chazal say that being angry is like serving avodah zarah. This is because a person becomes angry when he feels that his self-worth has not been properly valued or respected by others. He is also attributing occurrences to powers other than Hashem. By giving so much credit to his own or other people's existence, he is in essence denying that Hashem is the only important One.[55]

Time for Teshuvah This mishnah can also refer to the different ways that people make Hashem angry with aveiros and subsequently appease Him by doing teshuvah. There are those who sin often, angering Hashem, but follow up with teshuvah as well, thereby appeasing Him. Some people almost never do an aveirah, but when they do, they find it hard to admit to their mistake and do teshuvah. A rasha commits aveiros often and doesn't bother atoning for them, while the righteous commit few aveiros and always make sure to follow up with sincere teshuvah.[56]

Word Power

קָשֶׁה לִכְעוֹס וְנוֹחַ לִרְצוֹת, חָסִיד

The mishnah states that there are four temperaments among people. However, it does not include one who never gets angry, since that is far beyond regular human ability; someone like that is considered more angel than man. The highest level a regular person can achieve is that of a chassid, who might have rare outbreaks of anger, but which don't last long.[57]

Story

More Precious than an Esrog

R' Michel Zlotchover owned a special pair of tefillin he had inherited from his holy father. Many rich chassidim offered vast sums of money for them, but R' Michel refused to sell. His wife constantly begged him to sell them and use the money for desperately needed household expenses, but he remained firm in his decision.

One time, shortly before Sukkos, there was no esrog to be found in Zlotchov. Finally, on Erev Sukkos, a man came into town with a beautiful esrog but demanded to be paid not a penny less than fifty gold coins. R' Michel quickly found an eager buyer for his precious tefillin and bought the esrog with the proceeds. When his wife asked how he acquired such a beautiful esrog, he told her that he had sold his tefillin. She flew into a rage and screamed, "How can you do this? I've been begging you for years to sell them so we could have some money and you always refused. Now you sell it for an esrog?" She was so angry, she bit off the top of the esrog, rendering it passul. R' Michel calmly said, "Hashem, if You would like my esrog to be passul, I accept it with love."

His father appeared to him in a dream that night and informed him that the second sacrifice he made that day in controlling his anger was treasured even more than the act of selling his precious tefillin to buy the esrog![58]

There are four types of students:

1. One who is **quick to understand but quick to forget**—**his loss outweighs his gain** because he will remain with nothing.

2. One who is **slow to understand but slow to forget**—**his gain outweighs his loss** because he will eventually have much knowledge.

3. One who is **quick to understand and slow to forget**—**this** person has received **a good lot** from Hashem.

4. One who is **slow to understand and quick to forget**—**this** person has received **a bad lot**.

אַרְבַּע מִדּוֹת בַּתַּלְמִידִים:
מַהֵר לִשְׁמוֹעַ וּמַהֵר לְאַבֵּד,
יָצָא שְׂכָרוֹ בְּהֶפְסֵדוֹ.

קָשֶׁה לִשְׁמוֹעַ וְקָשֶׁה לְאַבֵּד,
יָצָא הֶפְסֵדוֹ בִּשְׂכָרוֹ.

מַהֵר לִשְׁמוֹעַ וְקָשֶׁה
לְאַבֵּד, זֶה חֵלֶק טוֹב.

קָשֶׁה לִשְׁמוֹעַ וּמַהֵר
לְאַבֵּד, זֶה חֵלֶק רָע.

Use What You've Got

A student who grasps a teacher's lesson quickly and remembers it for a while should thank Hashem for the special gift he was given. However, no matter what intellectual abilities you have, you must try your hardest to pay attention and learn to the best of your ability. No one is excused from trying.

One who finds it hard to understand, or forgets the material shortly after learning it, must not give up, but should constantly review the lessons.

One who finds learning easy should not credit himself, but should thank Hashem for his good fortune.

One who cannot grasp or remember his studies should realize that Hashem still wants him to try his best, using his limited capabilities.

 Connections

The Gemara says, "A Chacham who becomes angry loses his wisdom."⁵⁹ This shows us the connection to the previous mishnah: someone who doesn't get angry often or is easily appeased will also possess the good qualities mentioned in this mishnah. On the other hand, one who is angered easily and isn't easily appeased will find it hard to learn and will easily forget his knowledge.⁶⁰

 Did You Know?

Nonexistent The mishnah does not include in this list a person who never forgets, nor a person who is incapable of understanding—because neither of those students exist. Every single person is capable of learning Torah, just with varying amounts of effort. Even someone who remembers his learning for a long time must constantly review rather than rely solely on his natural ability.⁶¹

Story

No Excuses

A student once explained to R' Yechezkel Levinstein that he was exempt from learning because he was simply unable to learn. R' Yechezkel answered, "There are two types of people who don't learn: those who have an excuse and those who don't. It would seem that you are in the first group and therefore will not be punished for not learning. In truth, however, you are the one losing out by making excuses, because at the end of the day, you will still be ignorant."[62]

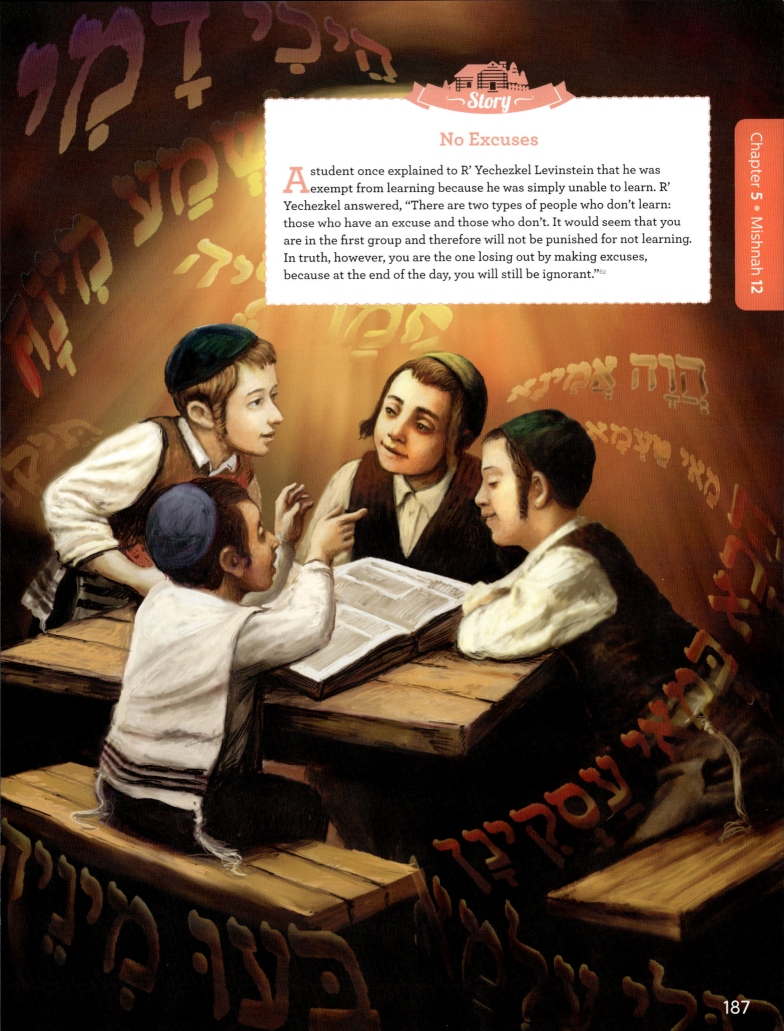

There are four types of people who give tzedakah:

1. One **who wants to give** tzedakah **but** does **not** want **others to give**—such a person **wishes bad on others,** and does not want them to benefit from the reward that comes from giving tzedakah.

2. One who wants **others to give** tzedakah, **but he** himself **does not want to give**—such a person **wishes bad on himself** by denying himself the reward that comes from giving tzedakah.

3. One who wants to **give** tzedakah **and** wants **others to give** is a **chassid**.

4. One who **does not** want to **give** tzedakah **and** does **not** want **others** to **give is a wicked person.**

אַרְבַּע מִדּוֹת בְּנוֹתְנֵי צְדָקָה:

הָרוֹצֶה שֶׁיִּתֵּן וְלֹא יִתְּנוּ אֲחֵרִים, עֵינוֹ רָעָה בְּשֶׁל אֲחֵרִים.

יִתְּנוּ אֲחֵרִים וְהוּא לֹא יִתֵּן, עֵינוֹ רָעָה בְּשֶׁלּוֹ.

יִתֵּן וְיִתְּנוּ אֲחֵרִים, חָסִיד.

לֹא יִתֵּן וְלֹא יִתְּנוּ אֲחֵרִים, רָשָׁע.

Penniless Tzedakah

Giving tzedakah means helping someone in need. Therefore, even someone who isn't wealthy can give tzedakah. You can help a friend who struggles with his homework, you can smile at the new kid in class, or you can stand up to the class bullies when you see them hurting someone. Opportunities for tzedakah are all around! Teaching others about mitzvos, visiting old people in the nursing home, or giving your parents nachas are all way to give tzedakah generously, even without spending a penny.

Connections

This mishnah connects to the previous one through the famous Yissachar-Zevulun partnership. Yissachar was a shevet of Torah learners supported by the businessmen from the shevet of Zevulun. A student is only able to learn if he is supported by generous sponsors and doesn't need to worry about financial concerns.[63] Through enabling Torah study, the businessman receives an equal share in the learning.

Word Power

לֹא יִתֵּן וְלֹא יִתְּנוּ The mishnah includes a person who does not give at all in the list of four types who give tzedakah. This is because it is the natural and innermost desire of every Jew to fulfill Hashem's will. However, this is sometimes covered up and not expressed. Yet the desire itself can never be extinguished; deep down, every Jew can be counted as a tzedakah giver. He may just need some time to discover and reveal that desire.[64]

Sparks

It's the Thought that Counts The mishnah does not categorize tzedakah donors by their actions, but by their intentions and mindset. Someone who gives a large donation but does so begrudgingly is not good, while someone who doesn't have any money to offer but consoles a pauper with kind words is righteous.[65] As the Gemara says,[66] "Someone who gives money to a poor person receives six blessings. Someone who also appeases the poor person with kind words receives eleven blessings."[67]

Give and Encourage to Give A chassid is someone who is not satisfied with fulfilling the basic halachah but always searches for ways to go beyond the letter of the law. Giving tzedakah himself is easy, and so he goes out of his way to encourage others to give as well.[68]

Learned from the Mishnah

The Noda Bi'yehudah was once approached by tzedakah collectors for a donation to help release a fellow Jew who was imprisoned.

"How much is needed?" he asked.

"1,000 coins," they replied.

The Rav went into the next room and brought back 990 coins. "Here is my donation," he said, handing them the sack.

"Excuse me, Rav," they asked him, "if you gave 990 coins so happily, why didn't you give ten more so we wouldn't have to collect from others?"

"You forget the mishnah," the Noda Bi'yehudah reminded them. "One who gives tzedakah but does not want others to give—such a person wishes bad upon others, for he does not allow them the opportunity to earn reward."[69]

Did You Know?

Jingle, Jingle, Smash, Crash It is better to give a large amount of tzedakah in small increments rather than all at once, because each time you give tzedakah, you are breaking your yetzer hara, who doesn't want you to part with your money.

There are four types of people who go to the Beis Medrash:

1. One who **goes** to the Beis Medrash **but does not** learn—**he is rewarded for going.**

2. One who **does** learn Torah at home **but does not go** to the Beis Medrash—**he is rewarded for** the learning he **did.**

3. One who **goes** to the Beis Medrash **and does** learn is a **chassid.**

4. One who **does not go** to the Beis Medrash and **does not** learn at home is a **wicked person.**

אַרְבַּע מִדּוֹת בְּהוֹלְכֵי בֵית הַמִּדְרָשׁ:

הוֹלֵךְ וְאֵינוֹ עוֹשֶׂה, שְׂכַר הֲלִיכָה בְּיָדוֹ.

עוֹשֶׂה וְאֵינוֹ הוֹלֵךְ, שְׂכַר מַעֲשֶׂה בְּיָדוֹ.

הוֹלֵךְ וְעוֹשֶׂה, חָסִיד.

לֹא הוֹלֵךְ וְלֹא עוֹשֶׂה, רָשָׁע.

On the Way

Sometimes, we start off doing something good with lots of energy and the best intentions, but halfway through we find ourselves intimidated and discouraged, and unable to follow through with our plans. Although it would be ideal to always fulfill our goals, we should know that Hashem cherishes both the action and desire to do it, and each are valuable to him.

Location, Location, Location

A person who sits idly in the Beis Medrash is rewarded simply for choosing to spend time there. Though he may not be actively learning, being surrounded by Torah on all sides will eventually have a positive effect.[70]

 Did You Know?

So Much Better Here There are many reasons why it is preferable to daven in a shul rather than in a private minyan in a home or office. Some of them are:

1. The awe of being in a holy place is not felt in a private home.
2. When the minyan runs a few minutes late in a shul, the congregants will use the time to say some Tehillim or learn from a sefer. In a house, they will feel less inclined to do so.
3. Once there is a gabbai collecting tzedakah in shul, poor people feel more welcome to come in and do the same.[71]

 Sparks

Full Immersion The one who neither goes nor does is held responsible for his actions because he doesn't even try to fully immerse himself in the Beis Medrash and give learning his best effort. If he had, he would have tasted the sweetness of Torah and would have wanted to continue.

Sparks

Call to Action The rasha mentioned in this mishnah is in the unfortunate situation of not even knowing that his actions are wrong. We therefore call him by such a harsh name to inform him, inspire him to action, and force him to give up the excuse of ignorance.[72]

Intent vs. Deed Good intentions and positive results are both important, which is why a person who completes only one of them is still rewarded. The title chassid, however, is reserved for someone who actually fulfills both.

Word Power

הוֹלֵךְ וְעוֹשֶׂה The word עוֹשֶׂה also means "to cause others to do." The four people in the mishnah can then be referring to:

1. הוֹלֵךְ וְאֵינוֹ עוֹשֶׂה—Someone who goes to the Beis Medrash to learn but does not encourage others to join;
2. עוֹשֶׂה וְאֵינוֹ הוֹלֵךְ—Someone who encourages others to go learn but does not go himself;
3. הוֹלֵךְ וְעוֹשֶׂה—Someone who goes and also encourages others to join;
4. לֹא הוֹלֵךְ וְלֹא עוֹשֶׂה—Someone who neither goes nor encourages others to go.[73]

Another explanation is that the "doing" in this mishnah refers to doing things to help the upkeep of the Beis Medrash. The four people in the mishnah can then be referring to:

1. הוֹלֵךְ וְאֵינוֹ עוֹשֶׂה—Someone who goes to the Beis Medrash but does not help in its upkeep;
2. עוֹשֶׂה וְאֵינוֹ הוֹלֵךְ—Someone who helps with the upkeep but does not go himself;
3. הוֹלֵךְ וְעוֹשֶׂה—Someone who goes and helps in its upkeep;
4. לֹא הוֹלֵךְ וְלֹא עוֹשֶׂה—Someone who neither goes nor helps with the upkeep of the Beis Medrash.[74]

Why Share it with a Horse?

Even the journey on the way to a mitzvah is holy.

The author of the Meir Nesivim was once walking to draw mayim shelanu to bake matzos, when he met the Maggid of Ostra'ah headed for the same destination. "Why don't you join me on my cart?" the Maggid offered. "There's no need for you to get all muddied."

"I have this mitzvah once a year," the other replied, "and you think I'm going to share it with a horse?"

The Maggid immediately descended from his wagon and the two continued together on foot.[75]

There are four types of students who sit before Chachamim—a sponge, a funnel, a strainer, and a sifter:

1. **A sponge** represents a student who **absorbs everything**.

2. **A funnel takes in** something **from one** end **and spills** it **out from the other** end. This represents a student who listens to his teacher but quickly forgets what he said.

3. **A strainer lets the wine** flow **through and collects the sediment**. This represents a student who forgets important lessons but remembers less important lessons.

4. **A sifter lets the flour-dust pass through and keeps the fine flour.** This represents a student who only remembers important lessons.

אַרְבַּע מִדּוֹת בְּיוֹשְׁבִים לִפְנֵי חֲכָמִים: סְפוֹג, וּמַשְׁפֵּךְ, מְשַׁמֶּרֶת, וְנָפָה.

סְפוֹג, שֶׁהוּא סוֹפֵג אֶת הַכֹּל.

וּמַשְׁפֵּךְ, שֶׁמַּכְנִיס בְּזוֹ וּמוֹצִיא בְזוֹ.

מְשַׁמֶּרֶת, שֶׁמּוֹצִיאָה אֶת הַיַּיִן וְקוֹלֶטֶת אֶת הַשְּׁמָרִים.

וְנָפָה, שֶׁמּוֹצִיאָה אֶת הַקֶּמַח וְקוֹלֶטֶת אֶת הַסֹּלֶת:

Take the Best of Everything

Each of the four types of learners (sponge, funnel, strainer, and sieve) have both positive and negative qualities. A person should strive to have the advantages of each of the four instruments:

1. Sponge (absorbs everything):
- Positive: Absorbs a lot of material quickly.
- Negative: Doesn't share his knowledge easily; needs to be "squeezed."

2. Funnel (keeps nothing inside):
- Positive: Passes on what he learned to others.
- Negative: Forgets what he learned quickly.

3. Strainer (keeps the bad and passes on the good):
- Positive: Discerns between important lessons and trivia and only passes on the important parts.
- Negative: Forgets important lessons but remembers trivia.

4. Sifter (keeps the good and passes on the bad):
- Positive: Discerns between important lessons and trivia, but only remembers the important stuff.
- Negative: Passes on only the non-essential lessons.[76]

Did You Know?

Four Stages The four types of students listed in this mishnah also represent four stages that every student goes through:

1. Sponge: When a child begins to learn, his mind absorbs everything, like a sponge. The teacher therefore needs to be careful to teach him only what is essential and correct.
2. Funnel: Eventually the child gets tired and loses focus, and the teacher's words begin to pass right through him. When that happens, the teacher gives the student a break.
3. Strainer: When the student matures and grows older, he gains the ability to distinguish between different kinds of information. However, because his mind is still developing, he cannot fully grasp deep concepts, which are compared to wine. He retains only the lower-level teachings.
4. Sieve: This is the highest level in a student's development. Not only does he have the ability to identify and forget unessential teachings—the flour-dust—but he also has the ability to understand and remember the fine flour—the deepest concepts.[77]

Word Power

בְּיוֹשְׁבִים לִפְנֵי חֲכָמִים The mishnah calls the four types of students "those who sit before Chachamim." This is because it is important to spend time in the presence of Chachamim and learn directly from them.[79]

In fact, even looking at the face of a righteous scholar has great benefits. Rabi Yehudah Hanassi once said that the reason he had such a good understanding of Torah was because he sat right behind Rabi Meir during shiurim. "Had I sat directly in front of him," he said, "I would have been even smarter."[80]

Sparks

Icing A teacher may use analogies or stories to make certain ideas more easily understood, or he might admonish the students or tell a joke (known as מִילְתָא דִּבְדִיחוּתָא) so that they pay attention. These are the parts of learning that the mishnah refers to as non-essential, for they are only an aid to teach the real Torah lessons.[78]

Story

An Empty "Kup"

A student once complained to R' Shlomoh Chaim Kesselman that although he was learning a lot, he didn't feel like any of it stayed with him. As the rav listened, he offered to make the student a tea and began to pour the hot water into a teacup. Instead of watching the cup however, he kept his eyes on the boy's face. The cup started to spill over onto the table, but R' Shlomoh Chaim didn't stop. At first the student didn't say anything out of respect for his teacher but after making quite a mess, the student respectfully pointed out that the tea was now spilling onto the floor.

"I don't understand," the rav asked, "why the water stayed in the cup at first but spilled over later on."

"When the cup is empty, it can be filled," the student replied, "but once it is full, the water will just spill over the sides."

"The same thing applies to your head," R' Shlomoh Chaim explained. "When it's filled with petty things, there is no room for Torah and it just spills out."

The student later told his friends that the lesson had penetrated deeply. He was always checking the latest headlines to keep up with the latest news, but when he realized how much it was interfering with his learning, he stopped.[81]

Any love that depends on a variable factor will cease when that factor ceases to be, and any love that does not depend on any variable factor will never cease.	כָּל אַהֲבָה שֶׁהִיא תְלוּיָה בְדָבָר, בָּטֵל דָּבָר בְּטֵלָה אַהֲבָה, וְשֶׁאֵינָהּ תְּלוּיָה בְדָבָר, אֵינָהּ בְּטֵלָה לְעוֹלָם.
What is an example of a love that depended on a variable factor? The love that Amnon had for Tamar, which was based on her beauty—a variable factor.	אֵיזוֹ הִיא אַהֲבָה שֶׁהִיא תְלוּיָה בְדָבָר, זוֹ אַהֲבַת אַמְנוֹן וְתָמָר, וְשֶׁאֵינָהּ תְּלוּיָה בְדָבָר, זוֹ אַהֲבַת דָּוִד וִיהוֹנָתָן.
What is an example of a love that did not depend on any specific thing? The love between Dovid Hamelech and Yehonasan. Yehonasan encouraged Dovid to be king, even though that prevented Yehonasan from being king, because he loved Dovid.	

Any argument that is for the sake of Hashem in heaven will have a lasting and meaningful outcome. But any argument that is for personal reasons, and not for the sake of Hashem in heaven, will not have a lasting and meaningful outcome.	כָּל מַחֲלוֹקֶת שֶׁהִיא לְשֵׁם שָׁמַיִם, סוֹפָהּ לְהִתְקַיֵּם, וְשֶׁאֵינָהּ לְשֵׁם שָׁמַיִם, אֵין סוֹפָהּ לְהִתְקַיֵּם.
What is an example of an argument that was for the sake of Hashem in heaven? The argument between Hillel and Shammai, who argued regarding halachos, yet their arguments were not personal; they cared only to determine the true halachah.	אֵיזוֹ הִיא מַחֲלוֹקֶת שֶׁהִיא לְשֵׁם שָׁמַיִם, זוֹ מַחֲלוֹקֶת הִלֵּל וְשַׁמַּאי. וְשֶׁאֵינָהּ לְשֵׁם שָׁמַיִם, זוֹ מַחֲלוֹקֶת קֹרַח וְכָל עֲדָתוֹ.
What is an example of an argument that was not for the sake of Hashem in heaven? The argument of Korach and his entire group with Moshe Rabbeinu, whose argument was rooted in a desire to rebel against authority.	

True Love

There are many people whom you may like. To test whether your love for them is unconditional, imagine if they were to stop talking to you, giving you gifts, or helping you out. What if they even made life harder for you? Would you still continue to love them?

A person does not stop loving his parents even if they are unable to provide for him. We must feel the same unchanging love toward Hashem.

Arguing the Holy Way

Arguing for personal gain is obviously something to be avoided. Even when arguing in matters of Torah, be careful to remember that it is Hashem's Torah and the argument is not about personal honor or being right. When both sides know that the only goal is to gain in Torah knowledge, the dispute becomes holy.

 ## Sparks

For the Right Reason Unconditional love for Hashem means performing the mitzvos just because Hashem said so. If you aren't yet at that level, doing mitzvos for other reasons is also good, because it will lead one to love Hashem.[82]

Cut from the Same Cloth An argument in Torah can be everlasting because the two opinions are themselves parts of Torah, which is eternal. Even if the halachah follows only one opinion, there is still a lesson to take from the others.

Selfish Love It is possible to help others for selfish reasons, such as to feel good about yourself, to be appreciated, or to feel important. A real act of love, however, is one that is done not for your benefit (however subtle) but purely for the benefit of the recipient.

It Takes Two When discussing a dispute that is l'shem Shamayim, the mishnah names both sides, Hillel and Shammai, since both had the same holy intention. The unholy dispute, however, mentions only Korach since he was in it only to win power for himself while Moshe's stance was l'shem Shamayim. So the dispute is only referred to as Korach's dispute.[83]

 ## Did You Know?

Still Not Final In the disputes between Hillel and Shammai, we generally follow the opinion of Hillel, but when Mashiach comes, we will follow that of Shammai instead.[85]

Love whom your Beloved Loves Having ahavas Yisrael helps you feel love toward Hashem because you are showing love toward those whom Hashem loves. Some siddurim have a proclamation accepting the mitzvah of ahavas Yisrael before davening, when we declare our love for Hashem.

 ## Connections

The ideas in these two mishnayos are connected: if the root of something is positive, it will succeed. Things rooted in evil will not last.[84]

Story

Leave it to the Experts

The Ba'al Shem Tov and R' Nachman Kosover differed in their opinions of the ideal way to serve Hashem. Once, R' Nachman overheard someone say something negative about the Ba'al Shem Tov's position.

"Let me tell you a story," he offered. "There was once a king who had two ministers. They decided to make a crown and present it to the king. They argued bitterly over the exact placement of the diamond and which position the king would like best. While they were discussing it, a commoner overheard them and told them, 'I agree with this minister. You should put the diamond there.'

"'Fool!' they answered him. 'Who do you think you are to give your opinion? We know the king and what he likes, so we can disagree. You don't know anything about it!'

"The same is true between me and the Ba'al Shem Tov," R' Nachman concluded. "We understand the greatness of Hashem and therefore, we argue about which way of service will please Him most. You don't understand anything about it, so who are you to offer your opinion?"[86]

כָּל הַמְזַכֶּה אֶת הָרַבִּים,
אֵין חֵטְא בָּא עַל יָדוֹ,
וְכָל הַמַּחֲטִיא אֶת הָרַבִּים, אֵין
מַסְפִּיקִין בְּיָדוֹ לַעֲשׂוֹת תְּשׁוּבָה.

One who tries to **bring merit to many people** is ensured by Hashem that **no aveirah is caused through him**. But **one who** tries to **bring many people to do aveiros** will **not be given an opportunity to do teshuvah** easily.

מֹשֶׁה זָכָה וְזִכָּה אֶת הָרַבִּים,
זְכוּת הָרַבִּים תָּלוּי בּוֹ,
שֶׁנֶּאֱמַר: צִדְקַת יְיָ עָשָׂה,
וּמִשְׁפָּטָיו עִם יִשְׂרָאֵל.

Moshe Rabbeinu is an example of the first type. He **had** many personal **merits** and he **brought merit to many** other **people** by teaching them Torah and guiding them. In addition, because he brought them merit, **he is given the credit for the merit of the many, as it says** in the Torah: Moshe Rabbeinu **did the righteous** mitzvos **of Hashem and** fulfilled **His laws with** B'nei **Yisrael**.

יָרָבְעָם בֶּן נְבָט חָטָא
וְהֶחֱטִיא אֶת הָרַבִּים,
חֵטְא הָרַבִּים תָּלוּי בּוֹ,
שֶׁנֶּאֱמַר: עַל חַטֹּאות
יָרָבְעָם אֲשֶׁר חָטָא,
וַאֲשֶׁר הֶחֱטִיא אֶת יִשְׂרָאֵל.

Yeravam ben Nevat is an example of the second type. He **did aveiros and led many others to do aveiros** by convincing them to worship idols. Because he caused their aveiros, **he is given the credit for the aveiros of the many people, as it says** in Melachim: **Yeravam** was punished **for the aveiros that he did and for the aveiros** that **he caused** B'nei **Yisrael** to do.

Be a Positive Influence

Our lives are so busy and there's always so much to get done! Sometimes, it seems impossible to make time to help a friend as well. Just remember that while you are very important, helping others should always be a top priority. The merit of causing others to do mitzvos is tremendous, and Hashem protects you from anything bad when you do so.

In contrast, being a bad influence is the worst thing you can do. If a person chooses to do aveiros on his own, that is his own business and he will be held accountable by Hashem. Causing others to sin though, is unforgivable.

Make sure that you are always a positive influence on your surroundings, and cause others only to do good things.

Sparks

To Teach is to Do Moshe fulfilled all the mitzvos he could, but some can only be practiced in Eretz Yisrael, where Moshe never stepped foot. Therefore, when B'nei Yisrael fulfilled the mitzvos based on Moshe's teachings, it was considered as if he himself had fulfilled them.[87]

Big or Small or None at All It doesn't matter if the mitzvah you helped others perform was big or small, or even if they didn't accept your offer! If you put in effort to help others improve their service of Hashem, Hashem will assist you in your service.[88]

Never Closed It's never impossible to do teshuvah, as the gates of teshuvah are never closed, no matter what.[89] The mishnah states that a person who has caused others to sin will receive no extra Divine intervention to aid him, but if he tries very hard, he can still do teshuvah.[90]

Word Power

אֵין חֵטְא בָּא עַל יָדוֹ The mishnah doesn't mean that the person will never sin again, because that would eliminate his free choice. Rather, the mishnah means that he will be protected from committing an unintentional sin.

All's Well That Ends Well

There was once a man named Nechunya who realized that the Jews traveling up to Yerushalayim for the Yom Tov had no water along the way and suffered terribly. He spent a long time digging wells along the roadsides so that the travelers would have fresh water. One day, his daughter was playing near one of those wells and fell inside. The family ran to Rabi Chanina ben Dosa, who calmly assured them that the girl would be saved. A while passed with no change and they grew frantic again, but Rabi Chanina just repeated his statement firmly.

A short time later, Rabi Chanina proclaimed, "The girl has been taken out of the well!"

The amazed parents hugged their daughter tightly and asked her how she had been rescued. "An old man with a ram came and pulled me out," she told them. Little did she know that she had been saved by Avraham Avinu himself. Rabi Chanina's students turned to him and asked how he had known the girl's future. "I am neither a prophet nor the son of a prophet," he declared. "I just knew it was impossible for Nechunya to suffer from the wells he dug to help others."[91]

One who has the following three traits is considered **a student of Avraham Avinu** who has learned from his ways, **and** one who has **three other traits** is considered **a student of the wicked Bilam.**	**כָּל** מִי שֶׁיֵּשׁ בּוֹ שְׁלֹשָׁה דְבָרִים הַלָּלוּ, הוּא מִתַּלְמִידָיו שֶׁל אַבְרָהָם אָבִינוּ, וּשְׁלֹשָׁה דְבָרִים אֲחֵרִים, הוּא מִתַּלְמִידָיו שֶׁל בִּלְעָם הָרָשָׁע.
The traits of **students of Avraham Avinu: a good** and generous **eye**—they are not jealous, but are happy for another's success, **a humble spirit, and a modest soul**—they avoid unnecessary luxuries.	תַּלְמִידָיו שֶׁל אַבְרָהָם אָבִינוּ: עַיִן טוֹבָה, וְרוּחַ נְמוּכָה, וְנֶפֶשׁ שְׁפָלָה.
The traits of **students of the wicked Bilam: a bad** and unsatisfied **eye**—they are jealous of others and are unsatisfied with what they have, **an arrogant spirit, and a greedy soul.**	תַּלְמִידָיו שֶׁל בִּלְעָם הָרָשָׁע: עַיִן רָעָה, וְרוּחַ גְּבוֹהָה, וְנֶפֶשׁ רְחָבָה.
What is the difference **between Avraham Avinu's students and the wicked Bilam's students? Avraham Avinu's students** will **eat** and enjoy the benefits of their good traits **in this world and** will **inherit** the greatest part of their reward in **the World to Come. As it says** in Mishlei: Hashem said: I will **cause those who love Me to inherit** the World to Come, **and I will** also **fill up their storehouses** in this world.	מַה בֵּין תַּלְמִידָיו שֶׁל אַבְרָהָם אָבִינוּ לְתַלְמִידָיו שֶׁל בִּלְעָם הָרָשָׁע, תַּלְמִידָיו שֶׁל אַבְרָהָם אָבִינוּ אוֹכְלִין בָּעוֹלָם הַזֶּה, וְנוֹחֲלִין הָעוֹלָם הַבָּא, שֶׁנֶּאֱמַר: לְהַנְחִיל אֹהֲבַי יֵשׁ, וְאֹצְרֹתֵיהֶם אֲמַלֵּא.
But the wicked Bilam's students will inherit Gehinom and go down into a pit of destruction, as it says in Tehillim: **And You, God, will bring them down to a pit of destruction. Men** who are bloodthirsty and **liars do not** live for even **half** the **days of their** lives. **But I will trust in You.**	אֲבָל תַּלְמִידָיו שֶׁל בִּלְעָם הָרָשָׁע יוֹרְשִׁין גֵּיהִנֹּם וְיוֹרְדִין לִבְאֵר שַׁחַת, שֶׁנֶּאֱמַר: וְאַתָּה אֱלֹהִים תּוֹרִידֵם לִבְאֵר שַׁחַת, אַנְשֵׁי דָמִים וּמִרְמָה לֹא יֶחֱצוּ יְמֵיהֶם, וַאֲנִי אֶבְטַח בָּךְ.

Living Lessons

Inside Out

Being jealous of a friend's new gadget is not merely a wish to own the same thing, but generally an indication of the envy we feel for him deep in our hearts. Jealous people can never have a happy and satisfying life because they always feel they are missing something. Generous people who can tolerate and even be happy for other people's good fortune have happy lives! What kind of life do you want to live?

Sparks

Bilam Today The mishnah finishes with a part of the passuk, "I will trust in You," which seems irrelevant to the mishnah and could have been omitted. It is included, however, to assure those who come into contact with creatures like Bilam not to despair, and trust that Hashem will carry out their due punishment.

A Life Half Lived No matter how long Bilam's follower lives for, he will always feel empty inside and will pass away having only lived his life to half its potential. A student of Avraham may not enjoy the best in this world, but he retains his faith in Hashem and knows that his life was lived to its fullest.⁹²

It's All About Attitude There are many "students of Avraham" who seem to suffer hard lives and do not enjoy the results of their good middos in this world as promised in the mishnah. However, because they are able to see everything with a good eye, they do not consider their portion in life bad and are truly happy with their lot.⁹³

Word Power

עַיִן טוֹבָה Having a good eye also means being able to see Hashem's hand in everything that occurs, and trusting that even the bad things that happen are for a good reason.⁹⁴

Did You Know?

Not Even Half a Life The mishnah says that evil people won't live half of their lives. In Tehillim it says that a person's average lifespan is seventy years. Some say that Bilam lived to be thirty-three or thirty-four years old, not even half of that time!⁹⁵

Never Enough

There was once a wealthy non-Jewish man who threw a large, fancy party. Among his invited guests was Rabi Dostai. The banquet hall was bedecked in tapestries, the tables set with the finest china, and the menu packed with every type of delicacy. The host kept looking at the serving plates on the table, growing visibly upset. Suddenly, he stood up with a roar and destroyed the entire feast, breaking the expensive decorations and ruining the food.

"There are no soft-shelled nuts!" he bellowed in fury.

Rabi Dostai asked him gently why such a small omission should ruin the whole feast, with such a vast array of other foods available.

"You don't understand," his host informed him. "You Jews know that whatever you enjoy in this world is only temporary and you have yet to receive reward in the world to come. We have but one world to take pleasure in, so there can be no second chances—everything must be perfect!"

Rabi Dostai compared it to the passuk in Mishlei: "The stomach of the wicked shall lack." They have both the opportunity and the means to acquire whatever they want, but no matter how much they have, they are never satisfied.⁹⁶

199

Yehudah ben Teima says:
Be bold as a leopard, not to be intimidated by people who mock you for doing the right thing. Be **light** and swift **as an eagle**, not letting laziness win over you. **Run as** quickly and enthusiastically as **a deer** to perform mitzvos, **and** be **strong as a lion** to overcome any obstacles in your path. Mimic the positive traits of these four creatures **to fulfill the will of your Father in Heaven.**

Yehudah ben Teima **would** often **say:**
A brazen, arrogant person will go **to Gehinom, while a bashful,** humble person will go **to Gan Eden.**

May it be Your will, Hashem, **our God and the God of our fathers, that the Beis Hamikdash be built quickly in our days and** that You **give us our portion in Your Torah.**

יְהוּדָה בֶּן תֵּימָא אוֹמֵר:
הֱוֵי עַז כַּנָּמֵר, וְקַל כַּנֶּשֶׁר,
רָץ כַּצְּבִי, וְגִבּוֹר כָּאֲרִי,
לַעֲשׂוֹת רְצוֹן אָבִיךָ
שֶׁבַּשָּׁמָיִם.

הוּא הָיָה אוֹמֵר:
עַז פָּנִים לְגֵיהִנֹּם,
וּבוֹשֶׁת פָּנִים לְגַן עֵדֶן.

יְהִי רָצוֹן מִלְּפָנֶיךָ, יְיָ אֱלֹהֵינוּ
וֵאלֹהֵי אֲבוֹתֵינוּ, שֶׁיִּבָּנֶה בֵּית
הַמִּקְדָּשׁ בִּמְהֵרָה בְיָמֵינוּ,
וְתֵן חֶלְקֵנוּ בְּתוֹרָתֶךָ.

Learn From Them

The four animals in this mishnah teach us important lessons for dealing with temptations of sin:

- Be as brave as a leopard with the knowledge that Hashem gave you the strength to overcome any temptations.
- When a tempting situation arises, be light as an eagle to flee from it immediately. The longer you stay, the harder it will be to avoid.
- Run like a deer, who constantly looks back to ensure that it is out of danger. Don't rely on the fact that you defied a temptation once, because the yetzer hara will never give up trying to trap you.
- Be strong as a lion to free yourself from the clutches of temptation. If you have already fallen for the temptation, don't think it's too late. You can break free and run away at any time![97]

Bold Across the Board

The need to be bold and firm applies on many levels. In general, one should carry oneself as a proud Jew, without trying to hide it. On a personal level, one must remain true to his beliefs no matter the circumstance.

In social situations, you may have to stand up and defend your principles. Sure, it's easier to follow your friends when they make fun of someone, but it's more important to be courageous and stop the bullying. It's fun to go along when the class decides to give someone the "silent treatment," so standing up firmly and telling them that you won't go along with it takes a lot of strength. It takes bravery to be a leopard, but standing up for the right thing is worth the price.

Biography

Rabi Yehudah ben Teima is mentioned just this one time in the Mishnah. Some say he is the Tanna Rabi Yehudah ben Dama who was killed by the Romans as one of the Asarah Harugei Malchus.

Connections

We must certainly be proud and bold in our fight against the yetzer hara. However, we must not take this boldness too far and let it make us arrogant. The second part of the mishnah reminds us that we must still be humble before others and be willing to learn from them.[98]

Word Power

וְקַל כַּנֶּשֶׁר The eagle is a relatively heavy bird. Some species weigh up to fifteen pounds! Why then, does our mishnah tells us to be **light** as an eagle?

The word קל has another meaning—easy. An eagle has very long and powerful wings, which give it the ability to soar to great heights בְּקַלּוּת—with ease.[99]

This is a lesson for all of us who face challenges in our avodas Hashem: Even if our challenges seem heavy, as an eagle actually is, by giving ourselves wings—being positive and having a good attitude—we can overcome them with ease.[100]

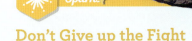
Spark

Don't Give up the Fight
The fight against the yetzer hara is hard and to strike a fatal blow requires the strength of a lion.[102] If one is unable to do that, at least a temporary defeat is necessary. Every time you strike your yetzer hara, you bring Hashem great pleasure.

Lesson in Everything
The fact that the mishnah teaches such valuable lessons from these animals shows us that everything in this world can teach us something. Hashem makes everything happen for a reason, so everything you see and hear contains a lesson that Hashem wants you to learn. Even if it seems petty and insignificant, we can use the experience to improve our service of Hashem.

Story

Look Who's Talking

R' Naftali of Rupshitz once described his morning struggle with the yetzer hara. "The yetzer hara comes to me and says, 'Naftali, it's still early, just go back to sleep.'

"'I'll learn from you,' I retort. 'You got up extra early to do your job. I'll do the same!'"[101]

Ben Bag-Bag says:

Delve into the Torah and delve into it again, always trying to uncover more and understand deeper, because everything is in it. With it you will see the truth.

Learn Torah forever, even as you grow old and worn out. Never move away from it, because it connects you to Hashem, and there is nothing better that you can have.

Ben Hei-Hei says: The reward for a mitzvah is increased in proportion to the amount of strain and hard work you experience when fulfilling it.

בֶּן בַּג בַּג אוֹמֵר:

הֲפָךְ בָּהּ וַהֲפָךְ בָּהּ,
דְּכֹלָּא בָהּ, וּבָהּ תֶּחֱזֵי,

וְסִיב וּבְלֵה בָהּ, וּמִנַּהּ לָא תָזוּעַ, שֶׁאֵין לְךָ
מִדָּה טוֹבָה הֵימֶנָּה.

בֶּן הֵא הֵא אוֹמֵר:
לְפוּם צַעֲרָא אַגְרָא.

Living Lessons

Scuba Lessons

A diver searching for underwater treasures inspects his equipment thoroughly before each dive, because he knows that a single loose part can be deadly. Throughout his trip, he must constantly breathe fresh oxygen; the air he inhaled above the water will not hold him for very long. Once he discovers the precious items, he doesn't suffice with one trip but returns to the bottom again and again, collecting more and more hidden treasures.

Torah learning works exactly the same. We must check that our connection to Torah remains strong since we cannot remain without it for even a second. Torah is a vast, undiscovered treasure that can be delved into time and again, each time yielding greater treasures.

Biography

Ben Bag-Bag According to many opinions, ben Bag-Bag and ben Hei-Hei are in fact two names for the same person—Rabi Yochanan ben Bag-Bag. His last name בַּג בַּג stands for בֶּן גֵּר בֶּן גִּיּוֹרֶת, indicating that he was a son of converts, while הֵא הֵא represents the fact that he was a child of Avraham and Sarah, both of whom had a ה added to their names.

He lived during the time of Hillel and merited the revelation of Eliyahu Hanavi.

Word Power

הֲפָךְ בָּהּ Since this mishnah refers to the daily routine of a Jew's life, it is written in Aramaic—the daily language in those times.[103]

Another reason: because ben Bag-Bag was a convert, his mother tongue was not Hebrew, but Aramaic. The statements were therefore recorded in that language.[104]

הֲפָךְ בָּהּ There are several reasons given as to why the mishnah uses the phrase הֲפָךְ בָּהּ–analyze it, twice:

- Everything in Torah can be understood on two levels: the basic, simple meaning and the deeper meaning.[105]
- Not only do we need to become familiar with the words, but we also need to delve into the reasoning behind them.[106]
- Not only must we analyze it ourselves, but we should also encourage others to analyze it.[107]
- Not only should we analyze what we learn when we are young, but we should re-analyze it when we are older and wiser.[108]
- The mishnah is simply telling us to analyze the Torah again and again, because there is no end to what we can find in it.[109]

Layers Every part of Torah can be explained on four different levels: פְּשָׁט, רֶמֶז, דְּרוּשׁ and סוֹד. Torah is never-ending; there is always another explanation to learn, another lesson to unearth.[110]

Fitting Reward The Torah was given so we could bring holiness into mundane acts and items. All of the time and energy that is put into one's Torah learning is transformed to holiness, so the more one puts in, the more is elevate.

Connections

The mishnah teaches us that we should never give up analyzing and learning the Torah, no matter how tiring or difficult it may be, because the reward is in proportion to the effort. However hard it may be for us to do, Hashem will take the effort into account and reward us accordingly.[111] This rule also applies to the effort put in to fulfilling mitzvos.[112]

Especially Now

R' Shlomoh Eiger and R' Zalman Posner were successful businessmen and accomplished Talmidei Chachamim. Their reputation for honesty and hard work attracted lots of contracts from the government. Unfortunately, some the workers they hired were not as honest as they were, and many of them stole money that was supposed to be used for the projects. R' Shlomoh and R' Zalman were placed on trial to prove their innocence. They sat together for hours, brainstorming ways to exonerate themselves. One night, after a fruitless session, R' Zalman left R' Shlomoh's house still pondering ways out of their dilemma. He suddenly thought of an idea he was sure would work. He ran back to the house and pounded on the door but R' Shlomoh didn't answer. Seeing the lights still lit, he opened the door and saw his friend learning so intensely that he didn't hear anything around him. He shook his shoulder and asked him, "I don't understand. How could you learn with such intensity at a time like this?"

"It is especially now that I should be learning," R' Shlomoh explained. "If not, our difficulties would only double."[113]

Yehudah ben Teima **would** often **say**:	**הוּא** הָיָה אוֹמֵר:
A **five-year-old** is of age **to** learn **Chumash**.	בֶּן חָמֵשׁ שָׁנִים לַמִּקְרָא,
A **ten-year-old** is of age **to** learn **Mishnah**.	בֶּן עֶשֶׂר שָׁנִים לַמִּשְׁנָה,
A **thirteen-year-old** is obligated **to** fulfill **mitzvos**.	בֶּן שְׁלֹשׁ עֶשְׂרֵה לַמִּצְוֹת,
A **fifteen-year-old** is of age **to** learn **Gemara**.	בֶּן חֲמֵשׁ עֶשְׂרֵה לַגְּמָרָא,
An **eighteen-year-old** is of age **for marriage**.	בֶּן שְׁמוֹנֶה עֶשְׂרֵה לַחֻפָּה,
A **twenty-year-old** is of age **to pursue** a livelihood.	בֶּן עֶשְׂרִים לִרְדּוֹף,
A **thirty-year-old** is of age of full **strength**.	בֶּן שְׁלֹשִׁים לַכֹּחַ,
A **forty-year-old** is of age **for understanding**.	בֶּן אַרְבָּעִים לַבִּינָה,
A **fifty-year-old** is of age **to offer advice**.	בֶּן חֲמִשִּׁים לָעֵצָה,
A **sixty-year-old** is of age **of maturity** and wisdom.	בֶּן שִׁשִּׁים לַזִּקְנָה,
A **seventy-year-old** is of a ripe **old age**.	בֶּן שִׁבְעִים לַשֵּׂיבָה,
An **eighty-year-old** is of age that shows that he has a **strong** and healthy body to survive to this age.	בֶּן שְׁמוֹנִים לַגְּבוּרָה,
A **ninety-year-old** is of age **of becoming bent over**.	בֶּן תִּשְׁעִים לָשׁוּחַ,
A **hundred-year-old** has lost the use of most of his natural abilities and is therefore considered **dead**. He is **removed from and ceases** to care about the physical pursuits **of this world,** and recognizes Hashem's presence in the world.	בֶּן מֵאָה כְּאִלּוּ מֵת וְעָבַר וּבָטֵל מִן הָעוֹלָם.

Mazal Tov for Now

Passing a milestone is a happy event, but one must realize that it's only a step toward bigger and better things. Imagine a child learned to crawl, and his parents were so pleased with that accomplishment that they never encouraged the baby to walk. The same goes for the milestones enumerated in this mishnah. Once a child finishes Chumash, he must move on to the next goal, and then the next, and the next. You can look back at your accomplishments with pride, but remember that you must keep pushing forward!

Never Miss a Moment

The underlying message of this mishnah is that we should use each period of our lives to its fullest potential, and not waste our time. When a person loses something like money or other belongings, there is always a chance he will get it back one day, whether it will be found, or he will get another one of the same. When time is lost, however, it can never be replaced. For this reason our mishnah teaches us this important lesson—to live our lives fully, with purpose.[114]

Story

A Fair Hearing

During the bar mitzvah of R' Yisrael Ruzhiner, one of the guests asked him, "How have you been able to stand up to your yetzer hara for so long? You didn't even have help from the yetzer tov as you only received it in its full strength today!"

"It's very simple," the young boy answered. "Whenever the yetzer hara would come to me, I would tell him that according to halachah, both sides need to be present in order to decide a ruling. I just kept pushing him off."[115]

Did You Know?

Who Wrote It? There are different opinions as to the author of this mishnah. Some say it was Shmuel Hakatan, and others say it was Yehudah ben Teima. There are also different opinions as to the placement of this mishnah, whether it goes before the mishnah of ben Bag-Bag or after.

Sparks

Equals Out The passuk says in regard to a Kohen Gadol marrying, "וְהוּא אִשָּׁה בִבְתוּלֶיהָ יִקָּח—and he should take a young maiden as a wife." The word וְהוּא has a numerical value of eighteen, corresponding to the age of marriage specified in this mishnah.[116]

Chapter 5 • Mishnah 22

205

Say this mishnah upon completing each perek:

Rabi Chananya ben Akashya says:

The Holy One, blessed be He, wanted to make B'nei **Yisrael** have many **merits.**

He therefore gave them an abundance of Torah and mitzvos, so that they would have many opportunities to connect to Him.

As it says in Yeshayah: **Hashem wanted, for the sake of** increasing B'nei Yisrael's **righteousness, that the Torah be made great and glorious.**

רַבִּי חֲנַנְיָא בֶּן עֲקַשְׁיָא אוֹמֵר:
רָצָה הַקָּדוֹשׁ בָּרוּךְ הוּא
לְזַכּוֹת אֶת יִשְׂרָאֵל
לְפִיכָךְ הִרְבָּה לָהֶם
תּוֹרָה וּמִצְוֹת
שֶׁנֶּאֱמַר: יְיָ חָפֵץ לְמַעַן
צִדְקוֹ יַגְדִּיל תּוֹרָה וְיַאְדִּיר.

Endnotes

1. הוספות לביאורים
2. לקו"א פכ"א
3. מדרש שמואל
4. שער היחוד והאמונה. מדרש תהלים
5. שמועות וסיפורים ח"ב סיפור כט
6. רבינו יונה
7. מדרש שמואל
8. סנהדרין קט, א. מחזור ויטרי. ראב"ן
9. סיפורי חסידים, תורה - ואתחנן
10. ביאורים
11. מהר"ל
12. רבינו מתתיה המצרי
13. פרקי משה
14. מדרש. אבות דרבי נתן. רש"י
15. רשימות דברים חלק ד ע' 35
16. אברבנאל, רש"י על מ"ג, אבות דרבי נתן פל"ג ה"ב
17. שפת אמת
18. רמב"ם. וראה אבות דרבי נתן לט. מדרש תנחומא, בשלח
19. רש"י
20. מדרש שמואל
21. מדרש שמואל
22. חסדי אבות
23. אור החיים במדבר יד, יב
24. שמועות וסיפורים מרבותינו הקדושים חלק א', סיפור האחרון על הבעש"ט
25. ערכי הכנויים ערך נחש
26. ביאורים
27. מגן אבות
28. מדרש שמואל
29. אוה"ת קדושים
30. רע"ב
31. דף על הדף ברכות סג, א (ע' תיג)
32. גיטין סח, א
33. ביאורים
34. לקו"ת פ' חקת
35. סוטה יג, ע"ב
36. חסדי אבות
37. מדרש שמואל
38. סיפורי חסידים, תורה - קרח
39. מדרש שמואל
40. אברבנאל. מדרש שמואל
41. הר' יוסף יעב"ץ
42. הר' יוסף יעב"ץ
43. ר' שמחה מויטרי. המאירי
44. משלי כב, כב
45. תוס' תענית ט, א ד"ה עשר תעשר
46. דברים טו, י
47. הר' יוסף יעב"ץ
48. נוצר חסד
49. דרך חיים
50. ר' שמחה בונים מפשיסחא
51. סיפורי חסידים - תורה, וירא
52. מדרש שמואל
53. אברבנאל
54. פסחים קיג, ב
55. הר' יוסף יעב"ץ. לב אבות
56. מגן אבות
57. מדרש שמואל
58. סיפורי חסידים מועדים - סוכות, אתרוג
59. פסחים סו, ב
60. מגן אבות
61. מדרש שמואל
62. שפתי חיים - מועדים, חלק א' ע' שח
63. מדרש שמואל
64. מדרש שמואל
65. משמועות מרבינו יונה
66. בבא בתרא ט, ב
67. משמועות מרבינו יונה
68. מדרש שמואל. לחם יהודה
69. מסכת אבות ע"פ יינה של תורה ע' שב
70. עטרת אבות חלק ב' ע' 157
71. המאירי
72. חיים שיש בהם על פרקי אבות ע' ריד
73. ביאורים
74. מדרש שמואל
75. מקוה ישראל
76. חיים שיש בהם על פרקי אבות ע' תצ
77. מדרש שמואל
78. ביאורים
79. ראשי אבות
80. מדרש שמואל
81. עירובין יג, ב. מילי דאבות
82. המשפיע ר' שלמה חיים קסלמן ע' 557
83. ביאורים
84. מדרש שמואל. נחלת אבות. עץ יוסף
85. מדרש שמואל
86. יערות דבש ח"ב דרוש ח
87. שבחי הבעש"ט (ירושלים-תרצ"א) ע' קצב
88. תפארת ישראל
89. חסדי אבות
90. רבינו יונה. מאירי. תפארת ישראל. תויו"ט
91. שפת אמת
92. בבא קמא נ, א
93. תפארת ישראל
94. רש"י
95. שפת אמת
96. סנהדרין קו, ועי' רש"י שם
97. במדבר רבה - כא, יח
98. מדרש שמואל
99. מדרש שמואל
100. עלי שור
101. עלי שור
102. פרדס האבות ע' קטז
103. רע"ב
104. מדרש שמואל
105. תוס' יו"ט
106. מדרש שמואל. נחלת אבות
107. ספר המוסר
108. מילי דאבות
109. פרקי משה. תפארת ישראל
110. המאירי
111. ענינה של תורת החסידות
112. רש"י
113. רע"ב
114. הוא היה אומר ח"ב ע' 725
115. מדרש שמואל
116. עטרת אבות ח"ב ע' 185
117. המאירי

פֶּרֶק שִׁשִּׁי

Chapter Six

Kol Yisrael

Say this mishnah before beginning each new perek:

All B'nei **Yisrael have a portion in the World to Come.**

As it says in Yeshayah regarding B'nei Yisrael upon Moshiach's arrival: **Your people are all tzaddikim,** and **they will all inherit Eretz** Yisrael **forever**—they will never be exiled from it again.

All will recognize that they are **the branch of My planting and the work of My hands,** in which I, Hashem, **take pride.**

כָּל יִשְׂרָאֵל יֵשׁ לָהֶם חֵלֶק לְעוֹלָם הַבָּא,

שֶׁנֶּאֱמַר: וְעַמֵּךְ כֻּלָּם צַדִּיקִים, לְעוֹלָם יִירְשׁוּ אָרֶץ,

נֵצֶר מַטָּעַי מַעֲשֵׂה יָדַי לְהִתְפָּאֵר.

The Chachamim taught the following perek of Braisos **in** Lashon Hakodesh, **the language of the Mishnah. Blessed** is Hashem, **Who chose the** Chachamim **and their teachings.**	**שָׁנוּ** חֲכָמִים בִּלְשׁוֹן הַמִּשְׁנָה, בָּרוּךְ שֶׁבָּחַר בָּהֶם וּבְמִשְׁנָתָם.
Rabi Meir says: Whoever involves himself **in Torah** learning **for its own sake,** because it is a mitzvah to learn Hashem's Torah, **will merit many** good **things. In fact, the** creation of the **entire world is worthwhile** just **for him.**	רַבִּי מֵאִיר אוֹמֵר: כָּל הָעוֹסֵק בַּתּוֹרָה לִשְׁמָהּ זוֹכֶה לִדְבָרִים הַרְבֵּה, וְלֹא עוֹד, אֶלָּא שֶׁכָּל הָעוֹלָם כֻּלּוֹ כְּדַאי הוּא לוֹ.
Some of the many things he merits: **He is called a** friend **and beloved** of Hashem. **He loves** Hashem **and he loves** Hashem's **creations. He makes Hashem happy and he makes people happy.** The Torah **clothes** and surrounds him **with humility and awe** of Hashem. **It prepares him to be righteous, dedicated** to Hashem, **upright, and trusted. It** also **distances him from aveiros and brings him close to merit.**	נִקְרָא רֵעַ, אָהוּב, אוֹהֵב אֶת הַמָּקוֹם, אוֹהֵב אֶת הַבְּרִיּוֹת, מְשַׂמֵּחַ אֶת הַמָּקוֹם, מְשַׂמֵּחַ אֶת הַבְּרִיּוֹת, וּמַלְבַּשְׁתּוֹ עֲנָוָה וְיִרְאָה, וּמַכְשַׁרְתּוֹ לִהְיוֹת צַדִּיק, חָסִיד, יָשָׁר, וְנֶאֱמָן, וּמְרַחַקְתּוֹ מִן הַחֵטְא, וּמְקָרַבְתּוֹ לִידֵי זְכוּת,
People enjoy his good **advice, wisdom, understanding, and strength. As it says** in Mishlei: Good **advice and wisdom are mine,** says the Torah. **I am understanding; strength is mine,** and the Torah gives these good qualities to those who learn it. It also **gives him royalty and authority, and** the ability to **judge properly.**	וְנֶהֱנִין מִמֶּנּוּ עֵצָה וְתוּשִׁיָּה, בִּינָה וּגְבוּרָה, שֶׁנֶּאֱמַר: לִי עֵצָה וְתוּשִׁיָּה, אֲנִי בִינָה, לִי גְבוּרָה, וְנוֹתֶנֶת לוֹ מַלְכוּת וּמֶמְשָׁלָה, וְחִקּוּר דִּין,
The secrets of the Torah are revealed to him. He becomes like a fountain that flows with ever-increasing strength, and like a river that never stops flowing.	וּמְגַלִּין לוֹ רָזֵי תוֹרָה, וְנַעֲשֶׂה כְּמַעְיָן הַמִּתְגַּבֵּר וּכְנָהָר שֶׁאֵינוֹ פוֹסֵק,
He becomes modest, patient, and forgiving when he is insulted. The Torah **makes him great and it raises him above all things.**	וְהֹוֶה צָנוּעַ, וְאֶרֶךְ רוּחַ, וּמוֹחֵל עַל עֶלְבּוֹנוֹ, וּמְגַדַּלְתּוֹ וּמְרוֹמַמְתּוֹ עַל כָּל הַמַּעֲשִׂים.

Living Lessons

A Better Person

Unlike any other wisdom, Torah refines the character of those who learn it. This is because Torah is Hashem's wisdom and not human wisdom. The more Torah you learn, the more refined your behavior can become, and the closer you can become to Hashem.

Did You Know?

For the Sake of a Spark The word לִשְׁמָהּ has the same letters as the word לְמֹשֶׁה, since someone who learns Torah for its own sake lights up the spark of Moshe Rabbeinu's neshamah that exists within him.[1]

Mishnayos and Braisos The first five perakim of Pirkei Avos are Mishnah while this perek is Braisa. Braisa comes from the Aramaic word בְּרָא—outside, since Rabi Yehudah Hanassi did not include them as official mishnayos.[2] This perek begins with the introduction that these lessons were taught "in the language of the Mishnah," because they are not actually Mishnah.[3]

Sparks

No Time to Sin People sin when they have free time on their hands. A person who spends all his time learning will be preoccupied with it even when he is taking a break. Keeping one's mind busy with Torah prevents sinful thoughts from entering the mind.[4]

One Friendship, One Goal Involvement with negative things usually stems from selfish motives, which are usually unique to each individual. In contrast, when people are involved with positive things, there is a common motive—to do good, which brings together everyone involved. When you are involved with learning Torah and doing mitzvos, you are bound to have many friends who are all reaching for the same ambition, bringing true friendship.[5]

Know it, Teach it The mishnah starts off with the words שָׁנוּ חֲכָמִים—the Chachamim taught, teaching us that knowledge is meant to be shared. Even if you don't fit in the category of Chachamim, you can fulfill the directive of this mishnah and teach whatever you do know to someone who doesn't know it yet.[6]

Word Power

נִקְרָא The mishnah uses the word נִקְרָא—he is called because when a person learns Torah for the right reasons, a Heavenly voice proclaims his elite status.[7]

Story

An Altruistic Understanding

R' Zalman Fradkin, rav of Lublin, was famous for his photographic memory. In fact, booksellers wouldn't allow him to browse through the books before he paid for them, for once he read a book, he no longer needed to own it.

Each time he visited his Rebbe, the Tzemach Tzedek, he would share some of his original Torah thoughts. One time, after hearing R' Zalman's presentation, the Rebbe told him that although his arguments were sound, they were contradicted by a mishnah. R' Zalman instantly reviewed the entire Shas in his head but could not figure out which mishnah contradicted his idea. The Rebbe told him which mishnah it was, but when R' Zalman repeated the mishnah in his head, he couldn't figure out what the Tzemach Tzedek was referring to. The Rebbe then began to recite the mishnah and R' Zalman was finally able to understand how a deeper understanding of the mishnah refuted his explanation. He later remarked that since the Rebbe learned Torah truly lishmah—purely for its own sake, he was able to understand its core principles and point out the flaw in R' Zalman's thesis.[8]

Rabi Yehoshua ben Levi says: Every single day, **a heavenly voice** that is heard by the neshamah **comes out from Har Chorev** (Har Sinai). **It announces and says, "Woe is to people who insult the Torah** by not learning with feeling." They are to be pitied **because anyone who does not** fervently **devote** himself **to Torah is called shameful. As it says** in Mishlei: **A beautiful woman** (the Torah) **without flavor** (without feeling and enjoyment) **is like a golden ring on a pig's nose.** Torah learning must be filled with passion and devotion.	אָמַר רַבִּי יְהוֹשֻׁעַ בֶּן לֵוִי, בְּכָל יוֹם וָיוֹם בַּת קוֹל יוֹצֵאת מֵהַר חוֹרֵב וּמַכְרֶזֶת וְאוֹמֶרֶת: אוֹי לָהֶם לַבְּרִיּוֹת מֵעֶלְבּוֹנָהּ שֶׁל תּוֹרָה, שֶׁכָּל מִי שֶׁאֵינוֹ עוֹסֵק בַּתּוֹרָה נִקְרָא נָזוּף, שֶׁנֶּאֱמַר: נֶזֶם זָהָב בְּאַף חֲזִיר, אִשָּׁה יָפָה וְסָרַת טָעַם.
There is another advantage of being occupied with Torah, as **it says** in the Torah: **The Luchos are Hashem's work, and the writing is Hashem's writing engraved on the Luchos. Do not read** the word as חָרוּת—**engraved but** as חֵרוּת—**freedom, because there is no person who is free** from social pressures and temptations, and able to reach his full potential **except one who involves** himself **in Torah** learning.	וְאוֹמֵר: וְהַלֻּחֹת מַעֲשֵׂה אֱלֹהִים הֵמָּה, וְהַמִּכְתָּב מִכְתַּב אֱלֹהִים הוּא, חָרוּת עַל הַלֻּחֹת, אַל תִּקְרֵי חָרוּת אֶלָּא חֵרוּת, שֶׁאֵין לְךָ בֶּן חוֹרִין, אֶלָּא מִי שֶׁעוֹסֵק בְּתַלְמוּד תּוֹרָה,
Whoever involves himself **in Torah learning is uplifted. As it says** in the Torah: **B'nei Yisrael traveled from Matanah to Nachaliel, and from Nachaliel to Bamos.** The Chachamim explain the significance of the names of these places: When a person uses the Mattanah—the gift of Torah, Hashem becomes his Nachaliel—his inheritance, which brings him to Bamos—an elevated place.	וְכָל מִי שֶׁעוֹסֵק בְּתַלְמוּד תּוֹרָה, הֲרֵי זֶה מִתְעַלֶּה, שֶׁנֶּאֱמַר: וּמִמַּתָּנָה נַחֲלִיאֵל, וּמִנַּחֲלִיאֵל בָּמוֹת.

 Did You Know?

Soul's Calling Although the Heavenly voice may seem pointless if no one can hear it, in truth the neshamah hears it, and feels a strong desire to connect to Hashem. We see the results of this when a person suddenly feels a strong pull to do teshuvah without knowing the cause.[9]

 Sparks

A Ring of Wisdom Beauty is a metaphor for wisdom. When it is used appropriately in Torah, it acts like a ring, beautifying the finger it is placed on. However, when the wisdom is used to justify bad behavior, it is likened to a ring in a pig's nose, losing its beauty because of its worthless setting.[10]

Living Lessons

Truly Free

Living with Hashem's Torah and mitzvos is truly liberating. There are many ways in which Torah makes us truly free people:

- **Free from Social Pressure:** Someone who does not have the Torah as his guide is under constant social pressure to behave according to his neighbors' expectations. One who follows the Torah has clear direction as to the correct way to behave, no matter what. He knows that he is doing the right thing, regardless of the changing ideas of the rest of the world.

- **Free from Worldly Troubles:** A free person isn't necessarily free of all hardship. A free person is one who isn't weighed down by his difficulties or controlled by them. One who is sincerely devoted to Torah will not get pulled down by material losses because he knows that everything comes from Hashem and that whatever He does is for the best. He also knows that his Torah will forever remain with him, unlike physical possessions, which can be lost in an instant.[11]

- **Free to be Your True Self:** Although in a sense the Torah is a yoke upon a person, it is still the only thing that makes a Jew truly free. The Gemara teaches that one way the Egyptians inflicted strenuous labor upon B'nei Yisrael was by giving the women the work of the men, while the men had to do the work of the women.[12] This was extremely difficult, since each party had to do something against their nature.[13] When a Jew isn't serving Hashem through Torah and mitzvos, he is going against his true nature. Therefore, even if it may seem as if he is free, in reality he is enslaved to the yetzer hara, which is forcing him to do something against his true will. Only when he is involved in Torah, even if it seems like hard work, is he really free, since he is following his true nature.

A Wrong-Way Ticket

R' Elchanan Wasserman was once visited by an old yeshivah friend who had since gone on to law school and become a successful lawyer.

"You should have come with me," his friend told him. "With your intelligence you would be even more rich and successful than I am."

R' Elchanan didn't reply. He accompanied his friend back to the train station and watched him board an old, rickety train. "Why don't you go on that one?" he asked, pointing across the platform to a much nicer train headed in the opposite direction.

"I'm heading the other way," his friend replied.

"But isn't it better to be more comfortable?" R' Elchanan persisted.

"It doesn't matter how comfortable you are if you're headed in the wrong direction," his friend patiently explained.

R' Elchanan smiled. "Why would it have helped me to join you and live a comfortable life if that takes me in the opposite direction of where I want to be?"[17]

Biography

Rabi Yehoshua ben Levi was an early amora (or, according to some, the last of the Tannaim) known as a chassid whose prayers were always answered. He once asked Eliyahu Hanavi when Mashiach will come. Eliyahu told him to ask Mashiach himself. He went to the gates of Rome and found Mashiach sitting there and asked him. Mashiach replied "הַיּוֹם—Today!" When the day passed, Rabi Yehoshua came to Eliyahu Hanavi and asked why Mashiach had not come. Eliyahu answered with the rest of the passuk in Tehillim: "הַיּוֹם, אִם בְּקוֹלוֹ תִּשְׁמָעוּ—Today, if you will heed His (Hashem's) voice."[14]

The Gemara relates that when it came time for Rabi Yehoshua ben Levi to pass away, he tricked the Malach Hamaves and entered Gan Eden alive.[15]

Behind the Quote

This mishnah refers to Torah learning beyond ordinary measures. Rabi Yehoshua ben Levi frequently displayed such great devotion to the Torah that he even taught people who were suffering from contagious diseases, although no one else dared approach them.[16]

הַלּוֹמֵד מֵחֲבֵרוֹ פֶּרֶק אֶחָד, אוֹ הֲלָכָה אַחַת, אוֹ פָּסוּק אֶחָד, אוֹ דִבּוּר אֶחָד, אוֹ אֲפִילוּ אוֹת אַחַת, צָרִיךְ לִנְהָג בּוֹ כָּבוֹד, שֶׁכֵּן מָצִינוּ בְּדָוִד מֶלֶךְ יִשְׂרָאֵל, שֶׁלֹּא לָמַד מֵאֲחִיתֹפֶל אֶלָּא שְׁנֵי דְבָרִים בִּלְבַד, קְרָאוֹ רַבּוֹ אַלּוּפוֹ וּמְיֻדָּעוֹ, שֶׁנֶּאֱמַר: וְאַתָּה אֱנוֹשׁ כְּעֶרְכִּי, אַלּוּפִי וּמְיֻדָּעִי.

One who learns a single perek, a single halachah, a single passuk, a single statement, or even a single letter of Torah from his friend must treat him with honor. As we learn from Dovid Hamelech, B'nei Yisrael's king, who learned only two things from Achisofel: to learn together with others rather than alone, and to walk with others and enthusiastically when going to learn, and he called him his rabbi, his leader, and his teacher. As Dovid Hamelech says to Achisofel in Tehillim: You are a man on my level; you are my leader and my teacher.

וַהֲלֹא דְבָרִים קַל וָחֹמֶר, וּמַה דָּוִד מֶלֶךְ יִשְׂרָאֵל שֶׁלֹּא לָמַד מֵאֲחִיתֹפֶל אֶלָּא שְׁנֵי דְבָרִים בִּלְבַד, קְרָאוֹ רַבּוֹ אַלּוּפוֹ וּמְיֻדָּעוֹ, הַלּוֹמֵד מֵחֲבֵרוֹ פֶּרֶק אֶחָד, אוֹ הֲלָכָה אַחַת, אוֹ פָּסוּק אֶחָד, אוֹ דִבּוּר אֶחָד, אוֹ אֲפִילוּ אוֹת אֶחָת, עַל אַחַת כַּמָּה וְכַמָּה שֶׁצָּרִיךְ לִנְהָג בּוֹ כָּבוֹד.

This leads to an obvious conclusion: If Dovid, king of B'nei Yisrael, learned only two things from Achisofel and still called him his rabbi, his leader, and his teacher, then if an ordinary person learns a single perek, a single halachah, a single passuk, a single statement, or even a single letter of Torah from his friend, he must surely treat him with honor.

וְאֵין כָּבוֹד אֶלָּא תוֹרָה, שֶׁנֶּאֱמַר: כָּבוֹד חֲכָמִים יִנְחָלוּ, וּתְמִימִים יִנְחֲלוּ טוֹב. וְאֵין טוֹב אֶלָּא תוֹרָה, שֶׁנֶּאֱמַר: כִּי לֶקַח טוֹב נָתַתִּי לָכֶם, תּוֹרָתִי אַל תַּעֲזֹבוּ.

Honor is earned only for Torah. As it says in Mishlei: The Chachamim will inherit honor; the perfect ones will inherit good. And only Torah is truly good. As it says in Mishlei: I, Hashem, have given you a good teaching; do not forsake My Torah.

A Teacher for Life

We owe gratitude and respect to anyone who has taught us and guided us in our lives, no matter how insignificant a lesson it may have been. Even years later, when you may have surpassed them in level, you must show them the proper respect.

Dovid Hamelech was a great Tzaddik and Talmid Chacham, and yet he showed tremendous respect for Achisofel, who taught him two small things. We, who are certainly much lesser than Dovid, must certainly respect our teachers.

Connections

The previous mishnah ended with the message that a person who studies Torah is elevated. Our mishnah demonstrates just how exalted it can make him: it raises him to the extent that he must be honored even if he's taught someone no more than one letter.[18]

Did You Know?

My Friend My Teacher The Talmidei Chachamim of Bavel would rise when their colleagues would enter the room, and tear their garments upon the death of a fellow student, just as they would for a teacher. This was due to the fact that their constant studying together brought them many opportunities to learn from each other.[19]

Sparks

The Personal Portion Every day in davening we say the words "וְתֵן חֶלְקֵנוּ בְּתוֹרָתֶךְ—Grant us our lot in Your Torah." Every Jew has a particular part in Torah that is connected to his individual soul. We must therefore show respect toward anyone who teaches us anything, even an insignificant lesson, since it may be the key to our personal portion in Torah.[20]

Story

With All Your Might

The Ba'al Shem Tov was once informed by Heaven that there was a simple shepherd whose service to Hashem was more outstanding than his. Eager to witness it for himself, he took along a few students and traveled to the pasture to watch events unfold.

Soon they observed the shepherd rise up and speak to Heaven. "Master of the Universe, You are so great, and I am so small. I wish I knew how to serve You properly but I was never taught Torah. Instead, I offer to You whatever talents I possess." The Ba'al Shem Tov and his students watched in amazement as he took out a shofar and blew with all his might, until he collapsed in exhaustion. Then he stood up again and began cartwheeling and somersaulting with endless energy. Finally, he turned once more to Heaven. "G-d Almighty, I don't have much else to offer You. But last night, the nobleman made a feast and gave all his servants a silver coin. I want to give it to You." He withdrew a coin from his sack and threw it up into the air with all his might.

The students watched the coin but could not see where it fell.

"A Heavenly hand grabbed it," the Ba'al Shem Tov informed them. "I have learned from this simple shepherd how to truly love Hashem with all your heart, soul, and might."[21]

This is the way to master Torah:

Eat bread with salt, drink small amounts of water, sleep on the ground, live a life of hardship without indulging in physical pleasures, and work hard in Torah.

It says in Tehillim that if you do so, "You will be fortunate and it will be good for you"— You will be fortunate in this world and it will be good for you in the World to Come.

כָּךְ הִיא דַּרְכָּהּ שֶׁל תּוֹרָה: פַּת בְּמֶלַח תֹּאכֵל, וּמַיִם בִּמְשׂוּרָה תִּשְׁתֶּה, וְעַל הָאָרֶץ תִּישָׁן, וְחַיֵּי צַעַר תִּחְיֶה, וּבַתּוֹרָה אַתָּה עָמֵל,

אִם אַתָּה עוֹשֶׂה כֵּן, אַשְׁרֶיךָ וְטוֹב לָךְ, אַשְׁרֶיךָ בָּעוֹלָם הַזֶּה, וְטוֹב לָךְ לָעוֹלָם הַבָּא.

Living Lessons

Be Strong

Our bodies today are weaker than in previous generations. Back then, people were able to endure prolonged fasts, but we are not. Fasting makes us weak and irritable, and interferes with our learning. Therefore, it is important to eat healthy food and sleep enough. There are, however, other small pleasures of which we must indeed deprive ourselves, in line with the lesson of this mishnah. We can hold back a disparaging comment we really wanted to say, turn away from an interesting but meaningless conversation, or decline dessert. Unnecessary Indulgences should be limited, but the basic practices that allow us to learn well are not to be shunned.[22]

Living the Good Life

We aren't expected to give up on all physical comforts in life, but we should be sure to keep our priorities straight. Torah is the most enjoyable thing in the world. It's better than nosh, games, and sports! It is sweeter than honey and more precious than gold! Learning Torah makes you thirst for more, shifts your focus and makes you realize that you already possess the most valuable treasure.[23]

Sparks

The Best Bed The people of Kovno were shocked one day when they arrived in shul to find a young bochur sleeping on a bench after a long night of learning. They shook their heads in pity, until R' Yisrael Salanter stopped them. "You think he is the pitiable one? Those of you who slept in beds are truly the unfortunate ones. He has fulfilled the braisa 'You should sleep on the ground... and it will be good for you in this world and in the world to come.'"[24]

Connections

This braisa continues teaching the proper approach toward learning Torah. The last few braisos taught about love of learning and love for teachers of even small amounts of Torah. Now we are learning about sacrifice for the sake of Torah learning.[25]

Sparks

Good and Happy The braisa promises that in this world, "You will be happy," while in the next, "It will be good for you." The only true goodness comes in Olam Haba. Even the best of this world is fleeting and can't be described as being truly good. The most you can get here is happiness.[26]

Deep Pain Thinking about the greatness of Hashem in relation to our lowly existence can bring one to feel pained at how far we are from Him. This can be remedied by learning Torah, which brings us closer to Hashem, and allows us to be happy and fortunate in this world.[27]

It's the Effort that Counts

The braisa specifically discusses working hard in Torah, rather than simply learning, because some people understand it quickly, while others take more time. Yet you aren't rewarded for the time or amount that you learn, but by the effort you put in to do so.[28]

Word Power

בִּמְשׂוּרָה The word בִּמְשׂוּרָה can refer either to a small liquid measure,[29] or the name of a small vessel.[30]

Tasteless

R' Schneur Zalman of Liadi, the Ba'al Hatanya, was once visited by his esteemed colleague, R' Shlomoh of Karlin. His wife, daughter, and Jewish housekeeper each wanted the privilege of cooking for their holy guest, so they divided the work between them. However, they forgot to assign the job of salting the food, so each one individually decided to add it.

When the two Tzaddikim finally sat down to eat, R' Schneur Zalman ate his entire bowl of soup, while poor R' Shlomoh could barely swallow a spoonful. When asked why he wasn't eating, R' Shlomoh replied that it was extremely salty and thus inedible. The women realized what had happened and felt terrible, apologizing profusely.

R' Shlomoh, however, could not understand how R' Schneur Zalman ate the entire bowl without flinching, despite the intense flavor.

R' Schneur Zalman explained, "Ever since I learned in Mezritch from the great Maggid, I worked on myself not to feel the taste of food."[31]

Do not seek greatness for yourself and do not desire honor.	**אַל** תְּבַקֵּשׁ גְּדֻלָּה לְעַצְמְךָ, וְאַל תַּחְמוֹד כָּבוֹד,
The good deeds **you do should** be greater than your Torah **learning**.	יוֹתֵר מִלִּמּוּדְךָ עֲשֵׂה,
Do not desire the table of kings and their riches, **because your table**—the spiritual greatness you achieve through serving Hashem—**is greater than their** fancy **tables** and physical riches, **and your crown** of glory—your connection to Hashem through learning His Torah—**is greater than their** physical **crown**.	וְאַל תִּתְאַוֶּה לְשֻׁלְחָנָם שֶׁל מְלָכִים, שֶׁשֻּׁלְחָנְךָ גָּדוֹל מִשֻּׁלְחָנָם, וְכִתְרְךָ גָּדוֹל מִכִּתְרָם,
Hashem, **Your Boss, can be trusted** to **pay you the reward for your work** of serving Him.	וְנֶאֱמָן הוּא בַּעַל מְלַאכְתֶּךָ שֶׁיְּשַׁלֶּם לְךָ שְׂכַר פְּעֻלָּתֶךָ.

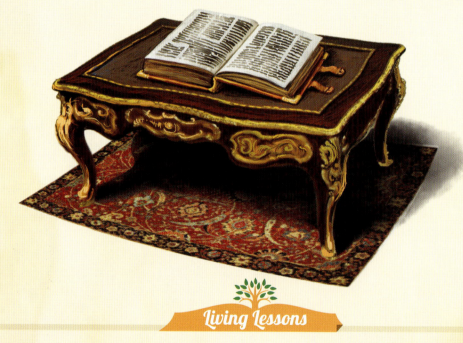

Living Lessons

Degrading Excuses

The yetzer hara is a master at excuses. He loves diverting our attention from the right thing by giving us reasons for doing something else. The most convincing argument he uses is to tell us that our friends will look down on us if we do the right thing. He tells you things like, "Don't be friends with the new kid. Everyone will think you are weird."

If you hear these thoughts playing into your mind, remind yourself that in fact, people respect a person who does the right thing more than one who does whatever it takes to become popular. This braisa encourages us to remember that honor and popularity are only temporary and do not really count for anything real. Be confident, and don't let worthless opinions stop you from doing the right thing.

Sparks

Commensurate Action Sometimes you might look ahead at all of the Torah that you haven't yet learned, and feel discouraged in the thought that you might never master it all. The braisa here comes to reassure you that Hashem treasures your efforts and will reward you for the work you put in by enabling you to eventually understand your learning.[32]

A Guiding Hand The braisa reminds us that our deeds should exceed our learning. This seems to be asking the impossible—for how can a person fulfill those mitzvos he hasn't yet learned about, or did not properly learn their halachos? However, as long as one does his part and sincerely desires to do Hashem's will, he is guided from Above and led to do the correct actions, even if he never learned them.[33]

Connections

The previous braisa warned against delving into physical pleasures. This braisa adds honor as another negative desire to be avoided.[34]

Did You Know?

The Crown of Crowns Kings always fear a rebellion that would threaten their crown. Someone in possession of the crown of Torah, however, holds it forever.[35]

Word Power

לְעַצְמְךָ The braisa tells us, "Do not desire greatness for yourself." It would have held the same message had it said simply, "Do not desire greatness." The extra word "for yourself" teaches us that only for yourself is it inappropriate to seek prestige. For others, you can and should seek it.[37]

Sparks

Not in Your Heart We are not told to refrain from actively seeking honor, as that is obviously inappropriate. We are instructed here to not even desire it in our hearts! This is a command that requires a great refinement of character, bringing you to genuinely despise honor, even deep in your heart.[38]

Embarrassing Honor

R' Yisrael of Ruzhin explained the correct attitude toward honor with the following story:

There was once a minister who received a lot of respect from the citizens, and all would bow when he approached.

The king himself, however, usually stayed out of the public eye, so much so that no one knew what he looked like. Once it happened that the two of them were out walking together, and all who saw them bowed to the minister while ignoring the unknown person at his side. The minister was beside himself with embarrassment. Each bow felt like a dagger to his heart because it was disrespecting his beloved king.

A Jew that receives honor from other people should feel the same embarrassment and pain. Who is he to receive admiration while the King of all kings is walking at his side, all but unnoticed?[36]

Torah is greater than being a kohen or king, because being a king comes with thirty special privileges and responsibilities, such as the prohibition against anyone else sitting in his place or riding on his horse; being a kohen comes with twenty-four gifts that must be given to kohanim, such as bikkurim, challah, and terumah. Whereas acquiring and mastering the Torah requires forty-eight qualities. They are:

גְּדוֹלָה תּוֹרָה יוֹתֵר מִן הַכְּהֻנָּה וּמִן הַמַּלְכוּת, שֶׁהַמַּלְכוּת נִקְנֵית בִּשְׁלֹשִׁים מַעֲלוֹת, וְהַכְּהֻנָּה בְּעֶשְׂרִים וְאַרְבַּע, וְהַתּוֹרָה נִקְנֵית בְּאַרְבָּעִים וּשְׁמוֹנָה דְבָרִים. וְאֵלוּ הֵן:

בְּתַלְמוּד,	1	constant **learning,**	**בְּמִעוּט שִׂיחָה,**	20 limiting conversation,
בִּשְׁמִיעַת הָאֹזֶן,	2	careful listening,	**בְּמִעוּט שְׂחוֹק,**	21 limiting laughter,
בַּעֲרִיכַת שְׂפָתַיִם,	3	verbalizing what one learns,	**בְּאֶרֶךְ אַפַּיִם,**	22 being slow to anger,
בְּבִינַת הַלֵּב,	4	having an understanding heart,	**בְּלֵב טוֹב,**	23 having a good heart,
בְּאֵימָה,	5	awe,	**בֶּאֱמוּנַת חֲכָמִים,**	24 having faith in Chachamim,
בְּיִרְאָה,	6	fear,	**בְּקַבָּלַת הַיִּסּוּרִין,**	25 accepting suffering,
בַּעֲנָוָה,	7	humility,	**הַמַּכִּיר אֶת מְקוֹמוֹ,**	26 being one who knows his place, recognizing his strengths and weaknesses,
בְּשִׂמְחָה,	8	happiness,		
בְּטָהֳרָה,	9	purity,		
בְּשִׁמּוּשׁ חֲכָמִים,	10	serving Chachamim,	**וְהַשָּׂמֵחַ בְּחֶלְקוֹ,**	27 who is happy with what he has,
בְּדִבּוּק חֲבֵרִים,	11	having close friends,	**וְהָעוֹשֶׂה סְיָג לִדְבָרָיו,**	28 who makes a protective fence around his words by choosing his words very carefully,
בְּפִלְפּוּל הַתַּלְמִידִים,	12	discussing and debating Torah with fellow students,		
בְּיִשּׁוּב,	13	calmly and carefully analyzing what one learns,	**וְאֵינוֹ מַחֲזִיק טוֹבָה לְעַצְמוֹ,**	29 who does not take credit for his achievements,
בְּמִקְרָא,	14	knowing **Tanach,**	**אָהוּב,**	30 who is beloved by others,
בְּמִשְׁנָה,	15	knowing **Mishnah,**		
בְּמִעוּט סְחוֹרָה,	16	limiting business activities,	**אוֹהֵב אֶת הַמָּקוֹם, אוֹהֵב אֶת הַבְּרִיּוֹת,**	31 who loves Hashem and loves people,
בְּמִעוּט דֶּרֶךְ אֶרֶץ,	17	limiting worldly activities,	**אוֹהֵב אֶת הַצְּדָקוֹת,**	32 who loves righteousness,
בְּמִעוּט תַּעֲנוּג,	18	limiting worldly pleasure,	**אוֹהֵב אֶת הַמֵּישָׁרִים,**	33 who loves justice,
בְּמִעוּט שֵׁנָה,	19	limiting one's sleep,		

(continued on page 220)

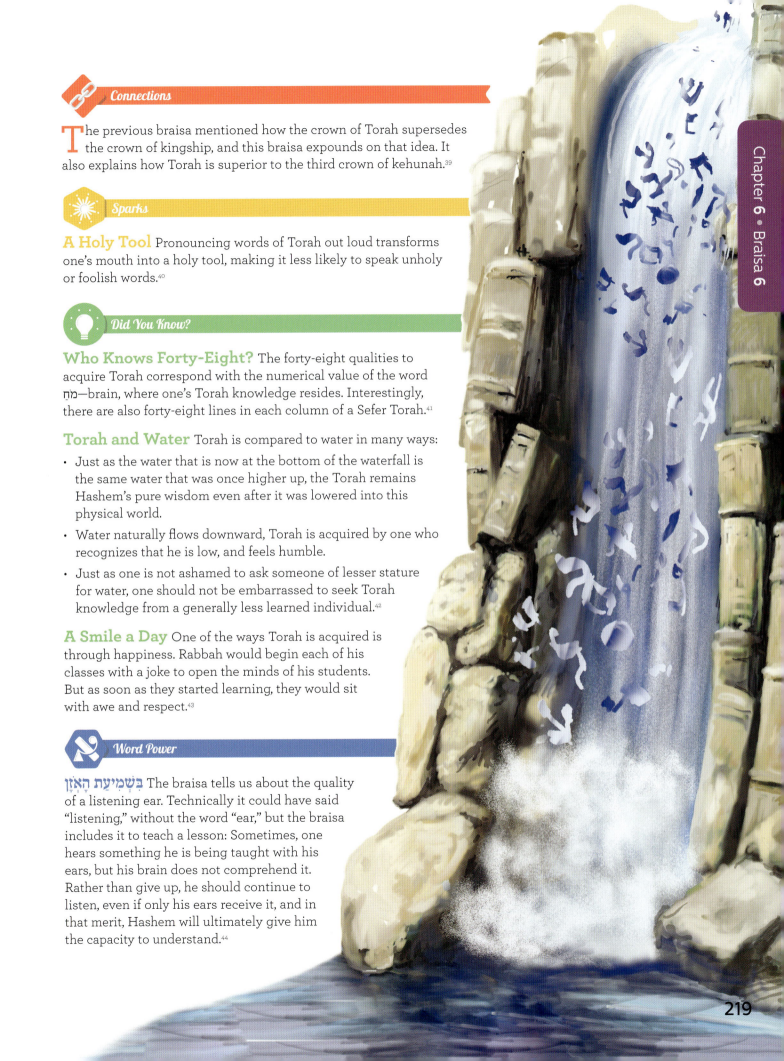

Connections

The previous braisa mentioned how the crown of Torah supersedes the crown of kingship, and this braisa expounds on that idea. It also explains how Torah is superior to the third crown of kehunah.[39]

Sparks

A Holy Tool Pronouncing words of Torah out loud transforms one's mouth into a holy tool, making it less likely to speak unholy or foolish words.[40]

Did You Know?

Who Knows Forty-Eight? The forty-eight qualities to acquire Torah correspond with the numerical value of the word מֹחַ—brain, where one's Torah knowledge resides. Interestingly, there are also forty-eight lines in each column of a Sefer Torah.[41]

Torah and Water Torah is compared to water in many ways:
- Just as the water that is now at the bottom of the waterfall is the same water that was once higher up, the Torah remains Hashem's pure wisdom even after it was lowered into this physical world.
- Water naturally flows downward, Torah is acquired by one who recognizes that he is low, and feels humble.
- Just as one is not ashamed to ask someone of lesser stature for water, one should not be embarrassed to seek Torah knowledge from a generally less learned individual.[42]

A Smile a Day One of the ways Torah is acquired is through happiness. Rabbah would begin each of his classes with a joke to open the minds of his students. But as soon as they started learning, they would sit with awe and respect.[43]

Word Power

בִּשְׁמִיעַת הָאֹזֶן The braisa tells us about the quality of a listening ear. Technically it could have said "listening," without the word "ear," but the braisa includes it to teach a lesson: Sometimes, one hears something he is being taught with his ears, but his brain does not comprehend it. Rather than give up, he should continue to listen, even if only his ears receive it, and in that merit, Hashem will ultimately give him the capacity to understand.[44]

PART II

אוֹהֵב אֶת הַתּוֹכָחוֹת,	34 who **loves criticism** because it helps him improve his ways,	**וּמִתְיַשֵּׁב לִבּוֹ בְּתַלְמוּדוֹ,**	42 who **thinks carefully** and deeply **in his studies,**
וּמִתְרַחֵק מִן הַכָּבוֹד,	35 who **keeps far from honor,**	**שׁוֹאֵל וּמֵשִׁיב, שׁוֹמֵעַ וּמוֹסִיף,**	43 who **asks** questions **and answers** others' questions, **listens** to his teacher, **and adds** to what his teacher says,
וְלֹא מֵגִיס לִבּוֹ בְּתַלְמוּדוֹ,	36 who **is not arrogant in his learning,**	**הַלּוֹמֵד עַל מְנָת לְלַמֵּד,**	44 who **learns in order to teach,**
וְאֵינוֹ שָׂמֵחַ בְּהוֹרָאָה,	37 who **does not enjoy** when he must give a halachic **ruling,**	**וְהַלּוֹמֵד עַל מְנָת לַעֲשׂוֹת,**	45 who **learns in order to** know what **to do,**
נוֹשֵׂא בְעוֹל עִם חֲבֵרוֹ,	38 who **carries the burden with his friend,**	**הַמַּחְכִּים אֶת רַבּוֹ,**	46 who **makes his teacher wiser** by asking good questions,
וּמַכְרִיעוֹ לְכַף זְכוּת,	39 who **judges** his friend **favorably** by giving him the benefit of the doubt,	**וְהַמְכַוֵּן אֶת שְׁמוּעָתוֹ,**	47 who **understands properly what he hears,**
וּמַעֲמִידוֹ עַל הָאֱמֶת,	40 who **places** his friend **on the** path of **truth,**	**וְהָאוֹמֵר דָּבָר בְּשֵׁם אוֹמְרוֹ.**	48 and who **quotes something in the name of** the person who said it.
וּמַעֲמִידוֹ עַל הַשָּׁלוֹם,	41 who **places him on the** path of **peace,**		

In fact, **you have learned: Whoever quotes something in the name of** the person **who said it brings redemption to the world, as it says** in Megillas Esther: **"And Esther told the king in Mordechai's name..."** that Bigsan and Seresh were planning to kill King Achashveirosh, which ultimately led to the miracle of Purim and the redemption of B'nei Yisrael.

הָא לָמַדְתָּ, כָּל הָאוֹמֵר דָּבָר בְּשֵׁם אוֹמְרוֹ, מֵבִיא גְאֻלָּה לָעוֹלָם, שֶׁנֶּאֱמַר: וַתֹּאמֶר אֶסְתֵּר לַמֶּלֶךְ בְּשֵׁם מָרְדֳּכָי.

Living Lessons

A Lifelong Lesson

One of the ways of acquiring Torah is constant learning. Torah has such an incredible breadth that one can never be satisfied with what he has already learned. In fact, the more you learn, the more you realize how vast it is, so that even after learning for your whole life, there will still be more to discover. Keeping this in mind should make you feel humble, which will increase your ability to learn even more.[45]

Sparks

One Good Turn Deserves Another Mordechai could have told the king about the assassination plot directly. However he chose to pass it on through Esther, hoping that the king would give her the credit for it. At the same time, Esther quoted Mordechai's name, hoping that he would receive the reward. We see here how Hashem helps us when we help others.[46]

The Ultimate Source A deeper meaning of the virtue of giving credit to the original author is attributing the Torah to its author and source—Hashem. While learning, one should keep in mind that Torah is not like any other subject, but the holy words and wisdom of Hashem.

This idea can be extended to recognizing that everything that exists comes from the words of Hashem that created the universe. Seeing Hashem as the source of everything reveals Hashem's presence in the world and brings the geulah.[47]

Connections

The last statement of the braisa is also connected to the qualities one might need to acquire Torah, because when the world is finally redeemed with the coming of Mashiach, many deeper levels of the Torah will be revealed, giving us a much more complete understanding of it all.[44]

Story

A Freezing Shiur

Hillel was very poor and only earned one tarpek (half a dinar) a day. He gave half of it to his wife to use for the family's needs, while he used the other half as the entrance fee to the Beis Medrash. One cold winter day, Hillel came home empty handed. The guard at the Beis Medrash refused to let him in, but Hillel refused to miss even one day of Torah learning. So he climbed up to the roof, leaned his head against the skylight, and listened carefully to the shiur taught below. He remained oblivious to the snow falling on top of him as he concentrated.

The next morning, the rabbis noticed that the hall was not as bright as it usually was. The guard was sent up to the roof where he discovered Hillel buried under a deep pile of snow.

Recognizing his determination to learn Torah, they allowed Hillel unrestricted access to the Beis Medrash from then on.[48]

Torah is great because it gives life, both in this world and in the World to Come, to those who learn it and do what it says. As it says in Mishlei: Because they—the words of the Torah—are life itself to the person who finds them, and they are a cure for his whole body. It also says there: The Torah will be a cure for your body and marrow for your bones, making them stronger.

It also says there: The Torah is a tree of life for those who hold onto it, and those who support Torah learning are fortunate.

It also says there: Words of Torah in your mind are like an elegant decoration for your head, and words of Torah spoken from your throat are a beautiful necklace for your neck.

It also says there: Torah will give your head an elegant decoration and it will give you a crown of beauty.

It also says there: Indeed, says the Torah, by learning me, your days will be increased, and years of life will be added to you.

It also says there: Long life is at the Torah's right. If we learn Torah for the correct reason—because it is a mitzvah—it will give us long life in addition to wealth and honor. Wealth and honor are at its left. Even if we learn Torah for other reasons, and not only because it is a mitzvah, it will still give us wealth and honor.

It also says there: The words of the Torah will add to the length of your days, the years of your life, and peace in your life.

גְּדוֹלָה תוֹרָה, שֶׁהִיא נוֹתֶנֶת חַיִּים לְעוֹשֶׂיהָ בָּעוֹלָם הַזֶּה וּבָעוֹלָם הַבָּא, שֶׁנֶּאֱמַר: כִּי חַיִּים הֵם לְמוֹצְאֵיהֶם, וּלְכָל בְּשָׂרוֹ מַרְפֵּא. וְאוֹמֵר: רִפְאוּת תְּהִי לְשָׁרֶּךָ, וְשִׁקּוּי לְעַצְמוֹתֶיךָ.

וְאוֹמֵר: עֵץ חַיִּים הִיא לַמַּחֲזִיקִים בָּהּ, וְתֹמְכֶיהָ מְאֻשָּׁר.

וְאוֹמֵר: כִּי לִוְיַת חֵן הֵם לְרֹאשֶׁךָ, וַעֲנָקִים לְגַרְגְּרֹתֶיךָ.

וְאוֹמֵר: תִּתֵּן לְרֹאשְׁךָ לִוְיַת חֵן, עֲטֶרֶת תִּפְאֶרֶת תְּמַגְּנֶךָּ. וְאוֹמֵר: כִּי בִי יִרְבּוּ יָמֶיךָ, וְיוֹסִיפוּ לְךָ שְׁנוֹת חַיִּים.

וְאוֹמֵר: אֹרֶךְ יָמִים בִּימִינָהּ, בִּשְׂמֹאלָהּ עֹשֶׁר וְכָבוֹד:

וְאוֹמֵר: כִּי אֹרֶךְ יָמִים וּשְׁנוֹת חַיִּים וְשָׁלוֹם יוֹסִיפוּ לָךְ.

Keep Holding On

The passuk states that "Torah is a tree of life for those who hold onto it." This means that we need to constantly review our learning so that we are able to maintain a strong grasp of it. Repeat the passuk one more time, review the mishnah again, and read the Rashi one more time. This will help ensure that your Torah learning endures.[49]

Sparks

Unearned Reward The passuk does not say that Torah gives life "לְלוֹמְדֵיהֶם—for those who learn it," but "לְמוֹצְאֵיהֶם—for those who find it." When you find something, it is not a payment for something you have done, and in no way did you earn the item. In a sense, our reward for learning Torah is similar to something we have found. One does not truly earn payment for learning Torah, since the benefit he reaps from it far outweighs the efforts puts in. Nevertheless, Hashem, in His great kindness, grants us the unearned reward anyway.[50]

Energizer It says that Torah injects life into those who do mitzvos. When one does not know the reason or significance behind a mitzvah that he does, it may be an empty and mechanical act. Learning reasons for the mitzvos fills those who do them with energy and vitality.[51]

 Word Power

לַעֲשׂוֹתָהּ When reading the passuk, "Torah gives life to those who do it," it seems that it should have said, "those who learn it." However, the phrasing of the passuk teaches us that the true goal of Torah is to bring what you learn into action—to fulfill the mitzvos and live your life according to the lessons of the Torah. In fact, Chazal say that if someone learns but does not do, it would have been better if he were never born.[52]

 **Did You Know?**

Best Medicine in Town Medication may heal one part of the body, but its side effects often harm other parts. Hashem's Torah, however, provides relief for the entire body.[53]

 **Story**

Like Fish to Water

Pappus ben Yehudah once saw Rabi Akiva teaching Torah to a large crowd, an act forbidden by the Romans and punishable by death.

"I don't understand," he cried. "How can you ignore the threat to your life by teaching so publicly?"

Rabi Akiva said, "Let me give you a parable. Once, a fox came across a river. Looking down, he noticed the fish swimming in a frenzy. 'What troubles you?' he asked them.

'There are fishermen upstream who are trying to catch us with their nets,' the fish replied.

'Oh, I can help with that,' replied the crafty and hungry fox. 'Why don't you come up on the bank with me, and I'll protect you.'

'Fool!' the fish cried back. 'True, we may die in the hands of the fishermen. But if we leave the water, we will surely die!'

The same is true of us Jews," Rabi Akiva concluded. "Although we may be at risk of the Romans' trap, leaving Torah will certainly cut us off from our source of life."[54]

223

רַבִּי שִׁמְעוֹן בֶּן יְהוּדָה מִשּׁוּם רַבִּי שִׁמְעוֹן בֶּן יוֹחַאי אוֹמֵר: הַנּוֹי, וְהַכֹּחַ, וְהָעֹשֶׁר, וְהַכָּבוֹד, וְהַחָכְמָה, וְהַזִּקְנָה, וְהַשֵּׂיבָה, וְהַבָּנִים, נָאֶה לַצַּדִּיקִים וְנָאֶה לָעוֹלָם,

Rabi Shimon ben Yehudah says in the name of Rabi Shimon bar Yochai: Beauty, strength, riches, honor, wisdom, maturity, old age, and children—these are **good traits for Tzaddikim** to possess so they can be more effective in influencing people to improve and in sanctifying Hashem's Name, which in turn **is good for the world.**

שֶׁנֶּאֱמַר: עֲטֶרֶת תִּפְאֶרֶת שֵׂיבָה, בְּדֶרֶךְ צְדָקָה תִּמָּצֵא. וְאוֹמֵר: תִּפְאֶרֶת בַּחוּרִים כֹּחָם, וַהֲדַר זְקֵנִים שֵׂיבָה.

As it says in Mishlei: **Ripe old age is a crown of beauty,** which also represents riches; **it can be found on the path of righteousness.** It also **says** there: **The beauty of young men is their strength, and the beauty of old men is ripe old age.**

וְאוֹמֵר: עֲטֶרֶת זְקֵנִים בְּנֵי בָנִים, וְתִפְאֶרֶת בָּנִים אֲבוֹתָם.

It also **says** there: **Grandchildren are the crown of the elderly, and the glory of children are their fathers.**

וְאוֹמֵר: וְחָפְרָה הַלְּבָנָה וּבוֹשָׁה הַחַמָּה, כִּי מָלַךְ יְיָ צְבָאוֹת בְּהַר צִיּוֹן וּבִירוּשָׁלַיִם, וְנֶגֶד זְקֵנָיו כָּבוֹד.

And it says in Yeshayah: Due to their painful **embarrassment and shame,** the wicked will see even **the moon and sun** as dark **when Hashem,** God of all creations, **rules on Har Tziyon and in Yerushalayim,** and honor is given **before His mature** and wise elders.

רַבִּי שִׁמְעוֹן בֶּן מְנַסְיָא אוֹמֵר: אֵלּוּ שֶׁבַע מִדּוֹת שֶׁמָּנוּ חֲכָמִים לַצַּדִּיקִים, כֻּלָּם נִתְקַיְּמוּ בְּרַבִּי וּבְבָנָיו.

Rabi Shimon ben Menasya says: These seven traits the Chachamim listed as fitting **for Tzaddikim, were all fulfilled by Rabi** Yehudah Hanassi **and his sons,** who possessed them all.

It's in Your Hands

The qualities listed here can have either a good effect or the opposite, depending on how they're used. Tzaddikim use these characteristics for Torah and mitzvos, while others might use them for their personal honor or even to put down others. Wealth, for example, can be used either to give tzedakah, or to control less wealthy people. The same is true with every trait Hashem grants a person. It's up to him to choose to use this trait positively.

Biography

Rabi Shimon ben Yehudah was a younger colleague of Rebbi and one of the Tannaim who helped compile the Mishnah. He was one of the younger students of Rabi Shimon bar Yochai. Not much is known about his life, other than that he lived in Akko, and is often referred to as אִישׁ כְּפַר עַכּוֹ—the Great One of the town of Akko.

Rabi Shimon ben Menasya was a student of Rabi Meir and a colleague of Rebbi. He was also one of the teachers of Rabi Shimon ben Yehudah. He lived to a very old age and watched Rebbi's children and their great qualities. He would split his day into three parts: a third to learn, a third to daven, and a third for work. Some say that he would learn the entire winter and work only during the summer.[55]

Behind the Quote

The fact that this statement is quoted in the name of Rabi Shimon bar Yochai makes it even more powerful. Rabi Shimon was know for being as far removed from physicality as a person could be, and yet he understood and taught about the importance of beauty and honor for a Talmid Chacham—it increases his standing in the eyes of others and allows his influence to spread more easily.[56]

Sparks

Use it, Don't Abuse it All of the qualities mentioned in the braisa have the potential to lead a person down a dangerous road. A person might think that it's better to live without them rather than to be tested with their power. The mishnah here teaches us that they bring great benefit both to himself and to the world at large, and so one should not avoid them, but be sure to utilize them properly.

This is why the braisa calls them מִדּוֹת, although technically strength, wealth, honor, and old age are assets, not character traits. Only one who has good character traits can achieve positive things through them; they are not even assets for an ill-mannered person.

Did You Know?

Useful Wealth Rabi Yehudah Hanassi (Rebbi) was extremely wealthy. Nevertheless, he only used his wealth to serve Hashem, and never for his own benefit. When he was about to pass away, he lifted his fingers toward the heavens and exclaimed, "Ribono Shel Olam, you know that even my little finger hasn't derived personal pleasure from it all!"[57]

A Strongman of Torah Rabi Yochanan once had an encounter with a bandit named Shimon, who possessed incredible strength. Knowing that Torah study requires exceptional might, Rabi Yochanan urged him to channel his strength for Torah. Shimon heeded the call and eventually became the great Talmid Chacham, Reish Lakish.[58]

It Helps to Be Brilliant

R' Yonasan Eibeshitz once had to visit the ruler of his city to beg him to revoke a decree of expulsion. Despite all his arguments, the anti-Semitic ruler refused to budge. With just one hour left before the decree would be enacted, R' Yonasan told the smug ruler, "Don't think that you will overcome the Jews. עַם יִשְׂרָאֵל חַי לְעוֹלְמֵי עַד! The Jewish nation will live forever more!"

"Very well," sneered the evil man, "If you can write that sentence one time for each Jewish citizen in this city, on a piece of paper no bigger than a mezuzah, I will revoke the decree. But remember, time is ticking! You have one hour!"

Indeed, an hour later, a triumphant R' Yonasan reappeared, waving the paper in his hands. He had brilliantly fulfilled the challenge, arranging the letters and words precisely so they could be read exactly the required number of times.[59]

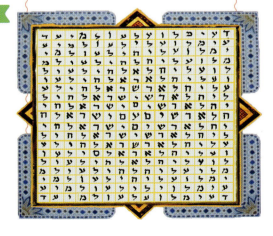

9

אָמַר רַבִּי יוֹסֵי בֶּן קִסְמָא: פַּעַם אַחַת הָיִיתִי מְהַלֵּךְ בַּדֶּרֶךְ, וּפָגַע בִּי אָדָם אֶחָד, וְנָתַן לִי שָׁלוֹם, וְהֶחֱזַרְתִּי לוֹ שָׁלוֹם, אָמַר לִי: רַבִּי, מֵאֵיזֶה מָקוֹם אַתָּה, אָמַרְתִּי לוֹ: מֵעִיר גְּדוֹלָה שֶׁל חֲכָמִים וְשֶׁל סוֹפְרִים אָנִי. אָמַר לִי: רַבִּי, רְצוֹנְךָ שֶׁתָּדוּר עִמָּנוּ בִּמְקוֹמֵנוּ, וַאֲנִי אֶתֵּן לְךָ אֶלֶף אֲלָפִים דִּנְרֵי זָהָב וַאֲבָנִים טוֹבוֹת וּמַרְגָּלִיּוֹת. אָמַרְתִּי לוֹ: אִם אַתָּה נוֹתֵן לִי כָּל כֶּסֶף וְזָהָב וַאֲבָנִים טוֹבוֹת וּמַרְגָּלִיּוֹת שֶׁבָּעוֹלָם, אֵינִי דָר אֶלָּא בִּמְקוֹם תּוֹרָה, וְכֵן כָּתוּב בְּסֵפֶר תְּהִלִּים עַל יְדֵי דָוִד מֶלֶךְ יִשְׂרָאֵל: טוֹב לִי תוֹרַת פִּיךָ, מֵאַלְפֵי זָהָב וָכָסֶף.

וְלֹא עוֹד, אֶלָּא שֶׁבִּשְׁעַת פְּטִירָתוֹ שֶׁל אָדָם, אֵין מְלַוִּין לוֹ לְאָדָם לֹא כֶסֶף וְלֹא זָהָב וְלֹא אֲבָנִים טוֹבוֹת וּמַרְגָּלִיּוֹת, אֶלָּא תוֹרָה וּמַעֲשִׂים טוֹבִים בִּלְבַד, שֶׁנֶּאֱמַר: בְּהִתְהַלֶּכְךָ תַּנְחֶה אֹתָךְ, בְּשָׁכְבְּךָ תִּשְׁמֹר עָלֶיךָ, וַהֲקִיצוֹתָ הִיא תְשִׂיחֶךָ. בְּהִתְהַלֶּכְךָ תַּנְחֶה אֹתָךְ, בָּעוֹלָם הַזֶּה. בְּשָׁכְבְּךָ תִּשְׁמֹר עָלֶיךָ, בַּקֶּבֶר. וַהֲקִיצוֹתָ הִיא תְשִׂיחֶךָ, לָעוֹלָם הַבָּא. וְאוֹמֵר: לִי הַכֶּסֶף וְלִי הַזָּהָב, נְאֻם יְיָ צְבָאוֹת.

Rabi Yosei ben Kisma says: I was once walking on the road while reviewing Torah, **and a** certain **man met me**. I didn't notice him, and so **he greeted me** first. He said, **"Shalom!"** and I answered **back to him, "Shalom!"**

He said to me, "Rabi, from which place are you?"

I told him, "I am from a great city of Torah **scholars and sages,** and my purpose in life is to be occupied with Torah."

He said to me, "Rabi, if you would **be willing to live with us in our place, I would give you a million golden dinar** coins, as well as **precious stones and pearls** so you can be free to learn, and even give a lot of tzedakah."

I told him, "Even **if you would give me all the silver and gold and** all the **precious stones and pearls in the world, I would only live in a place of Torah."**

And that is what is **written in the book of Tehillim by Dovid** Hamelech, King of B'nei **Yisrael**: Hashem—**the Torah of Your mouth is more precious to me than** the **thousands of gold and silver** pieces that I own.

Indeed, when a person passes away, no silver, gold, precious stones, or pearls join him in the World to Come. **Only his Torah** learning **and good deeds** accompany him, as Shlomoh Hamelech **says** in Mishlei: **When you walk,** the Torah **will guide you; when you lie down, it will watch over you; when you wake up, it will speak for you.** Meaning:

"When you walk, it will guide you"—in this world. "When you lie down, it will watch over you"—in the grave, after you pass away. **"And when you wake up, it will speak for you"—in the World to Come.**

And it **says** in Chaggai: **The silver is Mine and the gold is Mine, says Hashem,** God of all **creations,** so a person cannot truly own gold and silver. Whereas Torah becomes part of a person, and therefore remains with him in the World to Come.

Living Lessons

True Wealth

Treasures of gold and silver may be appealing, but the riches of Torah far outweigh them. Wealth can come and go, but the Torah you learn is yours forever.

Every minute in our lives is like time spent in a hall filled with precious gems, each moment a chance to acquire more jewels of Torah. Utilize every minute to its utmost.

Biography

Rabi Yosei ben Kisma

Rabi Yosei ben Kisma was a friend and colleague of Rabi Chanina ben Tradyon. He was well connected in Roman circles and respected by Jews and Romans alike. He was able to perform miracles and often used them to help his fellow Jews.

A story is told that he once visited a Roman and offered him 100 dinar to release two Jewish children the Roman had captured. The man refused and threw Rabi Yosei out of his house. Shortly afterward, he began to experience terrible pains and fever. Realizing what had happened, the Roman sent for Rabi Yosei, who cleverly negotiated with him until he agreed to release the children, this time without any payment. "You owe them money for the work they did for you while in captivity," Rabi Yosei reminded him. By now the Roman knew who he was dealing with, and he paid the children and set them free.

 **Behind the Quote**

This is not the only place where Rabi Yosei extols the virtues of Torah. In another place in the Gemara, he states that the two legs a person stands on in his youth are better than the three (with the addition of a walking stick) he uses in his old age.[60] What this means is that something achieved alone is greater than what is achieved with the help of others. This ability to accomplish on your own applies to Torah specifically, because even when you are alone you can learn Torah, whereas to perform mitzvos you need other items or people to fulfill them.[61]

 Connections

The previous braisa praised the value of riches and wealth. This braisa warns not to abandon Torah for them.[62]

 Sparks

Refuse for the Right Reasons

Rabi Yosei's refusal in this mishnah may seem selfish, until you look more closely at the request. The man was asking Rabi Yosei on behalf of his neighbors to come to **our** town and live with **us**. They weren't interested in changing their town into a holier place, but simply wanted the zechus of a Tzaddik to protect them. Rabi Yosei refused to leave a place of Torah unless the destination was willing to become a haven of Torah as well.[63]

 Did You Know?

Mysterious Messenger

Some say that the man that Rabi Yosei met was Eliyahu Hanavi.[64] According to others, it was actually a shliach of the Satan trying to get him to leave a city of Torah.[65]

Grab Every Chance

There was once a country that had an interesting custom. Every year they would hold elections to appoint a new king, but only foreigners were eligible for the position. However, the new king was not told one thing: the position was intended for only one year, after which he had to leave the country empty-handed, just as he came.

Most often, the king would invest in building himself beautiful palaces, some even transferring all their possessions from elsewhere into the country. Then, after receiving the news that they had to leave without taking anything, they were left devastated and destitute. One king, however, discovered the secret and immediately began sending anything valuable out of the country. He didn't waste any time seeking honor and prestige in the country, because he knew it was only for one year. Indeed, when his year was over he left the country a rich man.

This story is a parable for this world. A person who focuses on making his life in this world comfortable and prepares nothing for after his time will end up with nothing when it really counts! He leaves with nothing and regrets the wasted time on temporary things.

A smart person, on the other hand, uses his time to guarantee a future and does many mitzvos and learns Torah, which connects him to Hashem forever, so he leaves this world a rich man.[66]

חֲמִשָּׁה קִנְיָנִים קָנָה הַקָּדוֹשׁ בָּרוּךְ הוּא בָּעוֹלָמוֹ, וְאֵלּוּ הֵן: תּוֹרָה, קִנְיָן אֶחָד. שָׁמַיִם וָאָרֶץ, קִנְיָן אֶחָד. אַבְרָהָם, קִנְיָן אֶחָד. יִשְׂרָאֵל, קִנְיָן אֶחָד. בֵּית הַמִּקְדָּשׁ, קִנְיָן אֶחָד.

תּוֹרָה מִנַּיִן, דִּכְתִיב: יְיָ קָנָנִי רֵאשִׁית דַּרְכּוֹ, קֶדֶם מִפְעָלָיו מֵאָז.

שָׁמַיִם וָאָרֶץ מִנַּיִן, דִּכְתִיב: כֹּה אָמַר יְיָ, הַשָּׁמַיִם כִּסְאִי וְהָאָרֶץ הֲדֹם רַגְלָי, אֵי זֶה בַיִת אֲשֶׁר תִּבְנוּ לִי וְאֵי זֶה מָקוֹם מְנוּחָתִי, וְאוֹמֵר: מָה רַבּוּ מַעֲשֶׂיךָ יְיָ, כֻּלָּם בְּחָכְמָה עָשִׂיתָ, מָלְאָה הָאָרֶץ קִנְיָנֶךָ:

אַבְרָהָם מִנַּיִן, דִּכְתִיב: וַיְבָרְכֵהוּ וַיֹּאמַר: בָּרוּךְ אַבְרָם לְאֵל עֶלְיוֹן, קֹנֵה שָׁמַיִם וָאָרֶץ.

יִשְׂרָאֵל מִנַּיִן, דִּכְתִיב: עַד יַעֲבֹר עַמְּךָ יְיָ, עַד יַעֲבֹר עַם זוּ קָנִיתָ, וְאוֹמֵר: לִקְדוֹשִׁים אֲשֶׁר בָּאָרֶץ הֵמָּה, וְאַדִּירֵי כָּל חֶפְצִי בָם.

בֵּית הַמִּקְדָּשׁ מִנַּיִן, דִּכְתִיב: מָכוֹן לְשִׁבְתְּךָ פָּעַלְתָּ יְיָ, מִקְּדָשׁ אֲדֹנָי כּוֹנְנוּ יָדֶיךָ, וְאוֹמֵר: וַיְבִיאֵם אֶל גְּבוּל קָדְשׁוֹ, הַר זֶה קָנְתָה יְמִינוֹ.

The Holy One, blessed be He, took ownership of five possessions in His world. They are: Torah, one possession; heaven and earth, one possession; Avraham Avinu, one possession; B'nei Yisrael, one possession; the Beis Hamikdash, one possession.

From where do we know that Hashem took ownership of the Torah? Because it is written in Mishlei: Hashem took ownership of the Torah before the creation of the world, before His work long ago.

From where do we know that Hashem took ownership of the heaven and earth? Because it is written in Yeshayah: Hashem says as follows: The heaven is My throne and the earth is My footstool, so what house can you build for Me? And where is My resting place? And as Dovid Hamelech says in Tehillim: Hashem, how numerous are the works of Your hands! You made them all with great wisdom; the earth is full of Your possessions.

From where do we know that Hashem took ownership of Avraham Avinu? Because it is written in the Torah: And Malki Tzedek blessed him and said: Blessed is Avraham who belongs to Hashem, the Highest, Owner of heaven and earth.

From where do we know that Hashem took ownership of B'nei Yisrael? Because it is written in the Torah: Hashem, drive away any enemies until Your nation crosses over, until this nation, of which You took possession, crosses over the Yarden river and safely enters Eretz Yisrael. And it says in Tehillim: The holy people who are buried in the land—the mighty ones, B'nei Yisrael—all My delight is in them, says Hashem.

From where do we know that Hashem took ownership of the Beis Hamikdash? Because it is written in the Torah: You will bring Your people, B'nei Yisrael, to the place that You, Hashem, made as a dwelling place for Yourself—the Mikdash that You, Hashem, set up with Your hands. And it says in Tehillim: And Hashem brought B'nei Yisrael to the place of His holiness, the mountain that His right hand acquired.

Personal and Precious

Hashem owns everything in this world, but specifies these five as His personal possessions since they enable His nation to serve Him. Each minute of Torah that we learn and each mitzvah we perform is a chance for us to be counted among Hashem's private assets.

Sparks

Like Owner, Like Purchase When something is bought, the item itself does not change, but simply comes under different ownership. In the same way, Hashem's personal assets do not inherently change when they descend into the physical world. They still retain the ability to reveal Hashem's power. The heavens, home to the sun, moon, and stars, show that Hashem's might never grows old, and the earth that grows new produce shows Hashem's capacity to create something from nothing.[67]

Holy Mountain The passuk discussing the acquisition of the Beis Hamikdash actually refers to the Har Habayis rather than the building itself. This is because the sanctity of the mountain remains even after the destruction of the Beis Hamikdash.[68]

Word Power

קִנְיָנִים Even though Hashem doesn't need to buy anything, as they were never owned by anyone else, the braisa specifically uses the word acquisitions—a term for things that are bought—rather than possessions, which are simply owned. This is because when a person spends money to acquire an object it becomes more precious to him than if he had received it for free. These assets are similarly precious in Hashem's eyes, and are therefore called acquisitions.[69]

We're Your Precious Children

R' Levi Yitzchak of Barditchev was known for his emphasis on the preciousness of B'nei Yisrael to Hashem. Every year on Erev Yom Kippur, he would accept a kvittel from each member of his town with the names of his family to be included in R' Levi Yitzchak's prayers for a good year. Each kvittel was customarily accompanied by a small amount of money for tzedakah that served as a zechus for the petitioner.

One year shortly before Yom Kippur, R' Levi Yitzchak instituted a new rule: each name submitted for the kvittel had to be accompanied by no less than two groshen for tzedakah, to be presented on the spot. When the townspeople came to present their kvittels, many tried to negotiate the price, but the gabbai was under strict orders from the Rebbe to allow no exceptions. One of the supplicants was a poor widow who told the gabbai that she had no money, but promised to pay the four groshen for herself and her son as soon as she could. Moved by her appeal, the gabbai told her to ask the Rebbe directly, but he refused. "No exceptions!" he insisted.

The hours passed and the stream of people slowed. It was almost time for Kol Nidrei, but R' Levi Yitzchak kept glancing out the window, as if waiting for something. At the final moment, the widow reappeared, holding two groshen. "Please Rebbe," she begged. "Accept this on behalf of myself and my son and I promise to repay the other two groshen as soon as I can. I ran around the entire town trying to borrow just these two. Please accept it."

R' Levi Yitzchak remained unyielding. "Two groshen will cover one name," he insisted. "Who would you like me to daven for, you or your son?"

With tears in her eyes, the woman asked him to daven that her son be inscribed for a year of life, health, and happiness. Hearing this, R' Levi Yitzchak grasped the two groshen in one hand, the kvittel in the other and raised his hands to Heaven. "Father in heaven," he cried. "Look at the self-sacrifice this mother has for her child. Are You going to be less merciful to Your children? Can You look at this woman and refuse to grant Your children a year of life, health, and happiness?" Then turning to the widow and the gabbai, he said, "Come, now we can go to Kol Nidrei."[70]

Everything that the Holy One, blessed be He, created in His world, He created only in order to reveal His glory, as it says in Yeshayah: Everything that is called by My name, I have created, formed, and made for My glory. And it says in the Torah: Hashem will rule as king forever and ever, and all of Hashem's creations are for the purpose of revealing His glory.

כָּל מַה שֶּׁבָּרָא הַקָּדוֹשׁ בָּרוּךְ הוּא בְּעוֹלָמוֹ, לֹא בְרָאוֹ אֶלָּא לִכְבוֹדוֹ, שֶׁנֶּאֱמַר: כֹּל הַנִּקְרָא בִשְׁמִי וְלִכְבוֹדִי, בְּרָאתִיו יְצַרְתִּיו אַף עֲשִׂיתִיו. וְאוֹמֵר: יְיָ יִמְלֹךְ לְעֹלָם וָעֶד.

Mission Possible

By virtue of the fact that it was created by Hashem, every single creation has a mission: to demonstrate and bring glory to Hashem's name. Every item, animal, person, and event was created only because Hashem considered it important. We must recognize this and strive to use everything around us to further sanctify Hashem's name. Imagine if you had created a fun toy, and someone decided to use it to bang in some nails or stir a bucket of cement, totally ruining it. Hashem creates many amazing and powerful things. We must make sure they are used for their intended purpose. For example, we can use modern technology to access millions of Torah thoughts or to communicate with a friend and share what we learned in school. As technology advances more and more, we can come up with even more ways to use it to reveal Hashem's presence in this world.

Connections

After reading the previous braisa, we may think that since there are five things specifically mentioned as created with purpose, everything else might be a random design. This braisa corrects that impression, informing us that even the tiniest creation was created to manifest Hashem's glory.[71]

Sparks

Two Opposites After a perek replete with descriptions of the greatness of Torah, it might seem irrelevant or inappropriate to discussing ordinary creations. It is for this reason that the braisa specifically places these two topics together, teaching that Torah reaches its ultimate purpose only by affecting the world, uplifting it and making it a fitting home for Hashem.[72]

Did You Know?

Four Words, Four Worlds The different terminology in the passuk, בִּשְׁמִי וְלִכְבוֹדִי בְּרָאתִיו יְצַרְתִּיו אַף עֲשִׂיתִיו, refer to the four worlds: the higher, spiritual worlds of Atzilus, Briyah, Yetzirah, and the lowest world in which we live, known as Asiyah. It seems obvious that the three higher worlds were created to sanctify Hashem's name, but our lowly world of Asiyah seems distant from that lofty goal. The passuk therefore emphasizes אַף עֲשִׂיתִיו—even Asiyah was made to proclaim Hashem's glory, through our performance of Torah and mitzvos.[73]

A Lesson from Technology

A chassid once asked R' Avraham Yaakov of Sadigura, "If it is true that you can learn a lesson from everything in the world, what can we learn from a train?"

"That you can be just one second late and miss everything," he replied without hesitation.

"And what about a telegraph?" the chassid continued.

"That every letter and word is counted and paid for," answered his Rebbe.

"And the telephone?" persisted the chassid.

"Whatever is said here is heard there," was the reply.[74]

Say this mishnah upon completing each perek:

Rabi Chananya ben Akashya says:

The Holy One, blessed be He, wanted to make B'nei **Yisrael** have many **merits.**

He therefore gave them an abundance of Torah and mitzvos, so that they would have many opportunities to connect to Him.

As it says in Yeshayah: **Hashem wanted, for the sake of** increasing B'nei Yisrael's **righteousness, that the Torah be made great and glorious.**

רַבִּי חֲנַנְיָא בֶּן עֲקַשְׁיָא אוֹמֵר:
רָצָה הַקָּדוֹשׁ בָּרוּךְ הוּא
לְזַכּוֹת אֶת יִשְׂרָאֵל
לְפִיכָךְ הִרְבָּה לָהֶם
תּוֹרָה וּמִצְוֹת
שֶׁנֶּאֱמַר: יְיָ חָפֵץ לְמַעַן
צִדְקוֹ יַגְדִּיל תּוֹרָה וְיַאְדִּיר.

Endnotes

1. חסדי אבות להחיד"א
2. מדרש שמואל
3. רש"י
4. ר' ישראל, הובא במדרש שמואל
5. פרקי משה להר' משה אלמושנינו
6. ראה הל' ת"ת להרמב"ם פ"א ה"ב
7. מגן אבות לר"י, הובא בספר מעם לועז
8. ספר השיחות תרפ"ח-תרצ"א ע' 87
9. בעל שם טוב
10. דרך חיים להמהר"ל
11. פרקי משה להר' משה אלמושנינו
12. סוטה יא, ב
13. ראה רמב"ם הל' גירושין סוף פ"ב
14. סנהדרין צח, א
15. כתובות עז, ב
16. כתובות עז, ב
17. מסכת אבות ע"פ יינה של תורה ע' שנה
18. דרך חיים להמהר"ל
19. בבא מציעא לג, א, וברש"י שם
20. מהר"ם שיק
21. אמרות צדיקים להאדמו"ר מקלויזענבורג ע' קפט
22. אגרות קודש חלק י"ג ע' 465-466
23. ראה פתח עינים להחיד"א
24. היא שיחתי ח"א ע' קסט
25. פרקי משה להר' משה אלמושנינו
26. מדרש שמואל
27. לקו"ת אחרי כז, ד
28. הר' יוסף יעב"ץ, הובא במדרש שמואל
29. רש"י. מחזור ויטרי
30. ר' מתתיה היצהרי
31. לקו"ש חי"ח ע' 106
32. לחם שמים להר' יעקב עמדן
33. שפת אמת
34. מילי דאבות להר' יוסף חיון
35. פרקי משה להר' משה אלמושנינו
36. סיפורי חסידים - תורה, ויגש
37. מדרש שמואל
38. חסדי אבות להחיד"א
39. אבות פ"ד מי"ג
40. ילקוט יהודה
41. דרך חיים להמהר"ל
42. שה"ש רבה א, ב
43. שבת ל, ב
44. לחם שמים להר' יעקב עמדן
45. מדרש שמואל
46. ירים משה להאלשיך
47. ביאורים
48. יומא לה, ב
49. ר"י נחמיאש, וראה ברכות לב, ב
50. דרך חיים להמהר"ל
51. ביאורים
52. מדרש שמואל, בפירוש הא'
53. עירובין נד, א
54. ברכות סא, ב
55. קהלת רבה ט, (ט) א
56. ראה בית הבחירה להמאירי
57. כתובות קד, א
58. בבא מציעא פד, א
59. שרי המאה עמ' 141
60. שבת קנב, א, וברש"י שם
61. ביאורים
62. תפארת ישראל
63. לחם שמים להר' יעקב עמדן, וראה גם דרך חיים להמהר"ל
64. מרכבת המשנה להר' יוסף אלאשקר
65. מדרש שמואל
66. חובת הלבבות שער שלישי פרק תשיעי
67. ביאורים
68. מדרש שמואל
69. מילי דאבות להר' יוסף חיון, וראה מהר"י יוסף אלאשקר במרכבת המשנה
70. לאורם נתחנך ח"ב ע' 182
71. תפארת ישראל
72. ביאורים
73. מדרש שמואל
74. חיים שיש בהם על פרקי אבות ע' שיט

Glossary

A

Achashveirosh Ahasuerus, king of Persia during the time of the story of Purim

Acher Literally "Other," referring to Elisha the son of Avuyah, who became a heretic

Adam Harishon Adam, the first man

Aggadah The nonlegal Talmudic discussions, such as parables, maxims, or anecdotes

Aharon Hakohen Aaron, brother of Moses, the first High Priest

Ahavas Yisrael Love of a fellow Jew

Akeidah Literally "the binding," referring to the binding of Isaac

Akeidas Yitzchak The binding of Isaac

Alef, Beis, Gimmel, Daled, Hei, Vov, Zayin, Ches, Tes, Yud The first 10 letters of the Hebrew alphabet

Alef-Beis Hebrew alphabet

Amalek Amalekites, an ancient civilization and perpetual enemy of the Jewish people.

Amnon The oldest son of King David

Amora Sage of the Talmudic era

Amorah Ancient city of Gomorrah

Amos The book of Amos

Anshei Knesses Hagedolah The Great Assembly – a group of 120 sages who enacted many laws and practices around the time of the Second Temple.

Antoninus A Roman emperor. Some say that this was Marcus Aurelius

Apikoros Heretic

Apter Rav Rabbi Avraham Yehoshua Heshel of Apt (1748-1825)

Arizal Rabbi Isaac Luria (1534-1572)

Asarah Harugei Malchus The ten martyrs murdered by the Romans for their religious adherence and Torah study

Asher Bara Elokim "That G-d created..." (Genesis 2:3)

Atzilus, Briyah, Yetzirah, and Asiyah The four spiritual worlds described in Kabbalah

Av Beis Din Head of the Jewish court of law

Aveirah Sin

Aveiros Plural of Aveirah

Avodah Zarah Idol worship

Avodah Service

Avodas Hashem Service of G-d

Avos Our forefathers—Abraham, Isaac, and Jacob

Avraham Avinu Our father Abraham

Avraham Abraham

B

Ba'al Hatanya The author of the Tanya, Rabbi Schneur Zalman of Liadi, founder of the Chabad chassidic movement (1745-1812)

Ba'al Shem Tov Literally the "master of a good name," referring to the founder of the Chassidic movement, Rabbi Yisrael son of Eliezer (1698-1760)

Bar Kochba Leader of the rebellion against the Romans in the early second century of the Common Era

Bas Kol A Heavenly voice

Batei Din Plural of Beis Din

Bava Basra Literally "The last gate," referring to the last of three finance related tractates in the Talmud; it mainly discusses Jewish real estate law

Bavel Babylon

Bein Hashmashos A time between dusk and nightfall that is in doubt as to whether it is truly night and, therefore, has a unique set of laws

Beis Din Jewish court of law

Beis Hamikdash Holy Temple in Jerusalem

Beis Hillel The students of Hillel

Beis Medrash House of Torah study

Beis Shammai The students of Shammai

Beitar The city containing the fortress of Bar Kochba's revolt and the place where his rebellion was quashed

Bigsan and Seresh Officers of king Ahasuerus who plotted to kill him and were in turn discovered and killed

Bikkurim The first fruits to ripen each year, brought before G-d as a thanksgiving offering

Bikur Cholim Visiting the sick

Bilam Balaam

Birkas Hamazon Grace after the meal

Birkas Kohanim The priestly blessing

B'nei Beseirah Leaders of the Jewish supreme court who handed over their position to Hillel the Elder

B'nei Yisrael Literally "The children of Israel," a common name for the Jewish people

Bochur An unmarried man

Bochurim Plural of Bochur

Brachah Blessing

Brachos Plural of Brachah

Braisa A text that was not included in the final compilation of the Mishnah

Braisos Plural of Braisa

Bris Bein Habesarim "Covenant between the parts," which G-d made with Abraham, promising to guard his descendants

Bris Milah The covenant of Circumcision

Bris Literally "Covenant," usually referring to circumcision

C

Chachamim Torah sages

Chafetz Chaim Rabbi Yisrael Meir Kagan (1838-1933)

Chaggai The prophet Haggai

Chalitzah If a husband dies childless, his brother has an obligation to marry and support the widow if she so desires. If she chooses not to, she must perform a ceremony termed Chalitzah, which allows her to marry someone else

Challah A piece of dough separated and given to a Kohen (Priest) or burned, as is done today. Also refers to the traditional loaves of bread eaten during Sabbath and festival meals.

Chametz Leavened bread or other grain based products forbidden to us on Passover

Chanukah Hanukkah

Chashmona'i Hasmonean

Chassid Literally "Pious one," someone who serves G-d beyond the letter of the law. Colloquially used to describe a follower of the Chassidic movement

Chassidim Plural of Chassid

Chavah Eve, the mother of all mankind

Chazal The Talmudic sages

Chevra Kadisha A Jewish burial society

Chidushei Harim Rabbi Yitzchak Meir Rotenberg-Alter, founder of the Gur chasidic dynasty (1798-1866)

Chilul Hashem Desecration of G-d's Name

Chol Hamoed The intermediary days between the first and last days of Passover and Sukkot

Chozeh of Lublin Literally "The seer of Lublin," Rabbi Ya'akov Yitzchak Horowitz of Lublin (1745-1815)

Chumash The five Books of Moses

Churban Destruction, usually referring to the destruction of the Temple in Jerusalem

Chutzpah Audacity

D

Daven Pray

Davening Praying

Derech Eretz Respect

Din Torah A court case of Torah law

Dovid Hamelech King David

E

Eichah Book of Lamentations

Ein Yaakov A collection of Aggadah, the non-legal material from the Talmud

Eisav Esau

Eitz Hada'as Tree of Knowledge

Eliyahu Hanavi Elijah the Prophet

Eretz Yisrael The land of Israel

Erev Pesach The day preceding Passover

Erev Shabbos The day preceding the Sabbath (Friday)

Erev Sukkos The day preceding the Festival of Sukkot

Esrog Citron fruit used for a mitzvah on the Festival of Sukkot

Ezra Hasofer Ezra the scribe

G

Gabbai Officer of the Synagogue

Galil The north of Israel

Galus Bavel Babylonian exile, during the years 422-352 BCE

Galus Exile

Gan Eden The Garden of Eden

Gaon Literally "Genius," typically refers to a great Talmudic scholar

Gehinom The place where souls go to be cleansed from their transgressions after leaving this world

Geirim Converts

Gemara Talmud

Gematria Numerical value

Gemilus Chassadim Acts of kindness

Gebroks Matzah that has become wet

Geulah Redemption

Groshen A historic minuscule measurement of currency in Europe

H

Halachah Jewish law

Halachic Pertaining to Jewish law

Halachos Plural of Halachah

Har Arbel Mount Arbel

Har Habayis The Temple Mount in Jerusalem

Har Meron Mount Meron in northern Israel

Har Sinai Mount Sinai

Har Tziyon Mount Zion in Jerusalem

Hashem G-d

Havdalah The ceremony that marks the conclusion of the Sabbath or the festival

I

Ir Miklat City of refuge and exile for people who committed accidental murder

K

Kabbalah The mystical parts of the Torah

Kabbalas Ol Malchus Shamayim Accepting the yoke of Heaven

Kalba Savua Literally "The satisfied dog," the nickname of one of the three richest men of 1st century Jerusalem, father of Rachel the wife of Rabi Akiva

Kalev Caleb

Kallahs Brides

Kaparah Atonement

Kashrus Jewish dietary laws. It is also used to indicate the permissibility of an item

Kedushah Holiness

Kehunah Priesthood

Kever Burial place

Kiddush Sanctifying the Sabbath or festival over a cup of wine

Kinim The laws of various bird offerings

Kodesh Hakadashim The Holy of Holies—the innermost and holiest chamber of the Holy Temple in Jerusalem

Kohanim Gedolim Plural of Kohen Gadol

Kohanim Plural of Kohen

Kohen Gadol The High Priest

Kohen Priest

Kol Nidrei Literally "All vows," the first prayer of Yom Kippur in which we nullify all vows of the previous year

Korban Asham Guilt offering

Korban Olah Burnt offering

Korban Pesach Paschal lamb offering

Korban An offering brought in the Holy Temple in Jerusalem

Korbanos Plural of Korban

Kosher Literally "Correct," usually refers to food that is permissible under the Jewish dietary laws. It is also used to indicate the permissibility or validity of an item

Kotzker Rebbe Rabbi Menachem Mendel of Kotzk (1787-1859)

Krias Shema Recitation of the Shema Prayer

Krias Yam Suf The splitting of the Sea of Reeds (the Red Sea)

Ksav Ashuri The holy script in which Torah scrolls, tefillin, and mezuzot are written

Ksav Sofer Rabbi Avraham Shmuel Binyamin Sofer, the oldest son of the famed Chasam Sofer, known for his primary halachic work—Ksav Sofer (1815-1871)

Kvittel A note with a petitionary prayer given to a Rebbe

L

Lag Baomer Literally "The 33rd day of the Counting of the Omer," traditionally a day of celebration.

Lashon Hakodesh The Holy Tongue – the Hebrew language of the Torah

Lashon Hara Evil gossip

Lech Lecha Literally "Go for you," referring to G-d's command to Abraham to leave his homeland, testing his obedience

Lechem Hapanim The showbread in the Holy Temple

Levi Levite

Lishmah For the sake of Heaven, with no ulterior motives

L'shem Shamayim For the sake of Heaven

Luchos The two tablets containing the Ten Commandments

Lulav A palm branch used for a mitzvah during Sukkot

M

Maaseh Action

Ma'aser Tithe. A tenth of one's earnings that goes to charity

Mabul The flood of Noah

Maggid of Kozhnitz Literally "The preacher of Kozhnitz," Rabbi Yisroel Hopstein (1737-1814)

Maggid of Mezritch Literally "The Preacher of Mezritch," Rabbi Dov Ber, the second leader of the Chassidic movement, primary student of the Ba'al Shem Tov (1704-1772)

Malach Hamaves The Angel of Death

Malach Michoel The angel Michael, the angel of kindness

Malach Rafael The angel Rafael, the angel of healing

Malachi The last book of the Prophets

Malachim Angels

Malbim Rabbi Meir Leibush son of Yechiel Michel Wisser (1809-1879)

Mann Mannah—food from heaven

Marah One of the places the Jews camped during their travels in the desert

Maseches Eruvin The tractate in the Talmud that deals mainly with the laws of carrying objects from one place to another on Sabbath

Mattan Torah The receiving of the Torah at Mount Sinai

Matzah Unleavened bread, which we are commanded to eat on Passover

Matzos Plural of Matzah

Mayim Shelanu Literally "Water that rested overnight," referring to the water used to bake Matzos

Mazalos Constellations

Mechilta Halachic Midrash on the Book of Exodus

Melachah Literally "Work," referring to the 39 activities that are forbidden on the Sabbath

Melachim The book of Kings

Menashe A wicked king who ruled over the kingdom of Judah during the era of the first Temple in Jerusalem

Menorah The seven-branched Candelabra in the Holy Temple in Jerusalem, or the eight-branched candelabra used to celebrate Hanukkah

Mesechta Tractate

Mesorah The unbroken tradition; the Torah laws that were transmitted from generation to generation.

Midbar Desert

Middah K'neged Middah Measure for measure

Middos Character traits

Midrash Body of interpretations of the Torah text along with homiletic stories and lessons

Midrashim Plural of Midrash

Megillas Esther The Book of Esther

Mikdash Holy Temple

Mikvah A ritual immersion pool

Minyan A quorum of ten Jewish men needed for certain prayers and ceremonies

Mishlei The Book of Proverbs

Mishnah A compilation of the Torah laws that were handed down from generation to generation. Compiled by the great sage Rabi Yehudah Hanassi (Rabbi Yehudah the prince). The term also refers to each individual passage

Mishnah Brurah The name of the Halachic work written by the Chafetz Chaim—Rabbi Yisrael Meir Kagan

Mishnayos Segments of the Mishnah

Mitzrayim Egypt

Mitzvah Commandment

Mitzvas Asei Positive Commandments

Mitzvos Plural of Mitzvah

Mizbeiach Altar

Modeh Ani Literally "I am thankful," referring to the prayer said immediately upon waking in the morning

Mordechai Mordecai, one of the main personalities in the Book of Esther

Moshe Rabbeinu Moses, our teacher

Moshe Moses

Moshiach The Messiah. Literally "the anointed one," who will usher in the final Redemption

N

Nachash The snake, referring to the snake that enticed Eve in the Garden of Eden

Nassi The president or the prince, usually referring to the chief judge of the Sanhedrin

Navi A prophet

Nazir A person who consecrates himself to G-d, signified by abstention from wine and letting his hair grow uncut

Neshamah Soul

Netilas Yadayim Ritual washing of the hands upon awakening in the morning, before eating bread, and after bathing

Nevi'im Prophets

Nevuah A prophecy

Nezirim People who consecrate themselves to G-d, signified by their abstention from wine and letting their hair grow uncut

Niddah The laws of purity pertaining to women

Noach Noah

Noda Bi'yehudah The noted Halachic authority Rabbi Yechezkel Landau (1713-1793)

O

Ohr Hachaim Commentary on the Torah authored by Rabbi Chaim Ibn Attar (1696-1743)

Olam Haba The World to Come

Omer Barley offering that was brought on the second day of Passover, permitting the consumption of the newly harvested grain

P

Paraoh Pharaoh

Pardes The deepest, mystical aspects of Torah

Parshas Weekly Torah portion

Passuk Verse

Passul Unfit for use

Perek Chapter

Pesach Passover

Pessukim Verses

Pirkei Avos Ethics of the fathers

Pirkei D'rabi Eliezer An Aggadic-Midrashic work

Pischei Niddah The calculations of the laws of Niddah

Pruzbul See Shmittah. A legal document allowing the collection of loans after the Shmittah year

Psak Halachic ruling

Purim The joyous festival of the delivery from Haman and his plot to destroy the Jews

R

Rabbanim Rabbis

Radvaz Acronym for Rabbi David Ibn Zimra (1479-1573)

Rambam Maimonides

Rasha A wicked person

Rashi Acronym for Rabbi Shlomo Yitzchaki, most noted commentary on the Torah and Talmud (1040-1105)

Rav Teacher; also the name of one of the greatest sages of the Talmud

Rebbe Rashab Rabbi Sholom Dovber, the fifth Rebbe of the Chabad Chassidic dynasty (1860-1920)

Reshaim Plural of Rasha

Rosh Hashanah The Jewish New Year

Ruach Hakodesh The divine spirit

S

Sancheiriv Sennacherib

Sanhedrin The Jewish Supreme Court

Satan The accusatory angel

Sedarim of Mishnah The six books of the Mishnah

Seder The Passover meal celebrating the Exodus from Egypt

Sedom Sodom

Sefarim Holy books

Sefer Daniel The Book of Daniel

Sefer Habahir A mystical book authored by Nechunya ben Hakanah

Sefer Hachinuch A scholarly work that enumerates and explains all of the 613 commandments

Sefer Torah A Torah scroll

Sefer Yoel The Book of Joel

Sefer Holy book

Semichah Rabbinic ordination

Shabbos Sabbath

Shalom Literally "peace," commonly used as a greeting

Shamash Beadle

Shas The entire collection of the Talmud

Shaul Hamelech King Saul

Shavuos One of the three major Jewish festivals for which there was a pilgrimage to the Holy Temple

Shechinah G-d's presence

Shechitah Jewish ritual slaughter

Shecht Slaughter

Sheim Hameforash G-d's most holy Name

Shema The prayer in which we affirm our belief in G-d

Sheva Brachos Literally "Seven blessings," recited at a wedding celebration and for the following seven days

Shevatim The twelve tribes

Shevet Levi The tribe of Levi

Shevet Yehudah The tribe of Judah

Shevet Tribe

Shiduchim Marital matches

Shiur Torah class

Shiurim Plural of Shiur

Shliach Messenger

Shlomoh Hamelech King Solomon

Shloshim The thirty day mourning period after someone passes away

Shmiras Halashon Literally "Guarding the tongue," not speaking badly about others

Shmittah The 7th year in the continuous 7 year cycle, in which all work of the land must cease in Israel, and all loans forgiven

Shmoneh Esreh The central prayer recited three times daily consisting of 19 blessings

Shmuel Hanavi Samuel the Prophet

Shochet A person certified to slaughter cattle and poultry in the manner prescribed by Jewish law

Shofar The horn of a ram, blown primarily on Rosh Hashanah

Shul Synagogue

Shulchan Literally "Table," referring to the vessel of the Holy Temple where the showbread was kept

Siddur Prayer book

Siddurim Plural of Siddur

Sifri A work of Halachic Midrash

Simchas Beis Hasho'eivah The festive and extremely joyous celebration accompanying the water drawing in the Holy Temple during the intermediary days of Sukkot

Sinas Chinam Senseless hatred

Sivan The third month in the Jewish calendar, containing the Festival of Shavuot

Sotah A woman suspected of committing adultery

Sukkah A temporary shelter in which we are commanded to dwell for eight days during the Festival of Sukkot, commemorating the protection G-d provided for the Jews while traveling in the desert

Sukkos One of the three major Jewish festivals for which there was a pilgrimage to the Holy Temple. The festival in which we sit in a sukkah

T

Tachrichim Burial shrouds

Taharah Ritual purity

Tahor Ritually pure

Talmid Chacham Torah sage

Talmidei Chachamim Plural of Talmid Chacham

Tamei Ritually impure

Tanach The 24 books of the Bible

Tanna Literally "Teacher." A sage of the period of the Mishnah

Tanna'im Plural of Tanna

Targum Yonasan Literally "The translation of Yonatan," referring to the commentary on the Torah written by Yonatan ben Uziel one of the greatest students of Hillel the Elder

Techias Hameisim Resurrection of the dead

Tefillah Prayer

Tefillin Shel Rosh Black leather box with scrolls inside that is worn on the head

Tefillin Shel Yad Black leather box with a scroll inside that is worn on the arm

Tefillin Black leather boxes with scrolls inside

Tefillos Prayers

Tehillim Psalms

Teivah Noah's ark

Terumah Gifts of produce given to a kohen

Teshuvah Returning to G-d

Teveriah Tiberias

Tikkun A rectification

Torah Sheb'al Peh The Torah laws and traditions handed down from generation to generation

Torah Shebiksav The written Torah

Torah The five books of Moses. Also refers to the complete body of Jewish law and tradition

Tumah Ritual impurity

Tzaddik A righteous person

Tzaddikim Plural of Tzaddik

Tzadokim Sadducees—people who believe only in the written Torah, but not the oral traditions

Tzedakah Charity

Tzemach Tzedek of Lubavitch The 3rd Leader of the Chabad Chassidic Dynasty, Rabbi Menachem Mendel Schneerson (1789-1866)

Tzitzis Ritual fringes or tassels

U

Ushpizin The souls of holy ancestors who alternate "visiting" the sukkah each night of Sukkot

Y

Yaakov Avinu Our father Jacob

Yaakov Jacob

Yam Suf The Sea of Reeds (the Red Sea)

Yamim Tovim Plural of Yom Tov

Yarden Jordan River

Yavneh A city in Israel that served as the Torah center around the time of the destruction of the Second Temple

Yechezkel Ezekiel

Yehonasan Jonathan

Yehoshua Joshua

Yericho Jericho

Yerushalayim Jerusalem

Yeshaya Hanavi Isaiah the Prophet

Yeshayah The Book of Isaiah

Yeshivah School of Torah learning

Yeshivas Plural of Yeshivah

Yetzer Hara The evil inclination

Yetzer Tov The good inclination

Yidden The Jews

Yiras Shamayim Fear of Heaven

Yirmiyahu The Book of Jeremiah

Yishmael Ishmael

Yisro Jethro

Yissachar-Zevulun Refers to a partnership between the tribes of Issachar and Zebulun wherein Issachar would occupy their time with Torah study and Zebulun would support them financially and receive half of their Heavenly reward

Yitzchak Avinu Our father Isaac

Yom Kippur The day of Atonement

Yom Tov A festival

Yosef Hatzadik Joseph the righteous one

Yosef Joseph

Yovel The 50th year following the 7th seven year cycle (see Shmittah). All loans are forfeited and all land is returned to its original owners.

Z

Zechariah The book of Zachariah

Zechus Merit

Zekeinim The elders

Zohar The book of Mysticism

Zugos Pairs

Zuz Measurement of money

Index

A

Abba bar Zamina, Rabi, 133
Ablat, 105
accountability for our actions, 163
Achashveirosh, 52, 221
Acher (Elisha ben Avuyah), 139, 158–159
Achisofel, 212
acquiring Torah in forty-eight ways, 218–221
acquiring Torah in three ways, 73
acquisitions, Hashem's five, 228–229
action, importance of, 40–41, 72, 100, 130–131, 140, 217, 223
action as Gemilus chassadim, 12
action as justice, 43
Adam Harishon, 39, 112, 168–169
Afos, Rabi, 48
age when learning, ramifications of one's, 158–159, 204
Aharon HaKohen, 30–31
Akavya ben Mahalel, 84–85
Akeidas Yitzchak, 12
Akiva, Rabi, 41, 43, 47, 65, 71, 79, 87, 89, 91, 97, 99, 107–115, 119, 125, 129, 133, 137, 139, 141, 143, 145, 147, 223
Alexander the Great, 13
aloud, learning Torah, 20, 98, 219
Amalek, 38, 142
Amnon, 194
anger, avoiding, 56–57, 68–69, 154–155, 168, 184–186
animals, learning from characteristics of, 200–201
Antignos, 14–17
Antoninus, King, 48
apikoros, answering an, 76–77
application of halachos, 10
appreciation, learning, 172

Apter Rav, 43
arguing for the sake of Hashem, 194–195
Aristotle, 119
Arizal, 75
Arpachshad, 169
arrogance, avoiding, 32–33, 110, 128, 134, 198, 201
Ashi, Rav, 38, 54
Avraham Avinu, 12, 36, 103–104, 168–172, 176, 179, 197–198, 203, 228
Avraham Yaakov, R., 231
Avtalyon, 26–30, 33, 85
Azarya, Rabi, 11, 103

B

Ba'al Shem Tov, 15, 55, 125, 151, 156, 163, 171, 173, 179, 195, 213
bad eye, avoiding a, 70–71
balancing needs of oneself and of others, 47
Bar Kochba, 105
Baysos, 15
beauty, wisdom as, 210
behavior vs. character, not confusing, 126
Ben Azzai, Shimon, 123–128
Ben Bag-Bag (Ben Hei-Hei), Rabi Yochanan, 202–203, 205
Ben Nanas, Shimon, 123
Ben Zoma, Shimon, 122–123, 125–127
benefit of the doubt, giving the, 21, 54, 127, 138
Bentzion, 89
Bigsan, 221
Bilam, 176, 198–199
boldness, learning, 200–201
books, importance of owning holy, 17

borrowing Hashem's possessions in this world, 96, 114, 182
borrowing money, 67
bravery, learning, 200
bribery, refusing, 107, 135, 162–163
Brisker, R. Chaim, 175
Bruriah, 87, 139
Bunim, R. Simchah, 51
burden of Torah vs. burden of worldly affairs, 92–93

C

Chafetz Chaim, 63, 91
Chagai, 11
Chaim of Sanz, Reb, 145
Chalafta ben Dosa, Rabi, 94–95
Chananya, 11
Chanina ben Chachinai, Rabi, 90–91
Chanina ben Dosa, Rabi, 81, 99–103, 197
Chanina ben Tradyon, Rabi, 86–87, 139, 227
Chanina Sgan Hakohanim, Rabi, 86–87
Chanoch, 169
character, refining through Torah, 208, 217
character vs. behavior, not confusing, 126
chattering with your wife, 18
Chavah, 112, 167
children, B'nei Yisrael as Hashem's, 110–111, 184, 229
Chiya, Rav, 11
Chozeh of Lublin, 51, 123, 131
collective power of learning Torah drop by drop, 81
compromise, importance of, 42, 134
conditional creation of the world, 62

connecting to Hashem through mitzvos, 124
connecting to Talmidei Chachamim, 17, 68–69, 147
connecting to the Torah always, 202
consequences of one's actions, 49, 140
consistency in performance of three pillars, 13
correct learning and teaching, care in, 144–145
credit, taking undue, 62, 65
crowns, acquiring three, 144–146

D

danger, learning as a zechus for avoiding, 90, 96, 98, 141
Daniel, 11
davening properly, 74–75
death, passing on Torah after, 61
derech eretz, learning, 116–117
desecration of Hashem's name, 128–129
devotion in Torah learning, 10, 89, 125, 210–211
diligence in Torah learning, 10, 76–78, 91
Dinah, 23
doing a lot, saying a little and, 36
Dosa ben Horkinas, Rabi, 102–103
Dostai bar Rabi Yannai, Rabi, 98–99, 199
Dov Ber of Radshitz, R., 79
Dov Ber, Reb, 151
Dovid Hamelech, 48, 96, 126, 194, 212, 226, 228
drinking the words of Torah, 16–17

E

effort, importance of, 77–78, 81, 92, 136, 163, 186, 191, 197, 202–203, 215, 217
Efron, 36
Eiger, R. Shlomoh, 203
Eisav, 48, 127
Elazar ben Arach, Rabi, 64–67, 76–78, 147

Elazar ben Azaryah, Rabi, 107, 116–117, 157
Elazar ben Durdaya, Rabi, 140
Elazar ben Rabi Shimon bar Yochai, Rabi, 89
Elazar ben Shamua, Rabi, 109, 127, 142–143, 159
Elazar ben Yehudah of Bartosa, 96–97, 155
Elazar Hakapar, Rabi, 160, 162
Elazar Hamoda'i, Rabi, 104–105
Eldad, 142
Eliezer ben Chisma, Rabi, 118–119, 129
Eliezer ben Horkenus (Hagadol), Rabi, 64–69, 71, 79
Eliezer ben Yaakov, Rabi, 140–141
Elimelech, Reb, 19
Elisha ben Avuyah (Acher), 139, 158–159
Elisha ben Shafat, 16
Eliyahu Hanavi, 16, 31, 77, 115, 129, 133, 147, 149, 171, 203, 211, 227
embarrassment, avoiding, 104–105, 126, 143, 154–155, 217
Enosh, 169
enthusiasm for mitzvos, 124–125
Esther, 52, 221
Ever, 169
excuses, avoiding, 21, 24, 30, 134, 136, 138, 144–145, 148, 187, 216
experience, learning from, 178
Ezra Hasofer, 11, 35, 117

F

fair judgment, 134–135, 137, 156, 162
fear vs. love of Hashem, 14–15, 100
fences around halachos, following, 108–109
five, significance of the number, 95
fool, identifying a, 178
forgetting the Torah, not, 11, 76–77, 98–100, 186
forgiveness, obtaining, 73, 93, 154–155, 157
Fradkin, R. Zalman, 209
free will, 112–113, 166–167, 197

freedom, Torah causing, 210–211
friend, acquiring a, 20–21, 24, 30, 66–67, 70, 146, 209

G

Gamliel, Rabban, 38–39, 89, 105, 107, 119, 157
Gamliel ben Yehudah Hanassi, Rabban, 50–51, 53–54, 73
Gamliel Hazaken, Rabban, 75
geirim, challenges of, 109, 111, 113
gift, Torah as a, 73, 110–111
good, seeing in everything, 66–69, 199
good deeds and wisdom, balancing, 102–103, 116
government, davening for the, 86–87
greeting others first, 148
groups, learning in, 86–87, 89, 94–95, 212–213
guests, importance of having, 18–19, 36, 103, 123, 171

H

habit, not davening out of, 74
habits, developing good, 116–117
Hagar, 171
happiness of others, enjoying the, 70, 198
head vs. tail, being the, 148–149
heart, having a good, 66–67
Hebrew, power of, 33
helping oneself, importance of, 34–35
Hillel ben Rabban Gamliel, 51
Hillel Hazaken, 30–35, 37, 39, 54, 56–60, 62–63, 103, 109, 130, 157, 194–195, 203, 221
honor, seeking, 19, 160
honor, treating one's own and others' equally, 68–69, 142–143
honor, true, 122
honoring the Torah, 132–133
honoring those who learn Torah, 212

humility, learning, 10–11, 26–27, 30–31, 33, 35, 41, 43, 48, 85, 87, 97, 110, 128–129, 138, 157, 198, 201, 216–218

Huna, Rav, 38, 135

I

ignorance, avoiding, 56–57, 144–145

image, man created in Hashem's, 110–111

impartial judgment, 134–135

indulgence, avoiding, 60

infinity of the Torah, 62–63, 136

influence, being a positive, 22–23, 30–31, 41, 128–129, 146–147, 196, 209

influence of Torah on our lives, 119

influences, avoiding bad, 22–24

inheriting the Torah, 73

intent, importance of having the right, 81, 131, 189–191

interruptions in learning, avoiding, 96–97, 99, 125

investigating witnesses, 24–25

Ivan, 89

J

jealousy, avoiding, 70–71, 160–161, 198

job, giving a fellow Jew a, 19

judging everyone favorably, 20–22, 127, 134–135

judging others as guilty, 24

judging without being in another's place, 54

judgment of Hashem, 112–115, 134–135, 162–163

justice, world's existence based on, 42–43

K

Kalba Savua, 137

Kalev, 95

Keinan, 169

Kesselman, R. Shlomoh Chaim, 193

kindness as one of three pillars, 12–13, 42

Kitzes, R. Zev, 179

Korach, 104, 176, 194–195

Kosover, R. Nachman, 195

Kotzker Rebbe, 87

Ksav Sofer, 21

L

layers of the Torah, 203, 221

learning Torah as one of three pillars, 12–13, 42

learning Torah, five steps in, 10

Lemech, 169

Levenstein, R. Yechezkel, 187

Levi, 126

Levi Yitzchak, R., 183, 229

Levitas, Rabi, 128–129

life, Torah's reward as long, 222–223

listening, importance of, 219

Lot, 171

love, conditional vs. unconditional, 194–195

love of others, 30–31

love vs. fear of Hashem, 14–15, 100

M

Maggid of Austria, 191

Maggid of Kozhnitz, 95

Maggid of Mezritch, 35, 135, 163, 215

Mahalalel, 169

Malachi, 11

Malbim, 53

Malki Tzedek, 228

Mana, Rav, 38

Margolis, Reb Efraim, 37

Mashiach, 37, 113, 136, 151–152, 179, 195, 211, 221

mastering Torah in forty-eight ways, 218–221

Masya ben Charash, Rabi, 148–149

material vs. spiritual gains, 60–61, 160, 216, 226–227

maximizing one's own potential, 78, 80, 110, 172, 199, 204

meals, learning Torah during, 88–89

meeting place for Torah, using your home as a, 16–17, 20

Meidad, 142

Meir, Rabi, 31, 87, 95, 98–99, 109, 138–139, 141, 143, 147, 155, 158–159, 193, 208, 225

Meir of Premishlan, R., 71

memory, importance of a good, 64–65, 67, 158

Menasheh, King, 54

Mesushelach, 169

Michel Zlotchover, R., 185

Michoel, Malach, 123

middah k'neged middah, 58–59, 102–103, 115, 122, 132–133, 135, 141, 156–157, 180–181, 221

miracles, ten, 172–176

Mishael, 11

misunderstandings, avoiding, 28–29, 54, 144, 146

mitzvos leading to more mitzvos, 124–125

moderation, everything in, 129

money, helping others increase their, 72–73

Mordechai Hatzaddik, 11, 52, 221

Moshe Leib, Reb, 153

Moshe of Kobrin, R., 67

Moshe Rabbeinu, 10–11, 31, 33, 58–59, 69, 73, 78, 80, 111, 117, 142, 145, 176–177, 194–197, 209

motivation for Torah and mitzvos, correct, 14–15, 25, 32–33, 92–93, 100, 124, 131, 152–153, 195, 208–209, 222

motivation for work, 50, 53

N

Nachor, 169

Nachum of Chernobyl, R., 65

Naftali of Rupshitz, R., 201

nature vs. nurture, 160

Nechemiah, 11

Nechemiah, Rabi, 147

Nechunya, 197

Nechunya ben Hakanah, Rabi, 92–93

Nehora'i, Rabi, 146–147
neshamah, infinity of the, 84–85
night, importance of learning at, 91
Nimrod, 171
Nittai of Arbel, 20, 22–24
Noach, 168–169
Noda Bi'yehuda, 189
nurture, nature vs., 160

O

Ohr Hachaim, 139
Olam Haba, 15, 31, 57, 60, 80, 85, 101, 104–105, 114, 122, 130, 140, 150–153, 160, 162, 198–199, 214–215, 222, 226
Oral and Written Torah, learning together, 109
overcoming obstacles, 12
overcoming physical desires, 62

P

Pappus ben Yehudah, 223
Paraoh, 58–59, 81, 171
path, choosing one's, 46–47, 66–67, 118
patience, learning, 10, 13, 30–31, 33, 57, 168–169, 171–173
peace, loving and pursuing, 30–31
peace, world's existence based on, 42–43
peace between man and Hashem, 61
peace between man and man, 102, 149
Peleg, 169
people, four types of, 182
personal benefit, avoiding use of Torah for, 32–33, 130–131
pillars that hold up the world, three, 12–13, 42
Pinchas ben Yair, Rabi, 126
Pinchas of Koretz, R., 103
poor, treating equally rich and, 18–19
positive, staying, 178, 198–199, 201
Posner, R. Zalman, 203

power, avoiding positions of, 26–27
power, being wary of those in, 52–53
Preida, Rabi, 57
preparation for a mitzvah, 176, 191
pride, importance of Jewish, 11, 129, 200
primary vs. secondary Torah knowledge, 118–119, 193
prioritizing Torah study, 36–37, 54, 68, 92, 159, 214
provider, Hashem as, 10, 93
punishment, dealing with, 22–23
punishment as a direct result of aveiros, 180–181
purpose of the world, 166, 176–177, 201, 230–231

Q

qualities, correctly using personal, 224–225
qualities to master the Torah, 218–221
questions, importance of asking, 56, 178

R

Rabba, 219
Rabbeinu Hakadosh. see Yehudah Hanassi, Rabi
Radvaz, 47
Rambam, 46, 140
Rashab, Rebbe, 141
Rav, 14, 149
Rebbi. see Yehudah Hanassi, Rabi
recognizing Hashem, 76, 174
Refael, 149
Reish Lakish, 225
repetition of good acts, 113
respecting others, 106, 126–128, 142–144, 148–149, 171, 175, 212–213, 216–217
respecting the Torah, 132–133
responsibility for others, 74, 90, 97, 103, 124, 127, 130, 141, 188–189, 196–197
Reu, 169

review, constant Torah, 32, 76–77, 98, 186, 218, 222
reward for Torah study, 78, 80–81, 169–170, 215, 217, 223
Rochel, 109, 137
Ruzhiner, R. Yisrael, 23, 205

S

sacrifice, rewards of, 137, 185, 214–215, 229
Salanter, Reb Yisrael, 157, 214
Sancheiriv, King, 27
Sarah, 36, 171, 203
Satan, 123, 149, 227
saying a little and doing a lot, 36
Schneur Zalman of Liadi, R., 215
secondary vs. primary Torah knowledge, 118–119, 193
self-esteem, developing a healthy, 20, 110
sensitivity to others, 155–156, 175
separation from Hashem, avoiding, 65
separation from others, avoiding, 54–55, 130
Seresh, 221
Serug, 169
serving Hashem as one of three pillars, 12–13, 42
serving Talmidei Chachamim, 16
Shabse, R., 95
Shach (Reb Shabsai Cohen), 39
Shalom of Belz, Reb, 123
Shammai, 30, 33, 36–37, 62, 103, 109, 194–195
sharing possessions, 182
sharing Torah with others, 10, 62, 123, 209
Shaul, Abba, 64–65
Shechinah, presence of the, 17, 33, 86, 94–95, 157
Shelach, 169
Shem, 169
Shes, 169
Shevna, 31
Shimon (biblical), 126

Index

Shimon bar Yochai, Rabi, 33, 43, 75, 88–89, 91, 109, 131, 144–145, 224–225

Shimon ben Elazar, Rabi, 154–155

Shimon ben Gamliel, Rabban (grandfather), 27, 40–41, 43

Shimon ben Gamliel, Rabban (grandson), 42–43, 47, 69, 87, 97, 99

Shimon ben Menasya, Rabi, 224–225

Shimon ben Nesanel, Rabi, 64–67, 74–75

Shimon ben Shatach, 21, 24–26, 85

Shimon ben Yehudah Hanassi, 51, 155

Shimon ben Yehudah, Rabi, 224–225

Shimon Hataimani, 123

Shimon Hatzaddik, 12–15

Shlomoh Hamelech, 148, 154, 160, 181, 226

Shlomoh of Karlin, R., 215

Shlomoh Zalman, R., 77

Shlomtziyon, 25

Shmayah, 26–27, 30, 33, 85

Shmuel, 105

Shmuel, R., 89

Shmuel bar Nachmani, Rabi, 137, 155

Shmuel bar Susarti, Rabi, 14

Shmuel Hakatan, 156–157, 205

Shmuel Hanavi, 10

Sholom Dovber, R., 89

shul vs. home, davening at, 190

silence, importance of, 40–41

sin, avoiding, 84–85, 209

sin, fear of, 64–65, 67, 75, 99–101, 103

size of mitzvos as of equal importance, 46–47, 197

smiling, importance of, 36–37, 106, 219

speech as Torah, 12

speech as truth, 43

spiritual exercise, importance of, 29, 35

spiritual vs. material gains, 60–61, 160, 216, 226–227

spirituality, combining physicality with, 88–89

standing up for one's beliefs, 129, 168, 188, 200, 205

statements, creation with ten, 166–167

strength, learning, 200–201

strength, true, 122–123, 125, 214

students, four types of, 186, 190, 192–193

suffering, rejoicing in others,' 156–157

surrounding yourself with Torah, 146–147, 190–191, 226–227

surveilance by Hashem, 48–50, 112–113, 126, 184, 199, 221

T

tail vs. head, being the, 148–149

talents, maximizing one's, 64–65, 80, 96, 114, 122

Tamar, 194

Tarfon, Rabi, 33, 43, 65, 78–80, 107, 145

teacher, acquiring a, 20–21, 38–39

teachers, honoring our, 142, 212–213

teaching Torah, importance of, 32, 50–51, 130, 133, 209

temperaments, four types of, 184–185

ten, significance of the number, 166–167, 169–170, 172–174, 176

Terach, 169

teshuvah, doing, 68, 114–115, 127, 140, 151–153, 155, 159, 162, 169, 185, 197, 210

tests of Hashem, 21, 106, 127, 170–173

thought as Avodah, 12

thought as peace, 43

time, doing things in their correct, 34–35, 74, 154–155

time, not wasting, 78–79, 90–91, 123, 176, 199, 204, 226–228

trusting only Hashem, 52, 102, 198–199

truth, acknowledging the, 178

truth, Hashem knowing all, 112, 115

truth, the Torah as, 202

truth, world's existence based on, 42–43

Turnusrufus, 111

Tzadok, 15

Tzadok, Rabi, 130–131

tzedakah, giving, 18–19, 32, 60–61, 96–97, 109, 111, 113, 115, 117, 123, 125, 181–183, 188–189, 229

Tzemach Tzedek, 73, 167, 209

U

understanding the Torah, 10, 20, 32, 39, 50, 56, 73, 86, 92, 102, 136, 147, 159, 186, 202–203, 215, 217, 219, 221

V

verification of halachos, 38–39

Vespasian, Caesar, 131, 159

W

Wasserman, R. Elchanan, 211

water, Torah compared to, 219

wealth, true, 122–123, 226–227

wicked, avoiding the, 22–23

will, making one's as Hashem's, 54–55

wine, Torah compared to, 29

wisdom, true, 122–123

wisdom and good deeds, balancing, 102–103, 116

wisdom as beauty, 210

wise person, identifying a, 178

words, watching your, 28–29, 126, 154–155, 179

work, combining learning with, 50, 131–132, 138–139

work, importance of hard, 26–27, 50, 72–73, 103, 215

world's existence for Torah and mitzvos, 12–13, 42

writing to remember better, 21

Written and Oral Torah, learning together, 109

Y

Yaakov, Rabi, 96, 150–153
Yaakov Avinu, 12, 23, 48, 73, 126
Yannai, King, 25
Yannai, Rabi, 148–149
Yechiel Michel, R., 55, 97
Yehonasan ben Shaul Hamelech, 43, 194
Yehoshafat, King, 16
Yehoshua, 10, 33, 95, 142
Yehoshua ben Chananya, Rabi, 64, 66–67, 69–71, 79, 97, 107, 119, 123, 129, 159
Yehoshua ben Levi, Rabi, 149, 160, 210–211
Yehoshua ben Prachyah, 20–21, 23–24
Yehudah Assad, Reb, 21
Yehudah bar Ilai, Rabi, 27, 109, 144–145, 159
Yehudah ben Bava, Rabi, 133, 143, 145
Yehudah ben Beseirah, Rabi, 143
Yehudah ben Tabbai, 24–26, 85
Yehudah ben Teima (Dama), Rabi, 200–201, 204–205
Yehudah Hanassi, Rabi, 17, 43, 46–48, 50–51, 53, 79, 97, 117, 133, 135, 139–140, 143, 149, 155, 159–160, 193, 209, 224–225
Yehudah Nesiah, Rabi, 51
Yeravam ben Nevat, 196
Yered, 169
Yeshayah Hanavi, 113
yetzer hara, subduing the, 20, 22, 26, 46, 49, 53–55, 61, 67, 70, 74–75, 88, 117, 122–123, 125, 138, 144, 149, 151, 162, 189, 200–201, 205, 211, 216
Yishmael, 171
Yishmael, Rabi, 28, 106–107, 129, 131, 137, 139, 149
Yishmael bar Rabi Yosei, Rabi, 130, 134–135
Yishmael Kohen Gadol, Rabi, 41, 87
Yisrael of Ruzhin, R., 217
Yisrael of Vizhnitz, Reb, 155
Yisro, 133
Yisrolik, 95
Yissachar, 189
Yitzchak Avinu, 12, 171, 176
Yitzchak Meir Alter, R., 169
Yochanan, Rabi, 112, 149, 179, 225
Yochanan ben Berokah, Rabi, 128–129
Yochanan ben Zakkai, Rabban, 33, 62–67, 69, 71, 73, 75, 77–78, 93, 101, 103, 105, 131
Yochanan Hasandlar, Rabi, 35, 140–141
Yonah, Rav, 38
Yonasan bar Yosef, Rabi, 136–137
Yonasan ben Uziel, 33
Yonasan Eibishetz, Reb, 135, 161, 225
Yosef Hatzaddik, 43, 58, 104
Yosef Yitzchak, Reb, 20
Yosei bar Yehudah (Yosei Habavli), Rabi, 158
Yosei ben Chalafta, Rabi, 95, 109, 132–133
Yosei ben Kisma, Rabi, 226–227
Yosei ben Yochanan, 16–20
Yosei ben Yoezer, 16–17, 19–21
Yosei Haglili, Rabi, 107
Yosei Hakohen, Rabi, 64, 66–67, 72–73
Yoshiya, Rabi, 137

Z

Zalman Aharon, R., 89
Zecharyah, 11
Zeira, Rabi, 23, 99
Zevulun, 189
Zushe, Reb, 19, 80, 93, 117, 135

נדפס לזכות

הרה"ח הרה"ת משה מאיר הכהן

וזוגתו פנינה שיחיו

ליפשיץ

ולזכות ילדיהם **מנחם מענדל הכהן, יאכא גאלדע,
גיטל** ובעלה **מנחם מענדל פייערשטיין** ובתם **איטא בילא,
לוי יצחק הכהן, ודבורה לאה**
שיחיו

שלוחי כ"ק אדמו"ר נשיא דורנו
בעיר פורט לודרדייל, פלורידה

לברכה והצלחה רבה, בכל אשר יפנו
בגשמיות וברוחניות

ISBN: 978-1-935949-35-0

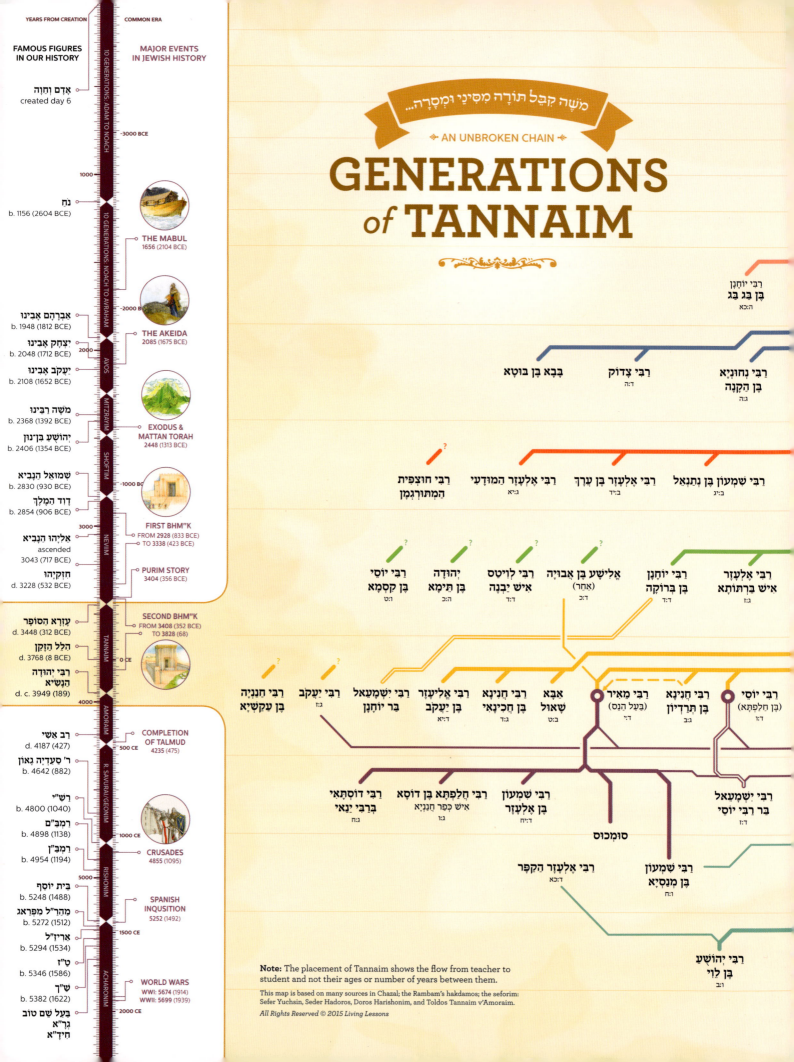